OPEN SOCIETY INSTITUTE
EU MONITORING AND ADVOCACY PROGRAM

Muslims in the UK:

Policies for Engaged Citizens

2005

Published by

OPEN SOCIETY INSTITUTE

Október 6. u. 12.
H-1051 Budapest
Hungary

400 West 59th Street
New York, NY 10019
USA

© OSI/EU Monitoring and Advocacy Program, 2005
All rights reserved.

TM and Copyright © 2005 Open Society Institute

EU MONITORING AND ADVOCACY PROGRAM

Október 6. u. 12.
H-1051 Budapest
Hungary

Website
www.eumap.org

ISBN: 1-891385-42-9

Library of Congress Cataloging-in-Publication Data.
A CIP catalog record for this book is available upon request.

Copies of the book can be ordered from the EU Monitoring and Advocacy Program
eumap@osi.hu

Printed in Gyoma, Hungary
Design & Layout by Q.E.D. Publishing

Table of Contents

Acknowledgements

The EU Monitoring and Advocacy Program of the Open Society Institute would like to acknowledge the role of the authors in researching and drafting these reports. Final responsibility for the content of the report rests with the Program.

Overview and Project Coordination	**Tufyal Choudhury**	*OSI UK Muslims Research Project Director*
Equality, Discrimination and Community Cohesion	**Maleiha Malik**	*Kings College, University of London*
Education	**Prof. J. Mark Halstead**	*University of Plymouth*
Labour Market	**Zamila Bunglawala**	*Policy Analyst*
Criminal Justice	**Dr. Basia Spalek**	*University of Birmingham*

In order to write this report, the authors have consulted with, and interviewed, a wide range of organisations and individuals. These include:

Fauzia Ahmad, Rosita Aiesha, Tahir Alam, Rushanara Ali, F. Amer, Janet Arkinstall, R. Arya, Mohammed Abdul Aziz, Diane Baderin, Runa Begum, Amir Bhatia, Major Lawrie Brown, Pat Brown-Richards, Meg Buckingham, Dr. N. Butt, Saraah Nehar Chowdhury, Fern Christensen, Barbara Cohen, Maurice Coles, Philip Colligan, R. Crawley, Sean Dempsey, Harpreet Dhami, Ali Dizaei, K. Drabu, Salah el-Hassan, Jamila Fernandez, Shareefa Fulat, Declan Gaffney, Sophie Gilliat-Ray, Jane Gordon, Rashid Gumra, H. Haleem, D. Harris, M. Hiley-Payne, Jane Howarth, Will Hutton, Detective Inspector Robert Lambert, Nick Isles, E. Izzidien, Maqbool Javaid, N. Jouied, Abdul Kader, Javid Kaliq, Khalil Kazi, Akram Khan-Cheema, Awais Khan, Humera Khan, Khalida Khan, N. Khan, Major Shagufta Khan, Michelynn Lafleche, Samar Mashadi, Gavin McGill, Jim McManus, Arzu Merali, Constable Mohammed Mahorouf, Dr M. Mukadam, Geoff Mulgan, Naheed Mushtaq, B. Mustafa, Fuad Nahdi, Max Nathan, Mike Nellis, Colm O'Cinnede, Nilesh Patel, Jonathan Portes, Mohibur Rahman, F. Rasool, E. Renier, Robin Richardson, Fiona Richmond, Bernabe Sanchez, Patricia Sellick, Christine Sheddon, Rashid Skinner, Ben Smith, Raschid Sohawon, Sarah Spencer, D. A. Syed, Clare Taylor, Seamus Taylor, Fariha Thomas, Chris Wade, Bill Wells, Stella Yarrow.

Al-Khoei Foundation, An-Nisa Society, Avenues School, London, (pupils and teachers), Belle Vue Girls' School in Bradford (staff and pupils), British Association of Women Police Officers (BAWP), Churches and Criminal Justice Forum, City Circle, Community Chaplaincy, Crown Prosecution Service, Faith Schools Scrutiny Review Panel, Forum Against Islamophobia and Racism (FAIR), Home Office Criminal Justice System Race Unit, IQRA Trust, Islamic Academy in Cambridge, The Islamic Human Rights Commission, JUSTICE, Muslim Unit Scotland Yard, Muslim Women's Helpline, National Association of Victim Support Schemes, National Probation Directorate, Northamptonshire Victim Support, Nottingham Victim Support, Oxford Centre for Islamic Studies, Oxfordshire County Council, Parliamentary Home Affairs Select Committee, Q-News, The Runnymede Trust, Victim Liaison Unit, West Midlands Probation area.

OSI held roundtable meetings for each of the four papers presented in chapters one to four of this report, in order to invite expert critique and commentary on the draft report from representatives of the Government, minority representatives, and civil society organisations and experts. We are grateful to the many participants at the roundtables who generously offered their time and expertise. We would also like to thank the organisations which hosted these meetings:

Equality, Discrimination and Community Cohesion	26 April 2004	Lewis Silkin law firm
Education	2 December 2003	Lewis Silkin law firm
Labour Market	11 March 2004	The Work Foundation
Criminal Justice	8 June 2004	DLA law firm

OSI would also like to thank The Runnymede Trust for their help in organising the launch event for this report, and Fiona MacTaggart MP for hosting this event.

EUMAP

Programme Director	Penelope Farrar
Deputy Programme Director	Miriam Anati
Program Officer	Katy Negrin
Program Officer	Alphia Abdikeeva
Program Coordinator	Andrea Gurubi
Admin. Assistant	Eva Kocsis

Preface

The Open Society Institute (OSI) Budapest is a private operating and grant-making foundation that develops and implements a range of programmes in civil society, culture, education, media and public administration, public health and human and women's rights, as well as social, legal and economic reform.[1]

In 2002, as part of its programme on minority protection in Europe, EUMAP, OSI's EU Accession Monitoring Program, now renamed the EU Monitoring and Advocacy Program,[2] published a volume of reports on minority protection in the five largest EU member states. The reports looked at the situation of Muslims in France, Italy and the United Kingdom and of the Roma/Sinti communities in Germany and Spain.

The UK report, *Monitoring Minority Protection in the EU: the Situation of Muslims in the UK,* launched by the then Home Office Minster Lord Filkin, was a snapshot of the situation of Muslims, in terms of minority rights and their experiences of discrimination and disadvantage. It identified the severe levels of disadvantage and discrimination that are experienced by British Muslims, and are significant barriers to their participation and integration in British society.

One underlying theme in the UK report was the need for policy makers in government and public bodies to ensure that their polices for tackling disadvantage and discrimination took account of the faith dimension in the identities of Muslim communities. The report made over 30 recommendations to the UK Government and other public bodies, calling upon them to take steps to encourage, facilitate and support participation in society by Muslims.

Following publication of the UK report, and noting the positive attitude to engagement in the issues raised by the report from the Government, the Open Society Institute is keen to ensure that the recommendations are taken forward. To this end, this report focuses on four areas: equality and discrimination, education, employment and criminal justice.

The four chapters of this report explore the most relevant issues for British Muslims in each of these areas, and the extent to which policy is presently addressing their needs as a group. Each paper also puts forward a number of recommendations aimed at

---

[1] Further information on the Open Society Institute is available on the OSI website at www.soros.org.

[2] Further information on OSI's EU Monitoring and Advocacy Program (EUMAP) and published reports are available on the EUMAP website at www.eumap.org.

supporting the development of more nuanced Government policy which is sensitive to the needs of Muslims. An overview chapter resumes the main general findings of these papers.

Overview

Table of Contents

OPEN SOCIETY INSTITUTE 2005

1. MUSLIMS IN THE UK: DEPRIVATION, DISADVANTAGE AND DISCRIMINATION

The Open Society Institute published its first report on Muslims in the UK in November 2002.[1] At this time there was very limited data specifically on the situation of UK Muslims. The report therefore relied mainly on available information on the approximately 60 per cent of UK Muslims from the Pakistani and Bangladeshi communities[2] to assess a range of issues affecting the broader Muslim population. Since then, data on faith groups in the UK has become more widely collected and has provided a more accurate picture of the present situation of Muslims. In particular, however, this data has revealed the extent and nature of the deprivation and disadvantage faced by Muslim communities in the UK.

As outlined in the first part of this section, the increasingly available data on Muslims in the UK serves to highlight the marginalisation faced by significant numbers of this group. Muslims in the UK are ethnically diverse with a young age profile. They are disproportionately represented in the most deprived urban communities and experience poor housing conditions. Data on education is not collected on the basis of religious affiliation, but the academic achievement of Bangladeshi and Pakistani pupils at GCSE level falls below the national average. Muslim children experience high levels of the risk factors associated with child poverty. A higher proportion of working age Muslims have no qualifications than for any other faith group. Muslims are by far the most disadvantaged faith group in the British labour market. They suffer from disproportionate levels of unemployment and inactivity and are over-concentrated in certain low-paying sectors of the economy. UK Muslims report higher rates of illness than all other faith groups and fare poorly on certain health indicators.

The second part of this section addresses the levels of discrimination experienced by Muslims in the UK. It notes the different ways in which discrimination can manifest itself and the impact this has on the everyday lives of Muslim. Particular areas of concern where Muslims feel they face discrimination are employment, education and the criminal justice system.

---

[1] Open Society Institute, *Monitoring Minority Protection in the EU: The Situation of Muslims in the UK*, EU Monitoring and Advocacy Program (EUMAP), OSI, Budapest, 2002, available on the EUMAP website at http://www.eumap.org/reports (accessed 21 September 2004), (hereafter, *2002 OSI Report*).

[2] According to data from the 2001 UK National Census, available on the website of the Office of National statistics at http://www.statistics.gov.uk/census2001/default.asp (accessed 2 November 2004), (hereafter, UK 2001 National Census).

1.1 Documenting Deprivation and Disadvantage among UK Muslims

According to the 2001 UK National Census (hereafter, 2001 Census) there are 1.6 million Muslims in the UK,[3] constituting three per cent of the UK population.[4] Muslims are the largest faith group after Christians and constitute 52 per cent of the non-Christian religious population.[5]

The UK Muslim population is ethnically diverse with the majority (73 per cent) of Asian ethnic background.[6] In 2001, 43 per cent were Pakistani, 16 per cent Bangladeshi, eight per cent Indian and six per cent of other Asian ethnic background.[7] In addition to this there are Arab, Afghan, Iranian, Turkish, Kurdish, Kosovar, North African and Somali Muslims. Although figures for these ethnic groups are not captured by existing census data, Muslims from some of these groups may account for the 12 per cent of Muslims who identified themselves as either 'White' UK or 'White' other in the 2001 Census.[8] In addition, six per cent of Muslims were of Black African origin. The main write-in response to the census 'Other' categories was 'Arab'.[9] Data from the census also reveals that 46 per cent of Muslims living in Great Britain were born in the

---

[3] Office of National Statistics, "Profiles", available on the ONS website at http://www.statistics.gov.uk/census2001/profiles/uk.asp (2 November 2004), (hereafter, UK 2001 National Census, *Profiles*). According to the 2001 Census, the total population of the UK was 58,789,194 million people.

[4] However, Ansari suggests that "the broad consensus considers two million as being more realistic since it is contended that a significant number of 'undocumented' and asylum seeking Muslims remain unaccounted for". See: H. Ansari, *The Infidel Within: Muslims in Britain since 1800*, London, Hurst, 2004, p. 172, fn. 12, (hereafter, Ansari, *The Infidel Within*).

[5] Of census respondents who stated that they had a religion, 42 million people described themselves as Christian, 1.6 million Muslim, 559,000 Hindu, 336,000 Sikh, 267,000 Jewish, 152,000 Buddhist, and 179,000 from other religions. A further 13.6 million people stated that they had no religion or did not state a religion. See: UK 2001 National Census, *Profiles*.

[6] For the ethnic and religious categories used in the UK 2001 National Census, see Appendix 1 Definitions.

[7] Office of National Statistics, *Focus on Religion*, London, ONS, 2004, p. 5, available at http://www.statistics.gov.uk/downloads/theme_compendia/for2004/FocusonReligion.pdf (accessed 20 October 2004), (hereafter, ONS, *Focus on Religion*).

[8] This includes the Turkish/Turkish-Cypriot population in the UK, which is estimated at between 125,000 to 300,000. See: Ansari, *The Infidel Within*, p. 169.

[9] See: Oxford Centre for Islamic Studies, *Muslim housing experiences*, London, Housing Corporation, 2004, p. 7, (hereafter, Oxford Centre for Islamic Studies, *Muslim housing experiences*).

UK, while 18 per cent were born in Pakistan, nine per cent in Bangladesh, nine per cent in Africa and three per cent in Turkey.[10]

Muslims have the youngest age profile of all faith groups in Great Britain. In 2001, one third of Muslims were under the age of 16 as compared to one fifth for the population as a whole.[11] The average age of Muslims is 28, 13 years below the national average. As a result of this younger age profile, Government policies aimed at children and young people will have a disproportionate impact on Muslim communities. It is vital, therefore, that Government departments and agencies implementing and delivering policy in relation to children and young people lead the way in ensuring that policy is sensitive to the needs of Muslims.

Muslims in the UK are disproportionately represented in the most deprived urban communities – 75 per cent live in 24 cities or authorities,[12] including around 38 per cent in London. Even within these cities, Muslims are highly concentrated spatially. For example, although in London Muslims represent eight per cent of the population, they are concentrated in a small number of London boroughs.[13] 67 per cent of people from minority ethnic communities live in the 88 most deprived districts in England, as compared to 37 per cent of the White population.[14] The concentration of Muslims in the poorest areas of cities is indicative of the marginalisation of Muslims, and means that the inter-faith and inter-ethnic interactions are often of a confrontational nature, resulting from fear and mistrust of the "other side".[15] It also means that a critical role will fall on departments and agencies developing and implementing Government strategies on sustainable communities and neighbourhood renewal.

Muslim households[16] are more likely than the general population to be married couple households with two or more children (28 per cent, compared to 11 per cent). At the same time, though, single-parent households make up a greater proportion of Muslim

---

[10] ONS, *Focus on Religion*, p. 6.

[11] ONS, *Focus on Religion*, p. 3.

[12] R. Richardson (ed.), *Islamophobia – issues, challenges and action: A Report by the Commission on British Muslims and Islamophobia*, Stoke on Trent, Trentham Books, 2004, p. 29, (hereafter, Richardson, Islamophobia).

[13] A quarter of London's Muslims live in Tower Hamlets and Newham, where they make up 36 and 24 per cent of the boroughs residents, respectively, see: Richardson, *Islamophobia*, p. 30.

[14] Neighbourhood Renewal Unit 2004, cited in *Strength in Diversity: Towards and Community Cohesion and Race Equality Strategy*, London, Home Office, 2004, p. 13.

[15] See: R. J. Pauly Jr., *Islam in Europe: integration or Marginalisation?*, Aldershot, Ashgate, 2004.

[16] The religion of a household refers to the religion of the household reference person.

households than is the case for the general population (12 per cent, compared to 10 per cent).[17]

Muslims are more likely to live in socially rented housing than all other faith groups (28 per cent live, as compared to 20 per cent for the general population). Muslims are also the most likely faith group to experience poor housing conditions: 32 per cent of Muslim households live in overcrowded accommodation, as compared to 22 per cent of Hindu, 19 per cent of Sikh and six per cent of Christian households.[18]

Muslim children experience high levels of the risk factors associated with child poverty: 42 per cent live in overcrowded accommodation, compared to 12 per cent for the population as a whole; 12 per cent live in households without central heating, compared to six per cent for all dependent children; and 19 per cent live in single parent households, compared to 23 per cent for all dependent children. Over one third (35 per cent) are growing up in households where there are no adults in employment, compared with 17 per cent for all dependent children, and 28 per cent live a household without a car or van, compared to 16 per cent for all dependent children.[19]

In education, data continues to be collected on the basis of ethnicity alone. Available data indicates that the levels of academic achievement of Muslim students are low, but improving. In 2002, 40 per cent of Pakistani children and 45 per cent of Bangladeshi children in England and Wales gained five or more GCSEs at grades A*-C, as compared to 50 per cent for the population as a whole.[20]

Almost one third of Muslims of working age have no qualifications, the highest proportion for any faith group.[21] A major study, published in 2004, examined the influences on participation in higher education on the achievement and transition to the labour market of minority ethnic students.[22] The study examines the experiences of different ethnic groups, so does not directly examine the experience of different faith groups. However, the study found that, with respect to students from other Asian groups, Pakistanis and Bangladeshis entering higher education have lower qualifications and are more likely to have vocational qualifications.[23] On the whole,

---

[17] Oxford Centre of Islamic Studies, *Muslim housing experiences*, p. 3.

[18] ONS, *Focus on Religion*, p. 11.

[19] Oxford Centre for Islamic Studies, *Muslim housing experiences*, p. 13, Table 3.

[20] G. Bhattacharayya, L. Ison and M. Blair, *Ethnic Minority Attainment Participation in Education and Training: the Evidence*, DfES, Nottingham, 2003, p. 12.

[21] ONS, *Focus on Religion*, p. 12.

[22] H. Conners, C. Tyers, T. Modood and J. Hillage, *Why the Difference? A Closer Look at Higher Education Minority Ethnic Students and Graduates*, Research Report 552, London, Institute of Employment Studies, 2004, (hereafter, Conners, *Why the Difference?*)

[23] Conners, *Why the Difference?*, p. 23.

minority ethnic students are more influenced than White students by the expected better labour market opportunities that higher education qualifications would bring.[24] Nonetheless, the initial unemployment level[25] amongst full-time[26] Pakistani graduates, at 14 per cent, is the highest of all ethnic groups and compares to six per cent for White graduates.[27]

Degree classification has a significant impact on employment. Nonetheless, even when comparing students with first and upper-second class degrees, Pakistani and Bangladeshi graduates had a higher unemployment rate than all other ethnic groups.[28] In fact, while, as a general rule, employment is lower among students with a higher degree classification than those with a low degree classification, this is reversed in the case of the Bangladeshi and "Asian Other" groups.[29] A higher percentage of Pakistani and Bangladeshi graduates go onto further study or training than White graduates.[30] The percentage of first-degree graduates entering into top three occupational groups is the lowest of all ethnic groups for Bangladeshis.[31]

Muslims are by far the most disadvantaged faith group in the British labour market. They are three times more likely to be unemployed than the majority Christian group. They have the lowest employment rate of any faith group (38 per cent) and the highest economic inactivity rate (52 per cent).[32] At 30 per cent, Muslim men had an economic

---

[24] Conners, *Why the Difference?*, p. 37.

[25] The study uses information from *First Destination Surveys*. These surveys ask students about their activities six months after obtaining their qualification, so reveal a snapshot of the students' initial employment situation.

[26] The study notes that there are no available statistics on part-time students' employment outcomes. However, it finds that "anecdotal evidence suggests that many (part-time students) are likely to stay working with their existing employers". See: Conners, *Why the Difference?*, p. 91.

[27] Conners, *Why the Difference?*, p. 88. The initial graduate unemployment rate refers to the level of unemployment within the first six months of graduation.

[28] Conners, *Why the Difference?* p. 94.

[29] Conners, *Why the Difference?* p. 93.

[30] Conners, *Why the Difference?* p. 89, Table 7.1. 17 per cent of White graduates go into further study or training after graduation, compared to 22 per cent for all minority ethnic groups and 23 and 24 per cent for Bangladeshi and Pakistani graduates.

[31] The top three groups are: professional, assistant professional and managerial. See: Conners, *Why the Difference?* p. 99. The percentage of Pakistani first degree students entering the top three occupational group is equivalent to that of White students.

[32] Figures provided by the Ethnic Minority Employment Division, Department for Work and Pensions, 2004, (hereafter, EMED, DWP).

inactivity rate almost twice that of Christians (16 per cent).[33] More than two thirds (68 per cent) of Muslim women of working age were economically inactive, the highest for any faith group. Of young people aged 16-24, Muslims have the highest unemployment rate of all faith groups; 17.5 per cent are unemployed, compared to 7.9 per of Christians and 7.4 per cent of Hindus.[34] Muslims also tend to be over-concentrated in certain sectors of the economy: 40 per cent of Muslim men in employment were working in the distribution, hotel and restaurant industry, as compared with 17 per cent of Christian men.[35] Moreover, 40 per cent of Muslims are in the lowest occupation groups, compared to 30 per cent of Christians. Muslim men are among the least likely to be in managerial or professional jobs and the most likely to be in low-skilled jobs.[36]

There are also indications that the deprivation and disadvantage experienced by many Muslims in the UK may also have implications for their health status. In the 2001 Census, Muslims reported the highest rates of illness of all faith groups. After taking the age structures of the population into account, it is found that 13 per cent of Muslim males and 16 per cent of Muslim females reported that their health was "not good", compared to 7 per cent for Christians. Compared to other faith groups, Muslims also have the highest rate of disability.[37] Health data on ethnic minorities reveal that Pakistanis and Bangladeshis had the highest rate of diagnosed heart disease.[38] There are also stark differences in the prevalence of diabetes in different ethnic groups. While Indians, African Asians and Black Caribbeans are three times more likely to have diabetes than Whites, Pakistanis and Bangladeshis are five time more likely to do so.[39]

---

[33] EMED, DWP, 2004.

[34] EMED, DWP, 2004.

[35] ONS, *Focus on Religion*, p. 14.

[36] OMS, *Focus on Religion*, p. 14.

[37] 24 per cent of Muslims females and 21 per cent of Muslim males had a disability, as compared to 15 and 16 per cent for Christian males and females, ONS, *Focus on Religion*, p. 8.

[38] While one in six ethnic minorities over the age of forty reported diagnosed heart disease or severe chest pain, the figure for Pakistanis and Bangladeshi was one in four. See: J. Nazroo, *Ethnicity, Class and Health*, London, Policy Studies Institute, 2001, pp. 74–77, (hereafter, Nazroo, *Ethnicity, Class and Health*).

[39] Nazroo, *Ethnicity, Class and Health*.

1.2   UK Muslims and Discrimination

The need for protection from religious discrimination has been a key demand of Muslim communities for over 20 years. The Home Office Citizenship Survey 2001 indicates that one third of Muslims felt that the Government was doing too little to protect the rights of people belonging to different faith groups in Britain.[40] Levels of dissatisfaction were higher among young Muslims (16-24 year olds), of whom 37 per cent felt that the Government was doing "too little".[41] When asked about the amount of respect employers showed for the customs of people belonging to different faith groups, one-third of respondents in all faith groups thought employers were doing too little.[42]

Research conducted prior to 11 September 2001 found that Muslims were the most likely to report "very serious" problems or experiences in relation to seven out of nine indicators of unfair treatment.[43] Recent research has concluded that in the post-September 11 environment, religion is more important than ethnicity in indicating which groups are more likely to experience racism and discrimination.[44] Religious discrimination can manifest itself in a number of different ways, including discounting

---

[40] Five per cent said the Government was doing 'too much' and 62 per cent felt the Government was doing 'the right amount'. However, this overall figure masks significant differences by gender and age: Muslim women (37 per cent) were more likely than Muslim men (30 per cent) to feel the Government was doing 'too little'. This gender difference is also found in the Christian, Hindu and Sikh groups. Among all respondents the response was: 'too much', 20 per cent; 'right amount', 54 per cent; and 'too little', 27 per cent. M. O'Beirne, *Religion in England and Wales: findings from the 2001 Home Office Citizenship Survey*, Home Office Research Study 274, London, Home Office, Research, Statistics and Development Directorate, 20004, p. 25, (hereafter, O'Beirne, *Religion in England and Wales*).

[41] However, this is lower than for others in this age group. O'Beirne, *Religion in England and Wales*, p. 26.

[42] O'Beirne, *Religion in England and Wales*, p. 30.

[43] The research identified nine indicators: ignorance, indifference, hostility, verbal abuse, physical abuse, damage to property, policies of organisations, practices of organisations and coverage in the media. Respondents were asked: How serious do you think the following problems/experiences are for people within your religion? Muslims were the most likely to say the problem was 'very serious' in relation to all indicators except verbal abuse (36 per cent of respondents from Sikh communities said this was very serious, compared to 35 per cent of Muslim respondents) and damage to property (here, 47 per cent of Hindus reported that this was a very serious problem, compared to 33 per cent of Sikhs and 30 per cent of Muslims). P. Weller, A. Fieldman and K. Purdam, *Religious Discrimination in England and Wales*, Home Office Research Study 220, London, Home Office, Research, Development and Statistics Directorate, 2001, pp. 106–105, available on the Home Office website at http://www.homeoffice.gov.uk/rds/pdfs/hors220.pdf (accessed 1 November 2004).

[44] See: L. Sheridan, *Effects of the Events of September 11th 2001 on Discrimination and Implicit Racism in Five Religious and Ethnic Groups*, Leicester, Leicester University, 2002.

the religious beliefs of others, religious jokes, compulsory religious services and exclusionary prayers and non-association due to the other person's religion.[45] Interviews with young Muslim men suggest that discrimination is focused on those who carry visible markers of being Muslim. Those interviewed suggested that young Muslim women suffered most discrimination in the aftermath of September 11 and that this was related to their dress choice.[46] Other studies found that "practising" young Muslim women encountered hostility from students, lecturers and employers, and that they faced "double discrimination based on the grounds of gender and religious adherence".[47]

In 2004, the BBC conducted a survey in which fictitious applications were made for jobs using applicants with the same qualifications and work experience, but different names. A quarter of the applications by the candidates with traditionally English sounding names – Jenny Hughes and John Andrews – were successful in securing an interview, compared to 13 per cent for the applicants with Black African names and only nine per cent of applicants with Muslim names.[48]

A 2003 survey of the perceptions of prejudice amongst young people found that they were almost twice as likely to think that there is a lot of prejudice against Asian people, than against Black people (39 per cent, compared to 20 per cent).[49] While the majority of young people believed that levels of racial prejudice would be unlikely to increase over the next five years, a survey of adults found that the majority (52 per cent) thought it would increase.[50] Another survey, conducted by several Muslim groups, found that since 11 September 2001, 80 per cent of Muslim respondents reported

---

[45] See: C. Huang and B. Kleiner, "New developments concerning Religious Discrimination in the Workplace", in *International Journal of Sociology and Social Policy*, vol. 21, no. 8-10, 2001, pp. 128–136.

[46] P. Hopkins, "Young Muslim men in Scotland: inclusions and exclusion", in *Children's Geographies*, vol. 2, no. 2, 2004, pp. 257–272.

[47] M. Parker-Jenkins, K. F. Haw, B. A. Irving and S. Khan, "Double Discrimination: An Examination of the Career Destinations of Muslim Women in Britain", *Advancing Women in Leadership*, 2:1 (1999)

[48] See: 'Shocking Racism in job market', BBC News, 12 July 2004, available on the BBC website at http://news.bbc.co.uk/1/hi/business/3885213.stm (accessed 28 November 2004). See also J. Wilson, "Muslim says he was sacked for wearing beard", *The Guardian*, 11 August 2004; and V. Dodd, "City Firm Sued for Bin Laden jibes", *The Guardian*, 9 April 2004.

[49] While 39 per cent perceived there was a lot of prejudice against Asian people, 49 per cent perceived "a little" and 11 per cent "hardly any". A. Park, P. Philips and M. Johnson, *Young People in Britain: The Attitudes of Experiences of 12 to 19 year olds*, London, National Centre for Social Research, 2004, p. 46, (hereafter, Park et al., *Young People in Britain*).

[50] Park et al., *Young People in Britain*, p. 47.

being subjected to Islamophobia; that 68 per cent felt they had been perceived and treated differently; and that 32 per cent reported being subjected to discrimination at UK airports.[51]

Attitudes and treatment based on stereotypes and prejudice are one of the ways in which Muslims encounter discrimination. Alexander suggests that Muslim young men have emerged as the new "folk devils" of popular and media imagination, being represented as the embodiment of fundamentalism. To be a British Muslim is defined "solely in terms of negativity, deprivation, disadvantage and alienation".[52] Archer notes that in public discourse Muslim men are not only conceptualised as "dangerous individuals" with a capacity for violence and/or terrorism, but also as "culturally dangerous" – as threatening "the British way of life/civilisation". She finds that "conceptualisations, assumptions and stereotypes about Muslim boys can have "real" effects and implications for pupils within schools".[53]

Other studies have picked up on the way in which stereotypes about Muslim women impact on the lives of these women. Gendered, class and racialised explanations reinforce dominant representations of young Muslim women as both oppressed and powerless, stereotypes that impinge directly on the lives of Muslim women. In one case, for example, a Muslim pupil interviewed for medical degree was questioned about her commitment to the profession. Muslim women find that they are often judged on the basis of being representatives of a stereotype, rather than as individuals.[54]

Discrimination in the criminal justice system, in particular with respect to police stop and search powers, continues to be of concern to British Muslim. Muslims report that they face religious profiling, and that they are being stopped and searched on the basis

---

[51] Forum Against Islamophobia and Racism, Al-Khoei Foundation and the Muslim College, *Counter-Terrorism Powers: Reconciling Security and Liberty in an Open Society: Discussion Paper – A Muslim Response*, London, FAIR, 2004, p. 22. The FAIR survey was based on questionnaires sent out to Muslim schools, Mosques, charities, Islamic students' societies, NGOS and members of the community. Over 200 people responded to the Survey, providing information on how they had been affected by Islamophobia.

[52] C. Alexander, *The Asian Gang, ethnicity, identity, masculinity*, Oxford, Berg, 2000, p. 6.

[53] L. Archer, *Race, Masculinity and Schooling: Muslim boys and education*, Maidenhead, Open University Press, 2003, p. 157, (hereafter, Archer, *Race, Masculinity and Schooling*).

[54] C. Dwyer, "Negotiating diasporic identities: young British South Asian Muslim women", in *Women's studies international forum*, vol. 23, no.4, 2000, pp. 475–486.

of their appearance.[55] It is difficult to obtain direct statistical evidence to support this, as data is not collected on the basis of religion. However, data on ethnicity shows, for example, that between 2001-02 and 2002-03, the number of White people stopped and searched under the Terrorism Act 2000 increased by 118 per cent, while the corresponding increase for Black people was 230 per cent and for Asian people 302 per cent.[56] The high number of stops and searches – and the gap between the number of stop and searches and that of actual arrests, charges and convictions – is leading to a perception among British Muslims of being unfairly policed, and is fuelling a strong disaffection and a sense of being "under siege".[57] The incarceration without trial, under anti-terrorism legislation, of detainees at HMP Belmarsh, also serves to further undermine Muslims' confidence in the justice system.[58]

According to the Forum Against Islamophobia and Racism (FAIR), the enforcement of anti-terrorism legislation "has led to the victimisation and stigmatisation of the Muslim community".[59] FAIR has also found that:

> "victimisation of Muslims under the anti-terrorism legislation has lead to increased incidences of Islamophobia and racism against Muslims. This has manifested itself in the form of vandalism of mosques, Muslim graves and homes" and that "the increased hostility towards Muslims has also seen an increase in hate campaigns against Islam and Muslims from far right groups".[60]

---

[55] Liberty, *Reconciling Security and Liberty in an Open Society – Liberty Response,* London, Liberty, August 2004, available on the Liberty website at http://www.liberty-human-rights.org.uk/resources/policy-papers/2004/liberty-and-security.pdf (accessed 2 November 2004), pp. 8–14, (hereafter, Liberty, *Reconciling Security and Liberty*). See also oral evidence given by the Muslim Council of Britain to the House of Commons Home Affairs Select Committee investigations into Anti-Terrorism Powers, 8 July 2004, available at http://www.publications.parliament.uk/pa/cm200304/cmselect/cmhaff/uc886-i/uc88602.htm (accessed 1 November 2004).

[56] Home Office, *Statistics on race and the Criminal Justice System: A Home office publication under section 95 of the Criminal Justice Act 1991,* London, Home Office, 2004, p. 28.

[57] See: Liberty, *Reconciling Security and Liberty,* p. 8. See also: S. Bates, "Anti-Terror measures alienate Muslims", *The Guardian,* 21 September 2004, available at http://www.guardian.co.uk/uk_news/story/0,,1309011,00.html (accessed 4 November 2004).

[58] Liberty, *Reconciling Security and Liberty,* p. 8. See also: *Concluding Observations/Comments of the UN Committee on the Elimination of Racial Discrimination,* para. 17, available on the UNHCR website at http://www.unhchr.ch/tbs/doc.nsf/0/cd515b6fbf9c7a12c1256e010056fdf4?Opendocument (accessed 1 November 2004)

[59] Forum Against Islamophobia and Racism, *A Submission to the Home Affairs Committee's Inquiry into Terrorism and Social Cohesion,* London, FAIR, 2004, p. 4, (hereafter, FAIR, *Terrorism and Social Cohesion*).

[60] FAIR, *Terrorism and Social Cohesion,* pp. 5–6.

Human Rights Watch has also found that the enforcement of the legislation "has harmed race and community relations" and undermined the willingness of Muslims in the United Kingdom to cooperate with police and security services.[61]

---

[61] Human Rights Watch, *Neither Just nor Effective: indefinite detention without trial in the United Kingdom under Part 4 of the Anti-Terrorism, Crime and Security Act 2001*, Human Rights Watch Briefing Paper, New York, HRW, 2004, pp. 14–15, available on the HRW website at http://hrw.org/backgrounder/eca/uk/anti-terrorism.pdf (accessed 29 October 2004).

2. THE RESPONSE OF UK MUSLIMS

This section addresses the response of UK Muslims to the deprivation, disadvantage and discrimination that many experience in their daily lives. Here, two key trends within Muslims communities can be highlighted. First, for some time now research has highlighted the growing importance to many UK Muslims of religious affiliation as a marker of identity. Many are now seeking recognition and acknowledgement of this in the public sphere. As outlined in the first part of this section, the tendency for religious identity to be prioritised over ethnic identity has important consequences in terms of addressing the needs of the (ethnically diverse) UK Muslim communities. As for other groups, British Muslims have many different identities. Nonetheless, it is a central premise of this report that it is legitimate to address the needs of British Muslims in terms of their membership of a distinct faith group.

A second trend, outlined in the second part of this section, is the development by British Muslims of a distinct discourse of "British Muslim citizenship". This is a positive attempt contribute to debates on citizenship by drawing upon Islamic traditions and ideas. Here Muslim groups and organisations have played an important role, as has the emergence of second- and third-generation British Muslims, educated and socialised in Britain, who clearly see their future as active and engaged British citizens.

2.1 Religious Affiliation as a Marker of Identity

The Home Office Citizenship Survey 2001 indicated that, for Muslims, religion was a more important aspect of identity (second to family) than ethnicity.[62] This finding is supported by other research that has tracked the rise, since the 1980s, of religion as a more significant marker of identity amongst Muslims than ethnicity.[63] Different

---

[62] M. O'Beirne, *Religion in England and Wales*, p. 20. The survey asked participants to list the top ten things that would say something important about themselves. For Muslims, Hindus and Sikhs the top three were family, religion and ethnicity. For Christians, religion was seventh on the list.

[63] See: S. Bouchner, *Cultures in Contact*, New York, Pergamon Press, 1982; N. Hutnik, "Aspects of identity in multi-ethnic society", in *New Community*, 12(1), 1985, p. 298; J. Jacobson, "Religion and Ethnicity: dual and alternative sources of identity among young British Pakistanis", in *Ethnic and Racial Studies*, 20(2), 1997; A. Saeed, N. Blain and D. Forbes, "New ethnic and national questions in Scotland: post-British identities among Glasgow Pakistani teenagers", in *Ethnic and racial studies*, 22(5), 1999, pp. 821–844, (hereafter, Saeed et al, *New ethnic and national questions in Scotland*); and L. Archer, *Race, Masculinity and Schooling: Muslim boys and education*, Maidenhead, Open University Press, 2003, (hereafter, Archer, *Race, Masculinity and Schooling*).

explanations have been put forward for this. Muslim mobilisation may be a response to racism, in which Muslim identities provide a way to respond to inequalities and negative stereotypes.[64] It may also be a reaction to the public devaluation and disparagement of Muslims and Islam that has led to increased in-group solidarity.[65] Muslim political activism can also be seen as part the "politics of 'catching-up' with racial equality and feminism".[66]

There are significant gender differences in the way that Muslim identities are imagined and used. For young women, Muslim identities can provide a way to negotiate parental restrictions which they locate in ethnicity. Islamic teachings in this context can be an important source for resistance to parental and community restrictions on behaviour, that allow women to reject their parent's views as set within ethnic tradition.[67] It provides a pathway to greater integration in education, employment and civic participation.

---

[64] "Islam provides both a positive identity, in which solidarity can be found, together with an escape from the oppressive tedium of being constantly identified in negative term". K. Gardner and A. Shuker, "'I'm Bengali, I'm Asian and I'm living here': the changing identity of British Bengalis", in R. Ballard (ed.), *Desh Pardesh: The South Asian Presence in Britain*, London, Hurst and Company, 1994, p. 163.

[65] See: Saeed et al, *New ethnic and national questions in Scotland*, pp. 821–844 and p. 826. Here, it is noted that "majority group public devaluation of a personally important social identity results in more ingroup solidarity on the part of the minority devalued group, and that this is a mechanism which allows the minority group to increase intergroup differentiation and to maintain its self esteem. Thus for example, recent growing disparagement by non-Muslims may be expected to have resulted in greater unity among Muslims themselves". See also: Y. Samad, "The politics of Islamic identity among Bangladeshis and Pakistanis in Britain", in Y. Samad, T. Ranger and O. Stuart (eds.), *Culture Identity and Politics: Ethnic Minorities in Britain*, Aldershot, Avebury, 1996; and P. Mandaville, "Europe's Muslim Youth. Dynamics of Alienation and Integration", in S.T. Hunter and H. Malik (eds.), *Islam in Europe and the United States: A Comparative Perspective*, Washington, Centre for Strategic and International Studies, 2002, p. 22.

[66] T. Modood, "Muslims and the Politics of Difference", in *Political Quarterly*, 74 (1), 2003, pp. 100–115. (Simultaneous publication in Sarah Spencer (ed.), *The Politics of Migration*, Oxford, Blackwell, 2003). See also: P. Statham, "New Conflicts about Integration and Cultural Diversity in Britain: The Muslim Challenge to Race Relations", in R. Cuperus, K. A. Duffek and J. Kandel (eds.), *The Challenge of Diversity: European Social Democracy Facing Migration, Integration, and Multiculturalism*, Innsbruck, Studienverlag, 2003, pp. 126–149.

[67] See: Y. Ali, "Muslim Women and the Politics of Ethnicity and Culture in Northern England", in G. Sahgal and N. Yuval-Davis (eds.) *Refusing Holy Orders: Women and fundamentalism in Britain*, London, Virago Press, 1992, p. 113; and S. Glynn, "Bengali Muslims: the new East End radicals?", in *Ethnic and racial studies*, 25, 6, p. 969, 2002.

For example, studies by Dwyer of South Asian Muslim female pupils have found that, while "Asian" dress signified difference from "Englishness", Islamic dress came to be seen as a way of bridging the gap, allowing the young women to wear what would otherwise be regarded as "English dress". The women wore trousers and long skirts rather than *shalwar kameez* on the basis that it was Islamic. Such dress challenged the supposed opposition between English and Asian clothes, creating a new fused identity that is both "Western" and "Islamic". Dwyer found that fashionable "western" and yet Islamic dress codes were particularly important for those young women who had begun to explore an alternative "new" Muslim identity. This reasserted Muslim identity offered an alternative gender identity, with respect to their ethnic identity, that emphasised not restrictions but greater possibilities for women. By showing themselves to be "good Muslims", the women gained greater freedom to pursue other interests. By evoking Islamic authority, individuals were able to argue that not only should they be able to dress in a style which was both "western" and "Islamic", but that they should also have greater freedom to go out, to go on to higher education and be fully involved in the choice of their marriage partner.[68] These findings confirm those of other studies of young Muslim women which found that they "desire to achieve equality within Islam, not without it, engaging in a discourse of what it means to be a Muslim woman and articulating their sense of equality within the religion".[69]

Archer's study of young Muslim men finds that the construction of Muslim male identities is intimately tied up with issues of masculinity. Here as elsewhere, masculinity is constructed through various positioning of self and others. In some cases, young Muslim men constructed a "strong" Muslim identity as a way in which to resist stereotypes of "weak passive Asians". The young men challenged this stereotype of Asian men by replacing it with an alternative association of Muslim masculinity with strength. They emphasise the brotherhood that this identity provides:

> The boys' construction of a 'strong' Muslim brotherhood might more usefully be read in terms of intertwining of racial and patriarchal themes, through which boys resist popular stereotypes of 'weak' and 'passive' Asian masculinity. The boys identifications could be seen as straightforwardly challenging this

---

[68] See: C. Dwyer, "Negotiating diasporic identities: young British South Asian Muslim women", in *Women's studies international forum*, 23(4), 2000, pp. 475–486; C. Dwyer, "Veiled meanings: young British Muslim women and the negotiation of differences", in *Gender, place and culture*, 6(1), 1999, p. 5; C. Dwyer, "Contradictions of community: questions of identity for young British Muslim women", in *Environment and Planning A*, 31(1), 1999, pp. 53–68; and C. Dwyer, "Contested Identities: Challenging Dominant Representations of young British Muslim Women", in T. Skelton and G. Valentine (eds.), *Cool Places: Geographies of Youth Cultures*, London, Routledge, 1997, pp. 50–65.

[69] M. Parker-Jenkins and K. F. Haw, "Equality within Islam, not without it: The views of Muslim girls in Britain", in *The Muslim Educational Quarterly*, 13, 3, 1996, pp. 17–34.

stereotype, replacing it with an alternative association of Muslim masculinity with strength. The boys' associations between Muslim identity, unity and strength challenge contemporary western ideals of individualistic white masculinity and elsewhere the boys differentiated between 'strong' collective Muslim families and unstable, highly individualistic western/white family structure.[70]

Archer found that Muslim male identity was at times racialised, and that young Pakistani Muslim men viewed being Muslim as a contrast to being White. The Muslim identity of these young men provided an important element of the defence of local male power. The talking up of race provided a way for them to "assert themselves in relation to white men".[71]

Research in Scotland found that Muslim men identified themselves as Scottish Muslims rather than British Muslims and did not see a contradiction between being Scottish and being Muslim.[72] Muslim men drew upon the different markers of "Scottishness" in ways that simultaneously included themselves in the perimeters of "Scottishness", whilst also excluding themselves from belonging completely within its boundaries. Inclusive markers of Scottishness included the accent, drinking Iron-Bru (a popular Scottish soft drink), and liking football and the natural environment. When asked if there were certain things that they would say are not Scottish about themselves, the most frequent response from the young Muslim men in this research related to drinking alcohol and being part of the "pub and club" culture that they saw as being an important part of Scottish culture.[73]

As with other forms of masculinity, one aspect of male Muslim masculinity is its role in the control and policing of women. Male discussion of female behaviour as being "un-Islamic" allows men to define themselves against women and place themselves as the authentic speakers. At the same time, it allows them to create the boundaries of Muslim and western society in terms of alternative perceptions of acceptable behaviour in women. Thus, the young men use "women" as a particular discursive arena for

---

[70] Archer, *Race, Masculinity and Schooling*, p. 50.

[71] Archer, *Race, Masculinity and Schooling*.

[72] P. Hopkins, "Young Muslim Men in Scotland: inclusions and exclusions", in *Children's Geographies*, 2(2), 2004, p. 257, (hereafter, Hopkins, *Young Muslim Men in Scotland*); and P. Hopkins, *Young Muslim men and 'blue squares': Negotiating Citizenship and Nationality in Scotland*, paper presented at the Royal Geographical Society at the Institute of British Geographers Annual Conference, London, 3-5 September 2003, (hereafter, Hopkins, *Young Muslim men and 'blue squares'*). See also: A. Saeed, N. Blain and D. Forbes, "New Ethnic and national questions in Scotland: post-British identities among Glasgow Pakistani teenagers", in *Ethnic and Racial Studies*, vol 22, no 5, 1999, pp. 821–844.

[73] See: Hopkins, *Young Muslim Men in Scotland*; and Hopkins, *Young Muslim men and 'blue squares'*.

drawing divisions and negotiating power between themselves and other white men. The women's perceived "inauthenticity" is rooted in their Britishness and western way of life, which is positioned as incompatible with Islam.[74] For young men, the policing of women is an important means for maintaining and asserting their own adolescent masculine ethnic and religious identities. Young Muslim men can mobilise religious discourses in order to legitimise their authority.[75]

The complexity of identity means, however, that caution is required in viewing Muslims as having neatly "bounded" Muslim identities. Archer, for example, found that while young Muslim men asserted specifically Muslim masculinities in the political sphere, and patriarchal Asian identities in relation to gender, these were both rejected in relation to youth culture, where the preference was for reggae, soul and rap music.[76]

2.2 Developing British Muslim Citizenship

An increasing political assertiveness by British Muslims should not be mistaken for a desire for separateness. Studies of different ethnic communities in the UK have found that similar levels of Pakistanis and Bangladeshis identified themselves as being "British" as black Caribbeans.[77] As Stratham has noted, "although British Muslims are politically assertive, they see themselves as being just as British as other minorities, and so importantly, they are for the most part being assertive *within* the British political community".[78] In the 2002 OSI Report, for example, it was noted that few Muslim responded to negative media coverage by making complaints to press and television regulators.[79] Since 2002, however, there have been several instances in which Muslims have mobilised to complain about particular articles or programmes in the media. In

---

[74] Archer, *Race, Masculinity and Schooling.*

[75] See also: M. Macey, "Religion, male violence and the control of women: Pakistani Muslim men in Bradford, UK", *Gender and Development* vol 7, no. 1, 1999, pp. 48–55.

[76] Archer, *Race, Masculinity and Schooling.*

[77] Asked whether they thought of themselves as British, 66 per cent of Pakistanis and 60 per cent of Bangladeshis said yes, compared to 62 per cent of Indians and 64 per cent of Caribbeans. See: T. Modood and R. Berthoud, *Ethnic Minorities in Britain: Diversity and Disadvantage*, London, Policy Studies Institute, p. 329.

[78] P. Statham, "New Conflicts about Integration and Cultural Diversity in Britain: The Muslim Challenge to Race Relations", in R. Cuperus, K.A. Duffek, J. Kandel (eds.), *The Challenge of Diversity: European Social Democracy Facing Migration, Integration, and Multiculturalism*, Innsbruck, Studienverlag, 2003, p. 138.

[79] *2002 OSI Report*, p. 130.

two cases, complaints by Muslims and others have led to action against individuals.[80] Muslim organisations are increasingly submitting responses to Government consultations, and submitting and presenting evidence to Parliamentary enquiries.

Commentators have also noted the emergence within Muslim groups and organisations of a discourse of British Muslim citizenship.[81] The development of this discourse has been attributed to the emergence of a younger generation of British born Muslims, educated and socialised in Britain and embedded in communities whose future is in Britain.[82] Lewis, whose study focuses on Bradford, shows how this shift is taking place across a whole range of Muslim groups.[83] Critical debates are taking place within active Muslim youth groups. The debate is often led by young educated professional Muslims who are developing an understanding of Islam that addresses the social and moral

---

[80] When Robert Kilroy-Silk, the presenter of the BBC 1 daytime discussion programme, published an article in the *Sunday Express* newspaper in which he called Arabs "suicide bombers, limb-amputators and women oppressors", his show was suspended by the BBC and eventually cancelled, due in part to complaints by Muslims. See: "CRE calls for Kilroy Apology", BBC News, 11 January 2004, available on the BBC website at http://news.bbc.co.uk/go/pr/fr/-/1/hi/uk/3387599.stm (accessed 26 October). Similarly, the British Council fired a senior press officer, Harry Cummins, after it was discovered that he was the author of a series of anti-Muslim articles in the *Sunday Telegraph*. See: W. Cummins, "Muslims are a threat to our way of life" *Sunday Telegraph*, 25 July 2004, available at http://www.telegraph.co.uk/opinion/main.jhtml?xml=/opinion/2004/07/25/do2504.xml (accessed 2 November 2004). See also: "The Tories must confront Islam rather than kowtowing to it" *Sunday Telegraph*, 18 July 2004, available at http://www.telegraph.co.uk/opinion/main.jhtml?xml=/opinion/2004/07/18/do1802.xml (accessed 2 November 2004). In particular, Muslim organisations have submitted responses to, and presented evidence before, inquiries concerning anti-terrorism legislation; proposals for a Commission for Equality and Human Rights; and changes to religious offences legislation.

[81] There is also a developing discourse around European Muslim citizenship. See, for example: T. Ramadan, *To be a European Muslim: a study of Islamic sources in the European context*, Leicester, The Islamic Foundation, 2002; J. Cesari, "Muslim Minorities in Europe, the Silent Revolution", in John L. Espoito and Francois Burgat (eds.), *Modernizing Islam, Religion and the Public Sphere in Europe and the Middle East*, London, Hurst, 2003; and S. Lathion, "A New Spectre? Islam and Muslims in Europe after 9/11", in *Islamica Magazine*, Summer/Fall 61, 2004.

[82] P. Lewis, "Beyond Victimhood: from the global to the local, a British case study", in J. Cersari, (ed.), in *European Muslims and the Secular State in a comparative perspective: final symposium report*, Network on Comparative Research on Islam and Muslims and Europe, Brussels, European Commission DG Research, 2003, (hereafter, Lewis, *Beyond Victimhood*).

[83] Lewis, *Beyond Victimhood*, p. 82.

issues that arise in their daily lives in Britain.[84] A key role here is played by media outlets that cater to second and third generation British Muslims, which create a public space in which issues of citizenship and belonging can be explored.[85]

Several authors have noted a significant shift in the discourse within many British Muslim organisations, from a defensive isolationism focused on the good of the Muslim community, towards discussion of Muslim contributions towards the "common good".[86] For example, Dr Manazir Ahsan, Director General of The Islamic Foundation, argues for the "need for British Muslims to define themselves in respect of their national and political loyalties and belonging with an emphasis on the mutualities and commonalities with the wider non-Muslim society".[87]

Within Muslim organisations, "the debate is no longer centred on rights and has moved on to responsibilities in the broader context of Islamic altruism. The reclamation of the Muslim contribution to social welfare, with a view to leading Muslims towards "making history" in a secularised context".[88] Home Office Minister Fiona MacTaggart has acknowledged that British Muslims "have consistently shown how it is possible to be British, Muslim and proud", and that:

> thoughout the country, Muslims, with their strong commitment to community development and with enterprise and dedication, are playing a vital role in building a strong and vibrant society.[89]

---

[84] S. McLoughlin, "Islam. Citizenship and Civil Society: 'New' Muslim Leaderships in the UK", in J. Cersari (ed.), *European Muslims and the Secular State in a comparative perspective: final symposium report*, Network on Comparative Research on Islam and Muslims and Europe, Brussels, European Commission DG Research, pp. 100–125.

[85] P. Mandaville, "Europe's Muslim Youth. Dynamics of Alienation and Integration", in S. T. Hunter and H. Malik (eds.), *Islam in Europe and the United States: A Comparative Perspective*, Washington, Centre for Strategic and International Studies, 2002, p. 23.

[86] See: S. McLoughlin, "Islam. Citizenship and Civil Society: 'New' Muslim Leaderships in the UK" in J. Cersari (ed.), in *European Muslims and the Secular State in a comparative perspective: final symposium report*, Network on Comparative Research on Islam and Muslims and Europe, Brussels, European Commission DG Research, p. 102, where McLoughlin notes the role in the Islamic Foundation, through its work with the Citizen Organising Foundation in "encouraging Muslims to move beyond the 'Pakistani' or even 'Muslim' good to some sort of 'common good'.

[87] M. S. Seddon, D. Hussain and N. Malik, *British Muslims – Loyalty and Belonging*, Leicester, The Islamic Foundation, 2003, p. viii.

[88] I. H. Malik, *Islam and Modernity: Muslims in Europe and the United States*, London, Pluto Press, 2004. See also: R. J. Pauly Jr., *Islam in Europe: integration or Marginalisation?* Aldershot, Ashgate, 2004.

[89] Speech by Home Office Minister Fiona MacTaggart, December 2003. Cited in Richardson, *Islamophobia*, p. 1.

3. THE GOVERNMENT POLICY RESPONSE

Just as Muslims have been active in developing a sense of engaged and active British Muslim citizenship, so Government policies have increasingly sought to respond to the demands and needs of Muslims. The Government has stated that "integration is not about assimilation into a single homogenous culture and there is space within the concept of 'British' for people to express their religious and cultural beliefs".[90]

This section examines the ways in which existing legislation and Government policy has addressed the deprivation, disadvantage and discrimination encountered by Muslims. It evaluates the degree to which Government policy has acknowledged the importance of addressing the specific needs of Muslims as a distinct group, as opposed to through the lens of ethnic affiliation.

A central prerequisite for designing effective policy is the collection of data. Increasing amounts of data are being collected and disaggregated on the basis of faith. The Office of National Statistics has begun analysing the 2001 Census data and has already published socio-economic data on faith communities.[91] The Labour Force Survey and the Home Office Citizenship Survey both ask questions on religion. However, significant knowledge gaps remain. In particular, data on the basis of religious affiliation is not collected in the key areas of education and, apart from in the Prison Service, of criminal justice.

Over recent years, there has been a significant evolution in legislation addressing discrimination based on religion. Legislation now prohibits direct and indirect discrimination, harassment and victimisation on the grounds of religion and belief, with respect to employment and vocational training. This legislation also applies to discrimination by institutions (including universities) which provide further or higher education.[92] The Government has announced its intention to bring legislation

---

[90] Home Office, *Strength in Diversity: Towards a Community Cohesion and Race Equality Strategy*, London, Home Office Communications Directorate, 2004, p. 5.

[91] See: ONS, *Focus on Religion*, p. 14.

[92] Employment Equality (Religion or Belief) Regulations 2003 (SI 2003/1660). The regulations came into force on 2 December 2003. They aimed to implement EU Council Directive 2000/78/EC of 27 November 2000 establishing a general framework for equal treatment in employment and occupation.

addressing discrimination on the ground of religion into line with that for discrimination on the grounds of race, sex and disability.[93]

Several measures have been taken to support the implementation of the EU Employment Directive.[94] For example, the Advisory, Conciliation and Arbitration Service (ACAS) issued guidelines for employers on meeting the requirements of regulations on religion and belief. The Department of Trade and Industry has funded several faith community organisations, including Muslim organisations to disseminate information about the new rights. The Government has published proposals for creating a Commission for Equality and Human Rights (CEHR),[95] although these have been rejected by the Commission for Racial Equality.[96] At the same time, however, the CRE appointed one of its commissioners Khurshid Ahmed, as a special Ambassador for Britain's Muslim communities and argued for comprehensive religious equality legislation.[97]

Government policy is only now beginning to address the discrimination and disadvantage experienced by Muslims as a group, with adjustments to meet the specific

---

[93] Speech by Prime Minister Blair at the Labour Party conference on 28 September 2004. The Prime Minister said that the Government would "change the law to make religious discrimination unlawful as we do race, gender and disability". See: "Full text: Blair's conference speech (part two)", *The Guardian*, 28 September 2004, available at http://politics.guardian.co.uk/labour2004/story/0,14991,1314765,00.html (accessed 2 November 2004).

[94] EU Council Directive 2000/78/EC of 27 November 2000 establishing a general framework for equal treatment in employment and occupation, (hereafter, EU Employment Directive).

[95] Department for Trade and Industry, *Fairness for All*, London, DTI, 2004.

[96] See: Commission for Racial Equality, *Fairness for All: A New Commission for Equality and Human Rights – a response Fairness for All: A New Commission for Equality and Human Rights – a response*, London: CRE, 2004. The CRE reached this position having posed three key tests. First, are the proposals right in principle; second, will they work in practice; and third, are they an improvement on the current Commission. The CRE answered these questions in the negative and found that a positive and conclusive case for a new body had not been made. They concluded that "the proposals would reduce our (or a successor body's) impact and authority; and the process of merger would destroy our capacity to reduce conflict within communities, to combat the rise of racist sentiment and organisations, and to meet the challenging objectives set for us by the government itself". Particular concerns included the reduced focus on legal enforcement in the new body and the absence of any proposals for a single equality act.

[97] See Commission for Racial Equality Press Releases: "Outlawing Religious Discrimination is CRE's top legislative priority", 22 July 2004, available at http://www.cre.gov.uk/media/nr_arch/2004/nr040722.html ; and "CRE gives special voice to Muslims", 31 March 2004, http://www.cre.gov.uk/media/nr_arch/2004/nr040331.html (both accessed 6 November 2004).

30

needs of Muslims. For example, the Treasury has changed the rules on Stamp Duty to allow financial institutions to offer *Sharia* compliant mortgages and loans. It is also looking at ways to remove barriers for those in social housing to accessing such financial products.[98] The Home Office has set up a Faith Communities Unit (FCU), which includes within its remit engaging with Muslim communities. The Government acknowledges that the record of Government engagement with faith communities has been patchy. Following a review of policy in this area, the FCU has published a guide for Government departments on how to improve consultation with faith communities.[99]

Soon after September 11, the Government passed legislation introducing a new provision in the 2001 Anti-Terrorism Crime and Security Act, to ensure that, in England and Wales, religious motivation for some violent offences would constitute a racially or religiously aggravated form of that offence (i.e. a separate offence).[100] Between December 2001 and March 2003, there were 18 prosecutions in England and Wales of religiously aggravated offences, of which ten involved Muslim victims.[101] In October 2003, the Attorney General's powers to challenge unduly lenient sentences were extended to include racially and religiously aggravated offences, following a recommendation by the Crown Prosecution Service Inspectorate. In July 2004, the Home Secretary announced the Government's intention to introduce legislation to outlaw incitement to religious hatred.[102]

As a response to the significant rise in stops and searches carried out against ethnic minority groups, the Government has established a Stop and Search Action team.[103] It

---

[98] See: *Hansard,* 16 September 2004, Col 1653W.

[99] Home Office, *Working Together: Co-operation Between Government and Faith Communities – Recommendations of the Steering Group Reviewing patterns of engagement between Government and Faith Communities in England,* London, Home Office Faith Communities Unit, 2004, see: http://www.homeoffice.gov.uk/docs3/workingtog_faith040329.pdf (accessed 29 October 2004).

[100] Crime and Disorder Act 1998, s. 28–32, as amended by Anti-terrorism, Crime and Security Act 2001, s. 39.

[101] The others were: two Sikh victims, two Hindu victims, one Jewish victim, one Jehovah's Witness victim, one Christian victim and one victim whose religion was not stated. See: Crown Prosecution Service, *Annual Report 2002–2003,* London, Crown Prosecution Service, 2003.

[102] Home Office, "Sideline the Extremists – Home Secretary", Press Release 222/2004, 7 July 2004, available at: http://www.homeoffice.gov.uk/n_story.asp?item_id=993 (accessed 2 November 2004).

[103] Home Office, "Government and police must engage communities to build a fairer criminal justice system", Press Release 220/2004, 2 July 2004.

has also announced a review of criminal justice statistics, with the aim to develop statistics that are "more informative, accessible and powerful at driving change".[104]

Government policy is not yet targeted at reaching individual faith groups. Government policy aimed at tackling socio-economic deprivation and improving life chances for the most disadvantaged should, indirectly, have a significant impact on Muslims. In addition, in some areas, like employment, policy is focused on minority ethnic communities and, as such, has the potential to reach Pakistani and Bangladeshi Muslims. However, such targeting does not extend to the 40 per cent of Muslims from other ethnic communities.

---

[104] Home Office, "New Challenges for Race Equality and Community Cohesion in the 21st Century", speech by the Rt. Hon. David Blunkett MP, Home Secretary, to the Institute of Public Policy Research, 7 July 2004, p. 14, available on the Home Office website at http://www.homeoffice.gov.uk/docs3/race-speech.pdf (accessed 2 November 2004).

4. IMPROVING POLICY FOR MUSLIMS IN THE UK

It is clear that, in designing and shaping public policy there is a move towards greater acknowledgement of the relevance of faith identities. At the same time, however, it is also clear that policy too often continues to focus on ethnicity alone, at a time when, for many Muslims, religion is becoming a more important marker of identity than ethnicity. It is in this context, that the policy papers in this report aim to support the Government in providing arguments and recommendations in favour of more nuanced policy which is sensitive to the needs of Muslim. The chapters in this report focus on four key policy areas: equality and discrimination, education, employment and criminal justice.

4.1 Recognising Muslim Identity

Chapter 1 of this report focuses on discrimination, equality and community cohesion. Its central premise is that religion is an important marker of identity for Muslims. It argues that it is important that Muslims see an accurate reflection of their sense of self in the public sphere. Citizens who sense that key legal and political institutions understand, accommodate and reflect their central concerns will feel a deeper sense of identification and belonging to these institutions. Recognition of identity by others is important for individual well-being. The failure to grant recognition (or the reflecting back to an individual a demeaning picture of themselves or the group from which they draw their sense of self) is a serious matter, which has implications for their well-being and autonomy. If Muslims see their sense of identity reflected in legal and political institutions, and their concerns being taken seriously by these institutions, they are more likely to comply with the obligations of these institutions without feeling coerced. It finds that the importance of recognising Muslims as a group based on religious affiliation is strengthened by the ways in which as a group they face social exclusion.

This chapter examines three forms of exclusion experienced by British Muslims: exclusion through violence, economic exclusion and exclusion from the public sphere. In relation to exclusion through violence, this paper argues for a broad definition of violence to also include less severe incidents of harassment and intimidation, including hatred expressed in speech ("hate speech") and vilification. At the same time, it recognises that the policy response to such violence cannot be the restriction of speech, except in severe cases where there is a risk of physical violence or public disorder. Instead, it is argued that the solution to the problem of the vilification of Muslims is to enable Muslims to enter into public debate. This includes, for example, investment that builds the capacity of Muslims to intervene in public discourse to be able to defend their group and faith and community. In short, what is needed is more speech, rather than the further regulation of free speech.

One consequence of the economic and social exclusion of Muslims is that they are heavy users of public and welfare services. In fact, one of the main points of contact between Muslims and the State is their experience of the State as a provider of key services such as health, education, housing and welfare. The Government acknowledges that, in Britain, people's religious differences affect their experience of public services.[105] This paper recommends that any attempt to improve the relationship between Muslims and the State, and their feeling of being respected and belonging, must therefore give this issue the highest priority.

4.2 Improving Policy on Education, Employment and Justice

Chapter 2 of this report argues that education is crucial for integration and social cohesion for several reasons. First, the school system is the first mainstream institution with which young people come into sustained contact. The extent to which schools respect and accommodate diversity send out strong signals about the value society, as a whole, places on diversity. Second, educational attainment is a key determinant of opportunities for finding employment and improving future life chances. Third, schools provide an opportunity to develop bonds and friendships across different ethnic and faith groups, and the education curriculum is itself a mechanism by which pupils are able to develop an understanding of the different groups within their community. This paper examines the key educational issues concerning Muslim parents, including the continuing poor academic results of Muslim children and the need to eradicate racism and racist and Islamophobic bullying in schools. The recommendations in relation to education are based on the premise, that a commitment to inclusive education requires both a willingness to listen to the ways that minority communities like Muslims define their own needs, and a determination to respond to those needs. It is argued that this approach will equally serve the well-being of the Muslim community and the interests of the broader, multicultural society.

Chapter 3 examines employment and participation in the labour market. Employment remains key to integration, empowerment and participation. The chapter outlines the context of Muslim participation in the labour market, in particular with respect to the labour market attainment of British Muslims. It identifies the barriers that Muslims face in entering and progressing in the labour market and the present gaps in public policy in this area. It argues that the Government should commit itself to policy which

---

[105] Home Office, *Strength in Diversity: Towards and Community Cohesion and Race Equality Strategy*, London, Home Office, 2004, p. 13.

has the clear aim of integrating Muslims into the mainstream labour market. It recommends that policy-makers should develop an inclusive and integrated strategy for Muslims to support their labour market entry and progression, and help overcome the barriers they encounter.

Chapter 4 examines policing and criminal justice, an area of growing concern, both in light of the high risk of Muslim experiencing crime as victims, the growing numbers of Muslim prisoners and the impact of anti-terrorism legislation on policing and on the Muslim communities sense of justice. Confidence in the criminal justice system is central to a sense of belonging and inclusion in society. This chapter examines the extent to which the criminal justice system presently addresses the needs of Muslims and makes recommendations aimed at improving the confidence of Muslims in the system. It looks across the board at all aspects of the contacts between Muslims and the criminal justice system, whether as victims of crime, witnesses, offenders, employees or volunteers.

4.3   General Findings

While policy is moving in the right direction with respect to meeting the needs of Muslims as a group, progress is still not enough to enable some of the real and rapid changes now required. This report makes a number of recommendations in the areas of equality and discrimination, education, employment and criminal justice. At the heart of these recommendations, however, is an underlying need for policy, as a whole, to become more responsive, sensitised and proactive with respect to engagement with Muslim communities. To achieve this, however, there is a need for the experiences of Muslim communities to be adequately understood and researched. Some of the general recommendations this report makes are:

- Improved data collection on the basis of faith (as well as ethnicity).

- More research on the specific needs of British Muslims as a group. For example, research to understand the barriers which Muslim women may face in accessing employment opportunities, and how these differ across generation and class.

- Strengthened engagement by Government agencies and public bodies with local Muslim communities, which should in turn feed into policymaking.

- Greater capacity building among Muslims and Muslim voluntary sector groups, to support greater participation and engagement in civic life.

- Better Muslim representation (for example, within the education and criminal justice system).

From the recommendations in these reports, three broad areas of work can be identified:

1. Policy aimed at tackling the socio-economic disadvantage experienced by Muslim communities should be better targeted to meet the specific needs of Muslims as a group (rather than through the lens of ethnic affiliation), to ensure that it reaches individuals from Muslim communities.

2. Policy aimed at addressing the discrimination encountered by Muslims, as a result of the prejudice and stereotypes that others have about them. In particular, anti-racism and diversity training should also cover anti-Muslim racism; and ethnic monitoring should, where possible, also include monitoring of religious affiliation, in order to identify ways in which policies can, unintentionally, operate to disadvantage Muslims.

3. Policy that views faith identities as a positive resource, which should be respected and acknowledged. For example, in education, supporting the interests of Muslim pupils by offering Arabic as a foreign language option or by including Muslim civilisation in the study of history.

Appendix 1: Definitions

Religious categories in the 2001 Census: the UK 2001 National Census asked an optional question on religious affiliation. The data is disaggregated into the following nine categories: Buddhist, Christian, Hindu, Jewish, Muslim, Sikh, any other religion, no religion and religion not stated.

Ethnic categories in the 2001 Census: the UK 2001 National Census contained a 16-point structure: White (British, Irish or Any Other White Background); Mixed (White and Black Caribbean, White and Black African, White and Asian or any other Mixed Background); Asian or Asian British (Indian, Pakistani, Bangladeshi, Any Other Asian Background); Black and Black British (Caribbean, African, any other Black background); Chinese or other ethnic group (Chinese, any other).

"Ethnic minorities": in this report, the use of the term "ethnic minority" as a broad "umbrella" label, is deliberate, to signify reference to a wide variety of ethnic minority groups. Where greater precision is required, reference to specific component groups within the ethnic minority population is made in the text. There is, inevitably, considerable debate and disagreement on the question of race, ethnicity and nomenclature. No specific political or sociological inference should be drawn from the use of related terminology in this report.

"White": as with the term "ethnic minority", the generic label "White" should be used with some caution. The existence of distinctive ethnic groups within the "White" category is gradually being acknowledged. Notably, in the UK 2001 National Census, people of Irish descent are recognised as a separate ethnic group.

Appendix 2: Bibliography

Alexander, C., *The Asian Gang: Ethnicity, identity, masculinity* (Oxford: Berg, 2000)

Ansari, H., *'The Infidel Within': Muslims in Britain since 1800* (London: Hurst, 2004)

Archer, L., *Race, Masculinity and Schooling: Muslim boys and education* (Maidenhead: Open University Press, 2003)

Ballard, R. (ed.) *Desh Pardesh: The South Asian Presence in Britain* (London: Hurst and Company, 1994)

Bhattacharayya, G., L. Ison and M. Blair, *Ethnic Minority Attainment Participation in Education and Training: the Evidence,* (Nottingham: DfES, 2003)

Bouchner, S., *Cultures in Contact* (New York: Pergamon Press, 1982)

Cersari J. (ed.), *European Muslims and the Secular State in a comparative perspective: final symposium report* (Brussels: European Commission DG Research, Network on Comparative Research on Islam and Muslims and Europe, 2003)

Commission for Racial Equality, *A Formal Investigation of the Police Service of England and Wales: an Interim Report* (London: CRE, 2004)

Commission for Racial Equality, *Fairness for All: A New Commission for Equality and Human Rights – a response* (London: CRE, 2004)

Conners, H., C. Tyers, T. Modood and J. Hillage, *Why the Difference? A Closer Look at Higher Education Minority Ethnic Students and Graduates,* Research Report No. 552 (London: Institute of Employment Studies, 2004)

Crown Prosecution Service Inspectorate, *Thematic Review of CPS Casework with a Minority Ethnic Dimension* (London: CPSI, 2002)

Crown Prosecution Service Inspectorate, *A Follow-up Review of CPS Casework with a Minority Ethnic Dimension* (London: CPSI, 2004)

Crown Prosecution Service Inspectorate, *Annual Report 2002–2003* (London: CPSI, 2003)

Crown Prosecution Service Inspectorate, *Guidance on Prosecuting Cases of Racist and Religious Crime* (London: CPSI, 2003)

Cuperus, R., K. A. Duffek and J. Kandel (eds.), *The Challenge of Diversity: European Social Democracy Facing Migration, Integration, and Multiculturalism* (Innsbruck: Studienverlag, 2003)

Department for Trade and Industry, *Fairness for All* (London: DTI, 2004)

Dwyer C., "Negotiating diasporic identities: young British South Asian Muslim women", *Women's Studies International Forum*, 23:4 (2000), 475–486

Dwyer, C., "Contradictions of community: questions of identity for young British Muslim women", *Environment and Planning A*, 31:1 (1999)

Dwyer, C., "Veiled meanings: young British Muslim women and the negotiation of differences", *Gender, Place and Culture*, 6:1 (1999)

Espoito, J. L. and F. Burgat (eds.), *Modernising Islam, Religion and the Public Sphere in Europe and the Middle East* (London: Hurst, 2003)

Forum Against Islamophobia and Racism, *A Submission to the Home Affairs Committee's Inquiry into Terrorism and Social Cohesion* (London: FAIR, 2004)

Forum Against Islamphobia and Racism, Al-Khoei Foundation and the Muslim College, *Counter-Terrorism Powers: Reconciling Security and Liberty in an Open Society: Discussion Paper – A Muslim Response* (London: FAIR, 2004)

Glynn S., "Bengali Muslims: the new East End radicals?" *Ethnic and racial studies*, 25:6 (2002)

HM Prison Service, *Implementing Race Equality in Prisons: A Shared Agenda for Change* (London: HM Prison Service, 2004)

Home Office, *Improving Public Satisfaction and Confidence in the Criminal Justice System Framework Document* (London: Home Office, 2003)

Home Office, *New Challenges for Race Equality and Community Cohesion in the 21st Century*, A speech by the Rt. Hon. David Blunkett MP, Home Secretary, to the Institute of Public Policy Research (London: Home Office, 2004)

Home Office, *Statistics on race and Race and the Criminal Justice System: A Home office publication under section 95 of the Criminal Justice Act 1991,* (London: Home Office, 2004)

Home Office, *Strength in Diversity: Towards a Community Cohesion and Race Equality Strategy* (London: Home Office Communications Directorate, 2004)

Home Office Faith Communities Unit, *Working Together: Cooperation Between Government and Faith Communities – Recommendations of the Steering Group Reviewing patterns of engagement between Government and Faith Communities in England* (London: Home Office Faith Communities Unit, 2004)

Hopkins, P., "Young Muslim men in Scotland: inclusions and exclusion", *Children's Geographies* 2:2 (2004), 257–272

Hopkins, P., *Young Muslim men and 'blue squares': Negotiating Citizenship and Nationality in Scotland*, a paper presented at the Royal Geographical Society with the Institute of British Geographers Annual Conference, London, 3-5 September 2003

Huang, C. and B. Kleiner, "New developments concerning Religious Discrimination in the Workplace", *International Journal of Sociology and Social Policy*, 21:8-10 (2001), 128–136

Human Rights Watch, *Neither Just nor Effective: indefinite detention without trial in the United Kingdom under Part 4 of the Anti-Terrorism, Crime and Security Act 2001*, Human Rights Watch Briefing Paper (New York: Human Rights Watch, 2004)

Hunter, S.T. and H. Malik (eds.), *Islam in Europe and the United States: A Comparative Perspective* (Washington, Centre for Strategic and International Studies, 2002)

Hutnik, N., "Aspects of identity in multi-ethnic society", *New Community*, 12:1 (1985)

Jacobson, J., "Religion and Ethnicity: dual and alternative sources of identity among young British Pakistanis", *Ethnic and Racial Studies*, 20:2 (1997)

Lathion, S., "A New Spectre? Islam and Muslims in Europe after 9/11", *Islamica Magazine*, 61 (Summer/Autumn 2004)

Liberty, *Reconciling Security and Liberty in an Open Society – Liberty Response* (London: Liberty, 2004)

Macey, M., "Religion, male violence and the control of women: Pakistani Muslim men in Bradford, UK", *Gender and Development*, 7:1 (1999), 48–55

Malik, I. H., *Islam and Modernity: Muslims in Europe and the United States* (London: Pluto Press, 2004)

Modood, T. and R. Berthoud, *Ethnic Minorities in Britain: Diversity and Disadvantage* (London, Policy Studies Institute, 1997)

Modood, T., "Muslims and the Politics of Difference", *Political Quarterly*, 74:1 (2003), 100–115

Nazroo, J., *Ethnicity, Class and Health* (London: Policy Studies Institute, 2001)

O'Beirne, M., *Religion in England and Wales: findings from the 2001 Home Office Citizenship Survey*, Home Office Research Study No. 274 (London: Home Office, Research, Statistics and Development Directorate, 2004)

Office of National Statistics, *Focus on Religion* (London: ONS, 2004)

Open Society Institute, *Monitoring Minority Protection in the EU: The Situation of Muslims in the UK* (Budapest: Open Society, EUMAP, 2002)

Oxford Centre for Islamic Studies, *Muslim housing experiences* (London: Housing Corporation, 2004)

Page, B., R. Wake and A. Ames, *Public Confidence in the Criminal Justice System: Home Office Research Findings 221* (London: HMSO, 2004)

Park, A., P. Philips M. and Johnson, *Young People in Britain: The Attitudes of Experiences of 12 to 19 year olds* (London: National Centre for Social Research, 2004)

Parker-Jenkins, M. and K. F. Haw, "Equality within Islam, not without it: The views of Muslim girls in Britain", *The Muslim Educational Quarterly* 13:3 (1996), 17–34

Parker-Jenkins, M., K. F. Haw, B. A. Irving and S. Khan, "Double Discrimination: An Examination of the Career Destinations of Muslim Women in Britain", *Advancing Women in Leadership*, 2:1 (1999)

Pauly, R. J., Jr. *Islam in Europe: integration or Marginalisation?* (Aldershot: Ashgate, 2004)

Ramadan, T., *To be a European Muslim: a study of Islamic sources in the European context* (Leicester: The Islamic Foundation, 2002)

Richardson, R. (ed.) *Islamophobia – issues, challenges and action: A Report by the Commission on British Muslims and Islamophobia* (Stoke-on-Trent: Trentham Books, 2004)

Saeed, A., N. Blain and D. Forbes, "New Ethnic and national questions in Scotland: post-British identities among Glasgow Pakistani teenagers", *Ethnic and Racial Studies*, 22:5 (1999), 821–844

Sahgal, G. and N. Yuval-Davis (eds.), *Refusing Holy Orders: Women and fundamentalism in Britain* (London: Virago Press, 1992)

Samad, Y., T. Ranger and O. Stuart (eds.), *Culture Identity and Politics: Ethnic Minorities in Britain* (Aldershot: Avebury, 1996)

Seddon, M.S., D. Hussain and N. Malik, *British Muslims – Loyalty and Belonging* (Leicester: The Islamic Foundation, 2003)

Sheridan, L., *Effects of the Events of September 11th 2001 on Discrimination and Implicit Racism in Five Religious and Ethnic Groups* (Leicester: Leicester University, 2002)

Skelton, T. and G. Valentine (eds.), *Cool Places: Geographies of Youth Cultures* (London, Routledge, 1997)

Spencer, S. (ed.), *The Politics of Migration* (Oxford: Blackwell, 2003)

Weller, P., A. Fieldman and K. Purdam, *Religious Discrimination in England and Wales*, Home Office Research Study No. 220 (London: Home Office Research, Development and Statistics Directorate, 2001)

British Muslims –
Discrimination, Equality
and Community Cohesion

Table of Contents

List of Acronyms

ACAS	Advisory, Conciliation and Arbitration Service
BCS	British Crime Survey
CEHR	Commission for Equality and Human Rights
CPS	Crown Prosecution Service
CRE	Commission for Racial Equality
DfES	Department for Education and Skills
DCMS	Department of Culture, Media and Sport
DTI	Department of Trade and Industry
EOC	Equal Opportunities Commission
PIU	Performance and Innovation Unit
RRA	Race Relations Act 1976
RR(A)A	Race Relations (Amendment) Act 2000
WEU	Women and Equalities Unit

1. EXECUTIVE SUMMARY

Community cohesion is seen as a way to establish a greater sense of citizenship, through the promotion of greater knowledge, respect and contact between people from diverse cultural backgrounds. A cohesive community is one where there is a common vision and all communities have a sense of belonging, where diversity is appreciated and positively valued. This paper argues that Government policy on British minority communities, including Muslims, needs to actively promote community cohesion (and, in turn, political stability) while at the same time ensuring principles of justice. Together, these two principles can serve to promote an inclusive vision of citizenship that allows individuals to simultaneously identify themselves as members of a particular ethnic or religious group, while also feeling a sense of belonging to Britain.

While ethnically diverse, there is sufficient similarity amongst British Muslims to speak about them meaningfully as a "social group", whose membership is linked by common faith-based beliefs, sentiments, experiences and attitudes. In developing and implementing policy there may be times when it is important to recognise faith identities and Muslims as a distinct group, rather than relying uniquely on ethnic categories such as Bangladeshi or Pakistani. Of course, individual Muslims also have aspects to their sense of personal identity that are independent of this group identity. However, it is clear that religion is an important aspect of identity for Muslims and for a society to create a common vision and instil a sense of belonging, it must also recognise individuals as members of social groups that the individuals themselves consider meaningful and significant.

Citizens who feel that key legal and political institutions understand, accommodate and reflect their central concerns will have a deeper sense of identification and belonging to these institutions. However, merely recognising individuals as citizens is in itself insufficient as it ignores the group dimension. The public recognition of Muslim identity will allow individuals to feel that they are accepted by the State and in the public sphere. For British Muslims to have a sense of belonging to a wider political community, they must be able to identify with the key legal and political institutions *as Muslims*, and feel included in the public culture of Great Britain *as Muslims*. Whether this process is called accommodation, pluralism or multiculturalism is less important than the fact that it can create a stable future for Muslims in Britain.

This paper aims to explore the basis by which British Muslims should be treated as a distinct social group for policy purposes, and establish recommendations aimed at improving policy addressing the needs of Muslims as a group. In particular, it is recommended that the Government ensure that more comprehensive data is collected on the basis of individuals' religious identity, not only their ethnicity. One of the most important reasons why it is necessary to recognise Muslims as a faith-based social group is that they, as a group, face problems of social exclusion. The Government uses the term social exclusion to describe what can happen when people or areas suffer from a combination of related problems[1] including unemployment, unfair discrimination, poor housing or high crime rates. However, it is also useful to examine more specifically the three main types of social exclusion faced by British Muslims: *exclusion through violence, economic exclusion,* and *political and public exclusion.*

Social exclusion premised on *exclusion through violence* is driven not only by hate crimes, but also by less severe incidents of harassment and intimidation, including "hate speech". The Government response to hate crimes in the post-11 September environment has been promising, with an extension of legislation to specifically cover religiously motivated crime.[2] However, a continued focus on using ethnic categories may nonetheless hamper progress in tackling hate crimes. In particular, there remains a significant gap in the mechanisms in place for inspecting key aspects of the criminal justice system for anti-Muslim prejudice. The Government response to hate speech has been to propose an extension of hate crime legislation to also cover Muslims.[3] If implemented and enforced effectively, this legislation should send a clear message that those who commit acts of violence or harassment against Muslims out of hatred of their religious identity will receive tougher penalties under criminal law.

The importance of free speech in a liberal society places legitimate limitations on the ability of the State to regulate speech. Criminal law should therefore be used in only the most extreme cases and the Government should also investigate alternative policy options. In particular, the Government should look into ways to strengthen the capacity of Muslims to enter into public debate and defend their faith in the public sphere. For example, the Government should encourage and fund initiatives to enable Muslim organisations to challenge distorted images of Muslims. In short, what is needed is more speech, rather than the regulation of free speech.

The level of economic exclusion faced by many British Muslims is examined in more detail in Chapter 3 of this report, on British Muslims and the Labour Market. This chapter focuses, rather, on discrimination law and policy, in particular in employment and training. It also addresses policy on the provision of services in the private and public sector. This is particularly important, given that a direct consequence of the

---

[1] See: Office of the Deputy Prime Minister, *Tackling Social Exclusion: Taking Stock and Looking to the Future,* London, Social Exclusion Unit, ODPM, 2004.

[2] Crime and Disorder Act 1998, s. 28-32, as amended by the Anti-terrorism, Crime and Security Act (2001), s. 39.

[3] In July, the Home Secretary announced the government's intention to introduce legislation to outlaw incitement to religious hatred see: Home Office press release, 7 July 2004, available at: http://www.homeoffice.gov.uk/n_story.asp?item_id=993 [accessed 21 September 2004].

economic exclusion encountered by Muslims is that they are disproportionately reliant on public and welfare services.

The Government's main response to problems of discrimination is reliance on the Race Relations Act. However, even with the transposition of the provisions of the EU Employment Directive, there is a long standing anomaly by which ethnic religious minorities such as Sikhs and Jews receive direct protection as a group, while non-ethnic religious minorities such as Muslims are given only indirect, and in some areas, no protection. The Government has announced its intention to introduce new legislation to prohibit religious discrimination in the provision of goods and services. However, there are also extra-legal measures that could be taken. For example, measures can be taken to gain a better understanding of the specific needs of Muslims in relation to key public services. Information gathered directly on Muslims as a group, as opposed to that gathered indirectly, through the lens of ethnicity, may then be used to develop more nuanced policy aimed at addressing the social exclusion faced by British Muslims.

The third type of the social exclusion encountered by British Muslims is *political and public exclusion.* This paper argues for the creation of a common public sphere able to offer a sense of belonging to both majority and minority communities, and to promote coexistence and community cohesion. To this end, both the majority and minority groups must recognise that comprises will need to be made. For the minority, this means that their private identity cannot automatically be reflected in the public sphere without some limited assimilation to the shared values that are the agreed-upon basis for a common public life. In turn, the majority will need to accept a necessary transformation of the public sphere and of public institutions, to accommodate some of the needs of minorities such as Muslims. An important role of the Government in this process is to encourage and support measures and initiatives through which the most urgent needs of Muslims, and in particular the most marginalised Muslim groups, can be accommodated. Muslim organisations also have a crucial role to play in this process.

2. INTRODUCTION

This report focuses on issues of law, politics and social policy using the usual methods of the social sciences. It is not intended to communicate the status and significance of Islam in the lives of British Muslims. Rather, it sets itself the more modest task of suggesting one way in which public policy could start to think about Muslims in the UK.

General Government policy on ethnic minorities, as well as the recent policies on "community cohesion" created since the disturbances in May 2001 in the North of England, emphasise the need for political stability.[4] This report endorses the priority given to this aim, but its main conclusions are that policy should be formulated around two poles: (1) political stability – sometimes also called "community cohesion"; and (2) principles of justice. A liberal state must, of course, pay attention to justice as "the first virtue of political institutions",[5] but, in addition, it should be able to resolve disagreements in a reasonable and politically stable way, without resorting to violence.

These two principles that guide policy serve a wider vision toward which society must strive: the guarantee of a level citizenship that allows individuals to simultaneously identify themselves as Muslims and feel a sense of belonging to Britain. If Muslims are to have an inclusive and egalitarian basis for this sense of belonging to a wider political community, they must be able to identify with the key legal and political institutions *as Muslims,* and they need to feel included in the public culture of Great Britain *as Muslims.* Whether this process is called accommodation, pluralism or multiculturalism is less important than the fact that it can create a stable future for Muslims in Britain.

Although individuals remain the paramount unit for analysis of liberal politics, it is also crucial to recognise the reality and importance of groups. This chapter argues that, when it comes to developing social policy, Muslims should at times be recognised as a social group. It goes on to identify the ways in which they can experience social exclusion as a group. The subsequent sections highlight some of the key features of social exclusion.

Section 3 deals with issues of method and sets out definitions of key concepts used in this chapter. There is sufficient similarity amongst Muslims to speak about them meaningfully as a social group whose membership is linked by common faith-based beliefs, sentiments, experiences and attitudes. However, the fact that Muslims are a social group does not preclude individual Muslims from having aspects to their sense of personal identity that are independent of their group identity.

---

[4] For further details see: *Minority Protection in the EU: The Situation of Muslims in the UK,* Budapest, Open Society Institute, 2002, pp. 85–87, available on the website of the EU Monitoring and Advocacy Program (EUMAP), at http://www.eumap.org/reports.

[5] J. Rawls, *A Theory of Justice,* Oxford, Oxford University Press, 1999.

It is important that Muslims see an accurate reflection of their sense of self in the public sphere. Citizens who feel that key legal and political institutions understand, accommodate and reflect their central concerns will have a deeper sense of identification and of belonging to these institutions. Recognition of identity by others is important for individual well-being. Failing to grant an individual recognition – or reflecting back to an individual a demeaning picture of themselves or the group from which they draw their sense of self – is a serious matter that has implications for that person's well-being and autonomy. If Muslims see their sense of identity reflected in legal and political institutions, and they see their concerns being taken seriously by these institutions, they are more likely to comply with the obligations of these institutions without feeling coerced. Therefore, in order for Muslims to feel that their concerns are being accurately reflected, it is vital that policy-makers and legal and political institutions recognise Muslims as a distinct social group.

Section 4 explores the forms of social exclusion suffered by Muslims in the UK. One reason why it is so important to recognise Muslims as a group based on religious affiliation is that they face social exclusion as a group. The Government has defined social exclusion as a short-hand term for what can happen when people or areas suffer from a combination of related problems, such as unemployment, poor skills, low incomes, unfair discrimination, poor housing, high crime, bad health and family breakdown.[6] The experience of large numbers of Muslims in the UK falls within this definition, and this results in their *involuntary* exclusion from mainstream social, political and economic institutions. More specifically, the social exclusion of Muslims is a term that captures their experience as a group that has overwhelmingly suffered in the past, and continues to suffer, from a combination of linked socio-economic problems.[7] Furthermore, after September 11, the continuing debate about Muslims and Islam in the public sphere makes Muslims in Britain a group that is particularly at risk of being culturally alienated. Either their own beliefs are not represented at all in the public sphere or they are represented in ways that are distorted, inaccurate and demeaning.

---

[6] See: Office of the Deputy Prime Minister, *Tackling Social Exclusion: Taking Stock and Looking to the Future,* London, Social Exclusion Unit, ODPM, 2004, (hereafter, ODPM, *Tackling Social Exclusion*).

[7] The evidence of socio-economic disadvantage for Muslims has usually relied on data for the Pakistani and Bangladeshi community in the UK. Over 90 per cent of Pakistanis and Bangladeshis in the UK are Muslim. Together they form 60 per cent of the UK Muslim population. However, information about the socio-economic disadvantage of Muslims as a group is beginning to emerge. See: Office of National Statistics, *Focus on Religion,* London, ONS, 2004.

In order to more fully explore the social exclusion that Muslims face as a group, it is useful to use as a reference the "five faces of oppression" defined by Young.[8] These forms of oppression can in turn be translated into three distinct types of social exclusion: exclusion through violence, economic exclusion, and political and public exclusion. Each of these forms of social exclusion is treated in more detail in the next three sections of this report.

Section 5 focuses on exclusion through violence. The response of the State to hate crimes in the post-September 11 environment has been promising, and it includes an extension of the Crime Disorder Act (1998) to specifically cover religiously motivated crime.[9] However, a continued focus on using racial and ethnic categories alone could, nonetheless, hamper progress in this area. There is a significant gap in the mechanisms in place for inspecting key aspects of the criminal justice system for anti-Muslim prejudice – at exactly the time when there is a pressing need for such processes.[10] In particular, it is necessary to think imaginatively about how to fill the gap left by the anomalous coverage of the Race Relations (Amendment) Act (2000) (hereafter, RR(A)A). One possibility is to introduce a voluntary process, which need not be as formal as a code of practice, to evaluate these agencies of the criminal justice system in relation to the impact of their policies on Muslims.

To understand a group's experience of exclusion through violence, however, it is important to widen the definition of violence to also include less severe incidents of harassment and intimidation, including hatred expressed in speech ("hate speech"). The State response to hate speech has been to propose legislation extending hate crime legislation to cover Muslims.[11] If implemented and enforced effectively, this could send a clear and unequivocal message that those who commit acts of violence against, and harassment of, Muslims out of deliberate and conscious hatred of their membership of their religious group deserve special penalties under the criminal law. However, the importance of free speech in a liberal society places legitimate limitations on the ability of the state to regulate speech. Criminal law should be used in only the most extreme cases where there is a risk of either physical violence or public disorder that this sort of

---

[8] See Iris Marion Young, *Justice and the Politics of Difference*, Princeton, NJ, Princeton University Press, 1990, esp. Ch. 5, (hereafter, Young, *Justice and the Politics of Difference*).

[9] Crime and Disorder Act 1998, s. 28–32, as amended by the Anti-terrorism, Crime and Security Act (2001), s. 39.

[10] See the chapter of this report on Muslims and the Criminal Justice System in this report for a discussion of the low levels of confidence Muslims have in parts of the criminal justice system.

[11] In July, the Home Secretary announced the Government's intention to introduce legislation to outlaw incitement to religious hatred see: Home Office press release, 7 July 2004, available at http://www.homeoffice.gov.uk/n_story.asp?item_id=993 (accessed 21 September 2004).

activity should be regulated. The grievances of Muslims faced with hate speech and vilification against them as a group can also be addressed using alternative policy options. This includes, for example, investment that builds the capacity of Muslims to intervene in public discourse to be able to defend their group and faith and thereby communicate what they consider to be the truth of their religion within the public sphere. The solution to the problem of the vilification of Muslims is to enable Muslims to enter into public debate. In short, what is needed is more speech, rather than the regulation of free speech.

Section 6 focuses on economic exclusion and, more specifically, on discrimination law and policy, in particular in employment and training; and in the provision of services in the private and public sector. The Government's main response to the problems of discrimination on the basis of race is reliance on the Race Relations Act (1976) that has indirectly given protection to Muslims against discrimination in employment, education, housing and in private and public sector service delivery.[12] There was a long standing anomaly which directly protected ethnic religious minorities such as Sikhs and Jews, but gave only indirect and in some cases no protection to non-ethnic religious minorities such as Muslims. Even after implementation of EU Employment Directive Muslims *qua Muslims* (unlike Sikhs and Jews) will not be protected from discrimination in the following areas: social protection (including social security and health care); education; goods and services available to the public including housing; social advantages (such as housing benefits, student maintenance grants and loans, or benefits for senior citizens). The Government has announced its intention to introduce legislation to prohibit religious discrimination in relation to goods and services but has provided no further details.

One consequence of the fact that Muslims suffer from economic and social exclusion is that they are heavy users of public and welfare services. In fact, one of the main points of contact between Muslims and the State is their experience of the State as a provider of these types of key services such as health, education, housing and welfare. Any attempt to improve the relationship between Muslims and the State, and their feeling of being respected and belonging, must therefore give this issue the highest priority. Dependency on public services carries with it the risk of being subject to intrusive authority by serve providers, who have significant power. In meeting the needs of those whom they service these public agencies often construct the needs of the user based on limited experience and information. This has the potential to lead to breaches of principles such as respect, autonomy and privacy.

---

[12] The Race Relations (Amendment) Act (2000) amended the Race Relations Act of 1976 to prohibit public authorities from discriminating on the grounds of race in carrying out their functions.

The key legislative framework for ensuring that public authorities examine their policies for discrimination is the RR(A)A, but this does not directly cover Muslims as a group. Still, there are other measures that could be taken that would not involve reform of the legislation. The starting point must be a better understanding of the specific needs of Muslims in relation to key public services. The Social Exclusion Unit has recognised that Government policy is dramatically failing to reach Pakistanis and Bangladeshis and that there may be need to change policy in this area.[13] Better information, and research that targets the faith needs of these communities directly, rather than indirectly, may reveal problems in policy that the Government previously has not realised, due to officials' insistence on using race or ethnicity as the most appropriate categories for analysis.

Section 7 addresses political and public exclusion. This paper argues for the creation of a common public sphere, one that is neither neutral between cultures nor a perfect mirror for personal identity. This common culture will be influenced by a process of renegotiating between the diverse cultural groups within a political community. In order to develop "a sense of belonging" that remains attentive to both the majority and the minority, and to generate a common public culture within which different groups co-exist, the parties involved must make compromises and adjustments. For the minority, this means that their private identity cannot automatically be reflected in the public sphere without some limited assimilation to the shared values that are the agreed-upon basis for a common public life. For the majority, this re-negotiation carries with it significant costs. These costs will be an inevitable outcome of attempts to transform the public sphere and institutions – from exclusively reflecting the dominant culture, towards a common culture that also seeks to accommodate some of the most urgent needs of minorities, such as Muslims.

To achieve this kind of inclusion, legal and political institutions must show that they take the needs and concerns of Muslims seriously. This debate needs to be conducted within mainstream institutions, where negotiation with other groups and the majority can take place. Clearly, Muslims will need to make concessions and compromises in their demands. The same is true of majority institutions and structures, which will need to accommodate some of the key demands of Muslims. Accommodation through a recognition of some aspects of the needs of Muslims could ensure a greater coalescence between the experience of individual Muslims in their daily lives, where many are guided by Islamic legal rules, and their experience of majority legal and political institutions. This kind of accommodation provides freely chosen normative guidance in the lives of Muslim citizens, by allowing key institutions to recognise certain Muslim norms as important. The result may be a higher degree of willing co-operation and identification with these institutions and, therefore, more political

---

[13] ODPM, *Tackling Social Exclusion*, p. 19.

stability. Muslim communities' institutions need to use this insight as the starting point for their own analysis. Most importantly, Muslim institutions must acknowledge that the values of liberal democracy and constitutionalism are non-negotiable, and demands for accommodation must accept these core liberal constitutional values as paramount.

The response by many Muslims to the misrepresentation of Islam has not been to enter the public space with their preferred version but, instead, to argue for restraints on speech. This response underestimates the value of freedom of speech and its priority in a liberal democracy. A subtle political and cultural solution may be more effective than legal regulation. While a liberal state may hesitate before regulating speech, in a situation where a vulnerable minority group is faced with persistent vilification, the State can legitimately respond by using non-legal remedies. British Muslims can reasonably lobby institutions like the Department of Culture, Media and Sport (DCMS) to take their interests more seriously. Government resources can help Muslim communities build the capacity needed to intervene in the public sphere and the media, so that Muslims can redress distortions that prevail. Equally important is State support for cultural projects that allow Muslims to express themselves in variety of ways – not only through political, social and economic speech, but also through cultural forms, such as art, music and literature. Freedom of thought and conscience, as well as the availability of public and private resources for developing and disseminating culture, provide Muslims with a unique opportunity for self-development and communication. A DCMS consultation and policy paper on the way in which arts and culture can contribute to cohesion in communities sets out the criteria for supporting communities in this way.[14] This work needs to be revived in the specific context of Muslims.

---

[14] Department for Culture, Media and Sport, *Culture at the Heart of Regeneration – Consultation Paper*, London, DCMS, 2004, available on the DCMS website at http://www.culture.gov.uk/global/consultations/2004+current+consultations/cons_culture_heart_regeneration.htm (accessed 1 November 2004), (hereafter, DCMS *Culture at the Heart of Regeneration*).

3. TOWARDS COMMUNITY COHESION: RECOGNISING MUSLIMS AS A SOCIAL GROUP

This section argues that the recognition of Muslims as a social group is a key aspect of achieving community cohesion between the minority Muslim communities and the majority. Community cohesion is a term that has been used in Government documents and policy, and the Government gives value to greater community cohesion because it can contribute to a number of important objectives.[15]

Community cohesion is seen as a way to promote greater knowledge, respect and contact between various cultures, while establishing a greater sense of citizenship. A cohesive community is one where:

1. there is a common vision and all communities have a sense of belonging;

2. the diversity of people's different backgrounds and circumstances is appreciated and positively valued;

3. those from different backgrounds have similar life opportunities; and

4. people from different backgrounds develop strong, positive relationships in the workplace, in schools and within neighbourhoods.

This section argues that, if a society seeks to create a common vision, instil a sense of belonging and develop strong relationships, it must recognise individuals as members of social groups that the individuals themselves consider meaningful and significant. This public recognition of identity is important, because it allows individuals to feel that they are accepted by the State and the public sphere. Merely recognising individuals as citizens – the traditional liberal approach to the problem of minorities – is no longer sufficient, because it ignores this group dimension. An appropriate theory for addressing minority needs must take into account not only individual identity but also group affiliations that have importance for an individual's sense of self-respect. The work on social groups that has been done by Iris Marion Young provides a useful way to link the idea of community cohesion to traditional liberal concern with minorities.

---

[15] Home Office, *Community Cohesion,* summary from the official Home Office website, available at http://www.homeoffice.gov.uk/comrace/cohesion/index.html (accessed 25 October 2004), (hereafter, Home Office, *Community Cohesion*).

3.1   Muslims as a "Social Group"

The vexed question about whether or not, for the purposes of law and policy, Muslims should be considered as a racial/ethnic group – and related debate about a commonly accepted definition of what constitutes a "religion" – should not prevent recognition that, in practice, people can, and do, undertake definitions of Muslims as a group. Ordinary social science analysis meaningfully uses terms to describe groups defined by, for example, gender, age, race/ethnicity, nationality or class. However, although the *central* meaning of the distinguishing characteristic of membership of any social group may be clear, some *marginal aspects* of the definition may be less apparent. It may, therefore, be difficult to decide whether a particular individual is a member of a given group.

Because this paper focuses on policy analysis and recommendations, theoretical definitions of social groups, such as those of Young or others, are less important than functionalist and pragmatic considerations. Definitions of race, class and even gender break down in the face of difficult cases.[16] It seems reasonably clear that groups are a social phenomenon. Individuals often do associate with those with whom they share a cultural, social, religious or other affinity. According to Young, social groups are more than just a collection of individuals, they fundamentally shape the way in which individuals define themselves and the way in which they are viewed by others. A particular social group is differentiated from others by certain practices, cultural norms and ways of life. Each member of the group has an affinity with other members, due to shared experiences and ways of life that encourage them to associate with one another. Group identification often arises in contrast to, and in dialogue with, other groups, in other words, as a response to difference. The encounter of differences in experience between distinct groups can heighten this identification, despite the fact that each group is a member of the same society or political community.[17] It is possible to speak meaningfully about groups that organise themselves in a way that allows us to refer to them as social groups, whilst at the same time recognising the importance, and perhaps primacy, of individuals within a liberal political community.

Muslims share with other religious groups the fact that their association with one another is based around certain common beliefs that can be defined as "faith-based" beliefs. Faith-based narratives are a key aspect of social regulation for these sub-communities. Moreover, faith-based forms of knowledge characteristically determine a

---

[16] For example, Professor Modood notes that the category "Muslim" is "as internally diverse as 'Christian or Belgian' or 'middle-class', or any other category helpful in ordering our understanding of contemporary Europe; but just as diversity does not lead to the abandonment of social concepts in general, so with that of 'Muslim'". T. Modood, "Muslims and the Politics of Difference", in *Political Quarterly*, 2003, p. 100.

[17] See Young, *Justice and the Politics of Difference*, esp. p. 43.

minority's own criteria of validity, competence and application. For the individual, they define what can and should be said and done. Legitimacy is provided by the fact that people within that tradition listen to the narratives, recount them, give them authority and use them as the basis for their beliefs and conduct.[18] In addition, these normative criteria provide the background context for the exercise of choice in a wide range of matters that concern the individual. Commitments of faith may be critical, not only in their impact on the pragmatic choices about what to do and how to act, but also in their impact on the whole range of aesthetic and emotional experiences of the agent.[19] In these ways, a feature of faith is its influence on the motivations and inner states of consciousness, which guide belief and conduct in important areas of the life of Muslims.

It is a central premise of this paper that Muslims are a group whose membership is determined according to common faith-based beliefs, sentiments, experiences and attitudes. In short, there is sufficient similarity amongst Muslims to allow us to speak about them meaningfully as a social group. For some time, academic research has indicated that religion has become a more significant marker of identity than ethnicity for Muslims in the UK.[20] The Home Office *Citizenship Survey* (2001) also indicates that, for Muslims, religion is a more important aspect of identity than ethnicity, and is second only to family.[21]

Identifying Muslims as a social group does not determine the issue of how social policy should respond to this reality. It also does not mean that individual Muslims do not have their own distinct way of expressing their faith and sentiments. Nor does it mean that individuals are not able to transcend or reject their identity as Muslims. Furthermore, and most crucially for this chapter, the fact that Muslims are a social group does not preclude individual Muslims from having aspects to their sense of personal identity that are independent of their group identity as Muslims.[22]

---

[18] J. F. Lyotard, *The Postmodern Condition: A Report on Knowledge*, Manchester, Manchester University Press, 1986, pp. 18–23.

[19] See the discussion in: C. Taylor, "Self-interpreting Animals", in *Human Agency and Language, Philosophical Papers, Vol. I*, Cambridge, Cambridge University Press, 1985, p. 45, (hereafter, Taylor, *Self-interpreting Animals*).

[20] See, for example: L. Archer, *Race, Masculinity and Schooling: Muslim boys and education*, Maidenhead, Open University Press, 2003; and J. Jacobson, "Religion and Ethnicity: duel and alternative sources of identity among young British Pakistanis", in *Ethnic and Racial Studies* 20(2), 1997.

[21] M. O'Beirne, *Religion in England and Wales: findings from the Home Office Citizenship Study 2001*, Home Office Research Study 274, London, Home Office, 2004, p. 20, available at http://www.homeoffice.gov.uk/rds/pdfs04/hors274.pdf (accessed 16 October 2004).

[22] See: Young, *Justice and the Politics of Difference*, p. 45.

It is also worth pointing out that there are no clear rules that allow us to distinguish between different types of social groups. There is, and often will be, a considerable overlap between criteria such as race, ethnicity, national origin and religion. It can be difficult, on a theoretical level, to clearly demarcate social groups based on ethnicity from those based on religion. For example, it is hard to decide whether it is nationality or religion that best defines the identity of some Pakistani Muslims. For this reason, a pragmatic approach is needed. As a matter of practice, it will be more appropriate if law and policy does not place too great an emphasis on these fluid categories. So that, for example, access to important legal rights and public/social/economic goods should not be dependant on the rigid application of abstract definitions. Rather, what is more important is to identify the value of recognising the way in which certain individuals define themselves as part of a social group that can reasonably be defined and identified. This argument has a special importance in the context of Britain's Muslims, who have been denied direct access to important legal rights and public goods because of the view that, unlike Sikhs or Jews, Muslims are not an ethnic or racial group.[23]

So, does it matter whether the self-identification of Muslims is accurately reflected in law and politics? This paper argues that it matters very much that Muslims see an accurate reflection of their sense of self in the public sphere. It also seems to matter to Muslim community groups, who, for over a decade, have been asking the Government to recognise Muslims as a distinct category.[24] Moreover, it can be argued that recognition of Muslim identity can enhance political stability, community cohesion and principles of justice.

3.2   Political Stability and Community Cohesion

As indicated above, community cohesion is a key part of the Government's strategy towards minorities generally and Muslims in particular. Community cohesion has a number of aims, including fostering a sense of citizenship and belonging amongst minority groups and encouraging contacts between the majority and the minority communities. The Government's strategy focuses on issues such as political leadership, regeneration, employment, sports and culture, youth, policing, education and the

---

[23] See discussion below.

[24] Interviews with representatives of Muslim organisations, such as the Muslim Council of Britain and City Circle confirm these demands. Moreover, representative media, such as *Muslim News* and *Q News,* confirms that Muslims are keen to be recognised as a distinct group for the purposes of legal and political decision making.

media.[25] These issues are addressed in the main body of this report and in the sections that follow.

Here it is worth noting the process through which individuals can develop a meaningful sense of community and belonging. Common meanings and beliefs are embedded in contemporary social ways of life, and they often help constitute the social and political culture – the community – and its institutions.[26] These meanings and beliefs cannot be understood by merely noting their impact on, or importance for, individual agents. They are not just shared beliefs and attitudes of all the individuals in a society. They also form the basis for an appreciation of social practices and institutions that cannot be understood as anything but communal. The common meanings that sustain law and legal institutions are the basis for community. People have to share and participate in a language and understanding of norms that allows them to talk about these institutions and practices.[27]

If we accept the view that there is a stronger, constitutive, relationship between law and social practices, then law is not only connected to the community in that it attends to communal values. This view suggests that law actually has an important function to play, not only in reflecting, but also in creating and sustaining, social life and shared values. Moreover, the impact of legal and political institutions on life is not neutral. This alternative view also suggests that there is a causal relationship between private individual identity and public institutions. Citizens, who sense that key legal and political institutions understand, accommodate and reflect their central concerns will feel a deeper sense of identification and belonging to these institutions.

According to this analysis, the role of law and legal/political institutions goes beyond that of regulating disputes. Law functions as an institution that constructs behaviour, gives it sense and meaning, and influences the self-interpretation of beliefs and conduct of participants. This complex social function assigns to law and its institutions an important public role, as a bank of collective wisdom and as a public "ritual".

3.3 The Recognition of Identity

Another feature of contemporary liberal culture that is relevant to our discussion of community cohesion is the "politics of identity". This idea focuses attention on a

---

[25] See: Home Office, *Community Cohesion*.

[26] See: M. Malik, "Faith and the State of Jurisprudence", in *Faith and Law: Essays in Legal Philosophy*, Oxford, Hart Publications, 2000, (hereafter, Malik, *Faith and the State of Jurisprudence*).

[27] See: Taylor, *Self-interpreting Animals*.

number of recurring themes in contemporary political writing. It rejects an atomistic picture of individual freedom as radical detachment and recognises an important link between individual freedom and identity, on the one hand, and social practices and community, on the other. Two consequences follow from these connections. First, an important source of the well-being and self-respect of an individual arises out of their sense of who they are – through their identification with important beliefs, groups and attachments. Second, where these beliefs, attachments and groups are denigrated, this in turn undermines the sources of self-respect and well-being of the individual.

Key aspects of identity are formed in dialogue with the other people who are a significant presence in our lives. The resulting importance of values like respect and recognition makes issues of identity and group membership vital for the public sphere.[28] The link between recognition by others and individual well-being raises the stakes in the "politics of identity" debate. Failing to grant someone recognition – or giving that person incorrect recognition – can cause damage to the well-being of the individual. This moves the "politics of identity" debate from the private to the public sphere.

If recognition by others is important for individual well-being, then the failure to grant recognition – or the decision to reflect back to an individual a demeaning picture of themselves or the group from which they draw their sense of self – can be categorised as a serious matter. It has consequences for the well-being and autonomy of individuals.[29] Where the State and its institutions are implicated in creating and sustaining this distorted image, there is a strong argument suggesting that the requirements of respect and recognition have been breached.

A strategy that recognises Muslims as a social group may ensure the development of a common vocabulary in law and politics that has a deeper meaning for Muslims and that they develop in conjunction with all other British citizens. This will facilitate the process of encouraging Muslims to feel a sense of identification with key legal and political institutions, especially where these institutions recognise and accurately reflect their key concerns as Muslims. This sense of identification with legal and political institutions can provide Muslims with a basis for a sense of belonging to a political community that they can share with other citizens. This process has the potential to

---

[28] For a discussion of the untenability of Rawls' distinction between private and public reasons for action, see: J. Finnis, "Natural Law Theory and Limited Government", in R. George (ed.) *Natural Law, Liberalism and Morality*, Oxford, Clarendon Press, 1996, p. 9.

[29] See: Malik, *Faith and the State of Jurisprudence*.

generate a sense of belonging to local and national communities,[30] and, therefore, it can foster a greater level of community cohesion and national political stability. Recognition of their existence as a social group may also ensure that the self-identification of citizens as Muslims is accurately reflected in legal and political institutions, thereby satisfying Muslims' right to the recognition and respect that are part of what it means for a liberal state to treat citizens as autonomous and free. It is critically important that mainstream, rather than fringe institutions, provide this public space for recognition.

If Muslims see their sense of identity reflected in legal and political institutions, and see that their concerns are taken seriously by these institutions, they are more likely to comply with the obligations of these institutions without feeling coerced. The prospect of a greater convergence between the experience of individuals in their daily and practical lives and their experiences of normative legal and political institutions – and therefore of meaningful identification and a higher degree of willing co-operation with these institutions – would justify such an effort.

The argument of this section of the report is that it is time to reconsider the current orthodoxy of placing Muslims into racial categories. Such a change has been a longstanding and key demand of Muslim organisations, and it has been reiterated in interviews carried out with a range of Muslim representative organisations, such as the Muslim Council of Britain (MCB) and City Circle.[31] Both organisations, and other Muslim commentators, were emphatic in their conclusion that, if Muslims are recognised as a distinct group by legal/political institutions, and for the purpose of policy design, it would encourage Muslims to feel that their concerns were being accurately reflected, and it would thereby strengthen identification with these institutions.

Indirect indicators, such as race or ethnicity, are an insufficient and inaccurate way of analysing and accommodating Muslims as a social group. If we concentrate solely on

---

[30] For a more detailed discussion of the way in which this process could work see: A. Mason, "Political Community, Liberal-Nationalism and the Ethics of Assimilation", in *Ethics* 109(2), 1999, p. 261. See also: M. Malik, "Minority Protection and Human Rights", in Campbell, Ewing and Tomkins (eds.), *Sceptical Approaches to Human Rights*, Oxford University Press, Oxford, 2001.

[31] Interviews with the Muslim Council of Britain (MCB) and the organiser of the City Circle, London, March 2004. MCB is the largest umbrella organisation, with affiliates from across the country representing a diverse range of members of the Muslim community, including women and ethnic minorities within the Muslim community. City Circle is a body that was founded by a group of Muslim professional men and women who organise lectures that are open to Muslims and non-Muslims. City Circle also does grassroots work within the Muslim community.

ethnicity, we can make critical errors in analysis and miss important information that can only be captured when we use faith/religion as a category. This is not to say that there is no overlap between race and faith/religion, or to deny that, in some cases, one can act as an indicator for the other. The previous analysis merely sets out the argument in favour of a policy shift in our approach in relation to certain distinct areas of analysis. Abstract objections such as "how do we define religion" are less helpful than taking a pragmatic approach that recognises that Muslims are the largest religious minority group in the UK. This will inevitably raise important questions about their distinct needs, not only as political citizens, but also as workers and consumers of public and private services.

4. COMMUNITY COHESION AND SOCIAL EXCLUSION

Section 3 pointed out that there are overwhelming reasons to recognise Muslims as a distinct social group and category for policy analysis. Such recognition would, it is argued, make a considerable contribution to Muslims' sense of citizenship and belonging, thereby fostering community cohesion. Another important factor for ensuring stable communities is reducing social exclusion, which acts as a way of alienating particular social groups, such as Muslims, and acts a barrier to their integration within mainstream society. This section takes up social exclusion as the criteria that should be used to evaluate the status of British Muslims as a particular social group. Section 4.1 sets out a definition of the term social exclusion and examines its relevance for Muslims in Britain.

It is worth noting here that the study of groups raises particular challenges for traditional liberal political theory, which finds it difficult to incorporate groups rather than individuals into discussions about rights and justice. The usual standard that is demanded from a State in its treatment of citizens is the requirement of justice. In this case, justice is usually taken to mean individual justice, in the form of individual human rights or civil and political liberty. However, it is possible to take an alternative view, which emphasises justice for a group.

Young identifies a number of criteria, which she refers to as "the five faces of oppression", that allow us to evaluate whether or not a group is "oppressed".[32] These criteria can be summarised in the following way. *First,* a group is oppressed if it suffers systematic violence, in which members of the group are targeted and experience violence because they belong to that group. *Second,* a group is oppressed when its members experience exploitation due to the transfer of the results of their labour to another social group. For example, unskilled or marginal workers in a poorly paid profession are low paid compared with those in a more privileged employment positions. *Third,* a group is oppressed when it experiences marginalisation, such as when its members are either excluded or expelled from useful participation in the economic, political, cultural and institutional life of a society. *Fourth,* a group is oppressed if it lacks power over its own

---

[32] See: Young, *Justice and the Politics of Difference,* ch. 2.

ability to control participation in economic or political activity (powerlessness). *Fifth,* a group is oppressed if it experiences cultural alienation.[33]

Young's five criteria provide an invaluable benchmark for evaluating the legal and political status of Muslims in Britain. We can translate these categories into the vocabulary that the Government and policy-makers themselves use to analyse these issues: the paradigm of "social exclusion".[34] Young's first criterion, systematic violence, is equivalent to "exclusion through violence" and will be addressed in Section 5 of this report. The phenomena of marginalisation, exploitation and economic powerlessness will be treated under the term "economic exclusion", which is covered in Section 6. And cultural alienation and political powerlessness are addressed as "political and public exclusion" in Section 7. These three main categories – exclusion through violence, economic exclusion and political and public exclusion – together capture most of the sources of oppression and social exclusion that are problematic for minority groups like British Muslims.

4.1   Muslims and Social Exclusion

"Social exclusion" is a term that is often used as political rhetoric. However, because it is used with such consistency in the Government's agenda on minorities in general, and British Muslims in particular, any work on policy design for Muslims in Britain must take social exclusion seriously as a starting point for analysis.[35] Significantly, the term "social exclusion" is used to discuss Europe-wide action.[36] Domestic and EU documents

---

[33] See: Young, *Justice and the Politics of Difference,* ch. 6. Young defines cultural alienation as the experience among one group that (a) they cannot identify with the dominant meanings in their society and (b) they feel that the perspective of their own group is either stereotyped, or distorted, rendered invisible within the dominant discourse of the public culture of their community. It is the co-existence of both these feelings that contributes to cultural alienation and makes it such a powerful source of oppression for a group. This oppressed group feels culturally alienated because it is invisible within the public culture and public dominant discourse in the society. Paradoxically, when the group's experiences are included within the public domain, they are stereotyped or distorted in a way that is demeaning for the group.

[34] For an analysis of the shift in the Government's use of terminology, from equality to social exclusion, see: H. Collins, "Discrimination, Equality and Social Exclusion", in *Modern Law Review,* 2003.

[35] See: Office of the Deputy Prime Minister, *Preventing Social Exclusion,* London, Social Exclusion Unit, ODPM, March 2001.

[36] Decision No. 50/2002/EC of the European Parliament and the Council of 7 December 2001 establishing a programme of Community action to encourage cooperation between Member States to combat social exclusion, OJ L10/1, 12 January 2002.

make it clear that there is concern for groups who are socially excluded, because they have been effectively prevented from participating in the benefits of citizenship and mainstream society. Economic deprivation is one factor, but not the only relevant one, used to define social exclusion. Other factors include: poor educational opportunities, bad housing and membership of a disfavoured minority group.

Social exclusion is a complex phenomenon. It is multi-dimensional, and can pass from generation to generation. Social exclusion includes poverty and low income, but it is a broader concept and encompasses some of the wider causes and consequences of deprivation. The Government has defined "social exclusion" as a short-hand term for what can happen when people or areas suffer from a combination of related problems, such as unemployment, poor skills, low incomes, unfair discrimination, poor housing, high crime, bad health and family breakdown.[37]

The experience of large numbers of Muslims in the UK falls within this definition of social exclusion. Muslims encounter *involuntary* exclusion from mainstream social, political and economic institutions. More specifically, saying that Muslims are subjected to social exclusion captures their experience as a group of people who have overwhelmingly suffered in the past, and continue to suffer, from a combination of related problems. Compared to other faith communities, Muslim men and women in Great Britain had the highest rate of reported ill health in 2001. A total of 13 per cent of Muslim men and 16 per cent of Muslim women described their state of health as "not good" compared to around eight per cent for the population as a whole. Taking into account age structures, Muslims also had the highest rates of disability.[38] Compared to households of other faith groups, Muslim households are the most likely to be situated in socially rented accommodation, to experience overcrowding[39] and to lack central heating.[40] Compared to other religious groups, Muslims had the highest proportion of people in the working-age population without any qualifications. The unemployment rate of Muslims is three times that of the population as a whole.[41]

Fear of crime and the risk of being a victim constitute particularly acute aspects of social exclusion. Evidence from the 2000 *British Crime Survey* (BCS) shows that ethnic minorities run greater risks of crime than White people. This situation reflects the fact

---

[37] See: ODPM, *Tackling Social Exclusion.*

[38] ONS, *Focus on Religion,* p. 8.

[39] Overcrowding is measured by "occupancy rating". This relates the actual number of rooms to the number of rooms "required" by members of the household (based on a relationship between them and their ages). A household with a rating of -1 or less can be considered to be overcrowded.

[40] ONS, *Focus on Religion,* p. 9.

[41] See chapter in this report on British Muslims and the labour market.

that minority populations are concentrated in large cities, in particular in conurbations where the crime risks are high for everyone, regardless of ethnicity. The 2000 BCS also found that people from ethnic minorities worry more about crime than White respondents, a finding that held up even when taking into account the sort of area in which respondents lived and their direct and indirect experience of crime. Furthermore, an analysis of the survey found that "worry about crime was particularly salient among Bangladeshis and Pakistanis".[42] According to the survey, "Pakistanis and Bangladeshis, in particular, are more likely than others to say that they felt 'very unsafe' at night, both in their homes and walking alone in their neighbourhood".[43]

4.2   The Impact of September 11

The situation of Muslims in Britain before September 11 was characterised by poverty and alienation, which in some cases create the risk of social isolation.[44] Alexander notes that, even prior to September 11, Muslim young men had emerged as the new "folk devils" of popular and media imagination and were represented as the embodiment of fundamentalism.[45] Since September 11, international events have ensured that the British Muslim community has become the focus of public attention. The coverage given to the "war on terror" and the Al Qaeda movement has generated an ongoing debate about Islam and the status of British Muslims.[46] The predominant paradigm for the public discourse surrounding Islam and Muslims is one of security issues and the "war on terror".

There are legitimate security concerns that have to be acknowledged in any reasonable debate on the post-September 11 situation. It has to be recognised that the State will have to undertake heavier policing of the Muslim community, similar to the heavier policing of the Irish community that existed during the period of attacks by the Irish

---

[42]   A. Clancy, M. Hough, M., R. Aust, and C. Kershaw, *Crime, Policing and Justice: The Experience of Ethnic Minorities. Findings from the 2000 British Crime Survey,* Home Office, Research Study 223, London, Home Office, 2001, p. xii, (hereafter, Clancy et al, *Crime, Policing and Justice*).

[43]   Clancy et al, *Crime, Policing and Justic,* p. 90.

[44]   See, for example: N. M. Ahmed, F. Bodi, R. Kazim and M. Shadjareh, *The Oldham Riots: Discrimination, Deprivation and Communal Tension in the United Kingdom,* London, Islamic Human Rights Commission, 2001.

[45]   C. Alexander, *The Asian Gang: Ethnicity, Identity, Masculinity,* Oxford, Oxford University Press, 2000.

[46]   See: The Runnymead Trust, *Islamophobia: A Challenge for Us All,* available at http://www.runnymedetrust.org/publications/pdfs/islamophobia.pdf (accessed 24 October 2004).

Republican Army in the UK. However, one of the consequences of the overlap in the public discourse on Islam/Muslims and violence/terrorism is that it will contribute to reinforcing existing prejudice against Muslims within Britain.

Although some sections of the media and the State have acted responsibly in attempting to distinguish the war against terrorism/Al Qaeda/bin Laden and Afghanistan, on the one hand, from Islam and British Muslims, on the other, there is a clear risk that this ongoing public discourse will have a negative impact.

More specifically, the situation is likely to result in negative stereotypes, which may manifest themselves in individual attitudes and conduct in a number of different ways. First, there can be greater violence and harassment by perpetrators who specifically target Muslims, or those perceived to be Muslims, and make them victims of systematic violence.[47] Second, there is a risk of increased discriminatory treatment, and perception of discriminatory treatment, of Muslims by law enforcement agencies, such as the police, Customs and Excise, immigration officials, and the Crown Prosecution Service. This problem will exacerbate already difficult relationships between these agents of the State and Muslim communities, and it is of particular importance given the reality of heavier policing of Muslim communities as part of the "war on terror". Third, these negative stereotypes may result in an increase in discriminatory attitudes and conduct by individual actors and institutions in the public and the private sector, especially as anti-Muslim prejudice is a growing strand of racism.[48] A recent study explored the impact of September 11 on discrimination and racism on different religious and ethnic groups. It noted that non-Muslim groups, such as Sikhs and Hindus, had experienced increases in racism and discrimination since September 11, but Muslims still had the greatest risk of being victims of racism and general discrimination. The study found that religion is more important than ethnicity in

---

[47] Jørgen S. Nielsen and Christopher Allen, *Summary Report on Islamophobia in the EU after September 11 2001*, Vienna, EUMC, May 2002. Available on the website of the EUMC at http://eumc.eu.int/eumc/material/pub/112001/Synthesis_report-en.pdf (accessed 1 November 2004).

[48] The PSI study in 1997 suggested that anti-Asian (which is used as the category from which to extract anti-Muslim attitudes) are a significant aspect of discriminatory attitudes towards ethnic minorities. See: T. Modood, R. Berthoud, J. Lakey, P. Smith, S. Virdee and S. Beishon, *Ethnic Minorities in Britain: Diversity and Disadvantage*, London, Policy Studies Institute, 1997. See esp. pp. 129–135 and p. 134, Table 4.34, for details of "Views on which racial, ethnic or religious group faces most prejudice today", which includes categories of Muslim. See also T. Modood, *Not Easy Being British: Colour, Culture and Citizenship*, Trentham Books, 1992.

indicating which groups are more likely to experience racism and discrimination post-September 11.[49]

Muslims are concentrated in some of the poorest sections of society, and they are therefore disproportionately high users of public services. The way in which these stereotypes may affect the delivery of appropriate public services is of particular importance in this analysis. Furthermore, negative images of Muslims result in the formation of prejudiced attitudes, which are manifested as hate speech against Muslims. The combination of these factors only serves to add to the pre-September 11 position of Muslims as a socially excluded group.

---

[49] L. Sheridan, *Effects of the Events of September 11th 2001 on Discrimination and Implicit Racism in Five Religious and Ethnic Groups*, Leicester, University of Leicester, 2002.

5. EXCLUSION THROUGH VIOLENCE

This section focuses on how the use of systematic violence against a group is one cause of their exclusion and oppression. Clearly, cases of physical violence, such as hate crimes, fall within this category, but Young's definition of violence also encompasses "less severe incidents of harassment, intimidation, or ridicule simply for the purpose of degrading, humiliating or stigmatising a group member".[50] This definition, therefore, includes hatred expressed in speech ("hate speech"). Moreover, Young's analysis argues that it is less the acts themselves and more the social context that surrounds them that adds to their gravity as a source of oppression. Some of these social factors include the fact that the violence is systematic in nature and is a social practice that all the parties know will happen again –

> "[…] the daily knowledge shared by all members of oppressed groups that they are liable to violation, solely on account of their group identity. Just living under such a threat of attack on oneself or family or friends deprives the oppressed of freedom and dignity, and needlessly expends their energy".[51]

Finally, a critically important aspect of Young's definition of violence is her insight of the way in which cultural imperialism intersects with violence. The "culturally imperialised" may reject the dominant viewpoint and attempt to assert their own subjectivity, or try to point out that their cultural difference may put the lie to the dominant culture's claim to universality. The dissonance generated by such a challenge to the hegemonic cultural viewpoints can also be a source of irrational violence.[52] Much of the chaos in the confrontation between "fringe" Muslim organisations and those on the far right who react to Islam with xenophobia would fall within this category. However, the resulting clash also has consequences beyond these two fringe groups.

---

[50] See: Young, *Justice and the Politics of Difference*, p. 61.

[51] See: Young, *Justice and the Politics of Difference*, p. 62.

[52] See: Young, *Justice and the Politics of Difference*, p. 63.

5.1   Hate Crimes

There is evidence of racially aggravated crime motivated by hatred of Muslims in both the pre-[53] and post-September 11[54] period. The response of the State to this phenomenon has been promising. Pre-September 11, racially aggravated crime was a criminal offence, but, as a non-ethnic religious minority, Muslims were not specifically protected by legislation. After September 11, the Home Secretary, in December 2001, introduced within anti-terrorism legislation[55] an extension of the Crime Disorder Act (1998), which specifically includes religiously motivated crime.[56] The British Government has, therefore, acted very responsibly in relation to protecting its Muslims citizens in this area.

Between December 2001 and March 2003, there were 18 successful prosecutions for religiously aggravated offences, of which ten involved Muslim victims.[57] In 2002, a Crown Prosecution Service inspection found that the seriousness of racially motivated offences was routinely reduced, because the racial element of the crimes was not considered.[58] In 2003, the Crown Prosecution Service produced guidance on prosecuting cases of racially or religiously motivated crimes.[59] A follow-up inspection in 2004 found that police identification of racist incidents had improved, as had staff commitment to the Racist Incident Monitoring Scheme. There were also notable

---

[53] See: *Labour Research,* Vol. 80, no 10, October 1991, which concluded that there had been an increase in the levels of racial violence specifically targeting Muslims during the first Gulf War in the early 1990s. For a discussion of these issues, see M. Malik, "Racist Crime", *Modern Law Review,* 62, 1999, p. 409.

[54] European Monitoring Centre on Racism and Xenophobia, *Anti-Islamic reactions within the European Union after the recent acts of terror against the USA: A collection of the EUMC of country reports from RAXEN National Focal Points (NFPs),* Vienna, EUMC, 10 October 2001. Available on the EUMC website at http://eumc.eu.int/eumc/material/pub/112001/Initial-Report-041001.pdf (accessed 15 October 2004). This EUMC report summarises the UK position on anti-Islamic violence in the post-September 11 period. The UK evidence is submitted by the Commission for Racial Equality (CRE) and confirms verbal and physical attacks on Muslims and their property.

[55] Anti-Terrorism, Crime and Security Act (2001), s. 39.

[56] Crime and Disorder Act (1998), s. 28-32.

[57] There were also two Sikh victims, two Hindu victims, one Jewish victim, one Jehovah's Witness victim, one Christian victim and one victim whose religion was not stated. Crown Prosecution Service, *Racist Incident Monitoring Scheme: Annual Report 2002–2003,* London, CPS, 2003.

[58] HM Crown Prosecution Service Inspectorate, *Thematic Review of CPS Casework with a Minority ethnic Dimension,* London, HMCPSI, 2002.

[59] Crown Prosecution Service, *Guidance on Prosecuting Cases of Racist and Religious Crime,* London, CPS, 2003.

improvements in engagement with minority communities. However, there remained a significant proportion of cases in which the racial element to the charges were reduced inappropriately.[60] The Attorney General's powers to challenge unduly lenient sentences were extended in October 2003, to include racially and religiously aggravated offences, following a recommendation by the Crown Prosecution Inspectorate. In March 2004, following an appeal by the Attorney General, the Court of Appeal increased the sentence for offenders for racially aggravated violence.[61]

Despite these advances, however, some further efforts should be made to encourage law enforcement agencies to pursue criminal charges in cases of religiously aggravated crime. Law enforcement officers, such as police and prosecutors, have discretion in these matters. Therefore, some effort needs to be made to ensure that any potential increase in prejudice against Muslims within the general population does not manifest itself in discriminatory conduct by law enforcement agents within the criminal justice system. It is important to consider the treatment of Muslims by the police, the priority that the system gives to prosecuting anti-Muslim hate crimes and the treatment of these issues by judges and juries. While the Home Office and the Department for Constitutional Affairs are making a serious effort to deal with the risk of anti-Muslim discrimination of this type, pressure should be maintained to ensure more progress in the successful implementation and enforcement of hate crime legislation and policy.

There are a number of concrete changes that should be made to facilitate this process. In particular, a continued insistence on using only racial categories could hamper progress. For example, in the training of police officers, Crown Prosecution Service personnel and judges, anti-discrimination training that focuses on discrimination based on colour or race/ethnicity alone will fail to capture the reality of the post-September 11 context, and could allow stereotypes about Muslims to persist. The key issue is that the criminal justice system generally, and hate crimes legislation in particular, must be enforced in a way that is fair, just and reinforces confidence in the system. If hate crimes legislation is implemented and enforced effectively and strategically, it can send a clear and unequivocal message that those who commit acts of violence and harassment against Muslims, out of deliberate and conscious hatred of the membership of this religious group, deserve a special penalty under criminal law.

There is a significant gap in the mechanisms in place for inspecting key aspects of the criminal justice system for anti-Muslim prejudice, at exactly the time when there is a

---

[60] HM Crown Prosecution Service Inspectorate, *A Follow Up review of CPS Casework with a Minority Ethnic Dimension*, London, HMCPSI, 2004, p. 7.

[61] Attorney General's Chambers, "Hate crime data show confidence building efforts are yielding results", Press-release, 6 April 2004, available on the website of the Attorney General at http://www.lslo.gov.uk/pressreleases/rims_comment_06_04_04.doc (accessed 1 November 2004).

pressing need for such processes. The Commission for Racial Equality (CRE) has specific responsibilities to ensure that local authorities implement their duty under the RR(A)A, Section 71, to eliminate unlawful discrimination and to promote equality of opportunity and good relations between persons of different racial groups. However, this duty does not cover non-ethnic religious minorities, such as Muslims. In relation to racial and ethnic religious minorities, the CRE document, *A Framework for Inspectorates*, of July 2002, gave detailed guidance on "inspecting for the duty". The term "inspecting for the duty" is used to describe the monitoring of various inspectorates (e.g. those relating to police or prisons) that ensure that public institutions are meeting the required standards. Since the introduction of the RR(A)A, Section 71, one of the features that these inspectorates evaluate is whether or not these institutions are meeting their statutory obligations to eliminate unlawful discrimination and promote equality of opportunity and good race relations between persons of different racial groups. There have been grassroots meetings with criminal justice agencies, and in one case, there was a request to re-draft a Race Equality Scheme where it failed to comply with the Section 71 duty in relation to racial minorities.[62] The fact that Muslims are not specifically included within the "inspecting for the duty" process is unfortunate. It is necessary to think imaginatively about how to fill in the gap left by the anomalous coverage of the RR(A)A in relation to non-ethnic religious minorities such as Muslims.

5.2   Hate Speech

Another way in which prejudice against a particular group manifests itself is through an increase in hate speech. This can consist of expressions of pejorative views about Islam and Muslims in private speech. But the problem is more serious when such views are expressed in public speech. Publicly expressed hate speech against Muslims can incite certain individuals to specific acts of violence against Muslims and their property. An example of this kind of hate speech would be a leaflet at a political rally that says: "Kick a Muslim today!". Hate speech may also involve vilification of Muslims through statements such as: "Muslims are a violent group".

The importance of free speech in a liberal society places legitimate limitations on the ability of the State to regulate hate speech. In particular, there is a critical difference between hate speech directed against Muslims and legitimate criticism of Islam. Proposed legal responses include calls for an extension to the laws on blasphemy and

---

[62] Phone conversations with employees at the Commission for Racial Equality. The calls took place in April 2004 as part of this research.

calls for regulation using criminal law, in the form of legislation prohibiting incitement to religious hatred.

The extension of the law on blasphemy may not be an appropriate response to the problems of hate speech against Muslims. Because blasphemy legislation is a particularly blunt way of regulating free speech, the usual liberal objections to prohibiting free speech are especially relevant in this context. Arguably, Muslims in a liberal democracy must respect these principles. Moreover, definitions are difficult to establish. In relation to a complex theology such as Islam, it might be very difficult to answer the question of whether or not a specific statement is blasphemy. Despite these obstacles, the Muslim Council of Britain and other organisations have campaigned for the extension of the law prohibiting blasphemy, so that it includes Muslims.

In July 2004 the Home Secretary announced the Government's intention to introduce legislation to outlaw incitement to religious hatred.[63] A particular problem for incitement legislation is the fact that prosecutions are dependent on the permission of a member of the Government, the Attorney General. In order to reassure Muslims that their speech is not being uniquely targeted for prosecution by the State, the Government may want to consider *inter alia:* (a) publishing a clear code of practice that outlines the factors relevant to the exercise of the discretion of the Attorney General; and (b) asking the Attorney General to submit a full report, with a summary of the figures and an explanation, to one of the House of Commons Select Committees (e.g. the Home Affairs Select Committee) or the Joint Committee on Human Rights.

Within a liberal democracy, criminal law is perhaps the most coercive way in which the State restricts individual freedom. Therefore, criminal law should be used in only the most extreme cases, where there is a risk of either physical violence or public disorder. In most cases, the grievances of Muslims faced with hate speech and vilification of their group are more appropriately addressed using extra-legal policy options. These options could include, for example, investment that builds the capacity of Muslims to intervene in public discourse, so that they can defend their group and faith and communicate what they consider to be the truth of their religion in the public sphere. Thus, the solution to the problem of vilification of Muslims is to enable Muslims to enter into public debate. In short, what is needed is more speech rather than the regulation of free speech.

---

[63] Home Office, "Sideline the Extremists – Home Secretary", Press-release, 7 July 2004, available on the Home Office website at http://www.homeoffice.gov.uk/n_story.asp?item_id=993 (accessed 1 November 2004).

6. ECONOMIC EXCLUSION

The earlier sections of this report established that social exclusion and economic deprivation and exclusion are a reality for large numbers of Muslims in Britain. This section concentrates on issues relating to employment, training and public services. There are many cases in which the fact that someone is Muslim is not relevant in the workplace. Concern with discrimination should not lead us to ignore the importance of ensuring that the workplace and the public sphere have neutral spaces, where individuals can come together as persons and where issues of race or faith are irrelevant. However, there are certain key needs that Muslims will have because of their faith. Despite the need for common and neutral space in the public sphere, these differences are relevant to any discussion of the economic exclusion of Muslims whether in employment, education or access to private and public services.

The phenomenon of economic deprivation can be summarised as exploitation, marginalisation and powerlessness.[64] Government initiatives by the Social Exclusion Unit, the Performance and Innovation Unit (PIU) and individual Government departments have all considered the nature of the specific and persistent economic disadvantage of Pakistanis and Bangladeshis,[65] who are disproportionately unemployed or involved in low-paid forms of employment. Employment and education are addressed in more detail in other chapters of this report. The focus of this section is more specifically on discrimination law and policy, in particular in employment and training, and in the provision of services in the private and public sector. However, it is also worth noting that there are limits to the use of the anti-discrimination law, which, like all forms of legal regulation, is necessarily complex, reactive and does not deal in a proactive way with the deep structures of inequality faced by Muslim communities.[66] Supply-side investment measures that target deprivation in the Muslim community should be a critical focus for attention, alongside anti-discrimination law, which controls the demand-side of the behaviour of key actors, such as employers.

---

[64] See: Young, *Justice and the Politics of Difference*, ch. 6.

[65] 90 per cent of Pakistanis and Bangladeshis in the UK are Muslim. Together they constitute 60 per cent of Britain's Muslim population.

[66] On the need for reform of UK discrimination law, see: B. Hepple, M. Coussey, and T. Choudhury, *Equality: A New Framework – The Report of the Independent Review of the Enforcement of UK Anti-Discrimination Law*, Oxford, Hart Publishing, 2000.

6.1 Discrimination in Law and Policy

The Government's main response to the problems of discrimination based on race or religion is reliance on the Race Relations Act (1976), which has indirectly given Muslims protection against discrimination in employment, education, housing and private and public sector service delivery. However, there was a long-standing anomaly in that ethnic religious minorities, such as Sikhs and Jews, were protected directly, while non-ethnic religious minorities, such as Muslims, received only indirect protection, and in some cases no protection.

This gap between the nature of the protection extended to different types of religious minorities has been partially filled by the implementation of EU-wide legislation that prohibits religious discrimination in employment and training and that directly covers Muslims.[67] As a result of these regulations, Muslims are protected from discrimination in employment and working conditions, including dismissals and pay; vocational guidance and training; and membership of, and involvement in, employers' or workers' organisations or professional bodies – for example, trade unions and professional bodies, like the Law Society or British Medical Association. However, unlike Sikhs and Jews, Muslims are not directly protected from discrimination in the following areas: social protection, including social security and health care; education; goods and services available to the public, including housing; and social advantages, such as housing benefits, student maintenance grants and loans, or bus passes for senior citizens.

Several measures have been taken to support the implementation of the new EU directive. For example, the Advisory, Conciliation and Arbitration Service (ACAS) issued guidelines for employers on meeting the requirements on religion and belief regulations. The Department of Trade and Industry (DTI) has funded several faith community organisations, including several Muslim organisations, so that they can disseminate information about the new rights. However, there remains a lack of legal aid and institutional support for individuals bringing claims before employment tribunals. In effect, the Government is informing people about their new rights without providing them with the support necessary to enforce these rights.

A critically important gap in the present scheme for legal protection is the role of enforcement agencies, such as the CRE. At present, racial and ethnic religious minorities fall within the jurisdiction of the CRE. They are therefore given critically important support, through campaign work, investigations of discriminatory practice and guidance with individual litigation. This level of support from an enforcement

---

[67] The Employment Equality (Religion or Belief) Regulations 2003 (SI 2003/1660) came into force on 2 December 2003. The regulations are intended to implement the European Union's Council Directive 2000/78/EC establishing a general framework for equal treatment in employment and occupation.

agency is especially important, because the remedy for a breach of race relations legislation is usually in Employment Tribunals, where there is no legal aid to assist applicants. In October 2003, the Government announced its intention to establish a single Commission for Equality and Human Rights (CEHR). This body is unlikely to be up and running until 2006, at the earliest. Once established, however, the CEHR would have responsibility for the enforcement of legislation covering discrimination based on faith or religion.

Short of legislative reform, there are also alternative strategies that the Government and other non-government actors can undertake. In the face of clear evidence showing higher poverty and unemployment in the Muslim community, the Government should consider whether it is appropriate to launch a sustained campaign, in conjunction with business, aimed at shifting the culture and attitudes that act as a barrier to employing Muslims. Such an effort would demonstrate that Government Ministers and business people believe that diversity pays. Such an effort could, for example, focus on employment of Pakistani and Bangladeshi women, whose low rates of economic activity are consistently highlighted. The Home Office Citizenship Survey suggests that women are more likely to report experiences of racial prejudice. This Home Office Survey could be extended to track the experiences and treatment of religious minorities, whose differences may be visible, such as Muslim women who wear headscarves.[68] Rather than running a general campaign around race issues, the campaign could focus on the employment of women who are visibly Muslim, in particular, those who wear a *hijab* (headscarf).

6.2 Provision of Services in the Public Sector

As mentioned previously, economic deprivation can be summarised as exploitation, marginalisation and powerlessness. One interesting aspect of exclusion resulting from economic deprivation is that it creates new issues from the point of view of justice. Within a welfare economy like the one that exists in the UK, a group such as Muslims, who are concentrated amongst the lowest economic and social strata, is as a group disproportionately dependent on public and welfare services and institutions. In fact, a major point of contact – and one of the main sources of the relationship – between Muslims and the State is their experience of the State as a provider of the key services, such as health, education, housing and welfare. Any attempt to improve the

---

[68] C. Atwood, G. Singh, D. Prime, R. Creasey et al., *2001 Home Office Citizenship Survey: People Families and Communities,* Home Office Research Study 270, London, Home Office Research, Development and Statistics Directorate, September 2003, p. 42. Available on the Home Office website at http://www.homeoffice.gov.uk/rds/pdfs2/hors270.pdf (accessed 21 September 2004), (hereafter, Atwood et al, *2001 Home Office Citizenship Survey*).

relationship between Muslims and the State, and their feeling of being respected and belonging, must therefore give this issue the highest priority.

Interestingly, the 2001 Home Office Citizenship Survey suggests that there is a perception amongst minorities that they will be treated less well by public sector organisations.[69] The Home Office Citizenship Survey is a biennial empirical study, designed to be part of the evidence base of the Home Office's community policy area. It has two main aims: (a) to be a major policy tool, informing both the development of policy and its implementation; and (b) to provide information for Home Office performance measurement. The survey found that the organisations where many minority members expected they would get worse treatment than people of other races included: council housing departments, housing associations, local councils and the immigration authorities. It also indicated that respondents from minority groups were more likely than White respondents to say they would be treated worse than people of other races, particularly when engaging with the following organisations: police, the Prison Service, armed forces and immigration authorities.[70] Younger Black and Asian respondents, aged 16-49, were more likely than older Black and Asian respondents to feel that they would be treated worse by a range of public organisations. In addition, the survey found that members of minority ethnic groups who had previous experience with police, courts and the Crown Prosecution Service were more likely than those without such experience to say they would be treated worse than people of other races.[71]

Faith, along with other factors, such as age, gender and ethnicity, should be taken into consideration in developing appropriate service delivery. Muslims have distinct needs that must be met so they can access public services efficiently and appropriately. Taking into account the key needs of Muslims in this way is important, not only because it has the possibility of generating community cohesion through encouraging a sense of belonging for Muslims. It is also important as a matter of justice.

Those who depend on public services for their basic needs are most often subject to policies that are at risk of being patronising, demeaning and arbitrary. This type of dependency on public services also carries the risk of being subject to intrusive authority by service providers, who have large amounts of power. In meeting the needs of those whom they service, these public agencies often construct the needs of the user based on limited experience and information. There is the potential for grave invasion of important principles, such as respect, autonomy and privacy, when public officials are given the power to construct what they deem to be the appropriate needs of users of these services. Obviously, the risk that service providers will "get it wrong" is especially

---

[69] Atwood et al, *2001 Home Office Citizenship Survey*, p. 42.

[70] Atwood et al, *2001 Home Office Citizenship Survey*, pp. 22–25.

[71] Atwood et al, *2001 Home Office Citizenship Survey*, ch. 3.

high when the user is from a different culture, race or religion, with distinct and different needs from mainstream society. This point is especially important in relation to Muslims, because, along with being the largest minority religion, they are a religious group with certain very distinct needs that require accommodation, including daily prayers, fasting and some degree of segregation or modesty rules for Muslim women.

The Government's main response to this challenge of delivering public services to minorities in an appropriate way is the RR(A)A of 2000 and the Race Equality Schemes that are supervised by the CRE. This is critically important legislation, which provides a proactive rather than reactive response to problems of inequality and social exclusion. Moreover, this model is more concerned with substantial equality and is therefore more appropriate as a response to the complex and deep structural problems that cause social exclusion of the Muslim community. However, unlike Sikhs and Jews, Muslims, as a group, will not be covered by the RR(A)A (see Section 1 and 71) which:

a) prohibits direct and indirect discrimination by certain public bodies (e.g. the police) in the exercise and performance of public functions;

b) places an enforceable duty on specified public authorities to take positive steps to eliminate discrimination and promote equality;

c) includes monitoring to ensure that there are minority staff represented in important public institutions who can (i) give input into policy design; (ii) provide a source for minorities, such as Muslims, identifying with key public institutions;

The main problem is that UK discrimination law defines "racial group" to include ethnic religious minorities, such as Sikhs and Jews, but excludes non-ethnic religious minorities, such as Muslims.[72] The gap caused by this omission becomes clear when examining a range of Race Equality Schemes that have been submitted to the CRE and when interviewing relevant public officials with responsibility for these issues in local authorities with a high Muslim population.[73] Although the needs of Muslims may be taken into account informally, as a matter of best practice, there is no formal recognition of these needs, nor is there any legal obligation to take these needs into account. There is a real risk that the good practice of accommodating the needs of Muslims may give way to the necessity of limiting coverage only to those groups strictly covered by the RR(A)A. This is a special risk in situations where cash-strapped public bodies have to make difficult decisions, such as which group to prioritise and who to consult in a local area. This is exactly the problem identified with a number of

---

[72] See: *Mandla v. Dowell Lee,* (1983) 1 All ER 1062 (H.L.).

[73] Stated in conversation and interviews with employees at the CRE and Camden Council in April 2004. Significantly, Camden Council, which has a large Muslim population, does not specifically include Muslims in its Race Equality Schemes.

reports summarised by the Independent Review Team of the Home Office. These reports criticised the provision of public services in cities in the north of England.[74]

Concern about the consequences of this gap is shared with Muslim organisations themselves. The director of a key Muslim organisation providing welfare to young Muslims made this point in an interview.[75] When asked which policy reform would make the most dramatic impact to young Muslims, the director of the Muslim Youth Helpline stated that, for her clients, the key issue was ensuring that public service delivery took into account the faith, rather than ethnic, needs of Muslims. She went on to emphasise that, in her experience, young Muslims were reluctant to access services that were in the mainstream, despite the fact that some of these services were specifically geared towards Asians. Their main concern was that they related their lives and choices to their identity as Muslims, rather than their identity as Pakistanis or Bangladeshis. They wanted to be able to go to individuals and organisations that understood their faith and would not make them feel they have to apologise for being Muslims. A further point made by the director was that existing practice by organisations such as the Home Office to make statutory funding available on grounds of ethnicity and race rather than religion meant that many Muslim service providers were unable to access Government funding and were dependent on, sometimes *ad hoc*, non-statutory funding.

The persistent disadvantage suffered by Muslims in a range of areas, in particular housing, health and education, requires explanation and response. The Government has denied itself a major policy lever in failing to recognise that, in many cases, public service delivery to these communities needs to focus on faith rather than ethnic identity. CRE guidance in this area has tried to compensate for some of these gaps, but there is no substitute for ensuring that the coverage of the RR(A)A is extended to Muslims. The argument that it is difficult to define a religious group or define religious needs is hard to justify, given the great success in implementing the EU legislation on religious discrimination. Of particular note is the excellent summary of the key needs of Muslims in the ACAS Code of Practice, which was drafted pursuant to this legislation.[76] There is no reason why similar guidance cannot be issued to local authorities, to supplement their work to ensure equality in the delivery of public goods and services.

---

[74] Community Cohesion: A Report of the Independent Review Team, para 2.20 and 2.21; see http://www.homeoffice.gov.uk/docs2/pocc2.html#youth (accessed 24 October 2004).

[75] Interview with the director of the Muslim Youth Helpline, conducted on 14 April 2004.

[76] ACAS Code of Practice, now available in its final form at http://www.emplaw.co.uk/ (accessed 24 October 2004).

Short of reform of the law, there are other measures that could be taken. The starting point should be a better understanding of the specific needs of Muslims in relation to key public services. Better information and research that targets the faith needs of these communities directly, rather than indirectly, may reveal causes that have so far been missed because of the use of race or ethnicity as indicators.

Another option is to strengthen the CRE's work in relation to delivery of public services to minorities. The CRE has always insisted that it does not have the jurisdiction to deal with matters relating to religion. Where legislation clearly prohibits regulating conduct of private employers, such reticence may be understandable. However, there are very few persuasive arguments as to why the CRE cannot take on a more robust role in ensuring that public authorities are aware of the benefits of paying special attention to religious minorities. Through its work on the Codes of Practices, supervision of the Race Equality Schemes, advice to inspectors, or informal advice, the CRE can make clear the advantages public authorities will get from ensuring that there is adequate consultation and attention to the needs of minorities such as Muslims in the design and delivery of public services. In fact, there is a good argument that, in some cases, the promotion of good race relations under the RR(A)A statutory duty requires attention to issues relating to faith and religion. In order to fill this gap, the CRE will need to update its Codes of Practice under the RR(A)A, including its Codes to the Inspectorates, to make it clear that, sometimes, public bodies need to specifically attend to the faith needs of minorities.

6.3   Public Procurement

It is also of critical importance that the Government and CRE recognise that the gap in race relations legislation in this area is likely to be replicated by private actors. For example, in the work done on using procurement as a way of disseminating good equality standards, the current CRE guidance fails to make it clear that, in some cases where the Race Equality Schemes are used as a guide to procurement contracts, these will fail to cover Muslims. Public procurement becomes an important issue, especially where there is an increasing transfer of public services to the private sphere. The nature of the service and users does not change, so the disproportionate use of them by Muslims remains the key issue.[77]

---

[77] See for example the CRE guide on procurement that fails to deal with this issue in either its text or through the imaginative use of examples: *Public Procurement and Race Equality – Guidelines for local government* (www.http://www.cre.gov.uk/publs (accessed 15 October 2004).

6.4   Provision of Services via the Voluntary Sector

As part of its work to regenerate communities and encourage neighbourhood renewal, the Government has placed great emphasis on increasing voluntary and community sector activity. The Home Office's Public Sector Agreement (PSA) VIII reflects the fact that the Government has set a target for active communities in England to "increase voluntary and community sector activity, including increased community participation, by five per cent by 2006".[78]

However, the *Home Office Citizenship Survey* reveals a number of factors indicating that Muslims will be at a significant structural disadvantage when it comes to acting as volunteers and that there are specific reasons why they are less likely to undertake civic participation. In general, the survey found that "Asian people were less likely than Black people and White people to be involved in social participation, informal volunteering and formal volunteering." In particular, "Asian women were less likely than members of other sex and ethnic groups to be involved in civic participation, social participation and formal volunteering." The survey also found that "people who had the highest levels of education, were from higher socio-economic groups, had the highest levels of household income and were in employment were, in each case, more likely than others to be involved in all types of voluntary and community activities".[79] Muslims fall within the lowest levels for all of these indicators.

It is also noteworthy that, in the context of established voluntary sector activities, there is a long-standing tradition for Christian and other faith-based institutions to provide the infrastructure for involvement. It may be that Muslims will not feel able to access the existing structures and so become involved in voluntary and community services.[80]

For all these reasons, it is essential that the Home Office pay special attention to the distinct need to build capacity within the Muslim community, thereby encouraging Muslims to be involved in active participation within their own communities. This focus should include paying special attention to the needs of Muslims, by identifying barriers to active participation, by conducting research and consultation with groups and by providing specific financial and non-financial incentives for Muslims – and especially key groups like Muslim women – to become involved in participation in their communities. Recruitment into volunteering and participation may also need to specifically focus on Muslim organisations, mosques and other community institutions within the Muslim community.

---

[78] See Statement of Purpose and Aims of the Home Office, available on the website of the Home Office at http://www.homeoffice.gov.uk/inside/aims/ (accessed 24 October 2004).

[79] Atwood et al, *2001 Home Office Citizenship Survey*, pp. 80–87.

[80] The author is grateful to Patricia Sellick of the Oxford Centre of Islamic Studies for highlighting this point.

7. PUBLIC EXCLUSION

In the previous sections, it was argued that the recognition of key aspects of individuals' identity is important to their well being and autonomy. This section explores some of the implications of this need for recognition by Muslims in Britain. It should not be controversial to state that, at this time, Muslims are in a unique situation in Britain. As the largest religious minority, they are faced with a public culture in the national and international sphere that consistently links their religion to violence and terrorism. Despite the laudable efforts of public leaders and public institutions to maintain a distinction between Islam and violence/terrorism, the possibility remains that distorted and demeaning images of Islam and Muslims will prevail in the public sphere.

One consequence of this situation is the prevalence of prejudice and stereotypes about Muslims, which, as discussed previously in this paper, can manifest themselves in hate crimes, hate speech and discriminatory conduct. This section widens this argument by suggesting that there is also a need to consider initiatives that allow the accommodation of Muslims within the national public culture. The view set out earlier, that cultural alienation of a group can be a form of oppression and injustice, obviously provides an argument of principle to support this point. Furthermore, there are arguments of political stability that are relevant. A notion of citizenship that bases membership in a political community on a sense of belonging to public legal and political institutions is likely to be the most inclusive for Muslims.

7.1 Accommodation of Muslims[81]

Clearly, debate over whether, and how much, the interests of Muslims should be accommodated will remain an urgent issue. The way in which the interests of Muslims are accommodated is critically important for community cohesion. This section argues that, by encouraging debate about these issues between all interested parties in appropriate institutions, it is more likely that stakeholders will to generate a stable consensus, with which not only the minority Muslim community but also the majority can agree.

A feeling of "institutional belonging" – an individual's sense of attachment to key political and legal institutions – and the deeper psychological needs that this fulfils, is important to both minorities and majorities. A traditional liberal model that adopts an "assimilationist/neutral" approach, and requires groups such as Muslims to give up on their identity as Muslims altogether, will be experienced as coercive. Such a model is

---

[81] For a more detailed discussion of these issues and full reference to sources, see: Malik, *Minority Protection and Human Rights*.

unlikely to serve as a source of stable identification for citizens who are both Muslims and British. The same is also true of any "exclusive" version of multiculturalism, wherein overwhelming priority is given to accommodation of the private identities of minorities, and the needs of the majority within the public sphere are ignored. This model would not foster a sense of "institutional belonging" for *both* the majority and the minority.

In short, neither the "assimilationist/neutral" model nor the "exclusive" version of multiculturalism is fully inclusive, and so neither is likely to yield the benefits of institutional identification with key public institutions. Both models ignore the possibility of a common public sphere that is neither neutral between cultures nor a perfect mirror for personal identity. This common public culture will be influenced by a process of renegotiating between the diverse cultural groups within a political community. Developing "a sense of belonging" that remains attentive to both the majority and the minority, and generating a common public culture within which different groups can co-exist, requires compromise and adjustment by all parties. For the minority, this means that their private identity cannot automatically be reflected in the public sphere without some limited assimilation to the shared values that are the agreed basis for a common public life. For the majority, this re-negotiation carries with it significant costs. These costs will be an inevitable outcome of attempts to transform the public sphere and institutions from exclusively reflecting the dominant culture towards a common culture that also seeks to accommodate some of the most urgent needs of minorities, such as Muslims.

What is needed is a debate within key legal and political institutions, to show that they take the needs and concerns of Muslims seriously. Importantly, this debate needs to be conducted in mainstream institutions, such as central and local government or the popular media, where it is possible to stage negotiation between other groups and the majority. This debate impacts on the issue of institutional identification because, when these institutions open up a dialogue about the terms of the common good, and are seen to be a focus for its provision, there are also implications for the private identity of the citizen. The well-being of the individual is linked with the success of the institution. These substantive discussions also contribute towards creating a common language of beliefs and enabling collective action, which, in turn, provide the basis for sustaining community.[82]

Individuals cannot obtain certain types of collective public good – such as communal education or healthcare – through individual action, but they are still able to recognise these goods as valuable. Any discussion about the nature of these public goods is also a

---

[82] See also: C. Sunstein, *The Paritial Constitution*, Cambridge, MA, USA, Harvard University Press, 1993, ch. 6, for an argument in support of deliberative democracy.

source for creating "common meanings" within a community. These common meanings cannot be understood by merely noting their impact on, or importance for, individual agents. They are not an aggregation of the shared beliefs and attitudes of all individuals in a society. Rather, they form the basis for a comprehension of social practices and institutions that cannot be understood as anything but shared and communal. A strategy that avoids debate about substantive issues of the common good carries with it the risk that citizens will find it more difficult to identify with political institutions and decision-making. They are more likely to view political community as having an "instrumental" rather than a "constitutive" status in their lives. Minorities faced with public institutions in which neither their members nor their values are adequately represented and reflected will find it difficult to view them as structures of identification.

A public debate on the terms by which Muslims will be accommodated into British society requires participation by Muslims in mainstream political institutions. If Muslims and non-Muslims debate these issues and reach a compromise, it is more likely that *both* Muslims and non-Muslims will feel institutional identification with the decisions taken and the organisations involved. Clearly, Muslims will need to make concessions and compromise about their demands. Equally, majority institutions and structures will need to accommodate some of the key demands of Muslims. This accommodation, based on recognition of some aspects of the needs of Muslims, could ensure greater coalescence between the experience of individual Muslims in their daily lives, where they may be guided by Islamic legal rules, and their experience of majority normative legal and political institutions. The result may be a higher degree of willing cooperation and identification with these institutions, and, therefore, more political stability.

A public debate on accommodation requires participation by Muslims in mainstream political institutions. The Government's commitment to citizenship and the teaching of democracy already includes discussion of the way in which concepts such as "citizenship" and "democracy" can take on a more inclusive meaning in plural liberal democracies that include Muslim minorities.[83] There are now substantive improvements in the representation of Muslims within local and national political structures. Muslims serve as councillors and MPs/candidates for the major political parties. It is also promising that the Home Office Citizenship Survey finds that:

> [...] relatively high feelings of political influence expressed by people from minority ethnic groups compared with White people are a particularly interesting finding in the light of evidence elsewhere in the survey that

---

[83] See: Citizenship Advisory Group, "Education for citizenship and the teaching of democracy in schools", in *Final Report of the Advisory Group on Citizenship chaired by Sir Bernard Crick*, London, Qualification and Curriculum Authority, 1998.

minority ethnic people believe they are more likely than White people to experience discrimination in the provision of public services.[84]

The greater participation of Muslims in political structures is not an argument in support of quotas in representation of minorities like Muslims. Quotas and other forms of "forcing the pace" for Muslim political representation are not as urgent as a focus on ideas and issues.

Accommodation allows key institutions to recognise certain Muslim norms as important, because the institutions provide freely chosen normative guidance in the lives of their Muslim citizens. Muslim community organisations need to use this insight as the starting point for their own analysis. Most importantly, they must acknowledge that the values of liberal democracy and constitutionalism are non-negotiable, and that demands for accommodation must accept these core values as paramount. Muslim communities need to develop mechanisms for decision making that allow greater participation by a wide range of Muslims, especially those who have been previously marginalised in decision making, such as women and young people. There needs to be some recognition by decision-makers who represent Muslims that that their authority within and outside the Muslim communities derives from their acceptability to individual Muslims. The contemporary public space for developing an accommodation of the needs of Muslims – within the limits of democratic constitutionalism – provides British Muslims with some attractive opportunities.

7.2   Integrating the Concerns of Muslims into Policy Making

Policymaking by local and national institutions should: first, pay attention to the key concerns of Muslims; and, second, focus on consultation with, and inclusion of, Muslims in decision making. The key lever for ensuring that this happens, the RR(A)A, does not explicitly extend to Muslims as a group. However, another way to compensate for this gap could be changes in decision-making through civil service and local authority reform, to make these organisations more representative. The use of diversity and race equality indicators by the civil service in its assessment of the impact of policy could be extended to specifically include faith groups, such as Muslims. In particular, in key areas where Muslims are excluded – health, education, housing and employment – the relevant departments could be encouraged to pay special attention to the impact of their decision-making on Muslim communities.

The Government has taken seriously some of the pressing concerns of the Muslim community. Widespread and detailed consultation on the structure and scope of the new Faith Unit at the Home Office provides Muslims with opportunities to voice their

---

[84] Atwood et al., *2001 Home Office Citizenship Survey*, p. 19.

concerns and influence public decision making. Most recently, this has led to a review of the Government's interface with faith communities and a report entitled *Working Together: Cooperation between Government and Faith Communities* (March 2004).[85]

However, this approach does not fully compensate Muslims for the fact that, unlike racial and ethnic racial minorities, their concerns are not mainstreamed into the reform of the Government's decision making machinery. The Government's agenda for increasing participation in public decision making, as outlined in documents such as the White Paper *Modernising Government* (March 1999), continues to use the criterion of race, thereby excluding Muslims, and it has no mechanism to compensate for the resulting gap.[86] The issues facing individual departments and public agencies should make it clear that, instead of a narrow definition of race, it is necessary to give attention to a wider definition of diversity, which includes Muslims as a group. The Government should also encourage private business and civil organisations to follow this example and ensure the fair representation of people from all backgrounds, including Muslims. In addition, there is also need to address the gap in research and policy, as well as political leadership and responsibility, concerning this issue.

The urgency of this issue should be reflected in the information about Muslims that feeds into Government. This activity should not be limited to individual lead departments, such as the Home Office, where such concerns are clearly part of PSA Objective VI. It should also affect other parts of the Government machinery. Options for reform include: (1) coordination of research by the Social Exclusion Unit or the Policy Unit within the Cabinet Office; and (2) giving clear responsibility for this issue to one of the existing, or newly formed, Cabinet Committees, whose composition could reflect the interests of different departments in relation to this issue. For example, the Home Secretary, through the Home Office PSA Target VI, and the Deputy Prime Minister, through the ODPM/Social Exclusion Unit and, especially, Neighbourhood Renewal and Objective I PSA Targets, both have overlapping responsibility for some of these issues.

7.3 Promoting Speech

As was highlighted when discussing the issue of "hate speech" (see section 4.1), there are limits to the way in which the State can intervene to control the free speech of

---

[85] A breakdown of the UK population by religion (April 2001) is available on the Home Office website at http://www.homeoffice.gov.uk/comrace/faith/index.html (accessed 24 October 2004).

[86] *Modernising Government*, HMSO, March 1999. Available at http://www.archive.official-documents.co.uk/document/cm43/4310/4310.htm (accessed 1 November 2004).

others in a liberal democracy. However, there is nothing in the free speech principle that prevents a state from recognising that it can intervene in the public sphere through non-coercive and extra-legal means, to compensate for prejudice and stereotypes that create the risk of hate crimes and discrimination.

This level of State intervention in the public sphere can serve two ends. First, it can prevent the formation of ideas and attitudes that lead to hate speech, hate crime and discrimination against Muslims. Second, it can provide a powerful tool for overcoming cultural alienation of Muslims, by making them feel that their identity as Muslims is included within national definitions of culture. For non-Muslims, the advantage of this policy is that they are provided with an antidote to the usual discourse on Islam and Muslims, a discourse that often focuses on political issues, like international events, the war in Iraq and the Middle East and terrorism.

Some types of words and images that represent Islam and Muslims cause specific and recognised harm. The Government has accepted the argument for legal regulation of messages that specifically incite hatred of Muslims and cause a risk of public disorder or harm to Muslims. The Government has announced an intention to introduce legislation to prohibit incitement to religious hatred. This will provide a mechanism to address speech that incites religious hatred. However, consideration should also be given to the possible responses to speech that falls short of incitement. A subtle political and cultural solution may be more effective than legal regulation.

While a liberal State may hesitate before regulating speech, it can legitimately respond by using, other than legal, remedies when a vulnerable minority group is faced with persistent vilification. British Muslims can reasonably lobby institutions, such as the Department for Culture, Media and Sport (DCMS), to take their interests more seriously. Resources can be made available to facilitate capacity building within Muslim communities, to help them intervene in the public sphere and the media, so they can redress the distortions that prevail. Equally important is national State support for cultural projects that allow Muslims to express themselves in variety of ways, not only through political, social and economic speech, but also through cultural forms, such as art, music and literature. Freedom of thought and conscience, as well as the availability of public and private resources for developing and disseminating culture, provide Muslims with a unique opportunity for self-development and communication.

The debate on the legitimacy, extent and nature of Muslim public participation in liberal politics must pay special attention to the benefits, as well as the burdens, of public participation. Participatory politics is a reciprocal process, in which the ability to influence works both ways. Under current political conditions, there are opportunities for religious groups to use their freedom to engage in public life and discussion – which are among the greatest virtues of liberal politics – and so influence individual and public conceptions of the common good. At one level, this is simple participation in existing democratic political processes in an effort to bring about the common good of *the whole* political community. However, there is nothing to prevent Muslims from conveying a more distinctive message that is specific to Islam. They can make a unique and invaluable contribution to the marketplace of ideas in contemporary liberal multicultural societies. This requires a move away from the type of politics that prefers the safety of what Tom Stoppard's recent trilogy calls "the Coast of Utopia".[87]

Social criticism, when it is done well, is neither elitist nor parochial. It is not something that is limited to specialists, but is rather an activity that all Muslims naturally do, and should, embrace. And social criticism is not limited to any one community. Muslim community institutions need to consider more measures to speak in language and concepts that have a universal appeal, not only to "insiders" but also, and especially, to "outsiders". They also need to be part of the mainstream participatory, democratic process, to contribute not only to the "Muslim good" but also to the common good.

This process can be facilitated by Government policies. There are two aspects to this type of policy. First, there should be a clear policy to support public-sphere intervention that challenges distorted images of Muslims. This can be done by both Muslims and non-Muslims. Second, policies to promote representation in culture, media and sport require positive intervention by national and local organisations with responsibility for arts and culture, such as local authorities and the DCMS. Again, the DCMS and other funding bodies, like the Arts Council, are responsible for the strategy for funding, monitoring and evaluation of projects relating to culture, media and sport. Thus, the DCMS has a pivotal role to play in supporting community cohesion and creating a positive role in accommodating Muslims in the public sphere. Obviously, the lead for community cohesion work must come from the Home Office, but the DCMS can also pay special attention to the specific needs of Muslims as a faith rather than ethnic group.

The Social Exclusion Unit's recent work in this area, summarised in their report *Policy Action Team 10: A Report to the Social Exclusion Unit*, sets out some of the DCMS's guiding principles in the area of social exclusion and community cohesion. These principles helpfully describe the aims of the DCMS as "valuing diversity" and argue for the need to connect policy in this area to the causes of social exclusion of certain groups.[88] This provides a useful starting point for analysis of the way in which the work of the DCMS can assist in overcoming social exclusion in the Muslim community.

---

[87] For Tom Stoppard's most recent reflections on the role of ideas in politics, see his trilogy of plays: *Voyage, Shipwreck* and *Salvage*. See also: Tom Stoppard, *The Coast of Utopia*, London, Faber and Faber, 2002.

[88] Department for Culture, Media and Sport, *Policy Action Team 10: A report to the Social Exclusion Unit*, London, DCMS, 13 September 2004. Available on the ODPM website at http://www.socialexclusionunit.gov.uk/downloaddoc.asp?id=216 (accessed 1 November 2004).

More specifically, it is suggested that the use of arts, culture and sport to overcome social exclusion in this particular social group should pay attention to the following policy levers, which are relevant for analysis: project evaluation, longtitudinal surveys of community needs, local authority cultural strategies, the DCMS's sports strategy, Bursay schemes[89] to promote young talent, and monitoring and follow-through policy. The DCMS should use its sponsoring agreements with its sponsor bodies as a way of setting targets for the inclusion and use of facilities by Muslims.

Organisations such as the Department for Education and Skills (DfES), the DCMS, the Arts Council, Sport England and local authorities need to develop and publish concrete action plans to promote opportunities for arts and sport amongst Muslim communities, use of facilities by Muslims and measured outcomes relevant to their needs. This may help compensate for the previously mentioned gaps left in the Race Equality Schemes established in these organisations – gaps caused by the failure to cover Muslims in the RR(A)A.

There are several examples that serve to illustrate how special attention to faith can make a difference to analysis. For example, attention to the needs of Muslims may reveal that the use of lottery money and distribution as a way of facilitating arts and culture projects is inappropriate, as Muslims are unable to access these resources due to Islam's injunction against gambling. There should be a way to compensate Muslims and their organisations, as well as other religious groups who may face similar restrictions, for this exclusion. Another example may be a need to make explicit the fact that not only those from racial and ethnic minorities but also those who frame their projects according to faith, such as Muslims, can apply for Arts Council funding. At the moment, the criteria for Arts Council funding refers to issues of race and ethnicity, thereby not directly encouraging groups such as Muslims to apply for funding within the paradigm of projects that focus on faith rather than race issues. Further examples might include the special needs of some Muslim women in accessing sport facilities, due to religious principles on separation and modesty.

In its consultation and policy paper on the way in which arts and culture can contribute to cohesion in communities, the DCMS usefully set out criteria for supporting communities in this way.[90] This work needs to be revived in the specific context of Muslims. There are examples of good practice in this area at a local level: Many local projects, such as mounting exhibitions on Islamic Art and the recent Shakespeare and

---

[89] Financial aid to needy students.

[90] Department for Culture, Media and Sport, *Culture at the Heart of Regeneration – Consultation Paper*, London, DCMS, 2004. Available on the DCMS website at http://www.culture.gov.uk/global/consultations/2004+current+consultations/cons_culture_heart_regeneration.htm (accessed 1 November 2004).

Islam season at the Globe Theatre, show the way in which different types of art form can contribute towards a more positive debate about Islam. However, these *ad hoc* local initiatives are insufficient to compensate for national coordinated action in this area. A national Festival of Islam, a series of arts events based throughout the UK, would provide an opportunity to present the history, art and culture of Islam as a civilisation and make an invaluable contribution towards a number of goals of this paper.

8. RECOMMENDATIONS

8.1 Recognising British Muslims as a Social Group

1. The Government should recognise Muslims as a social group for the purposes of legal and political decision making. For example, research, monitoring and legal remedies should reflect the fact that Muslims have a distinct faith identity, which they often cite as their pre-dominant source for self-identification.

Better Information about Muslims

2. The Government, especially the Home Office and the Social Exclusion Unit, should take steps to ensure more frequent and comprehensive data collection, disaggregated not only by ethnicity but also by religion, where it is important to capture the specific and common experiences of Muslims. It should consult with relevant groups on:

   • whether there are any advantages in supplementing the category of ethnicity with that of religion/faith, through a voluntary question, whether all data should be tagged in this way and whether, if not all areas are appropriate for this disaggregation, some areas should be prioritised;

   • whether there is a need for (i) more frequent and targeted surveys and/or (ii) occasional large surveys that are representative of the entire population and specifically address non-ethnic religious minorities' needs;

   • whether there are any advantages in supplementing ethnic categories with religion for work done at the small-area level to specifically target local initiatives;

   • how to compensate for incomplete information because the question about religion is voluntary; and how to guard against the misuse of data on religion/about Muslims.

8.2 Addressing Exclusion through Violence

Strategic enforcement of hate crime legislation

3. The Government should ensure that legislation on hate crimes is used strategically, to criminalise the most serious and culpable forms of racist conduct of those who undertake criminal acts motivated by conscious religious hatred.

4. The Government should ensure the appropriate training of law enforcement officers about policing issues arising out of "religious" hate crimes.

5. The Government should ensure that there is careful supervision of the exercise of discretion by law enforcement agencies in relation to this type of criminal power.

6. The Government should ensure that law enforcement agencies are monitored, supervised and held accountable to an independent body that includes *inter alia* members of the Muslim community and other faith communities.

7. Agencies in the criminal justice system, such as the police or Crown Prosecution Service, should ensure that training, development of codes of practice and consultation recognise that dealing with issues relating to "racism" or "race discrimination" will not always be appropriate to challenge anti-Muslim prejudice. Specially tailored training, monitoring and consultation should be provided to ensure that the specific and distinct needs of the Muslim community – and the specific risk of anti-Muslim prejudice tainting the exercise of discretion – are taken into account.

8. Work should be done by, *inter alia*, the Home Office, the Association of Chief Police Officers and the Metropolitan Police Authority, to inform and discuss issues relating to policing of the Muslim community.

9. The Home Office should consider including guidance on hate crimes against Muslims, with analogous guides for other religious minorities, such as Jews, in its guidance for Crime and Disorder Partnerships.

Building capacity to respond to hate speech

10. A particular problem is the fact that prosecutions are dependant on the permission of a member of the Government (the Attorney General). In order to reassure Muslims that their speech is not being uniquely targeted for prosecution by the State, the Government should consider *inter alia:*

    • publishing a clear Code of Practice that outlines the factors relevant to the exercise of the discretion of the Attorney General; and

    • asking the Attorney General to submit a full report, with summary of the figures and an explanation, to one of the House of Commons Select Committees (e.g. the Home Affairs Select Committee) or the Joint Committee on Human Rights.

11. The Government should encourage and fund initiatives that aim to build the capacity of Muslims to intervene in public discourse. This could include partnerships with the media and positive action to encourage and facilitate

Muslim employment in the media. Such proactive measures could be supplemented by reactive measures and work by the Press Complaints Council, OFCOM and public broadcasters to pay attention to the special risks to Muslims of hate speech.

12. The Department for Culture, Media and Sport (DCMS), OFCOM and the Press Complaints Commission may want to consider that, in extreme cases, there may be a need for regulation of the most extreme forms of hate speech against Muslims (e.g. via a voluntary code of practice against vilification of high risk minority groups such as Muslims) by these stakeholders.

8.3   Addressing Economic Exclusion

Combating discrimination in law and policy

13. The Government should consider harmonising the protection available to all religious minorities, both ethnic and non-ethnic, by extending protection from discrimination to cover these additional areas through new equality legislation.

14. The Government should, in its review of a change in the work of enforcement agencies such as the CRE and the Equal Opportunities Commission, pay special attention to the gap in this area and ensure that there are interim measures in place to help groups like Muslims build capacity and enforce their rights under the new legislation. This can be done through funding organisations to disseminate information about rights and the new Advisory, Conciliation and Arbitration Service Code of Practice. In addition, the Government should also consider funding to certain key Citizens Advice Bureaus in areas with high Muslim populations, to run campaigns to make workers aware of their rights.

15. The Government should encourage organisations such as the TUC to take up issues relating to rights of Muslim workers in employment.

16. The Women and Equalities Unit, and organisations such as the Equal Opportunities Commission, need to ensure that they now move beyond their meetings and consultations with Muslim women and develop an action plan with deliverable results and outcomes on the needs of this visible and vulnerable group.

17. The Government and the Women and Equalities Unit should develop campaigns specifically addressing non-discrimination and equality for Muslim women, who are at special risk of multiple discrimination, due to gender, race

and religion. The campaigns should aim to raise their participation in public life and the economy.

Combating discrimination in private and public sector service provision

18. The Government – via the Commission for Racial Equality, the Social Exclusion Unit, the Department for Trade and Industry or the Confederation of British Industry – should undertake research and consult widely with industry, employers and the Muslim community, in order to determine the key areas in which Muslims suffer a disadvantage due to their faith in enjoying private services.

19. The Home Office and the Social Exclusion Unit should undertake consultation and research on the needs and delivery of public services to the Muslim community, in order to supplement the work of the Commission for Racial Equality and local authorities in relation to race, under the RR(A)A.

20. The Government should instigate a pilot scheme around key issues, such as service delivery in education, employment or housing. Such a pilot study could mirror the type of issues raised in Section 71 of the RR(A)A, but should target consultation and policy design specifically towards issues of faith/religion.

21. The Commission for Racial Equality should ensure that guidance to public authorities makes clear the advantages in ensuring that adequate consultation and attention is given to the needs of minorities, such as Muslims in the design and delivery of public services.

22. The Government should, as a priority, review its policy – and also that of the Commission for Racial Equality – on public procurement, to ensure that it deals effectively with the concerns of Muslims. It may be necessary to make clear in these cases that the term "race" will not capture the whole range of data, groups and concerns that need to be considered. The term "diversity", or a wider definition of "equality" may be suggested as an alternative to "race," to ensure protection of Muslims as a group and to address their specific concerns.

23. The Government should revise guidance on the award of subsidies for investment, such as the Regional Selective Assistance, to include the term "diversity" rather than "race".

8.4   Addressing Political and Public Exclusion

Encouraging accommodation of Muslims

24. The Government should ensure it is fully informed about the specific needs of Muslims in the public sector. All consultation documents should compensate for the fact that references to race will not be a sufficient indicator to gather specific information about the needs of Muslims.

25. The Muslim community, and organisations such as the Muslim Council of Britain, should develop procedures and methods for full participation, to inform the Government about the most pressing and urgent needs and demands of Muslims.

26. The Muslim community, and organisations such as the Muslim Council of Britain, should make more clear and effective efforts to ensure that marginalised groups of Muslims, such as women and people with disabilities, are fully involved in decision making within the Muslim community.

27. The Government should specifically support marginalised groups of Muslims, by giving funding for organisations and by ensuring that funding for Muslim organisations is made conditional on the inclusion of these marginalised groups in projects.

28. The Government should consider reform of the way in which information and decision making about Muslims is coordinated. The Home Office has lead responsibility in this area. Options for reform include:

    • coordination of research by the Social Exclusion Unit or the Policy Unit within the Cabinet Office; and

    • giving clear responsibility for this issue to one of the existing or newly formed Cabinet Committees.

Promoting speech

29. The Government should support intervention in the public sphere, to challenge distorted images of Muslims by:

    • capacity building within the Muslim community, including giving support for media scholarships for Muslims or for organisations that are involved in the dissemination of accurate information about Islam and Muslims;

    • including guidance in the Codes of Practice of organisations/regulators such as Ofcom; and

- providing remedies and redress via cooperation with agencies such as the Press Complaints Council, when there has been specific and significant hate speech in the media.

30. The Department for Culture, Media and Sport should take the lead – while working with the Department for Education and Skills, the Arts Council, Sport England and also local authorities – to develop and publish Action Plans to promote access to, and opportunities for, arts and sport amongst Muslim communities, including promoting their use of facilities and measured outcomes relevant to their needs.

31. The Department for Culture, Media and Sport should consider support and funding for a national Festival of Islam. Such a festival would compensate for the disproportionate and distorted presentation of Islam as being linked to political terror and violence. It could also act as a lever to challenge anti-Islamic stereotypes, before they become entrenched into prejudiced attitudes about Muslims that lead to hate crimes, hate speech and discrimination. Finally, it could make an invaluable contribution towards community cohesion and overcoming cultural alienation by allowing British Muslims to feel that their identity and source of self-respect are being given public space and recognition.

Appendix 1: Bibliography

Ahmed, N. M., F. Bodi, R. Kazim and M. Shadjareh, *The Oldham Riots: Discrimination, Deprivation and Communal Tension in the United Kingdom* (London: Islamic Human Rights Commission, 2001)

Alexander, C., *The Asian Gang: Ethnicity, Identity, Masculinity* (Oxford: Oxford University Press, 2000)

Archer, L. *Race, Masculinity and Schooling: Muslim boys and education* (Maidenhead: Open University Press, 2003)

Atwood, C., G. Singh, D. Prime and R. Creasey, *2001 Home Office Citizenship Survey: People Families and Communities,* Home Office Research Study 270 (London: Home Office, 2003)

Hepple, B., M. Coussey, and T. Choudhury, *Equality: A New Framework – The Report of the Independent Review of the Enforcement of UK Anti-Discrimination Law* (Oxford: Hart Publishing, 2000)

Campbell, T., K.D. Ewing, and A. Tomkins (eds.), *Sceptical Approaches to Human Rights* (Oxford: Oxford University Press, 2001)

Citizenship Advisory Group, *Final Report of the Advisory Group on Citizenship chaired by Sir Bernard Crick* (London: Qualification and Curriculum Authority, 1998)

Clancy, A., M. Hough, R. Aust and C. Kershaw, *Crime, Policing and Justice: The Experience of Ethnic Minorities. Findings from the 2000 British Crime Survey,* Research Study 223 (London: Home Office, 2001)

Collins, H., "Discrimination, Equality and Social Exclusion", *Modern Law Review,* 66:1, (2003), 16–43

Commission for Racial Equality, *Public Procurement and Race Equality – Guidelines for local government (London:* Commission for Racial Equality, 2003)

Commission on British Muslims and Islamophobia, *Islamophobia, a challenge for us all,* (London: Central Books, 1997)

Crown Prosecution Service Inspectorate, *Thematic Review of CPS Casework with a Minority ethnic Dimension* (London, Crown Prosecution Service Inspectorate, 2002)

Crown Prosecution Service, *Guidance on Prosecuting Cases of Racist and Religious Crime* (London: Crown Prosecution Service, 2003)

Crown Prosecution Service, *Racist Incident Monitoring Scheme: Annual Report 2002-2003* (London: Crown Prosecution Service, 2003)

Crown Prosecution Service Inspectorate, *A Follow-up Review of CPS Casework with a Minority Ethnic Dimension* (London: Crown Prosecution Service Inspectorate, 2004)

Department for Culture, Media and Sport *Culture at the Heart of Regeneration – Consultation Paper* (London: Department for Culture, Media and Sport, 2004)

Department for Culture, Media and Sport, *Policy Action Team 10: A report to the Social Exclusion Unit* (London: Department for Culture, Media and Sport, 2004)

Douglas-Scott, Sionaidh (ed.), *Faith and Law: Essays in Legal Philosophy* (Oxford: Hart Publications, 2000)

European Monitoring Centre on Racism and Xenophobia, *Anti-Islamic reactions within the European Union after the recent acts of terror against the USA: A collection of the EUMC country reports from RAXEN National Focal Points (NFPs)* (Vienna: European Monitoring Centre on Racism and Xenophobia, 2001)

George, R., ed., *Natural Law, Liberalism and Morality* (Oxford: Clarendon Press, 1996)

Home Office, *Community Cohesion: A Report of the Independent Review Team* (London: Home Office, Community Cohesion Unit, 2002)

Jacobson, J., "Religion and Ethnicity: duel and alternative sources of identity among young British Pakistanis", *Ethnic and Racial Studies*, 20:2 (1997), 238–256

Lyotard, J. F., *The Postmodern Condition: A Report on Knowledge* (Manchester: Manchester University Press, 1986)

Malik, M., "Racist Crime", *Modern Law Review*, 62:3 (1999), 409–424

Mason, A., "Political Community, Liberal-Nationalism and the Ethics of Assimilation", *Ethics* 109:2 (1999), 261–281

Modood, T., *Not Easy Being British: Colour, Culture and Citizenship* (London: Trentham Books, 1992)

Modood, T., "Muslims and the Politics of Difference", *Political Quarterly*, 74:1 (2003), 100–115

Modood, T., R. Berthoud, J. Lakey, P. Smith, S. Virdee and S. Beishon, *Ethnic Minorities in Britain: Diversity and Disadvantage* (London: Policy Studies Institute, 1997)

Nielsen, Jørgen S., and C. Allen, *Summary Report on Islamophobia in the EU after September 11 2001* (Vienna: European Monitoring Centre on Racism and Xenophobia, 2002)

O'Beirne, M., *Religion in England and Wales: findings from the Home Office Citizenship Study 2001,* Home Office Research Study 274 (London: Home Office, 2004)

Office of National Statistics, *Focus on Religion* (London: Office of National Statistics, 2004)

Office of the Deputy Prime Minister, *Preventing Social Exclusion* (London: Social Exclusion Unit, Office of the Deputy Prime Minister, 2001)

Office of the Deputy Prime Minister, *Tackling Social Exclusion: Taking Stock and Looking to the Future* (London: Social Exclusion Unit, Office of the Deputy Prime Minister, 2004)

Open Society Institute, *Minority Protection in the EU: The Situation of Muslims in the UK* (Budapest: EUMAP, Open Society Institute, 2002)

Rawls, J., *A Theory of Justice* (Oxford: Oxford University Press, 1999)

Sheridan, L., *Effects of the Events of September 11th 2001 on Discrimination and Implicit Racism in Five Religious and Ethnic Groups* (Leicester: University of Leicester, 2002)

Sunstein, C., *The Partial Constitution* (Cambridge, MA: Harvard University Press, 1993)

Taylor, C., "Human Agency and Language" *Philosophical Papers, Vol. I* (Cambridge: Cambridge University Press, 1985)

Stoppard, T., The Coast of Utopia: *Voyage, Shipwreck, Salvage* (London: Grove Press, 2003)

Young, I. M., *Justice and the Politics of Difference* (Princeton, NJ: Princeton University Press, 1990)

British Muslims and Education

Table of Contents

OPEN SOCIETY INSTITUTE 2005

List of Acronyms

BTEC	Business and Technology Education Council
DfES	Department for Education and Skill
EAL	English as an Additional Language
GNVQ	General National Vocational Qualifications
LEA	Local Education Authority
NPQH	National Professional Qualification for Headship
OFSTED	Office for Standards in Education
PGCE	Post Graduate Certificate in Education
PLASC	Pupil Level Annual School Census
SACRE	Standing Advisory Council for Religious Education
TTA	Teacher Training Agency
UCAS	Universities and Colleges Admission Services
VA	Voluntary-Aided (school)

1. EXECUTIVE SUMMARY

Education is crucial to integration and social cohesion in a diverse multicultural and multi-faith society. There are several reasons for this. First, the school system is the earliest mainstream social institution with which young people come into sustained contact, and the extent to which schools respect and accommodate diversity sends out strong signals about the value which society as a whole places on diversity. Second, educational attainment levels are a key determinant of opportunities for finding employment and improving future life chances. Third, schools provide an opportunity to develop bonds and friendships across different ethnic and faith groups, and the education curriculum is itself a mechanism by which pupils are able to develop an understanding of the different groups within their community.

One third of Muslims are under age 16 as compared with one fifth of the population as a whole. There are approximately half a million Muslim children and young people currently receiving education in British schools and colleges. Increasing numbers of Muslims are entering further and higher education. As a result of this younger age profile, Government education policies aimed at children and young people will have a disproportionate impact on Muslim communities. It is vital, therefore, that Government departments and agencies implementing and delivering these policies lead the way in ensuring that policy is sensitive to the needs of Muslims.

There is significant diversity in what Muslim parents want. While some would like to send their children to schools with an Islamic ethos, others merely want single-sex schooling; others again would be happy to send their children to community or church schools so long as these are respectful of their faith and supportive of their distinctive identity. The majority of Muslims in the UK attend community school. However, at present many Muslim parents feel that community schools are not meeting the needs of their children.

The key educational issues concerning Muslim parents are: the continuing poor academic results of Muslim children; the need to eradicate institutional racism and racist and Islamophobic bullying; the lack of recognition or support for their children's faith identity; and the inadequacy of spirituals and moral education that schools provide.

The levels of academic achievement of Muslim students are low, but improving. Explanations for these low levels are usually given in terms of poverty, social deprivation and language difficulties, but there are further obstacles to their full achievement of potential that relate more specifically to their experiences as Muslims. These include the prevalence of religious prejudice and Islamophobia; the lack of Muslim role models in schools; the low expectations that some teachers have of Muslim students; and the lack of recognition of students' Muslim identity. In addition,

Muslim children who attend community or church schools typically also attend mosque schools or other supplementary schools outside normal school hours in order to receive education in Islamic beliefs and practices. This places an additional burden on Muslim children, in terms of both time and intellectual effort.

The school curriculum has an important role to play in encouraging cross-cultural understanding. Two shifts in the curriculum might help to make this happen. The first is a more global focus, whereby European and Christian culture is contextualised in terms of world civilisation. The second is the inclusion of references to the Muslim contribution to European learning and culture, particularly in the fields of art, literature, mathematics, geometry, science, history, philosophy, astronomy and medicine. Schools should also ensure that the curriculum is more responsive to Muslim sensitivities and interests in particular areas. Many Muslim parents would appreciate the option for their children to study Arabic in school, and also for them to receive a form of Religious Education that gave them more opportunities to enrich their understanding of their own faith as well as studying others.

The Government has taken the lead in many issues relating to the needs of children from Muslim and other minority groups. Much good practice in responding to the specific cultural needs of Muslims is also to be found at the level of many local authorities. However, effective mechanisms are needed for sharing and spreading such good practice more widely. At present, education policy views minorities only in terms of race and ethnicity. In particular, although many Muslim children and young people experience Islamophobia both in and out of school, anti-discrimination policy in education tend to focus much more on racial or ethnic discrimination, rather than religious discrimination. Without the collection of data on the basis of religion, education policy will not be able to meet the needs of individuals from different faith communities.

Muslim community organisations and individuals also have a vital role to play. Greater participation by Muslims in all aspects of the education system is central to ensuring that educational policy is sensitive to their needs. The numbers of Muslim teachers and governors in schools are very low, and drop-out rates for Muslims on teacher training courses are higher than average. What is needed are ways to engage Muslims more fully with the education system and also to empower them, by helping them to contribute more effectively to the processes of educational decision-making.

The recommendations with which this chapter concludes (section nine) are wide-ranging. They are based on the premise that a commitment to inclusive education requires both a willingness to listen to the ways that minority communities like Muslims define their own needs, and a determination to respond to those needs. This approach will equally serve the wellbeing of the Muslim community and the interests of the broader, multicultural society.

2. INTRODUCTION

"Education represents for British Muslims a major area of struggle for equality of opportunity and assertion of identity. It was over education that Muslims became increasingly vocal in raising their demands in the early 1980s, and it is where they have succeeded best in having many of their needs recognised in the face of controversy and opposition from broad sections of British society"[1]

Education is crucial to integration and social cohesion. There are several reasons for this: first, the school system is the earliest mainstream social institution with which young people come into sustained contact, and the extent to which schools respect and accommodate diversity sends out strong signals about the value society places on diversity. Second, educational attainment levels are a key determinant of opportunities for finding employment and improving future life chances. Third, schools provide an opportunity to develop bonds and friendships across different ethnic and faith groups, and the education curriculum is itself a mechanism by which pupils are able to develop an understanding of the different groups within their community.

More than half of Britain's Muslims (52 per cent) are under age 25, as compared to only 31 per cent of the population as whole. The average age of Muslims in the UK is 28 years old, 13 years younger than the national average.[2] There are half a million Muslims currently receiving education in British schools. Organisations and individuals delivering and participating in the education system have a critical role in engaging with the new generation of British Muslims.

This chapter highlights some of the anxieties Muslim parents currently have about the British system of educational provision. These anxieties focus on four major inter-linked issues: the continuing poor academic results of Muslim children; the failure of the schools to eradicate institutional racism and racist and Islamophobic bullying; the lack of support for Muslim children's Islamic identity; and the inadequacy of the spiritual and moral education that the schools provide – an inadequacy that is seen as at least partly responsible for the growth of drug addiction, the increasing number of Muslims in custody and the inner-city riots of 2001.[3]

The substantive content of this chapter is contained in sections three to eight.

---

[1] H. Ansari, *The Infidel Within: Muslims in Britain since 1800*, Hurst and Co, London, 2004, p. 298, (hereafter, Ansari, *The Infidel Within*).

[2] A. Scott, D. Pearce, and P. Goldblatt, "The Sizes and Characteristics of Ethnic Populations of Great Britain", in *Population Trends*, vol. 105, 2001, pp. 6–15, (hereafter, Scott et al, *Ethnic Popuations*).

[3] See: C. Allen, *Fair Justice: the Bradford Disturbances, the Sentencing and the Impact*, Forum Against Islamophobia and Racism, London, 2003.

Section three contextualises the position of Muslims and their children within the UK. It sets out the number of Muslims in British schools and their distribution throughout the country. It outlines the diversity of the Muslim community in terms of ethnicity and traditions within Islam and sketches the particular features of home and community life that define the experiences of Muslim children.

Section four examines data collection in the education system – in schools, further education and universities – and notes that most data collected is based on ethnicity rather than religious identity.

Section five examines Muslims' experience of schooling. It outlines the types of schools that are open to Muslim pupils, including community schools, church schools and independent and State-aided Muslim schools, and considers the factors that affect the choice of school made by Muslim parents. In addition to looking at formal or compulsory schooling, the section goes on to explore the role and nature of supplementary schooling. It examines the attainment of Muslim pupils in schools and their subsequent participation and experience of further and higher education. Finally, it looks at the involvement of Muslims as teachers and school governors and at the issue of parent-school relations.

Section six looks at issues of identity and Islamophobia. It examines the implications of the official practice of discussing school achievement in terms of ethnicity but not religion. It also considers the evidence of Islamophobia in schools, including the stereotypes about Muslim girls. It suggests that the school curriculum and teacher training provide important mechanisms for tackling Islamophobia, by ensuring greater understanding of Muslim communities and of Islam.

Section seven examines the ways in which the curriculum can acknowledge and respect Muslim identity and ensure that Muslims are confident to take on all the rights and responsibilities of full British citizenship. It suggests a more global focus within the curriculum, so that European and Christian culture is contextualised in terms of world civilisation, and calls for discussion of currently neglected Muslim contributions to European learning and culture. Such a change would support the identity and self-concept of young Muslims within the context of European citizenship. The section goes on to consider specific issues, as they arise, in relation to the content and delivery of classes in religious education, languages, sex education, music and the performing arts.

Section eight sets out the current policy framework. It highlights the findings in recent policy reports relevant to Muslims, as well as policy initiatives at the national and local level.

Overall, this chapter argues that a commitment to inclusive education must involve a determination to meet the needs of children from diverse community backgrounds. This involves a willingness to listen to the way those communities themselves define their needs. The recommendations in *section nine* are intended to raise awareness of the implications that an acceptance of a policy of cultural diversity has for the education of Muslims. The recommendations are put forward in acknowledgement that there are important differences between Muslims and other minority groups and that any policies put forward for minority ethnic groups generally may not meet the specific needs of Muslim pupils. Some of the recommendations are particularly appropriate for areas where there are heavy concentrations of Muslims, but others have more general applicability, or may even be relevant in the case of isolated Muslim pupils.

3. CONTEXT AND BACKGROUND

There are about 500,000 Muslim children currently receiving education in British schools – between five and six per cent of the total school population.[4] The vast majority of these live in England, the combined total of Muslim students for the rest of the UK being about 22,000 children.[5] Because of the differences in the way statistics are gathered, some of the information below refers to the whole of the UK, some to England only and some to England and Wales.

Eighty per cent of the UK's Muslims live in the five major conurbations of Greater London, West Midlands, West Yorkshire, Greater Manchester, and East Midlands, while the same areas contain 50 per cent of the general population.[6] Approximately 40 per cent of Muslims live in Greater London.[7] Outside London, the largest numbers of

---

[4] The Muslim population of the United Kingdom is variously estimated as being between 1.6 and 1.8 million people, or about 350,000 households. The lower figure comes from the Office for National Statistics (ONS). (See: Office for National Statistics, *UK National Census 2001: Focus on Religion,* available on the ONS website at http://www.statistics.gov.uk/focuson/religion, (accessed 1 November 2004), (hereafter ONS, *Focus on Religion*)). The higher figure comes from M. Anwar, an expert on Muslim ethnography, quoted in *The Financial Times,* 23 January 2002. These figures represent approximately three per cent of the total population – more than the combined total of Hindus, Sikhs, Jews and Buddhists in the UK. (See: ONS, *Ethnicity and Religion).* Moreover, the age profile of Muslims is much younger than any other religious group: In all, 33.8 per cent of Muslims fall into the 0-15 age bracket, and a further 18.2 per cent are between 16 and 24 years old. (See: Scott et al, *Ethnic Popuations).* Assuming that 75 per cent of children in the 0-15 age bracket attend school, and 80 per cent of young people in the 16-18 age bracket are in school, the number of Muslims attending school in the UK is between 482,477 (if the total Muslim population is 1.6 million) and 542,786 (if the total population is 1.8 million). The ONS gives the figure of 371,000 Muslim children in England of compulsory schooling age, i.e. 5-16 year-olds. (See: ONS, *Focus on Religion,* Education, 11 October 2004, available on the ONS website at http://www.statistics.gov.uk/cci/nugget.asp?id=963 (accessed 1 November 2004)). The higher figure in the present report includes all the children who attend school outside the compulsory period of schooling, especially 4-5 year-olds and 16-18 year-olds, as well as Muslim children in the rest of the UK, and an estimate of the increase between 2001 and 2004.

[5] This figure is calculated on the basis of about 14,000 children in Scotland, about 7,000 in Wales and less than 1,000 in Northern Ireland. See: website of the General Register Office, Scotland at http://www.gro-scotland.gov.uk; and website of the Office for National Statistics at http://www.statistics.gov.uk (accessed 5 November 2004).

[6] See Chapter 3 of this report (British Muslims and the Labour Market).

[7] In Greater London, the biggest concentrations of Muslims are in the boroughs of Tower Hamlets, Newham, Waltham Forest, Hackney, Brent, Redbridge, Westminster, Camden, Haringey, Ealing, Enfield and Hounslow.

Muslims are found in Birmingham, Bradford, Blackburn with Darwen, Luton, Oldham, Leicester, Kirklees, Manchester, Sheffield and Leeds.[8]

In some of these districts, Muslim children form a high proportion of the total school population. In Bradford, for example, children from ethnic minorities comprise about 33 per cent of the total school population, and most of these minorities are Muslims of Pakistani and Bangladeshi origin. A significant number of inner-city schools in Bradford almost exclusively serve the Muslim population.[9] Research suggests that the level of ethnic segregation is higher in schools than in local neighbourhoods, and that ethnic segregation is particularly high for pupils of Pakistani and Bangladeshi origin, both at secondary school and in their neighbourhoods.[10]

Muslim children come from a wide diversity of ethnic backgrounds. Over 40 per cent are of Pakistani origin, and nearly 20 per cent of Bangladeshi origin. Of the remainder, about 15 per cent are of Indian or other Asian origin, up to ten per cent are from Turkish or Turkish Cypriot origin, and the rest are from the Middle East, East Asia, Africa, or the Caribbean, with about four per cent being of mixed ethnic origin.[11] In addition, there is a small group (perhaps less than one per cent) of White converts. Most recent waves of Muslim immigrants and refugees have come from Morocco, Somalia, Kosovo, Afghanistan and Iraq.[12] The result of this ethnic diversity is that Muslim children bring to school a wide range of cultural and linguistic experiences, as well as connections of various kinds with a wide range of countries. In the face of this ethnic diversity, religion is a key element that serves to bind them into a unified group

---

[8] Office for National Statistics, "Census 2001: Ranking: Ethnicity and Religion: Muslim", available on the ONS website at http://www.statistics.gov.uk/census2001/profiles/rank/ewmuslim.asp (accessed 1 November 2004).

[9] Office for Standards in Education, *Inspection of Bradford Local Education Authority, September 2002,* London, OFSTED, Audit Commission, 2002, (hereafter, OFSTED, *Inspection of Bradford LEA*). See also: D. Phillips, *The Changing Geography of South Asians in Bradford,* 2001, available at http://www.bradford2020.com/pride/docs/section5.doc (accessed 1 November 2004).

[10] S. Burgess and D. Wilson, *Ethnic mix: how segregated are English Schools?,* Bristol, Centre for Market and Public Organisation, 2004.

[11] The 2001 UK National Census lacked separate categories for people of Arab, Persian or Turkish origin, but it is likely that a majority of those Muslims who identified as "White British" or "Other White" (nearly 12 per cent of the total number of British Muslims) were in fact Turkish or Turkish Cypriot in origin. See http://www.salaam.co.uk/themeofthemonth/september03_index.php?l=2 (accessed 18 October 2004).

[12] Scott et al., *Ethnic Populations;* M. Anwar, quoted in *The Financial Times,* 23 January 2002.

with common concerns. Both the diversity and the shared concerns among Muslims are significant factors for policy-makers to take into consideration.

In terms of religious belief, there are important differences in affiliation, the most obvious being that between the Sunnis and the Shi'as. There are many different subgroups within the broader faith community of British Muslims, including (for example) the Barelwi, the Deobandi/Tablighi Jama'at, and the Jama'at-i Islami.[13]

There are also differences between Muslims in terms of religious practice and commitment. One report estimates that there are 760,000 "practising" Muslims in the UK,[14] and another notes that 74 per cent of Muslims say their religion is "very important" to them.[15] However, a division between "practising" and "non-practising" Muslims is problematic, for practice is always a matter of definition and degree, and there are different ways in which the religion can be practised.[16] The Association of Muslim Social Scientists, in its 2004 position paper *Muslims on Education,* adopts an inclusive approach to the term "Muslim", encompassing "not only practising adherents of Islam, but also those who identify themselves as such (without necessarily being practising) or who belong to a household or family that holds Islam as its descendant [*sic*] faith".[17] There are also differences in the extent to which religion is part of the daily life of Muslim children. However, most Muslim children will, through family and community activities and the very language they use, if not through more formal religious observances, come into contact with the religion of Islam on a regular basis.

The family life of Muslim children differs in significant respects from that of broader British society.[18] The statistical evidence on family life is generally presented in official documents with reference to ethnic origin rather than to religion, and so most of the information in the rest of this section relates to British Muslim children of Pakistani and Bangladeshi origin. Anecdotal evidence suggests that the experience of other Muslim groups – particularly recent migrants like the Kosovars, Somalis and Afghans –

---

[13] See: P. Lewis, *Islamic Britain; Religion, Politics and Identity among British Muslims,* I. B. Tauris, London, 1994.

[14] The Guardian Research Department, "Special Report: Muslim Britain, The Statistics", *The Guardian,* 17 June 2002, available on the Guardian website at http://www.guardian.co.uk/religion/story, (hereafter, *The Guardian, Muslim Britain*).

[15] T. Modood, R. Berthoud, J. Lakey, J. Nazroo, P. Smith, P., S. Virdee and S. Beishon, *Ethnic Minorities in Britain: Diversity and Disadvantage,* London, Policy Studies Institute, 1997, p. 301, (hereafter, Modood et al, *Ethnic Minorities in Britain*).

[16] IQRA Trust, *Meeting the Needs of Muslim Pupils: advice for teachers and LEAs,* IQRA Trust, London, 1991, p. 11, (hereafter, IQRA Trust, Needs of Muslim Pupils).

[17] Association of Muslim Social Scientists and other groups, *Muslims on Education: a position paper,* AMSS, Richmond, 2004, p.11 (hereafter, AMSS, *Muslims on Education*).

[18] M. Parker-Jenkins, *Children of Islam,* Stoke-on-Trent, Trentham Books, 1995.

is often not dissimilar, though Muslims of Indian (and East African) origin tend to have a higher socio-economic profile and higher levels of educational achievement.

In terms of family life, the large majority of UK Muslim children of Pakistani and Bangladeshi origin (90 per cent) live with both parents, a much higher percentage than for White or Afro-Caribbean children.[19] The average number of persons per household is larger than for any other UK ethnic group, at 4.9 persons. This compares to 2.3 persons for White households.[20] Within the home, most UK Muslim children speak a language other than English, the most common being Punjabi, Bengali, Gujerati, Urdu, Turkish or Arabic.[21]

Muslim children in the UK experience high levels of the risk factors associated with child poverty. Some 42 per cent live in overcrowded accommodation, compared to 12 per cent for the UK population as a whole. Twelve per cent of UK Muslim children live in households without central heating, compared with six per cent for all dependent children. A total of 19 per cent live in lone-parent households; this is close to the 23 per cent for all dependent children. Over one third (35 per cent) of UK Muslim children are growing up in households where there are no adults with employment, compared with 17 per cent for all dependent children. Some 28 per cent of UK Muslim children live in a household without a car or van, compared to 16 per cent for all dependent children.[22] Three-quarters of UK children of Bangladeshi and Pakistani origin live in households earning less than half the average income for the UK.[23] And 54 per cent of Pakistani and Bangladeshi homes receive income support, three times as many as other households in the UK.[24] Some 35 per cent of Pakistani children and 50 per cent of Bangladeshi children in the UK are eligible for free school

---

[19] See: *The Guardian,* 21 September 2001.

[20] M. Murphy, "Household and Family Structure among Ethnic Minority Groups", in *Ethnicity in the 1991 Census, Vol. I,* HMSO, London, 1996, Table 8.3. See also R. Penn and P. Lambert, "Attitudes towards Ideal Family Size of Different Ethnic/Nationality Groups in Great Britain, France and Germany", in *Population Trends 108,* Summer 2002, pp. 49–58.

[21] National Literacy Trust, "Languages Spoken by Pupils in London", 21 January 2000, available on the website of the National Literacy Trust at http://www.literacytrust.org.uk/Research/lostop3.html#40languages (accessed 1 November 2004); See also: J. M. Halstead, *Education, Justice and Cultural Diversity,* Falmer Press. London, 1988, p. 15, (hereafter, Halstead, *Education, Justice and Cultural Diversity*).

[22] Oxford Centre for Islamic Studies, *Muslim housing experiences,* London, Housing Corporation, 2004, p. 13, Table 3, (hereafter, OCIS, *Muslim housing experiences*).

[23] Department for Work and Pensions, *Households Below Average Income, 1994/95–2000/01,* London, DWP, esp. ch. 4. Available on the DWP website at http://www.dwp.gov.uk/asd/hbai/hbai2001/hbai2000_01.asp (accessed 1 November 2004).

[24] *The Guardian, Muslim Britain,* p. 1.

meals.[25] There are higher levels of unemployment among the parents of UK Muslim children, lower average earnings, and a higher proportion of fathers who lack formal educational qualifications and are semi-skilled manual workers.[26] The mothers of UK Muslim children are less likely than any other group to be in paid employment outside the house.[27] Older siblings of UK Muslim children are more likely than other groups to be unemployed.[28]

The effects of high levels of poverty and social deprivation, and of the discrimination encountered by many Muslims, are also important. A rising number of Muslim children are likely to have a family member in prison; the number of Muslim prisoners has grown significantly in recent years to nine per cent of all prisoners.[29] Outside the home, many Muslim children experience the effects both of racism and of social, ethnic and religious prejudice and bullying, even when living in areas their parents consider safe.[30]

---

[25] G. Bhattacharyya, L. Ison and M. Blair, *Minority Ethnic Attainment and Participation in Education and Training: the Evidence*, Department for Education and Skills, Nottingham, 2003, p. 9, (hereafter, Bhattacharyya et al, *Minority Ethnic Attainment*).

[26] Cabinet Office, *Ethnic Minorities and the Labour Market: final report*, Cabinet Office, Strategy Unit, London, 2003. See also, R. Berthoud, *The Incomes of Ethnic Minorities*, University of Essex, Colchester, 1998.

[27] F. Ahmad, T. Modood and S. Lissenburgh, *South Asian Women and Employment in Britain: the interaction of gender and ethnicity*, London, Policy Studies Institute, 2003.

[28] Office for National Statistics, "Social Focus in Brief: Ethnicity 2002", available at the ONS website at http://www.statistics.gov.uk/statbase/Product.asp?vlnk=9763 (accessed 1 November 2004).

[29] Commission on British Muslims and Islamophobia, *Islamophobia: issues, challenges and action*, Trentham Books, Stoke-on-Trent, 2004, pp. 38–39. See also: M. Elkins and J. Olagundoye, *The Prison Population in 2000: a Statistical Review (Home Office Findings 154)*, London, Home Office, 2001.

[30] Office of National Statistics, *Social Focus in Brief: Ethnicity 2002*, ONS, 2002, available on the ONS website at http://www.statistics.gov.uk/statbase/Product.asp?vlnk=9763 (accessed 1 November 2004).

4. DATA COLLECTION IN THE EDUCATION SYSTEM

The primary source of data on Muslim children is the 2001 UK National Census. The first census to include a question on religious affiliation, it has generated much information relevant to education. Information on religion previously had to be inferred from the question on ethnic group. A recent publication by the Office for National Statistics, *Focus on Religion* (October 2004),[31] has drawn on data from the census to provide, for example, information about the age profile of the Muslim community and the number of Muslim children of compulsory school age.

The second major source of data is the Annual School Census,[32] carried out in January each year. Every nursery, primary, middle, secondary and special school is required to give data for this census by submitting an electronic return, the Pupil Level Annual School Census (PLASC), which includes information about each pupil's ethnic group and first language. The source of the ethnic group information has to be indicated; in the case of younger children, it normally comes from the parents, while older children sometimes provide the information themselves, and in some cases, the information may be ascribed to the school. The return also includes information on each school's bilingual assistants, teachers of ethnic minorities and teachers of English as an Additional Language (EAL). The school's return is submitted to the Local Education Authority (LEA), and goes from there to the Department for Education and Skills (DfES).

This information is seen as central to the task of monitoring policy, raising standards and targeting educational funds. The data allows for factors such as eligibility for free school meals, exclusions, performance and special needs to be analysed in terms of ethnicity. The DfES Research and Statistics Gateway[33] lists many research publications that draw on this source of data. From a Muslim perspective, the major shortcoming of the PLASC data is that Muslims are not identified as a distinct group. The identity of some Muslims, such as Pakistanis and Bangladeshis, can be inferred from their ethnic group, while others – including the 11 per cent of Muslims who are from "White" ethnic groups – cannot. Some schools, especially church schools, request information about pupils' religious affiliation outside of the PLASC returns, but this information does not feed into the official databases of the DfES.

---

[31] Office for National Statistics, *Focus on Religion*, October 2004, ONS, available at http://www.statistics.gov.uk/cci (accessed 25 October 2004).

[32] Department for Education and Skills, "Annual Schools Census", available on the DfES Teachernet website at http://www.teachernet.gov.uk/management/asc (accessed 26 October 2004).

[33] Department for Education and Skills, Research and Statistics Gateway, available at http://www.dfes.gov.uk/rsgateway (consulted 26 October 2004).

Universities and Further Education colleges use a similar system. Ethnic statistics are gathered by the University Central Admissions Service and the Graduate Teacher Training Registry, in order to monitor applications and admissions. University on-line enrolment requires details of ethnic origin. The information that all providers of teacher education are required to submit to the Teacher Training Agency includes ethnic origin. In none of these cases, however, are students required to answer questions about religion. All applications for jobs in universities and colleges of Higher or Further Education include questions on ethnicity. The personal data held on academic and support staff at universities and colleges typically includes questions on both ethnicity and religion, though the latter may be optional.

The ethnic categories used throughout the education system are gradually being standardised in line with the categories used in the 2001 UK National Census,[34] with the addition of the category "Parent/pupil preferred not to say". There is no reason, in theory, why data on religious affiliation could not be collected in the same way as data on ethnic origin throughout the education system. The main argument against this would be that many people consider religion, unlike ethnicity, to be a matter of choice rather than a matter of birth. While young children may be happy to be listed under the religion of their parents, this is less likely to be the case as children get older. In any event, whenever questions about religious affiliation are optional, experience suggests that many people prefer to keep their religion private.[35]

Further data is generated through educational research, funded by research councils or other sources. In such cases, the research may take the education of groups defined by religion, rather than ethnicity, as its central focus. The analysis of such research about the education of Muslim children and young people is at the heart of the present chapter, though there are many topics where the required research has not yet been done, or has not been done with sufficient thoroughness. Such research involves the analysis of national data; the administration of questionnaires and other wide-ranging surveys; observations of teaching and other school activities; scrutiny of policies and other documentation at school, LEA or national level; the study of life histories; group and individual interviews with Muslim children, parents, teachers, community representatives and others; and other methods.

Qualitative research clearly has some advantages over quantitative forms of data collection, in that it is more likely to allow the Muslims being interviewed to define their terms, explain their meaning and identify their own priorities. This is important where there is a danger that the researcher may use categories with which the

---

[34] For ethnic categories in the UK 2001 National Census, see Appendix 1: Definitions.

[35] It would of course make the data unreliable if disproportionate numbers of people from minority faiths opted for the category "Prefer not to say".

interviewee is not comfortable. The issue of the primary identity of Muslims may be one such case where questions are regularly shaped in terms of ethnic identity rather than religious affiliation. This issue is discussed more fully in section six below. For many Muslims, it is clear that much of the data currently collected in the British education system is interesting but of limited value, because it uses ethnic categories alone and ignores religious categories, so that it fails to pick out specific Muslim factors and issues.

5. MUSLIM CHILDREN AND BRITISH SCHOOLING

In the UK, children are required to attend school between the ages of 5 and 16. Parents of children of compulsory school age must ensure that their children receive a suitable education through regular attendance at a school, or that the children are taught adequately at home. Under the Human Rights Act (1998), State schools, as public authorities, are required to adhere to the requirements of the European Convention on Human Rights, such as the right to freedom of religion; the right of parents to schooling for their children, in line with their religious and philosophical beliefs; and the protection of pupils from discrimination on the grounds of religion.[36]

This section examines Muslims' experience of schooling. It outlines the types of schools that are open to Muslim pupils, including community schools, church schools and independent and State-aided Muslim schools, and considers the factors that affect the choice of school made by Muslim parents. In addition to formal or compulsory schooling, the section goes on to explore the role and nature of supplementary schooling. It examines the attainment of Muslim pupils in schools and their subsequent participation and experience of further and higher education. Finally, it looks at the involvement of Muslims as teachers and school governors and addresses the issue of parent-school relations.

5.1 Compulsory Schooling

Choice and diversity in schooling

There are approximately 25,000 State-funded schools in Britain.[37] Muslim children are found in every kind of British school, from public schools, to foundation schools, to city technical colleges, city academies and special schools.[38] A small, but growing, number – certainly still under one per cent of all Muslim children – are home-schooled.[39] Some parents send their children abroad for education, often to Pakistan,

---

[36] European Convention on Human Rights and Fundamental Freedoms (ECHR), art. 9 and 14, and Additional Protocol no. 1 to the ECHR, art. 2.

[37] P. Wintour, "Religious Schools 'must integrate in the community'", *The Guardian*, 14 November 2001.

[38] The educational systems of England, Wales, Scotland and Northern Ireland all have significant differences. Most of the discussion below refers to England, or to England and Wales, since most British Muslim children reside there.

[39] The Islamic Home Schooling Advisory Network (IHSAN) was set up by a group of Muslim women in 2000 to support parents choosing this option. The IHSAN website is available at http://www.islamichomeeducation.co.uk (accessed 2 November 2004).

but no data on this phenomenon is available.[40] However, the vast majority of Muslim pupils are educated in three kinds of schools: community schools, church schools or Muslim schools.[41] Many Muslim parents prefer single-sex schools at the secondary level, especially for their daughters.[42] However, the number of single-sex schools in the UK continues to decline.

Parents' final choice of school depends largely on what is available locally, as well as on their own educational priorities.[43] There are several possible constraints on the choice available. For example: first-choice community schools may be oversubscribed; church schools may give priority to the children of Christian parents; there may be no Muslim schools in the vicinity of the home; parents may not be able to afford the fees for private schooling; and no single-sex schools may be available.

There is significant diversity in what Muslim parents want, and indeed in how Muslims conceive of education. Traditionally, the purpose of Muslim education has been described as the creation of a "good human being".[44] However, many Muslims now prioritise academic success, seeing it as their Muslim duty to provide schooling that offers the best chance of obtaining good examination results.[45]

Those parents for whom the language needs of their children are a top priority may prefer community schools, because these often have facilities for easing the transition from mother tongue to English in the early years of schooling and for providing appropriate English as an Additional Language (EAL) support.[46] However, EAL provision is sometimes criticised for doing no more than helping children to "get by" in English rather than helping them to achieve their full potential. EAL has also been

---

[40] J. M. Halstead, *Education, Justice and Cultural Diversity*, p. 34.

[41] See Appendix 1 for definitions of these terms as used here.

[42] K. Hawe, "Muslim Girls' Schools – a conflict of interests?" *Gender and Education*, 6, 1 (1994) (hereafter, Hawe, *Muslim Girls' Schools*), pp. 63–76. See also: J. M. Halstead, "Radical Feminism, Islam and the Single-Sex School Debate", *Gender and Education*, 3, 3 (1991), pp. 263–278, (hereafter, Halstead, *Radical Feminism*).

[43] J. M. Halstead, "Parental Choice: an overview", in J. M. Halstead (ed.), *Parental Choice and Education*, Kogan Page, London, 1994.

[44] See, for example: S. M. N. al-Attas, "Preliminary Thoughts on the Nature of Knowledge and the Definition and Aims of Education", in S. M. N. al-Attas (ed.) *Aims and Objectives of Islamic Education*, Hodder and Stoughton, London, 1979.

[45] N. Hashmi, *A Muslim School in Bristol: an Overview of the Current Debate and Muslim School Children's Views*, Centre for the Study of Ethnicity and Citizenship, University of Bristol, 2003 (hereafter, N. Hashmi, *A Muslim School*), pp. 11–13.

[46] Over 90 per cent of children of Pakistani and Bangladeshi origin are registered as EAL. See: Bhattacharyya et al, *Minority Ethnic Attainment*, p. 13.

criticised for using materials that are not built around children's family and cultural experiences.[47]

Other parents prioritise spiritual and moral development or a traditional religious upbringing.[48] For some of these parents, a school with an Islamic ethos is essential,[49] while others are happy with community or church schools, so long as their children can also learn about Islamic beliefs and practices, either at home or at a local mosque school.[50]

The main implication of this diversity of educational priorities is that, as for other ethnic and faith groups in the UK, Muslims will benefit from as wide a range of school choice as possible. However, there is also a need for a better understanding of the factors that influence the choice of school by Muslim parents. One factor may be the impact of different kinds of schooling on the developing identity of Muslim children. (See below, section 6.1.)

This points to the need for more focused research investigating issues that are of real concern to the Muslim community. Possible research topics include: do pupils at single-sex schools achieve more? Do community schools prepare pupils better for citizenship than Muslim schools? Do Muslim values get a fair hearing in community schools? Do Muslim supplementary schools add value to the education of Muslim children? Such research might fit into the Teacher Training Agency's small grants scheme to enable teachers to carry out school-based case-study research, but equally, it might merit more large-scale funding within existing programmes run by the Department for Education and Skills and the Equal Opportunities Commission.

Community schools

The majority of Muslim children in the UK attend community schools. No precise figure is available, but it is almost certain that well in excess of 75 per cent of all Muslim children in the UK go to a community school. Nonetheless, there is no available data to indicate how many Muslim parents make a positive choice to send their children to community schools and how many send them there because they have

---

[47] This point was raised at the OSI roundtable meeting, London, 2 December 2003. *Explanatory Note: OSI held a roundtable meeting in London on 2 December 2003, hosted by Lewis Silkin, to invite critique of the present report in draft form. Experts present included representatives of the government, parents, and non-governmental organisations.*

[48] Learning and Culture Scrutiny Committee, *Faith in our Schools* (first draft), Oxfordshire County Council, 2004, p. 37.

[49] A *Guardian*/ICM poll of Muslims in March 2004 showed that nearly half of Muslim adults wanted their children to attend Muslim schools (*Guardian Weekly*, 18-24 March 2004, p. 9).

[50] T. Modood, *Ethnic Minorities*, p. 325.

no other option. At the secondary level, most of these are mixed comprehensive schools, though (as indicated below) many Muslim parents opt for single-sex education where this is available, especially for their daughters. Due to residence patterns, Muslim children tend to be concentrated in inner-city community schools in London boroughs and other major conurbations in England. Most Muslim children, therefore, attend schools with significant Muslim representation. Where grammar schools are available, the percentage of Muslim children attending is usually broadly in line with the percentage of Muslims within the local population. Comparatively few Muslim children attend schools where they are completely isolated from other Muslims.

While the Government has taken the lead on many issues relating to the needs of children from Muslim and other minority groups – including language needs, protection from discrimination and the monitoring of achievement levels – the response to specific cultural and religious needs has been largely left to local government. The reason for this is that Local Education Authorities (LEAs) are clearly in a better position to identify the cultural and religious needs of children within their district and to take measures to meet those needs. However, one unfortunate result of this delegation of responsibility has been that provision is uneven across the country. (Local government initiatives are discussed in section eight below).

Where LEAs offer guidance to schools on meeting the needs of Muslim pupils, schools still have considerable discretion on how far and how enthusiastically the guidelines are implemented. Policies and practices adopted by LEAs and individual schools in response to Muslim requests include: the provision of a room for midday prayer and special provision for Friday prayers; the adaptation of school uniform rules and sportswear requirements, and provision of appropriate showering arrangements, to take account of Islamic teaching about modesty and decency; the use of discretionary holidays to allow Muslim children permission to be away from school at the start of Ramadan and at 'Eid al-Fitr and 'Eid al-Adha; the provision of *halal* food for school lunches; single-sex groupings and classes; and sensitivity to Islamic beliefs in assemblies and other school activities.[51] Data is not available on how widespread these policies are or what proportion of the Muslim pupil population attend schools that adopt such policies.

Where Muslim children form a significant percentage of the school population, some schools, in addition to the above policies, try to ensure that there are Muslim teachers, governors and other school officials and employees. They also endeavour to provide a

---

[51] IQRA Trust, *Needs of Muslim Pupils*. However, several correspondents noted that such concessions are still unavailable to many Muslim pupils (see, for example, the written responses to this report from teachers and pupils at the Avenue School, London: J. Fernandez *et al.*, 22 January 2004).

school ethos and extra-curricular activities that are respectful to Islamic values.[52] However, such practices are by no means uniform across the country. Furthermore, they are often only granted after a prolonged campaign by Muslim communities.[53]

Many Muslim parents continue to feel that community schools are not meeting the needs of their children,[54] and a growing number of community leaders argue that schools with a large majority of Muslim children should be re-established as Muslim voluntary-aided schools.[55] In part, Muslim parents' dissatisfaction may be the result of a lack of understanding of their faith in the wider educational community and an unwillingness by schools, particularly in the aftermath of September 11, to engage openly in discussions with the Muslim community.[56] It may also be due to their perception of less favourable attitudes towards, and lower expectations of, pupils from minority faith communities.[57] In UK schools, proportionately more pupils of Pakistani

---

[52] Interview with head teacher of Belle Vue Girls School, Bradford, 26 March 1999. In a written response to the present report (8 October 2003), E. Renier , a Muslim parent and student at the University of Westminster, comments on the need for school toilets to be adapted to take account of the personal hygiene needs of Muslim students and also on the imbalance between the time spent celebrating Christian festivals and that spent on Muslim ones in multicultural schools. Many Muslims also have reservations about the use of National Lottery funds to support community education projects involving Muslims (see: AMSS, *Muslims on Education*, pp. 20–21).

[53] See: Ansari, *The Infidel Within*, pp. 318–323.

[54] This claim seems to be justified by recent findings reported in T. Cline et al., *Minority Ethnic Pupils in Mainly White Schools*, Department for Education and Skills, Research Brief No 365, 2002 (hereafter, Cline et al., *Minority Ethnic Pupils*). The problems are longstanding. In 1992, for example, a public examination was scheduled for the date of an important Muslim festival and schools were powerless to change it. (See: Hawe, *Muslim Girls' Schools*, p. 67). In a written response to the present report (10 October 2003), E. Izzidien, Executive Member and Campaigns Officer of the Federation of Student Islamic Societies, also noted that university examinations continue to be scheduled on Muslim festivals. The claim was also supported by several responses to this report from correspondents at the Avenue School, London (J. Fernandez *et al.,* 22 January 2004). For examples of teacher insensitivity to Muslim dietary and dress requirements, see: The Runnymede Trust, *Islamophobia: a challenge to us all,* Runnymede Trust, London, 1997, p. 43.

[55] This point was raised more than once at the OSI roundtable meeting.

[56] Written response to this report from R. Crawley, European Institute of Human Sciences, 24 March 2004.

[57] Written responses to this report from B. Mustafa, Oxford Centre for Islamic Studies, 16 October 2003; and H. Haleem, formerly of the IQRA Trust, 2 October 2003. See also: J. Eade and F. Zaman, *Routes and Beyond: Voices from Educationally Successful Bangladeshis*, Centre for Bangladeshi Studies, London, 1993, pp. 18–20; and T. Basit, *Eastern Values, Western Milieu: Identities and Aspirations of Adolescent British Muslim Girls*, Ashgate, Aldershot, 1997, pp. 114–164.

and Bangladeshi origin are recorded as having special educational needs, compared to White, Indian and Chinese pupils.[58] Other anxieties of Muslim parents include the continuing poor levels of achievement by Muslim children; the failure of schools to eradicate racist and Islamophobic discrimination, prejudice and bullying; the inadequacy of the spiritual and moral guidance which the schools provide; and the lack of support for their children's Islamic identity. All of these issues are discussed more fully later in this chapter.

Church schools

Church schools are the second largest provider of education for Muslim children, though again, precise figures are not available. Where they have the choice, many Muslim parents choose to send their children to Christian or other faith schools, whether voluntary-aided or voluntary controlled,[59] instead of choosing the more secular community schools.[60] In some cases, the reason is simply that there are more single-sex schools available in the church school sector, and many Muslim parents favour such provision. In other cases, it may be because a school with a religious ethos, even a non-Muslim one, is considered preferable, so long as no attempt is made to convert the children. It may also be because Christian schools often have a good academic reputation, and because the moral guidance they provide is rooted in religion.[61]

Catholic schools rarely admit more than ten per cent of Muslim children,[62] but Church of England schools, especially voluntary-controlled schools, which see it as their role to serve the local community, often place no limits on admissions. It is not

---

[58] Bhattacharyya et al, *Minority Ethnic Attainment*, pp. 17–18.

[59] For the main differences between these two kinds of State-funded faith school, see Appendix 1.

[60] About one third of all State-funded schools in England are faith schools, the vast majority of them Christian (mainly Church of England and Catholic), and they serve about 22 per cent of the school-age population. Muslims occasionally send their children to non-Christian faith schools; for example, there is one Jewish school in London where 50 per cent of the pupils are Muslim.

[61] Hawe, *Muslim Girls' Schools*, p. 68.

[62] Catholic schools are committed to nurturing the faith of Catholic children, but also, where appropriate, to serving the needs of the local community. Many Catholic schools in England and Wales have an upper limit for admissions of 10 or 15 per cent of non-Catholic children, and often priority within this percentage is given to parents seeking a specifically Christian upbringing for their children. See: Bishops' Conference of England and Wales, *Catholic schools and Other Faiths: a consultation paper*, Catholic Bishops' Conference of England and Wales, London, 1997.

unknown for inner-city Church of England schools to be majority Muslim.[63] In recommending an expansion in the numbers of secondary Church of England schools, the *Dearing Report* envisaged that these would be inclusive schools, catering for pupils from all faiths and no faith.[64]

Some Muslim parents may be anxious that, even though no overt attempts are made at proselytising, the hidden assumptions of the truth of Christianity that underpin the school's activities may influence their children.[65] However, there is no available research that explores the experiences of Muslim children in church schools or examines the effects, if any, on their beliefs, values and developing identity.

Single-sex schooling

According to a report by the IQRA Trust, the majority of Muslim parents support single-sex schooling for their daughters after puberty. There is some evidence that Muslim girls go along with parental support for single-sex schools: They talk of a "sense of sisterhood" and claim there are "fewer distractions".[66] Reports from Muslim head teachers and others also suggest that girls often get a better education in a single-sex context.[67]

Outside the Muslim community, there is growing evidence that mixed schools have not lived up to their promise of equal educational benefits for boys and girls.[68] The boys tend to dominate classroom interaction and compete more successfully for

---

[63] Blackburn with Darwen Borough Council, *Faith Schools and Cultural Diversity: Consultation Document*, Education and Lifelong Learning Department, Blackburn, 2001, (hereafter, Blackburn with Darwen Borough Council, *Faith Schools*). See also: R. S. Weston, "Food for Thought: Four Issues Confronting a School Governor in a Multicultural Area", in *Viewpoints*, 8, Spring 2001, (hereafter, Weston, *Food for Thought*).

[64] Church Schools Review Group, *The Way Ahead: Church of England Schools in the New Millennium (The Dearing Report)*, Church House Publishing, London, 2001.

[65] J. M. Halstead, "Muslim Perspectives on the Teaching of Christianity in British Schools", in *British Journal of Religious Education*, 15, 1, Autumn 1992, pp. 43–54.

[66] Interview with Muslim pupils C, D and E of Belle Vue Girls School, Bradford, 26 March 1999. Hashmi, on the other hand, found that only a few of the Muslim children she interviewed thought segregating the sexes important. See: N. Hashmi, *A Muslim School*, pp. 30–31. It is likely that the nature of the group consulted (in particular, whether or not they attended single-sex schools themselves) influenced the outcome of the consultations.

[67] R. W. Maqsood, "The Education of Muslim Women", in *Issues in Islamic Education*, Muslim Educational Trust, London, 1996, pp. 79–82; N. Mirza, "Educational Opportunities for Muslim Girls in Britain", in *Issues in Islamic Education*, Muslim Educational Trust, London, 1996, pp. 91–94.

[68] A. Burgess, "Co-education – the Disadvantages for Schoolgirls", in *Gender and Education*, 2, 1, pp. 91–95.

teachers' time and attention, with the result that girls' potential may not be fully developed. There are fewer women in authority to serve as role models for the girls. Boys thrive both academically and socially in a mixed school environment, while girls do not. There are also greater opportunities for boys to harass girls verbally and physically in mixed schools. Muslim parents are increasingly using these arguments to support their preference for single-sex schooling.[69]

State-maintained Muslim schools

Only five Muslim schools are currently in receipt of State funding. This compares to 4,716 State-funded Church of England schools; 2,110 Catholic; 32 Jewish; 28 Methodist; one Seventh Day Adventist; one Sikh; one Greek Orthodox; and a number of joint-faith schools, mainly Anglican-Methodist.[70] Less than half of one per cent of British Muslim children are educated in such schools, but their existence is of great symbolic value in the eyes of many Muslims, as a recognition that the Muslim community has the right in practice as well as in law to establish such schools. Two of these schools are secondary schools (Al-Hijrah VA School, Birmingham, and Feversham College, Bradford), and the other three are primary (Al-Furqan VA School, Birmingham; Islamia VA School in Brent, London;[71] and Gatton VA Primary school in Wandsworth, south-west London, which joined the State sector in September 2004).[72] Plans have recently been approved for a sixth State-funded Muslim school, in Leicester.

State-funded Muslim schools are required to teach the National Curriculum, but they are free to teach their own syllabus for religious education. In addition, they have a Muslim ethos and Muslim assemblies, and their teachers can provide a role model of belief and practice for Muslim pupils. Forty-eight per cent of Muslims support faith

---

[69] Halstead, *Radical Feminism.*

[70] J. M. Halstead, "Faith and Diversity in Religious School Provision", in L. Gearon (ed.), *Education in the United Kingdom: Structures and Organisation,* David Fulton, London, 2002, pp. 146–157.

[71] N. Darr (ed.), *Muslim Directory,* London, MDUK Media Ltd, 2003, pp. 144–160, (hereafter, Darr *Muslim Directory*). There have been many more unsuccessful than successful applications for State funding for Muslim schools so far, and both Islamia School and Feversham College tried several times over a period of more than ten years before gaining funding. Islamia School, for example, which was founded in 1983, first applied for funding in 1986, moved to new premises in 1991, applied twice more, was eventually given grant-maintained status in 1998 and became a voluntary-aided school in 1999.

[72] J. Darby, "SW London – Muslim Schools", available on the Families Online website at http://www.familiesonline.co.uk/topics/schooling/schools_sw_muslim.htm (accessed 2 November 2004), (hereafter, Darby, *SW London – Muslim Schools*).

schools within the State sector,[73] and all the Muslim voluntary-aided schools have long waiting lists. There are eight new applications for State funding currently under consideration by LEAs, for existing or new Muslim schools, and more are in the early stages of planning. The preparation of such applications is becoming much more sophisticated, particularly as applicants seek to meet new legal standards.[74] In some cases, sponsors are commissioning detailed research reports, to set out the case for such schools.[75]

In 2001, the Government committed itself in principle, in the White Paper *Schools Achieving Success,* to an expansion of the number of State-funded faith schools.[76] Many Muslims support the idea that independent Muslim schools should be incorporated into the LEA community of schools, either as voluntary-aided schools or as city academies.[77] Increasing the number of Muslim schools within the State sector would increase the choice of options available to Muslim parents, ensure equality of treatment for major religions and raise the quality of provision at the schools. For some, this may be seen as a point of principle and equity, even if they do not choose the option for their own children.[78] However, if Muslim schools are to be integrated as far as possible into the mainstream, some form of second-tier capacity-building funding will clearly be needed, to provide necessary support and expertise, both for staff training and development and for improving provision of resources.[79]

Independent Muslim schools

Currently, there are well over 100 independent Muslim schools in the UK, including one in Scotland and two in Wales, but none so far in Northern Ireland.[80] There is considerable diversity in terms of size, curriculum, teaching staff, educational

---

[73] T. Modood, *Ethnic Minorities,* p. 325.

[74] Education Act (2002) s. 157 and The Education (Independent School Standards) (England) Regulations 2003, SI 1910.

[75] See, for example, N. Hashmi, *A Muslim School.*

[76] Department for Education and Employment, *Schools Achieving Success (Cm. 5230),* London, HMSO, 2001, para. 5.30. The arguments for and against Muslim schools form part of a wider debate about the purpose and funding of faith schools in the UK and are discussed below.

[77] City academies are technically independent of the Local education Authority (LEA), but they can be developed in partnership with the LEA; play a part in LEA activities; and buy into LEA services and initiatives.

[78] This point was made at the OSI roundtable meeting, London, 2 December 2003.

[79] AMSS, *Muslims on Education,* pp. 9, 20.

[80] The figure of 120 schools is given in Commission on British Muslims and Islamophobia, *Islamophobia: issues, challenges and action,* Trentham Books, Stoke-on-Trent, 2004, p. 49.

philosophy and religious affiliation. For example, about a dozen of the schools are Darul Uloom institutions. These schools combine traditional Islamic religious education, based on models from the Indian sub-continent, with some mainstream English National Curriculum subjects. They are designed primarily to provide formal training for imams and teachers in Islamic institutions. Most of the Muslim schools, however, seek to prepare children for life and work in broader British society, while at the same time nurturing their Islamic faith.

Most independent Muslim schools are quite small, averaging about 150 pupils, which means that only about three per cent of Muslim pupils currently attend Muslim schools.[81] The number of schools is unstable, as there is a steady number of closures, usually because of a lack of financial viability. However, the general trend is upward, and the number has increased three-fold over the last ten years. They are funded privately, through the support of local mosques, other private funding and the fees paid by parents – which may vary from £100 to £4,200 (€143 to €6,000) per year. They are not required to follow the National Curriculum, though they typically do so in some subjects. Other subjects, such as history or art, may be given an Islamic flavour. A significant percentage of time may also be devoted to Islamic Studies and Arabic, and sometimes Urdu, for pupils of Pakistani origin.[82]

In the past, private Muslim schools have received critical reports from the Office for Standards in Education (OFSTED), particularly because of poor buildings, inadequate resources, the failure to meet good health and safety standards, inexperienced management, unqualified teachers and the low level of general education that they provide.[83] They have also been criticised for a failure to provide opportunities for their

---

[81] Iftikhar Ahmad, of the London School of Islamics, suggests that the average enrolment is 100 pupils, which would mean that only two per cent of British Muslim pupils attend Muslim schools. See: "Muslim Community Schools", *Local Government Chronicle,* 13 December 2002, available on the LGC website at http://www.lgcnet.com/pages/discuss/view.asp?ArticleID=273 (accessed on 2 November).

[82] J. M. Halstead, "Educating Muslim Minorities: some Western European Approaches", in W. Tulasiewicz and C-Y. To (eds.) *World Religions and Educational Practice,* Cassell, London, 1993, p. 169, (hereafter, Halstead, *Educating Muslim Minorities*).

[83] One of the most recent to receive a highly critical report from the HM Inspectorate of Education (HMIE) was Iqra Academy in Glasgow, which was inspected in February 2003 and has since closed. See: HM Inspectorate of Education, *Registration Inspection of IQRA Academy, Glasgow, 26 March 2003,* available on the HMIE website at http://www.hmie.gov.uk/institute.asp?ins=9047&typ=3 (accessed 2 November 2004). An even more recent highly critical report was received by Scotland's last remaining Muslim school, the Imam Mohammad Zakariya school, in Dundee, on April 2004. It was given six months to improve or face closure. See: *The Muslim News,* 17 October 2004. See also I. Hewitt, "Every Cloud Has a Silver Lining", *The Muslim News,* 26 September 1997.

students to mix with students from other faiths and backgrounds, an activity that is considered important for young Muslims to develop cross-cultural understanding and a broader view of British society.[84] However, the academic results of Muslim schools are improving (see section 5.3 below).

In spite of improving standards in Muslim independent schools and the growing support for them, recent legislation has led to fears within the Muslim community that many may be forced to close.[85] Previously, independent Muslim schools were able to obtain "provisional registration", which permitted them to open as educational establishments and gave them time to develop their resources and provision before applying for full registration. However, the new legislation now requires all new independent Muslim schools, like other independent schools, to apply to the Department for Education and Skills for registration, and the category of "provisional registration" is no longer valid. Such schools are required by the Education Act (2002) to meet the standards set out in the regulations[86] before they are allowed to open, and they must be inspected on a regular cycle.[87]

Existing schools have until September 2005 to meet the standards, and failure to do so may result in closure. The standards are very exacting, and in many respects are not different from the conditions that have to be met before voluntary-aided status can be granted. It is therefore likely that few existing schools will be able to meet these standards without considerable expenditure, the provision of additional resources and much expert advice and support.[88] The legislation is likely to have a disproportionately adverse affect on independent Muslim schools compared to other independent schools, perhaps mainly for socio-economic reasons. Opinion is divided within Muslim communities, between those who see the legislation as oppressive of parental freedom to educate their children in line with their own beliefs and values and those who see the

---

[84] Written responses to this report from Mrs Abdul Kader and Noshiena Khan of the Avenue School, London, 5 October 2003.

[85] This point was made more than once at the OSI roundtable discussion, London, 2 December 2003.

[86] The Standards for Registration cover: the quality of education provided by the school; the spiritual, moral, social and cultural development of pupils; the welfare, health and safety of the pupils; the suitability of proprietor and staff; the school's premises and accommodation; the provision of information; and the procedures for handling complaints. Full details are given in The Education (Independent School Standards) (England) Regulations (2003) Statutory Instrument No. 1910.

[87] The detailed regulations for inspection are contained in: OFSTED, *Inspecting Independent Schools: the Framework for Inspecting Independent Schools in England under Section 163 of the Education Act 2002. In use from September 2003,* Office of Her Majesty's Chief Inspector of Schools, London, 2003.

[88] This point was made at the OSI roundtable meeting, London, 2 December 2003.

legislation as improving standards in the independent Muslim schools that survive. By March 2004, only two Muslim independent schools in England had been inspected under the new system,[89] and neither fully met the required standards. Several further inspections are planned before the end of 2004.[90]

The debate about Muslim Schools

The growing number of case studies of Muslim schools[91] has helped to dispel some prevalent myths about them. These include the belief that they do not teach girls adequately, that they do not make any attempts to prepare children for citizenship in a multicultural society and that they do not teach children about other cultures or religions. However, the most important issue still remains the question of principle: should Muslims be free to establish their own schools whenever and wherever they choose to do so? Of course, Muslims' legal right to do so, subject to certain conditions, is enshrined in the 1944 Education Act. But unless decision-makers are convinced that such schools serve the interests of Muslim children and do not conflict with the interests of the broader society, they will never be whole-heartedly supported. This is one of the most controversial issues in contemporary educational policy, and it has generated a great deal of debate.

Some of the arguments about Muslim schools are the same as those about faith schools generally,[92] with opposition coming from academics and organisations like the

---

[89] These are Al-Hijrah (Primary) School, Birmingham (inspected 19-23 January, 2004) and the School of the Islamic Republic of Iran, Manchester (inspected 15-18 March 2004).

[90] All OFSTED inspection reports are available at the OFSTED website at http://www.ofsted.gov.uk/reports (accessed 2 November 2004).

[91] See, for example: T. Kücükan, "Community, Identity and Institutionalisation of Islamic Education: the Case of Ikra Primary School in North London," *British Journal of Religious Education*, 2, 1 (Autumn, 1998), pp. 32–43. See also: M. Haque, "Muslim Education in Britain: the King Fahd Academy, London", *Muslim Education Quarterly*, 17, 2, Winter 2000, pp. 69–72; and Y. Sasano, *The Creation of British Muslim Identity in the Islamic Schools of London*, unpublished MPhil thesis, Hitotsubashi University, Japan, 2003.

[92] Commission for Racial Equality, *Schools of Faith*, CRE, London, 1990; J. De Jong and G. Snik, "Why Should States Fund Denominational Schools?", *Journal of Philosophy of Education*, 36, 4, 2002, pp. 573–587; G. Grace, *Catholic Schools: Missions, Markets and Morality*, RoutledgeFalmer, London, 2002; F. Harris, "Do We Really Want More Faith School?", *Education Review*, 15, 1, 2002, pp. 32–36; R. Jackson, "Should the State Fund Faith-Based Schools? A Review of the Arguments", *British Journal of Religious Education*, 25, 2, 2003, pp. 89–102.

National Secular Society;[93] but others refer to specifically Muslim issues.[94] The debate may be approached differently by Muslims and non-Muslims.[95] Some of the arguments apply to all Muslim schools, whether independent or State-funded, while others refer only to the issue of State-funding. The arguments need to be distinguished carefully, since the debate about Muslim schools is characterised currently by much talking at cross purposes.

Leaving aside those who have tried, without justification, to link the issue of British Muslim schools with the events of September 11,[96] there are four main arguments against the establishment of Muslim schools.

First, it is claimed that they are socially and ethnically divisive, because they are not inclusive schools that serve the wider community. Even if they are willing in principle to accept non-Muslim pupils, this does not happen in practice. The effect is to isolate Muslims from the broader society and to hinder attempts at integration.[97] They may also affect the viability of other local schools.[98]

The second argument is that the processes of religious nurture and those of education are conceptually different. On the basis of this argument, some express concerns that efforts to nurture faith may lead, intentionally or otherwise, to indoctrination, with insufficient attention being paid to the development of critical judgement and

---

[93] The National Secular Society runs an extensive website on faith schools which, notwithstanding its principled opposition, contains much useful information; see: http://www.secularism.org.uk/ (accessed 2 November 2004). See also: Humanist Philosophers Group, *Religious Schools: the Case Against*, British Humanist Association, London, 2001, (hereafter, Humanist Philosophers Group, *Religious Schools: the Case Against*).

[94] C. Hewer, "Schools for Muslims", *Oxford Review of Education*, 27, 4 (December 2001), pp. 515–527, (hereafter, Hewer, *Schools for Muslims*).

[95] I. Hewitt, "The Case for Muslim Schools", in The Muslim Educational Trust, *Issues in Islamic Education*, MET, London, 1996, pp. 72–78 (hereafter, Hewitt, *Muslim Schools*); J. M. Halstead, *The Case for Muslim Voluntary-Aided Schools: some philosophical reflections*, Islamic Academy, Cambridge, 1986 (hereafter, Halstead, *The Case for Muslim Voluntary-Aided Schools*).

[96] H. Judge, "Faith-based Schools and State Funding: a partial argument", *Oxford Review of Education*, 27, 4 (December 2001), pp. 472–473. See also F. Beckett, "Holier Than Thou", *The Guardian*, 13 November 2001; and K. Sellgren, "Warning about 'Bin Laden Schools'", *BBC News Online*, 26 March 2002, at http://www.news.bbc.co.uk/hi/english/education/newsid_1893000 (accessed 25 October 2004).

[97] P. Toynbee, "Keep God out of Class", *The Guardian*, 9 November 2001.

[98] Interview with representatives of the Faith Schools Scrutiny Review Panel, Oxfordshire County Council, 22 October 2003.

openness to new ideas.[99] Muslim schools may teach ideas that are controversial or lack scientific credibility, such as creationism, as if they are truths.[100] There is no justification for spending public funds to support the maintenance of religious belief in schools – indeed it is a violation of conscience for those whose taxes fund faith schools against their will.[101] It should not be the role of a State-funded school to nurture any particular religious faith.[102]

The third argument is that Muslim schools may fail to prepare children adequately for democratic citizenship in a multicultural society, or indeed to prepare them at all for British citizenship.[103] They may also pay inadequate attention to the need for pupils to develop tolerance, respect and understanding of other faiths, for the most effective way for children to learn tolerance and cross-cultural understanding is to be educated alongside those of other religious and cultural backgrounds.[104]

Finally, it is claimed that Muslim schools may be inadequate in comparison with community schools, with respect to the development of personal autonomy.[105] They do not respect children's right to an open future, and restrict children's freedom to escape the constraints of their own cultural background.[106]

On the other side, there are four main arguments *in support of* the establishment of Muslim schools.

---

[99] Humanist Philosophers Group, *Religious Schools: the Case Against.*

[100] Hewer, *Schools for Muslims*, p. 522. See also: S. A. Mabud, "Aims and Objectives of an Integrated Science Curriculum for a Multi-faith, Multicultural Country", in *Muslim Education Quarterly*, 9, 4 (1992), pp. 14–24.

[101] L.S. Underkuffler, "Public Funding for Religious Schools: difficulties and dangers in a pluralistic society", *Oxford Review of Education*, 27, 4 (December 2001), pp. 577–592.

[102] cf. R. Pring, "Faith Schools: Can They Be Justified?", in J. Cairns and R. Gardner (Eds.) *Faith Schools: Conflict or Consensus?* Kogan Page, London, 2004 (hereafter, R. Pring, "Faith Schools").

[103] W. Kymlicka, "Education for Citizenship", in J. M. Halstead and T. H. McLaughlin (Eds.), *Education in Morality*, Routledge, London, 1999 (hereafter, W. Kymlicka, "Education for Citizenship"), pp. 88–90.

[104] F. Beckett, "We Should Abolish Faith Schools – they breed only intolerance and isolation", *Guardian Education*, 14 October 2003, p. 5; W. Kymlicka, "Education for Citizenship", pp. 88–90.

[105] cf. R. Pring, "Faith Schools".

[106] M. Mason, "Religion and Schools: a Human Rights-based Approach", *British Journal of Religious Education*, 25, 2 (Spring 2003), pp. 117–128.

First, they increase parental choice and enable Muslim parents to choose a school whose values are consistent with the home.[107] They demonstrate equity for Muslims in relation to other faith groups that already have their own State-funded schools.[108] They demonstrate equality of respect and recognition for Islam as a minority faith in the UK, which Muslims see as a prerequisite for greater integration.[109]

Second, from a Muslim perspective, they nurture faith – for example, by teaching religious education and other subjects, including art, sex education and history, from an Islamic point of view and by providing a school ethos that is supportive of faith – and thus provide a bulwark against the growth of secularism, materialism and relativism.[110] They remove barriers to Muslim religious observance that may be found in other schools, including: the lack of prayer facilities; the lack of *halal* food for school meals; problems of clothing and sportswear; inadequate facilities for Muslim requirements on hygiene and cleanliness; and the failure to celebrate Muslim festivals. They provide an appropriate spiritual environment in which clear moral teaching is possible, and thus avoid the problem found in community schools that Muslim children are exposed to moral values that conflict with their own faith.

Third, they provide an education which is in accordance with Muslim beliefs and values, such as providing single-sex schooling after puberty. They are thus a response to the danger of absorption into the dominant culture.[111] Single-faith schools are "a truer reflection of a multi-faith society than multi-faith schools",[112] in that the latter encourage all children to celebrate festivals from different faiths, whereas, in the real world, they will celebrate only those of their own faith.

Fourth, they provide an environment secure from Islamophobic bullying and other issues that cause Muslim children stress in community schools. They produce high academic results (see section 5.3 below). They solve the problem found in some community schools of unsympathetic treatment and low aspirations of, and expectations for, Muslim pupils. They help Muslim children to develop and retain

---

[107] Halstead, *Muslim Voluntary-Aided Schools.*

[108] S. A. Mabud, "Editorial: Can Muslim Faith Schools Be Divisive? *Muslim Education Quarterly,* 19, 2 (2002), pp. 1–3.

[109] J. M. Halstead and T. H. McLaughlin, "Are Faith Schools Divisive?", in J. Cairns and R. Gardner (Eds.) *Faith Schools: Conflict or Consensus?* Kogan Page, London, 2004, (hereafter, J. M. Halstead and T. H. McLaughlin, "Are Faith Schools Divisive?").

[110] Hawe, *Muslim Girls' Schools,* pp. 66–67; M. Somerville, "Faith Schools", in *Catholic Post,* 77, October 2001, p. 10.

[111] J. M. Halstead, "Towards a Unified View of Islamic Education", *Islam and Christian-Muslim Relations,* 6, 1 (June 1995), pp. 25–43.

[112] Hewitt, *Muslim Schools,* p. 75.

their Muslim identity, and it is only if Muslim children have a strong self-concept and sense of identity that they will be able to develop respect and tolerance for others and play a worthwhile role in an increasingly multicultural society.[113] They encourage the self-esteem of Muslim pupils by increasing awareness of Muslim contributions to knowledge in fields such as mathematics, medicine, science, geography and astronomy.[114]

It is clear that some of the arguments in support of Muslim schools effectively counter the arguments against – especially, for example, the points about divisiveness and intolerance.[115] Others, however, simply draw attention to the diversity of views about education in British society, including the existence of different views about the relationship between religion and education and about the role of the teacher as moral exemplar. Some of the things that Muslim schools successfully do could certainly be done by non-Muslim schools with appropriate policies. For example, non-Muslim schools could pay more attention to Muslim contributions to knowledge, could counter Islamophobic bullying in school more effectively, could support Muslim pupils' religious observances and could avoid low expectations of Muslim pupils. On the other hand, it would be very hard for non-Muslim schools to present values that are fully consistent with those of a Muslim home or to provide a bulwark against secularism and loss of faith. As noted above, different parents have different priorities, and their needs can only be met through a range of options.

5.2 Supplementary Schools

In addition to compulsory education, parents and community groups are free to provide any other schooling or education they feel is necessary to meet the needs of their children. The organisations or institutions that provide these are generally referred to as "supplementary schools". There are several different kinds of supplementary schooling available to Muslim children,[116] and these are often, but by no means always, provided in local mosques. The main kinds are: classes in the faith and practice of Islam; mother-tongue classes, especially in Urdu or Bengali, which are not necessarily Islamic in character; and classes run by mosques or community groups to help Muslim children with their homework or with basic skills. In addition, some organisations run what is effectively a kind of youth club; in Bristol, for example, the Muslim Cultural Society organises leisure activities on Saturday evenings.

---

[113] Hawe, *Muslim Girls' Schools*, p. 67.

[114] Hewer, *Schools for Muslims*, pp. 523–525.

[115] J. M. Halstead and T. H. McLaughlin, "Are Faith Schools Divisive?".

[116] AMSS, *Muslims on Education*, pp. 35–36.

The dominant pattern that has emerged in Britain for many Muslim children is to attend community or church primary schools in the daytime and also attend mosque or other Islamic schools for up to two hours every evening, to learn about their religion. This pattern has come about as a pragmatic response by Muslim parents and community leaders to the perceived gaps in State-funded education. Little research has been carried out into Muslim supplementary schools, and such information as is available draws on local experiences rather than providing a national overview. While many such supplementary schools are held in mosques, others are held in community centres, church halls, school halls hired for use outside of school hours, or private homes. Attendance figures are rarely available, and it is impossible to state with confidence what percentage of Muslim children attend supplementary schools. There appears to be considerable variation between districts and, to some extent, between different ethnic groups.[117] However, it is clear that many mosques and other Muslim organisations are very active in teaching children the principal beliefs and practices of Islam. In Bradford, for example, there are 63 Muslim supplementary schools registered with the LEA,[118] and in Bristol the Taleem-ul-Islam Trust organises religious lessons on Sunday mornings, with an attendance of about 400 boys and girls.[119]

Children typically receive supplementary schooling in Islam, from the age of four or five to the age of 13 or 14, although girls may stop attending earlier. They learn Arabic for the purposes of Qur'anic recitation, and they also study the principal beliefs of Islam and the basic requirements of the *Shari'a*.[120] Those who wish to memorise the whole Qur'an and become a *hafiz* may attend mosque in the morning as well.[121] It is worth noting that children do not learn Arabic as a modern language, although their study in the mosque might be useful preparation for doing so if the subject were to be offered at their regular school.

There are a number of reasons why this dominant pattern of education has, over many years, created problems and challenges for Muslim children in the UK.

---

[117] One source claims a 90 per cent attendance, but this is almost certainly an over-estimate; see J. Darby, *SW London – Muslim Schools*.

[118] Bradford District Race Review Team, *Community Pride, not Prejudice*, Bradford Vision, Bradford, 2001 (hereafter, *The Ouseley Report*), p. 44.

[119] N. Hashmi, *A Muslim School*, p. 21.

[120] C. W. North, *Islam in Schools and Madrasahs: a Field Study in Sparkbrook, Sparkhill and Part of Small Heath in Birmingham, 1983-85*, Unpublished MA Thesis, University of Birmingham, 1986.

[121] Redbridge Standing Advisory Council on Religious Education, *Briefing Paper 4: Muslim Madrasahs in Redbridge*, London Borough of Redbridge, 2003 (hereafter, Redbridge, *Muslim Madrasahs*).

First, the system continues to expose Muslim children to secular and un-Islamic values for most of their school day,[122] values which may be strongly criticised within the mosque. This exposure to diverse and incompatible values may create tensions in Muslim children, particularly in relation to their civic identity and loyalties.

Second, the additional demands the system places on Muslim children in terms of both time and effort have proven unacceptable to some Muslim parents, and this is another reason why a growing number of parents are coming to support the principle of separate Muslim schooling.[123]

Third, the quality of education provided in mosque or other Islamic schools has often been considered significantly inferior to that of community or church schools. The premises and resources are often inadequate, the teachers often unqualified and the methods, which include rote-learning and strict discipline, are often out of tune with contemporary educational thinking and practice.[124] As awareness of these problems increases, many Muslim groups are trying to improve the quality of provision, sometimes with the support of the LEAs. For example, in Redbridge, Greater London, members of the local Child Protection Scheme have worked with the leaders of the mosque schools, and a joint working group has been set up with the local education authority and mosque schools.[125] Other local authorities, including Birmingham, Manchester, Leicester and Watford, are offering training to teachers from mosque and other Islamic schools and encouraging links between supplementary schools and mainstream schools.[126]

Within mosque schools, teaching is often provided by local imams, who may be unfamiliar with current educational thinking and who may actually have received their training in *madrasahs* on the Indian subcontinent, or in other cultural contexts outside the UK. The need for imams who are trained in the UK, and are able to communicate and interact with young British Muslims, has become a prominent issue.[127] There are institutions in the UK that are seeking to cater for the training of imams, including: the Muslim College in Ealing, which offers a Diploma in Islamic Studies as well as a Masters degree for imams (validated by Birkbeck College, London); and the Markfield Institute of Higher Education in Leicestershire, linked to the Islamic Foundation,

---

[122] Halstead, *Muslim Voluntary-Aided Schools,* p. 15.

[123] Halstead, *Educating Muslim Minorities,* p. 171.

[124] Halstead, *Educating Muslim Minorities,* pp. 169–171; M. I. Coles *Education and Islam: a new strategic approach,* School Development Support Agency, Leicester, 2004, pp. 17–18 (hereafter, Coles *Education and Islam*).

[125] Redbridge, *Muslim Madrasahs.*

[126] Coles, *Education and Islam,* p. 18.

[127] J. Klausen, "Is There an Imam Problem?", *Prospect,* May 2004.

which offers MA, MPhil and PhD degrees in Islamic Studies (validated by the University of Loughborough) and the Certificate of Muslim Chaplaincy Training.[128] The Home Office currently has plans to not allow the recruitment of imams outside the UK unless they have a high-level qualification in English. This is likely to reduce recruitment drastically, because English is not part of the *madrasah* curriculum. Therefore, the demand for British diplomas and degrees for imams is likely to increase substantially over the next few years.

5.3   The Academic Achievements of Muslims

Of all ethnic minorities in the UK, people of Pakistani and Bangladeshi origin are the most likely to have no academic qualifications. Almost half of all Bangladeshi men and women, 27 per cent of Pakistani men and 40 per cent of Pakistani women do not have academic qualifications.[129] Low parental education levels, along with parental occupation, have been identified as key factors related to low achievement levels among Pakistani and Bangladeshi children.[130]

In 2000, only 30 per cent of the children of Pakistani and Bangladeshi origin in England and Wales gained five or more GCSEs at grades A*-C, compared to 50 per cent in the population as a whole. This made them the lowest achieving of all ethnic groups. The same level was achieved by 37 per cent of African Caribbean children, 62 per cent of Indian children and 70 per cent of "other Asian" (mainly Chinese) children.[131] By 2002, the success rate had risen to 40 per cent for Pakistani children and 45 per cent for Bangladeshi children, compared to about 51 per cent for the general population.[132] Yet these percentages mask a number of important points:

First, as in other communities, there are important and increasing differences in the achievement levels of boys and girls. The figures for Birmingham in 2003 illustrate the national trend: some 37 per cent of Pakistani boys achieved five or more GCSE passes at grades A*-C, compared to 50 per cent of Pakistani girls; and 43 per cent of Bangladeshi boys achieved the same level, compared to 58 per cent of Bangladeshi

---

[128] M. Haque, "Review of the Progress of Islamic Education", in *Muslim Education Quarterly*, 19, 4 2002, pp. 68–69.

[129] A. White, *Ethnicity 2002*, Office for National Statistics, London, available on the ONS website at http://www.statistics.gov.uk.

[130] M. Anwar, *British Pakistanis: Demographic, Economic and Social Position*, Coventry, CRER, 1996, pp. 47–48.

[131] *The Guardian, Muslim Britain*, p. 2.

[132] Bhattacharyya et al, *Minority Ethnic Attainment*, p. 12.

girls.[133] The Bangladeshi girls actually exceeded the average for White girls in Birmingham. However, what these figures highlight most clearly is the problem of the sense of alienation felt by many young male Muslims at school. Further evidence of this alienation and disaffection is found in a report commissioned by the IQRA Trust in 2000.[134] Evidence is also provided in the Runnymede Trust's *Parekh Report,* which identifies a worrying increase in exclusions of Bangladeshi, Pakistani and Somali boys in some LEAs and schools and recommends urgent steps to reduce such exclusions.[135] Among the report's recommendations are that schools should become more Muslim-friendly, and that the choice of schools available for Muslims should be increased, to better address the needs of this group and thereby improve their academic achievement.

Second, research findings support the view that there is a strong correlation between low academic achievement and the social factors mentioned in section three above, particularly: high levels of poverty, ghettoisation and residence in deprived neighbourhoods, parental unemployment and parental employment in unskilled or semiskilled jobs.[136] However, it has been suggested that, although Bangladeshis and Pakistanis continue to have a low level of achievement compared to national averages, when compared to their non-Muslim counterparts with the same socio-economic background, they are doing better than expected.[137] Free school meals provide a useful register of comparative social disadvantage. Unsurprisingly, pupils eligible for free school meals achieve considerably lower average grades than those who are not eligible, whether Muslim or not. Levels of eligibility for free school meals within Muslim communities are among the highest in the country.[138] It is also worth noting that,

---

[133] National Literacy Trust, "Ethnic Minority Achievement", available on the National Literacy Trust website at http://www.literacytrust.org.uk/Database/stats (accessed 2 November 2004). See also: W. Berliner, "Gifted but Black", *Education Guardian,* 14 October 2003, p. 2.

[134] D. Pye, B. Lee and S. Bhabra, *Disaffection amongst Muslim Pupils. Exclusion and Truancy,* IQRA Trust, London, 2000.

[135] The Runnymede Trust, *The Future of Multi-Ethnic Britain: Report of the Commission on the Future of Multi-Ethnic Britain, under the Chairmanship of Bhikhu Parekh,* Profile Books, London, 2000, p. 152, (hereafter, *The Parekh Report*).

[136] National Literacy Trust, "Poverty Statistics: the link between poverty and literacy", available on the National Literacy Trust website at http://www.literacytrust.org.uk/Database/stats (accessed 2 November 2004)

[137] Z. Haque, *British Muslims and Education,* paper presented at a seminar for the British Muslim Centre, September, 2003, p. 2, (hereafter, Haque, *British Muslims and Education*).

[138] Thirty-five per cent of Pakistani children and 50 per cent of Bangladeshi children are eligible for free school meals (See: Bhattacharyya et al, *Minority Ethnic Attainment,* p. 9). Within Muslim voluntary-aided schools, over 30 per cent of the children are eligible for free school meals – a significantly higher proportion than for the voluntary schools of any other faith. See: G. Hinsliff, 'Single Faith Schools Target Well-off', *The Observer,* 18 November 2001).

although children of Pakistani and Bangladeshi origin are over-represented among 16-year-olds with the poorest qualifications, they are also well represented proportionately in terms of entry to university.[139] This suggests that, where social and economic factors are not overwhelming, there are high levels of educational ambition among such students.

Third, there is a wide range of other factors that may, either singly or in combination, contribute to low achievement levels. Social class and levels of fluency in English are key issues linked to attainment, as are more nebulous factors, like parents' expectations, peer group pressure, individual motivation and school effectiveness.[140] However, numerous other factors that are more directly linked to religion may also contribute to Muslim children's levels of underachievement. These include: religious discrimination; Islamophobia; the lack of Muslim role models in schools; low expectations on the part of teachers; time spent in mosque schools; the lack of recognition of the British Muslim identity of the students; and the disaffection and disorientation resulting from the incompatibility of the values of the school and the home. These factors have been almost entirely neglected in the literature on achievement levels. OFSTED could play a bigger part in identifying and dealing with specific Muslim issues – which are distinct from more general "Asian" or minority ethnic issues – and thereby help to raise the achievement levels of Muslim pupils, but this may require more training for registered inspectors, especially on Islamophobia and issues of British Muslim identity.

Fourth, there are significant regional differences in the achievement levels of Muslim pupils. Again, this may be linked to the high levels of social deprivation in some regions. High concentrations of Muslims are found in the lowest ranking LEAs, and the poorest performing educational authorities are usually in the most deprived areas. For example, the most recent OFSTED inspection of Bradford LEA, in 2002, found its overall performance to be "currently unsatisfactory".[141] OFSTED is required, among other things, to assess LEA Educational Development Plans, which will include strategies for raising the achievement levels of under-achieving groups, but the current practice of identifying Muslim pupils by ethnic origin rather than by religious affiliation impedes the identification of the specifically religious factors mentioned above that may affect levels of achievement.

---

[139] *The Parekh Report*, p. 146; D. Owen, A. Green, J. Pitcher and M. Maguire, *Minority Ethnic Participation and Achievements in Education, Training and the Labour Market*, HMSO, London, 2000.

[140] See: Haque, *British Muslims and Education*, p. 3; and Bhattacharyya et al, *Minority Ethnic Attainment*, pp. 21–22.

[141] OFSTED, *Inspection of Bradford*, p. 5.

The academic achievements of pupils at Muslim schools – as opposed to those in community, foundation or church schools – vary considerably, but the best compare very favourably with non-Muslim schools. For example, in 2001, Islamia Primary School in Brent came third out of 51 schools in the district in Key Stage 2 SATs results, on one measure, and first out of 51, on an adjusted measure.[142] In the 2002 GCSE results, 100 per cent of the pupils entered at al-Furqan Community College in Birmingham, Leicester Islamic Academy, Madani School in Tower Hamlets, Tayyibah School in Hackney and Brondesbury College in Brent achieved 5 or more GCSE passes at grades A*-C, though the numbers entered were in some cases quite small. The rate at Feversham College was 53 per cent, slightly above the national average, and well above the Bradford average of 37 per cent. Other Muslim schools, like Zakaria Muslim Girls' School in Batley, have results only slightly lower, and they generally outperform local authority schools.[143]

No national initiatives for raising attainment levels currently target Muslim pupils as such, though several that are directed at raising the attainment of children living in inner-city areas – including Excellence in Cities, Sure Start, Extended Schools and Study Support – will potentially benefit areas with large Muslim populations.[144] In an attempt to narrow the achievement gap for minority ethnic pupils, the Department for Education and Skills has also launched two pilot schemes involving 15 LEAs. The Ethnic Minority Achievement Grant provides substantial funding to support children with EAL needs, and further funds are provided through the Formula Spending Share. Again, this support is of particular benefit to pupils from Pakistani, Bangladeshi and other Muslim communities. (See also section 8.2 below).[145]

5.4   Muslims in Further and Higher Education

Post-16 education

Statistics on religious affiliation are not kept in this sector, only statistics on ethnic origin. Compared to their White counterparts, a higher proportion of students of Pakistani and Bangladeshi origin stay on into the sixth form at school or pursue their

---

[142]   Key Stage 2 SATs are the national tests taken by children in Year Six (i.e. at the age of eleven). The education league tables for Brent are available on the BBC website at http://news.bbc.co.ukhi/english/statistic/education/school_tables_2001 (accessed 2 November 2004).

[143]   The results of Muslim schools are published on the website of the Muslim Parents Association (UK) at http://www.muslimparentsassociation.co.uk (accessed 2 November 2004).

[144]   Coles *Education and Islam,* pp. 18–19.

[145]   Haque, *British Muslims and Education,* pp. 5–6.

studies at a college of further education.[146] Three broad pathways are open to students in the 16-19 phase: the traditional academic route (leading to AS and A level examinations), the vocational route and the occupational route. Pakistani and Bangladeshi students are well represented on the academic route, and are twice as likely as White students to pursue GNVQ qualifications,[147] but they are less likely to follow the occupational route.

The further education sector includes sixth form colleges, tertiary colleges, colleges of further education, adult education and community education centres, university continuing education departments, and specialist colleges – in other words, all post-compulsory education outside the higher education sector. In 2003, there were 70,200 students of Pakistani and Bangladeshi origin (3.2 per cent of the total) enrolled in further education in England, and within this group, there was a significantly higher proportion of females than males. Yet, when it comes to work-based learning, the proportions are different. Only 4,100 students of Pakistani or Bangladeshi origin were enrolled in work-based learning (1.5 per cent of the total).[148]

Many of the points made in relation to Muslim student organisations at the end of the next section apply equally to students in further education as well as those in higher education.

Higher education

There are no official statistics on the number of Muslim students in higher education, though reports point out that the number of successful "Asian" applicants increased by more than 50 per cent between 1994 and 1999.[149] Many universities have only recently put in place more sophisticated ethnic monitoring systems, which identify, for example, numbers of students of Pakistani or Bangladeshi origin, and full ethnic statistics are not currently publicly available. Even when the figures are available for Pakistanis and Bangladeshis, they will not give a good indication of the total number of Muslim university students. However, the Federation of Students Islamic Societies

---

[146] Bhattacharyya et al, *Minority Ethnic Attainment*, p. 24.

[147] 28 per cent of Pakistani students and 27 per cent of Bangladeshi students are likely to have GNVQ or BTEC qualifications, compared to 13 per cent of White students. See: H. Connor, C. Tyers, S. Davis and N. Tackey, *Minority Ethnic Students in Higher Education*, DfES, London, 2003.

[148] Learning Skills Council, *Further Education and Work Based Learning for Young People: Learner Numbers in England on 1 November 2003*, LSC, Coventry, 2004.

[149] National Literacy Trust, "Ethnicity and Access to Higher Education", available on the website of the National Literacy Trust at http://www.literacytrust.org.uk/Database/stats, (accessed 2 November 2004), (hereafter, NLT, *Higher Education*).

(FOSIS) estimates that there are over 35,000 Muslim students attending universities, with significant numbers also coming from abroad.[150]

This figure may mask the under-representation of particular groups, such as Bangladeshi women, as well as the fact that Muslim students are particularly concentrated in a few universities.[151] While Muslim parents prefer single-sex schools during their compulsory schooling, many take a more pragmatic line by the time students reach university age, in the belief that young Muslims should be mature enough by that stage to study in a mixed-sex environment.[152] A few girls report being offered a university place but not being allowed by their parents to take it up; in some cases being able to continue living at home while studying makes a difference.[153] Some Muslim young women report that it is difficult for them to leave their home city to attend higher education courses elsewhere because of "parental concerns about distance and personal safety".[154]

Students from wealthier groups in society are generally much more likely to be accepted on degree courses than children from lower social classes, from poor areas and from families whose parents are unemployed or unskilled. To some extent, Muslim children are beginning to buck this trend. Bangladeshi and Pakistani children with unemployed parents are more likely to enter higher education than their White counterparts.[155] However, Pakistani and Bangladeshi undergraduates are less likely than their White counterparts to get a first or upper-second classification for their degree.[156]

In 2001, the most popular subject groups for male students of Pakistani and Bangladeshi origin were mathematical sciences and information technology. For female students from the same group, social studies and business and administration were most popular.[157] Medicine, law and medicine-related subjects are also popular.[158] One of the recommendations of the *Parekh Report* is that universities should seek ways to

---

[150] Federation of Student Islamic Societies, *Islamophobia on Campuses and the Lack of Provision for Muslim Students,* FOSIS, London, 2003, (hereafter, FOSIS, *Islamophobia*), p. 5.

[151] NLT, *Higher Education.*

[152] IQRA Trust, *Needs of Muslim Pupils,* p. 18.

[153] Interview with Muslim pupil B of Belle Vue Girls School, Bradford, 26 March 1999.

[154] Oldham Independent Review Panel, *Oldham Independent Review Panel Report: One Oldham, One Future, under the chairmanship of David Ritchie,* Oldham Borough Council, 2001, (hereafter, *The Ritchie Report*), p. 29.

[155] *The Guardian, Muslim Britain,* p. 2.

[156] Bhattacharyya et al, *Minority Ethnic Attainment,* p. 30.

[157] The Universities and Colleges Admission Service (UCAS) annual data set for 2001.

[158] Bhattacharyya et al, *Minority Ethnic Attainment,* p. 29.

ensure that potential students from Asian communities "apply for a wide range of courses".[159] This might involve making courses "culturally more inclusive" wherever possible.

According to estimates by FOSIS, at least 85 per cent of higher educational institutions in the UK have a sizeable number of Muslim students.[160] However, there are significantly higher proportions of Muslim, and other minority ethnic, students at the "new" (post-1992) universities in London and, to a lesser extent, other big cities.[161] According to a recent survey investigating the experiences of 1,000 candidates from each of the main ethnic groups in the UK, there is evidence of possible bias against Muslim candidates within the "old" universities. The probability of a candidate of Pakistani or Bangladeshi origin receiving an initial offer from an "old" university was 0.57, while that of a White candidate with equivalent qualifications was 0.75. No evidence of such bias was found in the "new" universities, where 60 per cent of Asian students pursue their degree courses – compared to only 35 per cent of White students.[162] Further research is needed to investigate the reasons for these differences.

FOSIS estimates that over 65 per cent of higher educational institutions in the UK have Islamic Societies. These societies organise social and religious activities; represent students' interests to the authorities, for example, by requesting that prayer facilities be made available to students; support student welfare; and encourage links with the local Muslim community outside the university.[163] Some Islamic Societies also organise Arabic classes; invite prominent Muslim speakers to address open meetings; hold classes for students who want to develop a deeper understanding of their faith; and have additional activities for female Muslim students.[164]

Current concerns that have been expressed by Muslim student organisations include: the need for a more systematic provision of prayer facilities for Muslims; the need for Muslim chaplains or counselling services; the need for student refectories to provide food that conforms to Islamic dietary requirements; the need to respect Islamic festivals and prayer times in planning events that require student attendance, such as examinations; the need to respect Islamic beliefs and practices, for example respecting

---

[159] *The Parekh Report,* p. 148.

[160] FOSIS, *Islamophobia,* p. 5.

[161] Bhattacharyya et al, *Minority Ethnic Attainment,* p. 28.

[162] M. Shiner and T. Modood, "Help or Hindrance? Higher Education and the Route to Ethnic Equality", *British Journal of Sociology of Education,* 23, 2, June, 2002, pp. 209–232.

[163] FOSIS, *Islamophobia,* p. 5.

[164] A. Sahin, "Studying Islamic Education at the School of Education of the University of Birmingham", available at http://www.studyoverseas.com/re/abdullah.htm (accessed 2 November 2004) (hereafter, Sahin, *Studying Islamic Education*).

rules about the consumption of alcohol by organising some induction events and Student Union activities that do not involve "pub crawls"; the need for official policies on Islamophobia and sensitive procedures for reporting incidents of religious harassment and discrimination; and the need for a system of student loans or grants that does not put Muslim students in a position where they are required to act against Islamic rules on paying and receiving interest.[165]

5.5   Muslims Working in the Educational System

School teachers

No accurate figures are available for the number of trained Muslim teachers in the UK, though one source estimates that there are fewer than 1,000.[166] There are also no accurate statistics on the number of Muslim students currently undertaking teacher training, whether through the undergraduate or Post Graduate Certificate in Education (PGCE) routes, though, again, it is likely that the numbers are very low. The percentage of school teachers in England from ethnic minorities is variously reported at between two and five per cent.[167] Teachers from ethnic minorities drop out from teacher training at a higher rate than their White counterparts, are seriously under-represented in senior posts and often feel isolated in the profession.[168]

The reasons for the low numbers of Muslim teachers and trainees may include the following: teaching is not a popular career for many young educated Muslims;[169] teacher training rarely contains any significant Muslim components; faculties of education rarely target recruitment at the Muslim population; and Muslim teachers regularly experience Islamophobia while they are training, and also when they are teaching in schools (see section 6.2 below).

---

[165] FOSIS, Islamophobia, pp.6, 8; Federation of Student Islamic Societies, *The Future of Higher Education Funding and its Implications for Muslim Students,* FOSIS, London, 2003.

[166] G. N. Saqeb, "Teacher Training in Islam: its importance and practicalities", in *Issues in Islamic Education,* The Muslim Educational Trust, London, 1996, p. 34, (hereafter, Saqeb, *Teacher Training*).

[167] For the lower figure, see: A. Ross *Ethnic Minority Teachers in the Teaching Workforce,* IPSE Occasional Paper, London, 2001. For the higher figure, see The Runnymede Trust, *Briefing Paper for GTC Teacher Meeting on Black and Minority Ethnic Issues in Teaching and Learning,* The Runnymede Trust, London, 2003.

[168] General Teaching Council for England, *Response to DfES Consultation "Aiming High: Raising the Achievement of Ethnic Minority Pupils",* GTC, London, 2003, pp. 8–9, (hereafter, GTC, *Response*).

[169] Saqeb, *Teacher Training,* pp. 34–35; GTC, *Response,* pp. 8–9.

The Faculty of Education at the University of Plymouth is one of a number of faculties currently carrying out research into the reasons for the very low numbers of ethnic minorities, especially Muslims, applying for their initial teacher training programmes.[170] Several universities, including the University of Birmingham, have recently introduced initial teacher-training courses specifically for Muslim teachers, as well as offering MA degrees in Islamic education, and other opportunities for research into the subject.[171]

School governors

All schools are required to include both parents and community representatives on their governing bodies. However, Muslim parents and community leaders currently play a disproportionately small part in school governance and in educational decision-making generally. For example, in Birmingham, 25 per cent of all pupils in the maintained sector are Muslim, but only six per cent of school governors are Muslim.[172]

The reasons why Muslims are poorly represented on governing bodies are partly that positive steps have not been taken by schools and LEAs to recruit Muslim governors, and partly that Muslims have often failed to put themselves forward for election, perhaps because of a lack of understanding of educational structures and procedures. A report on Bradford, for example, suggests that Asian and other ethnic minority communities find it difficult to contribute to the education agenda because of lack of knowledge of the system.[173] LEAs have an important contribution to make here, for example by publicising the fact that parent governors can be reimbursed, not only for travel and subsistence expenses, but also for other expenses, including childcare or babysitting, and by making it clear that support is available for governors whose first language is not English.

Muslims are often "consulted" by the decision-makers, but they need to be in a position where they join the body of decision-makers, so that they can influence the decisions that are made about Muslim school children directly.[174] Such empowerment will only be achieved if Muslim parents and community representatives receive training in the rights and responsibilities of school governors. This will enable them to work

---

[170] University of Plymouth, *Widening Participation Initiative in Initial Teacher Education,* Faculty of Education, University of Plymouth, 2003.

[171] Sahin, *Studying Islamic Education,* pp. 1–2. A few years ago, the Association of Muslim Schools of UK and Eire also set up its own PGCE courses in conjunction with Cheltenham and Gloucester College. This has now been replaced by a Graduate Teacher Programme course with the University of Gloucester.

[172] Information provided by Tahir Alam, Muslim Council of Great Britain.

[173] *The Ouseley Report,* p. 30 ff.

[174] AMSS, *Muslims on Education,* p. 16.

with the school in the education of their children, to campaign more effectively for change and to play a full part in the decision making process.[175]

Home-school links

Many schools in multicultural districts have developed effective policies for using community languages in notices around the school and in letters to parents. However, there is scope for both schools and LEAs to develop more appropriate strategies for consultation with Muslim parents – and indeed, Muslim young people – on matters of educational policy and practice. Muslim parents should be consulted about issues such as preferences for different kinds of schooling, ways of respecting Islamic culture, and meeting the needs of Muslim pupils. The consultation document issued by Blackburn with Darwen Borough Council provides a good example of the use of an independent market research company to survey the opinions of Muslim and Asian parents about schooling options prior to setting out recommendations.[176] At the school level, closer home-school links will enable schools to involve Muslim parents more fully in the activities of the school and to take fuller account of parents' views and wishes.

---

[175] Weston, *Food for Thought.*

[176] Blackburn with Darwen Borough Council, *Faith Schools.*

6. ISSUES OF IDENTITY AND ISLAMOPHOBIA

6.1   Religious and Ethnic Identity

The failure to acknowledge and recognise the faith identity of Muslim children may have particularly unfortunate consequences in schools. For example, in terms of educational planning, some community schools attempt to keep religion and faith out of school altogether, and this makes it more difficult for them to meet the distinctive spiritual, moral and cultural needs of Muslim children. The result is that Muslim children's unique religious identity may not be celebrated in schools, leading to a feeling that this identity is also not valued in broader society. Acknowledgement of the importance of faith identities can lead to the development of creative and effective solutions to issues concerning schools. For example, in East London, attendance rates at primary schools have increased since the Local Education Authority enlisted the assistance of the local mosque in emphasising the importance of children's education to parents at Friday prayers.[177] More research is needed on the ways in which different kinds of schooling impact on the developing identity of Muslim children, so that Muslim parents can make more informed choices.

The official practice of discussing school achievement only in terms of ethnicity and gender, but not in terms of religion, is not only potentially damaging to the developing self-concept of Muslim children, but it also means that possible links between faith identities and underachievement are ignored. For example, it has already been suggested that there may be a link between underachievement and the fact that Muslim students are exposed to divergent values at school and at mosque school. It may also be significant that Muslim students are liable to be bullied, teased and attacked, because of their religious and cultural background (see below, Section 6.2), and that Muslim students carry the additional burden of working an extra two hours or more at mosque school in the evenings, in order to preserve their religious identity (see above, Section 5.2). Further research is needed on these issues. The emphasis on ethnicity also reinforces the false idea that Muslims are a mono-ethnic group and that Muslim schools are mono-ethnic institutions.

The prominence of religion in the identity of young British Muslims is of enormous importance in schools, but it involves complex questions of intercultural relations in a multicultural society.[178] Ansari is right to suggest that a range of distinct identities is emerging among Muslims in Britain in the 21st century,[179] but most of these identities

---

[177] L. Ward, "Mosque improves pupils' attendance", *The Guardian*, 5 July 2004, p. 8.

[178] Ansari, *The Infidel Within*, pp. 17–22 .

[179] Ansari, *The Infidel Within*, p. 406.

have a strong religious dimension.[180] For all children, not just Muslims, a positive recognition of their self-defined sense of personal identity may be a prerequisite for their educational success, achievement of potential and full participation in society.

This issue can only be fully resolved by an acceptance of faith identities in official documentation, surveys and research. The implication is that attainment figures in the case of Muslims should be collected on the basis of religious as well as ethnic identity. A commitment to do this at all levels, from the DfES and OFSTED, to LEAs and individual schools, would be a major undertaking. Without it, however, it seems likely that the needs of Muslim children will never be fully identified, let alone met. OFSTED inspectors, for example, are required to assess "the extent to which the school actively enables pupils to develop self-knowledge and spiritual awareness [...] and appreciate their own and others' cultural traditions",[181] but the failure to mention religious identity makes it less likely that issues relating specifically to Muslim children will be raised.

6.2   Islamophobia in Schools and Universities

The concept of Islamophobia

Islamophobia has been defined as irrational hostility towards Islam and, therefore, fear or dislike of Muslims. The term also refers to the discrimination and social exclusion arising from this fear and hostility. The term was brought to public consciousness through the establishment of the Commission on British Muslims and Islamophobia, by the Runnymede Trust, and through the publication of the Commission's report in 1997.[182] Typical instances of Islamophobia include attacks on mosques and Muslim cemeteries, threatening phone calls to Muslim organisations and physical attacks and verbal abuse against individuals identified as Muslims by their dress or in other ways. Clearly, Islamophobia has much in common with racism, though it is targeted against

---

[180] J. Eade, "Identity, Nation and Religion: educated young Bangladeshi Muslims in London's East End", in *International Sociology*, 9, 3, 1994, p. 386; N. Hashmi, *From Ethnicity to Religion: the Shifting Identities of Young Muslims in Britain and France*, PhD Thesis, European University Institute, Florence, 2003.

[181] Office for Standards in Education, *Handbook for Inspecting Secondary Schools*, OFSTED, London, 2003, p. 54.

[182] Commission on British Muslims and Islamophobia, *Islamophobia: a Challenge for us all*, Runnymede Trust, London, 1997, (hereafter, Commission on British Muslims and Islamophobia, *Islamophobia*). See also: Commission on British Muslims and Islamophobia, *Addressing the Challenge of Islamophobia*, Uniting Britain Trust and Runnymede Trust, London, 2001.

people because of their religious affiliation rather than because of their membership of a racial or ethnic group.[183]

However, the term "Islamophobia" has not as yet been generally incorporated into official educational policies at either the national or local level. Since the Stephen Lawrence Inquiry report, LEAs have been required to collect information from schools about racist incidents, but there is no guidance about the inclusion of religious anti-Muslim hostility in such reports. As a result, Islamophobic incidents within schools are often not monitored or addressed – though valuable guidance has been given by some LEAs (including Ealing)[184] and by teachers' unions.[185]

Islamophobia in schools

Islamophobic attitudes may underpin much of the teasing and bullying that Muslim children experience at school. However, it is currently impossible to gain accurate statistics on Islamophobia in schools because, when schools log "racist" incidents, they make no distinction between racism, such as calling someone "Paki", and Islamophobia, such as making fun of someone because of their Islamic beliefs and practices – even assuming the latter kind of incident is logged at all. Statistics are not yet available that compare the levels of bullying experienced by pupils of Pakistani or Bangladeshi origin to the levels experienced by children from other minority ethnic groups.

Two important points are, however, clear from research evidence. First, it is not only other pupils who may display Islamophobic attitudes. Teachers may, for example, mock Islamic rules on dress.[186] Other adults may also be involved: in one incident, a schoolgirl had her headscarf pulled off by a woman at her school gates.[187] Second, the incidents that are reported – and there was a welter of reports in the aftermath of

---

[183] A report published by the University of Derby in conjunction with the Home Office in 2000 drew attention to the high levels of religious discrimination experienced by Muslims, see: K. Purdam and P.G. Weller (eds.), *Religious Discrimination in England and Wales: an interim report,* University of Derby/Home Office, 2000.

[184] Commission on British Muslims and Islamophobia, *Islamophobia,* p. 54.

[185] See, for example: National Association of Schoolmasters and Union of Women Teachers, *Islamophobia: advice for schools and colleges,* NAS/UWT, London, 2003. See also: National Union of Teachers, *The War in Iraq: the impact on Schools,* NUT, London, 2003.

[186] G. Bhatti, *Asian Children at Home and at School,* Routledge, London, 1999, p. 186 f.; Runnymede Trust, *Islamophobia: its Features and Dangers,* Runnymede Trust, London, 1997, p. 18.

[187] Islamic Human Rights Commission, *UK Today: the anti-Muslim backlash in the wake of 11th September 2001,* IHRC, Wembley, 2001, p. 3, (hereafter, IHRC, *UK Today*).

September 11[188] – may only be the tip of the iceberg, as students may not wish to make a fuss, draw attention to themselves or escalate the situation. Furthermore, students may have little faith in the school's response. The media must also carry some of the responsibility for the development of negative attitudes towards Muslims.[189] Schools need to counter this influence by helping all children to think critically about the media and to understand the ways in which the media influence and help to form public opinion.

In the same way that racism may be individual or institutional, so Islamophobia is not just a matter of individual discrimination, but can be found deeply embedded in institutional practices.[190] Muslim groups sometimes feel that their legitimate requests are met with a sophisticated web of excuses from schools and that schools sometimes obstruct normal scrutiny and discussion of their policies and procedures.[191]

The Federation of Students Islamic Societies (FOSIS) has highlighted the phenomenon of Islamophobia on university campuses. It finds expression in a number of ways, including: physical violence, such as perpetrators ripping off headscarves; verbal abuse; threats, like the bomb threat to the Muslim prayer hall at Manchester University; negative or patronising images in student newspapers; and a general sense that Muslim students are alienated and excluded.[192]

Many Muslim organisations have sought to combat Islamophobia in education. For example, the Islamic Human Rights Commission has produced many reports documenting the problems faced by Muslims, including problems encountered within schools.[193] The Commission has also produced an information pack containing several specimen letters, including letters challenging disrespectful remarks or urging the

---

[188] J. Henry, "Why Do Arabs Hate Americans, Miss?", in *Times Educational Supplement*, 28 September 2001. See also: Runnymede Trust, *Addressing Prejudice and Islamophobia*, Runnymede Trust, London, 2001; IHRC, *UK Today*; L. Sheridan, "Religious Discrimination: the New Racism", in *The Quest for Sanity: Reflections on September 11 and the Aftermath*, Muslim Council of Britain, Wembley, 2002; and C. Allen and J. Nielsen, *Summary Report on Islamophobia in the EU after 11 September 2001*, EUMC, Vienna, 2002.

[189] Commission on British Muslims and Islamophobia, *Islamophobia*, ch. 10. See also: E. Poole, *Reporting Islam: Media Representations of British Muslims*, London, I.B. Tauris, 2002.

[190] Commission on British Muslims and Islamophobia, *Islamophobia*, pp. 13–14.

[191] Written response to this report from T. Alam, Education Committee of the Muslim Council of Britain, 2 December 2003.

[192] FOSIS, *Islamophobia*.

[193] See, for example: IHRC, *UK Today*; and Islamic Human Rights Commission, *The Hidden Victims of September 11: the Backlash against Muslims in the UK*, IHRC, Wembley, 2002.

balanced representation of Islamic issues, for Muslim parents and community leaders to send to schools.[194]

Stereotypes of Muslim girls

Muslim girls have often been stereotyped as trapped in a patriarchal, oppressive system that allows them no freedom to express themselves or develop their full potential.[195] The *Swann Report* (1985) reinforced these stereotypes when it maintained that Muslims were advocating schools for their daughters that had

> a far more central focus in the curriculum on education for marriage and motherhood in a particular Islamic sense, with other subjects receiving less attention and with the notion of careers education being seen as irrelevant to the pattern of adult life which the girls were likely to pursue.[196]

If teachers were to approach the education of Muslim girls with such stereotypical views of what their parents wanted, it would be no surprise if the girls felt their needs were not being met.[197] However, the statistics on educational attainment mentioned above have already challenged some of these myths and prejudiced views, and perhaps they also indicate that many teachers have already rejected the stereotypes. Muslim girls are out-performing Muslim boys in school examinations at all levels, and are catching up quickly with, and even sometimes overtaking, their White counterparts. Increasing numbers of Muslim girls are being supported by their parents to continue their studies at university.[198] As one 16-year-old Muslim girl said, "education gives status and respect, as well as helping your employment prospects."[199]

A key issue is parental trust. The head teacher of one girls' school with a majority of Muslim pupils reported that most Muslim parents would allow their girls to engage in

---

[194] Information pack available on the website of the Islamic Human Rights Commission at http://www.ihrc.org (accessed 2 November).

[195] See: S. Khanum, "Education and the Muslim Girl", in G. Sahgal and N. Yuval-Davis (eds.) *Refusing Holy Orders: Women and Fundamentalism in Britain,* Virago, London, 1992, pp. 124–140; Hawe, *Muslim Girls' Schools,* pp. 69–72; S. Shaikh and A. Kelly, "To Mix or Not to Mix: Pakistani Girls in British Schools", in *Educational Research,* 31, 1, 1989.

[196] Department of Education and Science, *Education for All: Final Report of the Committee of Enquiry into the Education of Children from Ethnic Minority Groups, under the chairmanship of Lord Swann. Cmnd 827,* DES, London, HMSO, 1985, p. 505, (hereafter, *The Swann Report*). This was preceded by an interim report produced in 1981 under the chairmanship of Lord Rampton.

[197] Basit, *Eastern Values, Western Milieu.*

[198] F. Ahmad, "Modern Traditions? British Muslim Women and Academic Achievement", *Gender and Education,* 13, 2, 2001, pp. 137–152.

[199] Interview with Muslim pupil A of Belle Vue Girls School, Bradford, 26 March 1999.

inter-school sports; undertake work experience, including a police training course and work in a local newspaper office; and go on residential trips, including a trip to France, because they trusted the school and trusted their daughters.[200]

Official school policy regarding permitted dress codes has become more Muslim-friendly in recent years, as LEAs show more understanding of the Muslim requirements of modesty and decency.[201] The *hijab* is normally considered acceptable nowadays in State-funded schools, following a number of high profile cases where girls were suspended for wearing it. Other aspects of school uniform policy, however, continue to cause problems in some schools, where girls may not be allowed to wear trousers instead of skirts, or tracksuits on the sports field. These problems, of course, are not merely Muslim issues, but affect many non-Muslim girls as well.

In spite of the liberalisation of official policies, however, there are many reports that Muslim girls and university students, and sometimes teachers, continue to experience Islamophobic abuse, and sometimes sexual harassment, when they choose to wear the *hijab*.[202] In addition, young women who wear the *hijab* sometimes find this a barrier to employment, and they may feel obliged to remove it for university or job interviews.

There is clearly no room for complacency. There is little evidence that schools and universities are paying adequate attention to the particular needs of Muslim young women with regard to health education, sex education, sports and physical education, or, more generally, ways of preparing them for life as Muslim women in a western society.[203] In particular, female staff is needed for girls' physical education and

---

[200] Interview with head teacher of Belle Vue Girls School, Bradford, 26 March 1999; IQRA Trust, *Needs of Muslim Pupils,* IQRA Trust, p. 15.

[201] A recent case that received much media attention has helped to clarify the boundaries of what schools currently find acceptable in terms of Islamic dress. A girl in Luton was refused permission to wear the *jilbab* (ankle length dress) to school and in June 2004 the High Court ruled in favour of the school. The case caused considerable debate within the Muslim community. See: E. A. Buaras, "Muslim Pupil Fights Religious Dress Ban", *The Muslim News,* 27 February 2004; C. Milmo, "School ban on Islamic gown upheld by the High Court", *The Independent,* 16 June 2004, p. 14 (see also editorial on p. 30).

[202] FOSIS, *Islamophobia.*

[203] IQRA Trust, *Needs of Muslim Pupils,* pp. 16–18. A Muslim perspective on girls' development is contained in: A. Ghadiwala and A. Lasania, *Muslim Girl's Manual of Selfwatching,* Bolton Muslim Welfare Trust, Bolton, 1994.

games.[204] Specialist training is needed for those involved in pastoral care, to enable them to take a more pro-active role in respecting Islamic beliefs and values.[205]

6.3   Knowledge of Islam among Non-Muslims

The school curriculum has an important contribution to make in helping pupils to develop an understanding of the different groups within their community. Knowledge and understanding of Muslim communities and their faith helps to break down prejudice and counter Islamophobia. The main subject where such teaching takes place is religious education. In community schools, this is taught in accordance with either the Qualifications and Curriculum Authority syllabus or one of the locally agreed syllabuses. There are well over 100 of these syllabuses, and each includes the study of Islam.[206]

Therefore, at least in theory, every child in the country leaves school with some knowledge of Islam. But, of course, the quality of teaching and the quality of pupils' learning varies from school to school and from individual to individual. Indeed, it is not unknown for pupils to confuse elements of the six different world faiths they study at some stage in their school career,[207] and to retain very little long-term knowledge of Islam, unless they have studied it as a specialisation for GCSE or "A" level examinations. All the Examination Boards currently offer pupils the opportunity to take GCSE religious education in Islamic studies alone, though informal reports from schools suggest that this option is rarely taken by non-Muslim pupils.[208] At "A" level, Islam must generally be studied alongside other faiths or religious topics.[209] No statistics are currently available to show how widely these options are taken up by non-Muslims.

---

[204] Written response to this report from Mrs J. Fernandez, Principal of the Avenue School, London, 22 January 2004.

[205] Written response to this report from F. Amer, Head of Education and Inter-faith Relations at London Central Mosque Trust and Islamic Cultural Centre, 16 October 2003.

[206] Sahin, *Studying Islamic Education*, p. 1.

[207] R. Homan and L. King, "Mishmash and its Effects upon Learning in the Primary School", in *British Journal of Religious Education*, 15, 3, Summer, 1993, pp. 8–13; J. Hull, "Mishmash, Religious Education and Pluralism", in *British Journal of Religious Education*, 12, 3, Summer, 1990, pp. 121–125.

[208] Reports from individual schools suggest that options that combine the study of Islam with one or more other religious education topics are much more popular with non-Muslim students at GCSE.

[209] An argument for the establishment of an "A" level in Islamic Studies is included in AMSS, *Muslims on Education*, p. 18.

The Islamic component of religious education is usually taught by non-Muslims, and often by non-specialists, who have had little training in Islamic beliefs and values. There is, therefore, a danger of misrepresentation of the religion. This danger is compounded when classes employ books and resources that contain factual inaccuracies and misunderstandings.[210] For example, some books that are still in use contain pictures of the Prophet Muhammad. Schools have a responsibility to check the factual accuracy of representations of Islam in the textbooks and library books they use, especially, but not exclusively, in religious education. Where schools are unable to carry out such checks themselves, they can consult lists of approved books produced by the Muslim Council of Britain or other suppliers. In October 2004, the Muslim Council of Britain launched a scheme to provide a resource pack about Islam, for schools to use as a teaching aid.[211] Muslims do not necessarily object in principle to the idea that information about Islam can be taught by non-Muslims, so long as the information is accurate and it is taught respectfully. But they often feel that the limited understanding of Muslim issues on the part of many non-Muslim teachers makes it hard for them to teach Islam effectively. As one correspondent pointed out, their "lack of awareness of the immense diversity of views and culture within the Islamic paradigm has created crude stereotyping and a wrongly assumed cultural conformity".[212]

While it is possible within the framework of the National Curriculum to study aspects of Islamic art, history and literature, and the Islamic contribution to mathematics and science, this is the exception rather than the rule in most community schools. The new National Curriculum subject of "citizenship", made compulsory in secondary schools in 2002, has the potential to contribute to cross-cultural understanding, including Islamic issues. The National Curriculum programme of study requires pupils to be taught about "the origins and implications of the diverse national, regional, religious and ethnic identities in the United Kingdom, and the need for mutual respect and understanding".[213] However, despite some good practice and new ideas,[214] many schools have found it difficult to make space for this new subject. Instead, they have chosen to deliver the subject of citizenship largely through existing subjects. As a result,

---

[210] Written response to this report from H. Halim, formerly of the IQRA Trust, 2 October 2003.

[211] BBC News, "Muslims Launch School Books Drive", 12 October 2004, available at http://news.bbc.co.uk/1/hi/education/3736428.stm (accessed 1 November 2004).

[212] Written response to this report from D. A. Syed of the Avenue School, London, 3 October 2003.

[213] Department for Education and Employment, *Citizenship: the National Curriculum for England,* London, Qualifications and Curriculum Authority, DfES, 1999.

[214] M. Imran and E. Miskell, *Citizenship and Muslim Perspectives: Teachers Sharing Ideas,* Development Education Centre, Birmingham, 2003.

the opportunity to develop new and interesting approaches to cross-cultural understanding has been lost.

It is rare for non-religious education specialists on primary teacher training programmes to spend more than one day out of a four-year undergraduate education degree on the study of Islam and the needs of Muslim pupils, though they may spend more time studying related issues of racism, inclusion, multicultural education and equal opportunities.[215] For PGCE students, the period of study is likely to be much shorter than this, if they receive any at all. A study of teachers in mainly White schools in 2002 found that issues relating to meeting the needs of ethnic minority pupils simply had not been covered in most cases, either in initial training or in any recent in-service training.[216] Similarly, university teachers may receive no training at all on the subject.

School governors, OFSTED inspectors and other education specialists are unlikely to receive specific training in Muslim needs and Muslim issues in schools, except perhaps indirectly, through a course on racism or on raising ethnic minority achievement. There is clearly a need for both universities and LEAs to review their provision of in-service training for teachers, as well as training for school governors, in issues of policy and practice that affect Muslim pupils.

---

[215] See, for example, the BEd course documentation for the University of Plymouth primary teacher training programmes. Informal conversations suggest that this is not very different in other HE colleges and departments of education.

[216] Cline *et al, Minority Ethnic Pupils.*

7. CURRICULUM ISSUES

7.1 The Cultural Dimension of the Curriculum

It is undeniable that the cultural heritage that underpins the curriculum of British schools is European and Christian, and that, for many Muslim pupils whose families originate from other parts of the world and have a different cultural heritage, this leaves them disadvantaged in British schools.[217]

One response is to require Muslim students to cast off their own cultural heritage and aim for "cultural literacy"[218] in British traditions, language and way of life as quickly as possible. As one correspondent suggested, some teachers "see it as their mission to teach the pupils to look beyond their community and so deliberately exclude all Muslim-friendly options or make only token reference to them".[219] This approach is, in any case, made explicit by those liberal philosophers of education who see it as the role of the school to "liberate" children from the constraints of their present and particular circumstances.[220]

Another response is for Muslims to retreat into a few inner-city enclaves, where they can preserve their cultural heritage virtually untouched by the way of life in the broader society around them.

Most Muslims, however, would prefer a response in which they are both free to develop their distinctive Muslim identity and confident to take on all the rights and responsibilities of full British citizenship. Two shifts in the curriculum might help to make this happen. The first is a more global focus, where European and Christian culture is contextualised in terms of world civilisation. The second involves the inclusion of currently neglected Muslim contributions to European learning and culture, particularly in the fields of art, literature, mathematics, geometry, science, history, philosophy, astronomy and medicine. The effect of this would be both to enrich the curriculum for all students, by helping them to understand the interdependence of cultures and civilisations, and to support the identity and self-concept of young Muslims within the context of European citizenship.[221]

---

[217] Hewer, *Schools for Muslims*, p. 523.

[218] E. D. Hirsch, Jr, *Cultural Literacy: What Every American Needs to Know*, Vintage Books, New York, 1988.

[219] Written response to this report by Tahir Alam, Education Committee of the Muslim Council of Britain, 2 December 2003.

[220] C. Bailey, *Beyond the Present and the Particular: a Theory of Liberal Education*, Routledge and Kegan Paul, London, 1984.

[221] Hewer, *Schools for Muslims*, pp. 523–524.

Islamic literature, history and art

A recent survey found that comparatively little is done across the curriculum to support, or even recognise, the identity of young Muslims, or to increase knowledge generally of Muslim issues.[222] Much more could be done in literature classes to include Islamic authors and poets[223] and texts that call cultural stereotypes into question. In history classes at the secondary school level, there is the possibility to study the Crusades and the Muslim contribution to mathematics, science, medicine and architecture, within an optional Key Stage 3 study of "Islamic History and Civilisation 700–1250 AD". However, there is no research evidence available about how widely this option is adopted in schools, and anecdotal evidence suggests that take-up is minimal.

At primary school level, there are even fewer opportunities to study Islam. For example, there is currently no option to study classical Muslim civilisations instead of, or in addition to, the Greeks, the Egyptians or the Vikings. In any case, teachers generally have a very limited understanding of Islamic history. One correspondent pointed out that their "lack of awareness of the immense diversity of views and culture within the Islamic paradigm has created crude stereotyping and a wrongly assumed cultural conformity".[224] More could also be done in art to focus on Islamic forms, including calligraphy, architecture, geometrical designs and practical crafts.[225]

Arabic as a modern foreign language

Arabic could be offered as an optional modern foreign language, alongside the more usual French, German and Spanish. Since Arabic is the holy language of Islam, this would doubtless prove a popular option for Muslims, many of whom will have learned the rudiments of Arabic, or at least Arabic recitation, in Mosque schools. The economic benefits to the country from such a move could also be substantial.[226]

Such a change, however, would require considerable commitment on the part of Government departments, teacher training institutions, LEAs and schools. In order to introduce Arabic as a modern foreign language, universities would have to produce a

---

[222] L. Kaul-Seidman, J. S. Nielsen and M. Vinzent, *European Identity and Cultural Pluralism: Judaism, Christianity and Islam in European Curricula. Supplement: Country Reports*, Herbert-Quandt-Stiftung, Bad Homburg, Germany, 2003, especially pp. 14–89. This point was also repeatedly made by correspondents, including ,for example, the written response to the present report from J. Fernandez *et al.*, Avenue School, London, 22 January 2004.

[223] Written response to this report from Noshiena Khan, Avenue School, London, 3 October 2003.

[224] Written response to this report from D. A. Syed, Avenue School, London, 3 October 2003.

[225] IQRA Trust, *Needs of Muslim Pupils*, p.13; S. H. Nasr, "The Teaching of Art in the Islamic World", in *Muslim Education Quarterly*, 6, 2, 1989, pp. 4–10.

[226] G. Sarwar, *British Muslims and Schools*, Muslim Educational Trust, London, 1991, pp. 26–27.

sufficient supply of graduates in Arabic; the Teacher Training Agency would have to make places available on appropriate PGCE courses; the providers of PGCE courses would have to find school placements; OFSTED would have to appoint inspectors; LEAs would have to provide advisory and other support; schools would have to adjust their existing modern language provision, juggling with human and other resources; and examination boards may have to provide new GCSE and "A" level syllabuses.

English as an additional language

It has already been noted that many Muslim pupils speak a language other than English at home. Over 90 per cent of pupils of Pakistani and Bangladeshi origin are registered as having English as an Additional Language (EAL), and, of course, many other Muslim children fall into this category as well. Children studying EAL are more likely to come from low-income families, and their attainment levels, particularly in English, are lower than those of non-EAL pupils.[227] The needs of bilingual pupils feature highly in government plans to raise achievement levels,[228] and the Ethnic Minority Achievement Grant provides substantial funds to support these needs.[229] Undoubtedly, such support is part of what is required to help Muslim children achieve their full potential, but at the same time, their religious needs must not be forgotten. This implies not only that value be given to Muslim pupils' other language skills, whether Arabic or community languages, but also that EAL materials used in the classroom should respect Islamic values.

Sex education

The teaching of sex education in schools can be a continuing problem, not so much because it is thought to be a topic better taught at home than at school, but more because the values on which current sex education programmes are based often seem to contravene Islamic teaching. In particular, some of the materials and teaching approaches used in sex education are offensive to the Islamic principles of modesty and decency. Muslims may also be concerned that sex education can tend to undermine Islamic teaching about family life.

In view of these problems, some Muslim parents are likely to choose to exercise their right to withdraw their children from sex education in school, unless the programmes can be changed in order to demonstrate greater respect for Muslim beliefs. Many

---

[227] Bhattacharyya et al, *Minority Ethnic Attainment*, pp. 13–15.

[228] Department for Education and Skills, *Aiming High: Raising the Achievement of Ethnic Minority Pupils*, Ref DfES/0183/2003, Nottingham, DfES Publications, 2003, pp. 28–31.

[229] National Literacy Trust, "Overview of Ethnic Minority Achievement and Literacy", available on the NLT website at http://www.literacytrust.org.uk/Database/EALindex.html#Overview (accessed 2 November 2004).

Muslim parents would be reassured if single-sex classes were the norm for sex education and if Muslim perspectives on marriage, family life, premarital and extra-marital sexual relations, and other key issues, were given equal respect and prominence alongside other perspectives.[230]

Music and the performing arts

Many Muslims enjoy music in a variety of forms, but others think it is an inappropriate subject for the school curriculum. Some Muslims are involved in the performing arts and the entertainment industry, with rap groups like *Fundamental* and hip-hop bands like *Outlandish* achieving a high degree of popularity. Others prefer devotional music, like Quwalis and Berber music. Those who oppose music on the curriculum believe that it is, at best, a waste of time, a diversion from more important things in life, and, at worst, a dangerous enticement to believers to engage in forbidden activities. The belief has its foundations in a *hadith* of the Prophet Muhammad and in all four schools of Islamic law. Of course not all Muslims share these views, but schools must avoid putting those who do into a position where they are required to act against their deep convictions.

It would be helpful if there were an option to withdraw from music lessons, but in the absence of this, it would be prudent for schools to avoid making Muslim children study music with an erotic content or an overtly Christian message.[231] It would also be helpful if the music curriculum were adapted, to make it more inclusive of Muslims. Similar points apply to dance and other areas of the performing arts, and also to some aspects of the art curriculum.[232] In all these areas, the keynote is sensitivity to Muslim beliefs and a determination not to force Muslim pupils to undertake activities against their beliefs in the name of broadening their experience. The provision that allows schools to release pupils from some subjects, so that they can focus on others where they could achieve better, may be the way forward when Muslims feel their beliefs are

---

[230] J. M. Halstead, "Muslims and Sex Education", in *Journal of Moral Education*, 26, 3, September 1997, pp. 317–330; F. M. D'Oyen, *The Miracle of Life: a Guide on Islamic Family Life and Sex Education for Young People*, Islamic Foundation, Leicester, 1996; G. Sarwar, *Sex Education: the Muslim Perspective*, Muslim Educational Trust, London, 1992.

[231] J. M. Halstead, "Muslim Attitudes to Music in Schools", in *British Journal of Music Education*, 11, 2 July 1994, pp. 143–156.

[232] IQRA Trust, *Needs of Muslim Pupils*, p. 13–14.

being compromised.[233] In-service training would help teachers to respond appropriately to Muslim beliefs in these areas.[234]

Religious education

Schools must provide religious education for all registered pupils, though there is a legal right for parents to withdraw their children.[235] In England and Wales, schools other than voluntary aided schools or those of a religious character must teach religious education according to either the locally Agreed Syllabus or the Qualifications and Curriculum Authority Syllabus. Each Agreed Syllabus must reflect the fact that the religious traditions of Great Britain are in the main Christian, while taking into account the teachings and practices of the other principal religions represented in the country.[236] The development of the Agreed Syllabus within each LEA is delegated to the Standing Advisory Council for Religious Education (SACRE), made up of representatives from the Church of England, other religious denominations, the local Council and teachers' unions. Muslims are increasingly being appointed to local SACREs as representatives of "other religious denominations".

Most Muslims are usually happy for their children to learn about other faiths within a course on world religions, but some see such teaching as irrelevant to Muslim children and argue that the time would be better spent learning computing or mathematics.[237] Furthermore, Muslims do not want their children to be targeted for proselytisation by Christians or members of other faiths. Where Muslims perceive this as a danger, they can exercise their legal right of withdrawal from religious education and collective worship.[238] Some Muslims are concerned that, when Islam is taught to Muslim children by non-Muslim teachers as part of a world religions course, the children might end up confused or misinformed. As one correspondent put it, they "are frequently confronted with a basic misconception and flawed understanding of the Islamic faith.

---

[233] Written response to this report from T. Alam, a member of the Education Committee of the Muslim Council of Britain, 2 December 2003.

[234] Written response to this report from D. Harris, independent researcher on Muslims and music, 6 October 2003.

[235] For England and Wales, Education Act (1996), s. 386; for Northern Ireland, see Education Reform (Northern Ireland) Order (1989) SI 2406 (NI 20) and Education and Libraries (Northern Ireland) Order (1986) (NI 3); for Scotland, see Education (Scotland) Act (1980) and the Scottish Office Education Department Circular 6/91.

[236] Education Act (1996), s. 375. Similar guidance is given in the Scottish Office Education Department Circular 6/91.

[237] Ansari, *The Infidel Within*, pp. 330–331.

[238] IQRA Trust, *Needs of Muslim Pupils*, p. 24–25.

This can take the form of a trivialisation of the most important aspects of the religion and an exaggeration of the importance of its cultural manifestations."[239]

For many Muslims, however, the most important kind of religious education is that which nurtures children in their own faith.[240] In community schools, children are taught religious knowledge and respect for others, but the intention of such religious education is not to provide detailed understanding of, or to reinforce, their own faith. For this type of education, Muslim parents rely on supplementary schools. As indicated earlier, the system of supplementary schools has developed in an *ad hoc* manner, in response to the needs of Muslim communities. With the emergence of second- and third-generation British Muslims, there is now a need for a more coherent approach to the religious education of minority faith communities. This includes consideration of the respective roles of State schools and supplementary schools.

Many parents would like their children to have the opportunity to receive lessons about Islam within community schools, as part of the normal school day, preferably taught by an imam or qualified Muslim teacher.[241] Experiments with this approach have been tried in Bradford and elsewhere, but so far no LEA has adopted the German model, in which the children from individual faith groups are taught religious education classes separately for 70 per cent of the time – in the Muslim case, by a local imam who has responsibility for several schools – and then together for the remaining 30 per cent.

Pupils in State schools are required to take part in daily collective worship, which shall be "wholly or mainly of a broadly Christian character".[242] Parents have the right to withdraw their children from attending collective acts of worship. It is not unknown for schools to use the presence of Muslim students as a reason to not provide a daily act of collective worship. However, this is not in accordance with the wishes of most Muslim parents, because it removes a potentially important contribution to children's spiritual, moral and religious development. Comparatively few schools have opted for a "determination", which would free them from the legal requirement that collective worship should be "wholly or mainly of a broadly Christian character" and allow them to offer worship with an Islamic character. In Birmingham, for example, only 25 schools offer such provision.

---

[239] Written response to this report from D. A. Syed, Avenue School, London, 3 October 2003.

[240] M. A. Khan-Cheema *et al.*, *The Muslims and 'Swann'*, The Council of Mosques (UK and Eire), London, 1986.

[241] Written response to this report from B. Mustafa, Oxford Centre for Islamic Studies, 16 October 2003.

[242] Education Act (1996), s. 386; School Standards and Framework Act (1998), s. 70; The Scottish Office, Education Department Circular 6/91.

Extra-curricular activities

Lunch-time and extra-curricular activities enrich the school experience of all pupils, but when these are provided for Muslim pupils, care must be taken to avoid putting them in a position where they are expected to act against their beliefs and values. Where Muslims are members of school sports teams, issues may arise about sportswear and facilities for showers. Teachers and supervisors need to ensure that Muslim students feel comfortable with the arrangements and that their need for modesty and decency is respected. Sensitivity may also be needed when taking Muslim pupils on trips outside the school. Teachers should be sensitive about respecting prayer times, Muslim festivals and the Ramadan fast – as well as avoiding embarrassing Muslim pupils by asking them to take part in activities that they perceive as un-Islamic. Schools with large numbers of Muslim pupils may wish to be pro-active in their support of specifically Islamic activities and clubs. For example, they may choose to organise Islamic clubs like Young Muslims UK.[243]

7.2   Teacher Training

Many of the points made in this and the previous section have implications for teacher training. Teachers should be trained to meet the needs of Muslim pupils and to respond sensitively to Muslim beliefs and values in, and beyond, the classroom. This implies that they should have an adequate knowledge of Islamic beliefs and values, as well as contemporary religious and cultural practices, and they should be willing to incorporate such knowledge, where relevant, across the curriculum and in any extra-curricular activities they lead. It is important that teachers respect children's Muslim identity, avoid negative perceptions and less favourable expectations of Muslim pupils, and avoid stereotypical thinking about Islam and Muslims. Teachers should also be trained to offer support to Muslim pupils who are victims of Islamophobic behaviour and to deal appropriately with offending pupils. They should be encouraged to adopt assessment practices that respect cultural diversity. Examination questions should not assume a non-Muslim framework of values, and a non-standard response to questions about history, literature or other arts and humanities subjects that is written from a Muslim perspective should be respected as valid, in the same way that feminist, Marxist or post-modern responses are accepted.

Teacher training institutions should ensure that their widening participation initiatives encourage the pro-active recruitment of Muslim trainee teachers, as well as those from other ethnic minorities. Teacher training should be made more Muslim-friendly, and more support should be provided for Muslims training to be teachers, in order to

---

[243] Interview with deputy head teacher of Belle Vue Girls School, Bradford, 26 March 1999.

encourage long-term commitment to the profession. Only Muslim teachers can provide Muslim role models for Muslim students in schools, so there is a need for more Muslim teachers in positions of authority. Increasing the number of minority ethnic teachers does not in itself meet this need.

8. THE POLICY FRAMEWORK

There have been no official reports focusing exclusively on the educational needs of Muslim children and young people. Nevertheless, through their discussion of racism, ethnicity, community cohesion, educational disadvantage and faith schools, some reports and initiatives have addressed issues that are relevant to the needs of Muslim pupils and students. The policy responses for meeting the needs of Muslim pupils may be categorised under two headings: (1) equalising opportunities; and (2) supporting religious and cultural identity.

It is possible to identify four elements involved in equalising opportunities for Muslim pupils:

- ensuring that Muslim students have access to the opportunities offered by a general education;
- preparing them to live as full British citizens without fear of racism or other forms of prejudice and discrimination;
- helping them to compete in the employment market on an equal footing with other British citizens; and
- enabling them to generally enjoy the economic and technological benefits of modern life.

Supporting religious and cultural identity involves: recognising and respecting Islamic beliefs, values and ways of life; ensuring that Muslim children are never put in a position in school where they are expected to act in a way that is contrary to their deeply held beliefs; and celebrating and supporting their distinctive cultural identities and experiences.[244]

National policy tends to focus on the first category, equalising opportunity, which is uncontroversial and lies at the heart of race relations legislation, equal opportunities policies and community relations. Policy to equalise opportunity attempts to counter ethnic minority disadvantage and underachievement.

Local policy, while still primarily concerned with equalising opportunities, also sometimes extends to support for cultural identity. Some forms of such support, such as supporting community languages, are relatively uncontroversial, but supporting children's religious beliefs and cultural practices is much more controversial, and indeed there are many who question whether it can ever be the role of the school to do

---

[244] Halstead, *Education, Justice and Cultural Diversity,* p. 203 ff.

so.[245] Nevertheless, most educators agree that cultural values and assumptions are embedded in education, and that cultural domination by the majority can only be avoided by specific measures to support minority cultures.[246] On this basis, many LEAs have introduced multicultural initiatives that seek to respond positively to the needs and wishes of minority groups, including Muslims, so long as these are not perceived to be in conflict with the needs of broader society.

8.1   Policy Reports

The first significant national report to discuss the education of children from ethnic minority groups was the Department of Education and Science report, *Education For All*, (known as the *Swann Report*).[247] This report provides an extensive list of recommendations on racism, underachievement, multicultural education, the need to support children's linguistic and cultural identities and the employment of ethnic minority teachers, all of which have a bearing on the education of Muslims in Britain. However, it does not support bilingual education or separate faith schools, preferring rather to emphasise the need for all children, irrespective of their personal background, to be educated together, as a way of preparing them for life in a multicultural society. There is a degree of inconsistency, therefore, in its acceptance of single-sex education.

In line with its underlying liberal values, the *Swann Report* argues that "ethnic minority communities cannot in practice preserve all elements of their cultures and lifestyles unchanged",[248] because "education has to be something more than the reinforcement of the beliefs, values and identity which each child brings to school".[249] However, the report states that minorities must be free to maintain those elements of their culture that they consider most essential to their ethnic identity, so long as individual freedom of choice is preserved.[250] Some Muslims have argued that these underlying values are flawed, since they imply that Islamic culture can be broken down into its component parts, some of which can readily be discarded. The UK Council of Mosques, in its response to the *Swann Report*, argued that it was hard for Muslims to accept the values

---

[245] See, for example: W. Kymlicka, *Liberalism, Community and Culture*, Oxford, Clarendon Press, 1989, pp. 167–168.

[246] J. M. Halstead, "Schooling and Cultural Maintenance for Religious Minorities in the Liberal State", in K. McDonough and W. Feinberg (eds.), *Citizenship and Education in Liberal-Democratic Societies*, Oxford University Press, Oxford, 2003, pp. 273–295.

[247] *The Swann Report.*

[248] *The Swann Report*, p. 5.

[249] *The Swann Report*, p. 364.

[250] *The Swann Report*, p. 6.

on which the recommendations are based. The Muslim members of the committee that produced the report, along with most of its other ethnic minority members, wrote a note of dissent on the key issue of separate faith schools.[251]

The Commission on British Muslims and Islamophobia report, *Islamophobia: a Challenge for Us All*, contains a number of detailed recommendations on education.[252] Some of these have already been implemented, such as the review of Section 11 funding, and the review of the criteria for funding faith schools, but others await implementation. In particular, the report recommends that government departments and agencies should:

- collect data on the religious affiliations of pupils in all schools;
- issue a set of principles for teaching about religion and citizenship in a multi-faith society;
- provide similar guidance on the inclusion of Islamic issues in the teaching of history;
- give guidance to registered inspectors on what to look for in reporting on the extent to which schools meet the needs of Muslim pupils; and
- encourage more Muslims to train as teachers.

The report also recommends that LEAs and schools should:

- encourage Muslim representation on schools' governing bodies;
- develop mentoring schemes that will provide role models for Muslim pupils;
- ensure that there is an explicit reference to religion in all policies on racism; and
- produce written guidelines on meeting the pastoral, religious and cultural needs of Muslim pupils.

The report further highlights the need for coherent policies on religious education, school dress code, school meals, collective acts of worship, fasting periods, religious holidays, Friday prayers, single-sex groupings and classes, contacts with parents, contacts with mosques and mosque schools, physical education dress and showering arrangements.[253]

---

[251] *The Swann Report*, p. 515. See also: M. A. Khan-Cheema *et al.*, *The Muslims and "Swann"*, The Council of Mosques (UK and Eire), London, 1986.

[252] The Commission on British Muslims and Islamophobia was set up by the Runnymede Trust in 1996, under the chairmanship of Professor Gordon Conway, and published a major report, *Islamophobia: a Challenge for Us All*, the following year (Commission on British Muslims and Islamophobia, *Islamophobia*).

[253] Commission on British Muslims and Islamophobia, *Islamophobia*, p. 46.

The Commission on the Future of Multi-Ethnic Britain published its report *The Future of Multi-Ethnic Britain* (known as the *Parekh Report*) in 2000.[254] Although it deals with many other matters besides education, the report highlights the inadequacy of the lead set by government on issues of equality and diversity in schooling, a problem that is only partly offset by the activities of unions, independent bodies and LEAs. It also draws attention to the inadequacy of current ethnic monitoring procedures, which are criticised because the categories used blur significant differences between groups; the failure of the Ethnic Minority Achievement Grant to have an impact on current patterns of underachievement; and the poor record of OFSTED on race issues.

Of particular interest to Muslims are some of the *Parekh Report's* recommendations and comments on matters of religion and education. The report says that a statement of general principles should be drawn up on reasonable accommodation in relation to religious and cultural diversity in schools and that schools with a religious ethos should be encouraged. It also suggests the establishment of a commission on the role of religion in the public life of a multi-faith society, to make recommendations on legal and constitutional matters.[255]

A number of reports issued in response to the 2001 disturbances in Bradford, Oldham and Burnley make substantial comments on education in the context of a multicultural society. The Bradford Vision Report, *Community Pride, Not Prejudice* (known as the *Ouseley Report*) comments on the lack of consultation with ethnic minority communities over education, as well as the marginalisation of ethnic minority governors and teachers in schools.[256] This report also comments on the prevalence of Islamophobia in schools and the failure of "all-white and/or all-Muslim schools" to contribute to social and racial integration.[257] The report recommends a number of initiatives to promote social harmony, emphasise social inclusion, eliminate institutional discrimination, celebrate success and promote diversity. Citizenship education in schools is seen as a major way to carry forward this agenda, particularly by

---

[254] *The Parekh Report.*

[255] *The Parekh Report*, pp. 241–243.

[256] Bradford District Race Review Team, *Community Pride, not Prejudice*, Bradford Vision, Bradford, 2001, (hereafter, *The Ouseley Report*). One of the strengths of the report is that it incorporated the views of young people. Muslim pupils from Belle Vue Girls School made up a quarter of the Review Team that produced the report, and the report devotes significant space to young people's views about education and a description of successful community projects involving young people. Although the report is centrally about the growing ethnic divisions in Bradford and the "worrying drift to self-segregation", it has a lot to say about education.

[257] *The Ouseley Report*, p. 1.

teaching pupils about diversity and the need for mutual respect and understanding.[258] Bradford Council's action plan in response to the report was published in mid-2002. It included an enhanced curriculum for citizenship in Bradford, the establishment of a Youth Parliament with elections in September 2002, and the requirement that faith schools should produce a statement on their contribution to community cohesion.[259]

A report entitled *Community Cohesion* (widely known as the *Cantle Report*)[260] was one of two reports published by the Home Office that were concerned with issues of community cohesion.[261] It identified separate educational arrangements[262] as one of the main factors contributing to the "parallel lives" of different ethnic communities, and it argued that cross-cultural understanding would develop more easily if schools had a better mix of faiths and cultures.[263] The *Cantle Report* therefore recommended that all schools, whether faith schools or not, should limit their intake from one culture or ethnicity and should offer at least 25 per cent of their places to members of other cultures or ethnicities within the local area.[264] However, the difficulties of implementing this recommendation are acknowledged,[265] and the top priority set out is to promote contact with other cultures by any possible means.

The *Cantle Report* also recommends that, in teaching programmes and daily activities, schools should respect the needs of different faiths and cultures; that their activities should be inspected to this effect; that more ethnic minority teachers and governors should be recruited, especially males, because "Pakistani Muslim youths" need more

---

[258] *The Ouseley Report,* pp. 25–28.

[259] Audit Commission, *Bradford Metropolitan District Council: Corporate Assessment, December 2002,* London, Audit Commission, Comprehensive Performance Assessment Project Team, 2002, pp. 15–16.

[260] Home Office, *Community Cohesion: Report of the Independent Review Team Chaired by Ted Cantle,* London, Home Office, Community Cohesion Review Team 2001, (hereafter, *The Cantle Report*).

[261] The other was the Ministerial Group on Public Order and Community Cohesion, *Building Cohesive Communities, a Report of the Ministerial Group Chaired by John Denham,* Home Office, London, 2001. A further report on community cohesion was issued by the Local Government Association in 2002.

[262] There is an ambiguity in the terminology used that led people to believe that the problem being identified was Muslim schools rather than segregation in State schools resulting from admissions policies and parental choices. For a further critique of the *Cantle Report,* see: Commission on British Muslims and Islamophobia, *Islamophobia,* pp. 50–53 and Ch. 9.

[263] Shain and others have strongly criticised the report for "blaming the victim" by implying that "racism is *caused by* segregation rather than *causing* it". See: F. Shain, *The Schooling and Identity of Asian Girls,* Stoke-on-Trent, Trentham Books, 2003, pp. vii–viii.

[264] *The Cantle Report,* p. 33.

[265] *The Cantle Report,* p. 34.

role models in schools;[266] and that staff and governors need more "diversity training". The report states that Islamophobia was often identified as a problem, adding that some young people felt they were "being socially excluded because of their faith" and that "this was not being recognised or dealt with".[267] However, no suggestions are made in the report as to how such issues should be addressed.

The *Oldham Independent Review* (known as the *Ritchie Report*)[268] provides useful statistics on the ethnic dimensions of the borough's schools and levels of achievement, but appears to ignore the distinctive needs of Muslim children. Parents are blamed for most of the educational problems in the borough, including extended holidays to Pakistan and Bangladesh[269] and "misconceptions concerning the education of other ethnic groups".[270] No attempt is made to explore the reasons for parental actions or the potential educational value of the trips to countries of origin. The final recommendation for pre-16 education is "that all parents are mindful of their responsibility to equip their children in the most positive ways to develop the skills and attitudes needed to live in a multicultural society".[271]

A further report, *Burnley Speaks, Who Listens* (known as the *Clark Report*), contains only a small section on education, though there is a discussion of educational policies in an appendix, together with a comprehensive report from the Lancashire Education Authority.[272]

The year 2004 has seen a proliferation of reports on issues relating to the education of Muslim children in the UK. January 2004 saw the publication of a report by M. I. Coles, a senior adviser in Birmingham LEA, entitled *Education and Islam: a new strategic approach*. This report combines a valuable discussion of policy issues, particularly relating to LEA initiatives, with a statement of the principles that underpin a Muslim approach to education and an examination of current issues of concern. It presents 15 reasons why a new strategy is needed for dealing with Muslims in

---

[266] *The Cantle Report*, p. 36.

[267] *The Cantle Report*, p. 40.

[268] Oldham Independent Review Panel, *Oldham Independent Review Panel Report: One Oldham, One Future, under the chairmanship of David Ritchie*, Oldham Borough Council, 2001, (hereafter, *The Ritchie Report*).

[269] *The Ritchie Report*, p. 25.

[270] *The Ritchie Report*, p. 26.

[271] *The Ritchie Report*, p. 29.

[272] Burnley Task Force, *Burnley Speaks, Who Listens*, Burnley Borough Council, 2001. The Council's response to the report is contained in: Burnley Task Force, *A Neighbourhood Renewal Strategy for Burnley*, Burnley Borough Council, 2003.

education, and concludes with a further list of 15 components of the proposed new strategy. Perhaps the most important of these is the first:

> All those involved with education should seek and empathise with a greater understanding that goes beyond the daily practices and rules of Islam to an awareness of the centrality of the love and remembrance of God in Islam, and of the major issues faced by British Muslim pupils, their parents and their communities.[273]

The latest report from the Commission on British Muslims and Islamophobia contains a detailed review of progress over the last seven years. Its chapter on education includes a section setting out an agenda for further educational research,[274] based on the RAISE Project discussed below, and a discussion of issues affecting Muslim children arising from the recent wars in Afghanistan and Iraq.[275]

In Summer 2004, the RAISE Project[276] published a handbook for schools entitled *The Achievement of British Pakistani Learners: work in progress.*[277] This publication addresses the low attainment levels of pupils of Pakistani and Kashmiri heritage. It is based on a number of case studies carried out in Bradford, Derby, Kirklees, Leeds, Leicester, Manchester, Nottingham, Redbridge, Rotherham, Sheffield and Slough. The handbook deals with issues of identity, citizenship, parental involvement in schools, girls' progress, underachievement, and links between mainstream schools and mosque schools.

In June 2004, a consortium of Muslim organisations published a position paper, *Muslims on Education,* which aimed to open up dialogue between British Muslims and the Department for Education and Skills.[278] The paper has a chapter on general concerns, such as Islamophobia, parental choice and educational achievement. Further chapters in the paper cover issues arising in non-Muslim schools, in Muslim schools and in supplementary education. Some of the recommendations are familiar, such as halting the decline in single-sex provision, while others are innovatory, including tax incentives for Muslim children receiving home schooling, compulsory religious

---

[273] Coles, *Education and Islam,* p. 20.

[274] Commission on British Muslims and Islamophobia, *Islamophobia,* p. 51.

[275] Commission on British Muslims and Islamophobia, *Islamophobia,* pp. 54–56.

[276] A project set up in 2002 by the Uniting Britain Trust in conjunction with the Churches Regional Commission for Yorkshire and the Humber, and funded by Yorkshire Forward.

[277] RAISE Project, *The Achievement of British Pakistani Learners: work in progress,* Trentham Books, Stoke-on-Trent, 2004.

[278] AMSS, *Muslim on Education.* This report was prepared by the Association of Muslim Social Scientists (AMSS UK), the Forum Against Islamophobia and Racism (FAIR), For Education and Development (FED 2000) and the Muslim College UK.

education at Key Stage 4 and the appointment of Muslim observers to LEA meetings. This paper also places significant emphasis on the spiritual dimension of education:

> Qualitative aspects such as spirituality and independence of thought are as important as quantitative aspects such as key stage assessments and examination grades in setting a vision for education.[279]

8.2   Central Government Initiatives

Central Government initiatives are generally based on the identification of minority pupils in terms of racial group, ethnicity and mother tongue, rather than in terms of religious faith. Recent amendments to the 1976 Race Relations Act seek to "eliminate unlawful racial discrimination, promote equality of opportunity and promote good relations between people of different racial groups". According to these requirements, which became law in December 2001, schools must: draft a written policy explaining how they are promoting racial equality; monitor the ethnic balance of staff and pupils; monitor the achievements of pupils from different ethnic backgrounds; and develop policies to tackle the under-achievement of particular groups, where such under-achievement is identified.[280]

A number of recent Government initiatives, including the National Literacy Strategy, the National Numeracy Strategy, Beacon Schools, Specialist Schools and City Academies, have been introduced as a way of tackling low attainment. There have also been initiatives directed specifically at ethnic minorities. The Ethnic Minority Achievement Grant is intended to address any educational or other disadvantages experienced by ethnic minorities. As already noted, it is used, in particular, to support the language needs of refugee children and other pupils with a mother tongue other than English.[281] However, Zubaida Haque has reported that funding from this grant has "not been terribly effective so far in narrowing achievement gaps among minority ethnic groups".[282]

---

[279] AMSS, *Muslims on Education*, p. 9.

[280] The requirements of the Race Relations (Amendment) Act 2001 are set out in: Commission for Racial Equality, *Code of Practice on the Duty to Promote Race Equality*, CRE, December 2001. Non-statutory guidance is provided in: Commission for Racial Equality, *A Guide for Schools* and *A Guide for Institutions of Further and Higher Education*, CRE. Both documents are available on the CRE website at www.cre.gov.uk.

[281] National Literacy Trust, *Overview of Ethnic Minority Achievement and Literacy*.

[282] Haque, *British Muslims*, p. 7.

A consultation document entitled *Aiming High: Raising the Achievement of Minority Ethnic Pupils* was issued by the DfES in March 2003.[283] The overall aim was to equalise educational opportunities, particularly by paying attention to the needs of bilingual pupils, Afro-Caribbean pupils and "highly mobile" pupils. Detailed responses to this document have been published by the General Teaching Council for England,[284] the National Union of Teachers (NUT)[285] and other groups. Underpinning the *Aiming High* project, which was finally announced in October 2003,[286] is the fear that continuing underachievement may endanger social cohesion, as well as leaving personal and economic potential unrealised.[287]

From a Muslim perspective, what is particularly noticeable about this document, and the responses to it, is the failure to include a religious dimension. The shortage of "ethnic minority" teachers is discussed, and targets are set. However, unless the numbers of Muslim teachers are increased, Muslim pupils will continue to be without role models in schools. Although Pakistani and Bangladeshi pupils are identified as underachieving groups at all stages of education, no attempt is made to examine possible reasons for this underachievement, except for bilingualism. Only African-Caribbean pupils and mobile pupils are targeted for special attention. *Aming High* simply ignores key reasons for the underachievement of Pakistani and Bangladeshi pupils that relate to their religious affiliation, including religious prejudice, Islamophobia, the failure of schools to support their religious identity, the impact of supplementary schooling and their daily exposure to values different from those of the home. Instead, the answer to raising achievement is sought in strong leadership, effective teaching and learning, high expectations, an ethos of respect, including a clear approach to racism and bad behaviour, and parental involvement.[288]

8.3   Local Government Initiatives

Over the years, LEAs have devised a number of policies designed to respond to the need both to equalise opportunities and to preserve religious and cultural identity. For

---

[283] Department for Education and Skills, *Aiming High: Raising the Achievement of Ethnic Minority Pupils, Ref DfES/0183/2003*, DfES Publications, Nottingham, 2003, (hereafter, DfES, *Aiming High*).

[284] GTC, *Response*.

[285] National Union of Teachers, *Response to DfES Consultation "Aiming High: Raising the Achievement of Ethnic Minority Pupils"*, NUT, London, 2003 (hereafter NUT, *Response*).

[286] H. Muir, "Ethnic Minority Pupils Get More Help", *The Guardian*, 23 October 2003, p. 8.

[287] DfES, *Aiming High*, p. 4.

[288] DfES, *Aiming High*, p. 13.

example, Bradford Council produced a policy document in 1982 on educational provision for ethnic minorities, particularly Muslims, in Bradford.[289] The main issues covered were separate physical education lessons for girls; permission for Friday prayers for Muslims, led by imams, to be held in schools; permission for Muslim pupils to be absent on religious festivals and to wear traditional dress that met Muslim requirements for modesty and decency; permission for parents to withdraw their children from religious education and collective worship; and the provision of *halal* meat in schools. Most of these issues were not, however, implemented in practice, and the policy of merging single-sex schools and providing only co-education was also halted. Further guidance was issued by the same LEA the following year on how to recognise, challenge and correct racist behaviour in schools.[290] However, relations between Muslims and the broader community in Bradford were later damaged by a series of incidents, including the Honeyford affair[291] and the aftermath of Muslim protests against the publication of Salman Rushdie's *The Satanic Verses*.

These early ground-breaking initiatives at local-authority level were followed by similar initiatives in Birmingham and elsewhere.[292] Over the last 20 years, these initiatives have been added to, and made more sophisticated, elsewhere in the country. However, the impact of such policies has been mixed, partly because of limited commitment to the policies within the LEA, with the result that implementation has been uneven and many schools have felt free to ignore them.

In December 2001, Blackburn with Darwen Borough Council produced an important consultation document concerning provision for the educational needs of multicultural and multi-faith communities in the borough.[293] The document provides interesting statistics on the relationship between religion and education in the borough: 26 per cent of pupils in LEA schools are from ethnic minorities (mainly Muslim); 48 per cent

---

[289] City of Bradford Metropolitan Council, *Education for a Multicultural Society: Provision for Pupils of Ethnic Minority Communities (LAM 2/82)*, Bradford, City of Bradford Metropolitan Council, 1982.

[290] City of Bradford Metropolitan Council, *Racist Behaviour in Schools (LAM 6/83)*, Bradford, City of Bradford Metropolitan Council, 1983. See also: Halstead, *Education, Justice and Cultural Diversity*.

[291] See: Halstead, *Education, Justice and Cultural Diversity*.

[292] City of Birmingham District Council, *Guidelines on Meeting the Religious and Cultural Needs of Muslim Pupils*, Birmingham Council, 1986 (revised in 1999). For a discussion of this document, see: D. Joly, *Britannia's Crescent: making a place for Muslims in British Society*, Avebury, Aldershot, 1995, especially Ch. 7.

[293] Blackburn with Darwen Borough Council, *Faith Schools and Cultural Diversity: Consultation Document*, Education and Lifelong Learning Department, Blackburn, 2001 (hereafter, Blackburn, *Faith Schools*).

of the schools in the State sector are Christian schools (Catholic or Church of England), including eight Church of England primary schools with a majority of Muslim pupils; there are no Muslim schools in the State sector, but seven independent Muslim faith schools (with over 800 Muslim pupils between them). As part of the consultation, an independent market research company was commissioned to carry out small-scale research among parents in the borough. Some 176 families were interviewed, of which two-thirds were Asian.

From the main findings of the consultation listed below, it is clear that the parents consulted hold a wide range of views on the best form of education for their children:

- A number of "Asian heritage parents" expressed some dissatisfaction with LEA schools that were not meeting their religious, moral and cultural needs. Some wanted single-sex schooling at secondary level within the State system.

- There was support from a number of "Asian heritage parents" for Church of England schools, because these schools recognised the importance of faith. However, there was frustration at the lack of places available in such schools at the secondary level.

- There was a growing trend towards the use of independent Muslim faith schools. Various reasons were given for this, including academic standards, moral and spiritual ethos, single-sex schooling and the Muslim faith basis of the curriculum and policies of the schools.

- Some parents found the curriculum and opportunities in some independent Muslim schools to be narrow and oppressive, and they positively supported multicultural, multi-faith schools.

- Some groups and individuals wanted Muslim faith education to be provided within the State system.

- There was some evidence that young people felt less strongly about religious and cultural issues than their parents.[294]

In view of these findings, the document recommends that at least one of the existing independent Muslim faith schools should become a voluntary-aided school or a City Academy and that the possibility should be explored of changing the status of one Church of England or community primary school to a Muslim voluntary-aided primary school. The document also proposes exploring the possibility of transferring an existing high school into either a Church of England high school, welcoming pupils from all faiths, or a multi-faith City Academy. In addition, the report recommends that the LEA should continue to develop best practices in meeting the needs of all communities. These include: bilingual support for pupils; guidelines on school

---

[294] Blackburn, *Faith Schools*, p. 3.

uniform and sportswear; guidance on monitoring racist incidents; guidance on meeting the needs of Muslim pupils during Ramadan and extended leave from school; support for underachieving pupils; experimenting with single-sex teaching at Key Stage 3; employing more ethnic minority teachers; and providing professional development for teachers on the needs of minority pupils.

These recommendations are broadly in line with Government policy to diversify educational provision, increase parental choice and encourage the development of more faith schools.[295] Other local authorities are following suit and engaging in sometimes lengthy consultation exercises about the justifiability and practicability of granting voluntary-aided status to Muslim schools.[296]

---

[295] The outcome of the consultation, *Report into findings of the consultation on faith schools and cultural diversity,* is available on the website of the Blackburn with Darwen Borough Council at http://council.blackburnworld.com/council/executive_board/executive_board_documents/0 30116/pdf/faith_schools_brief.pdf (accessed 1 October 2004).

[296] See, for example: Learning and Culture Scrutiny Committee, *Faith in our Schools* (first draft), Oxfordshire County Council, 2004. This is a review of Council policy in the light of a recent application by a Muslim organisation to set up a faith school.

9. RECOMMENDATIONS

9.1 Muslim Children and British Schooling

9.1.1 Compulsory education

Choice and Diversity in Schooling

1. The Department for Education and Skills and Local Education Authorities should develop improved structures for consultation with Muslims, at both the national and local levels, on matters of educational policy and practice.

2. The Department for Education and Skills, the Teacher Training Agency and research councils should provide funds for focused research investigating issues that influence Muslim parents' choice of schools and are of real concern to the Muslim community. This should include such topics as the relationship between single-sex schooling and achievement levels; the compatibility of community schools with Islamic values; and the extent to which Muslim schools prepare students for British citizenship.

Community Schools

3. Local Education Authorities and schools should ensure that Muslim values are respected in schools, so that Muslim children are not put in a position where they are expected to act in a way that conflicts with their fundamental beliefs and values. Schools with Muslim pupils should carry out an audit of school policies, procedures and curriculum, to ensure that they are "Muslim-friendly".

4. The Department for Education and Skills should establish national guidelines on ways to meet the distinctive needs of Muslim pupils, incorporating best practice at the level of the Local Education Authorities. These should include issues of clothing; school meals; school attendance during, and acknowledgement of, Islamic festivals; Muslim needs during Ramadan; meeting Muslim hygiene and cleanliness requirements; providing prayer facilities for Muslim students for the midday prayer; and permission for attendance of a mosque for the Friday midday prayer.

5. Local Education Authorities should explore the possibility, wherever Muslims make up a large majority of the population of a particular community school, of re-establishing that school as a Muslim voluntary-aided school. Parental opinion should be investigated, along with the willingness of the local council

for mosques or other Muslim community organisations to manage the school, and the ability of such organisations to perform this role.

6. Local Education Authorities should establish procedures for disseminating good practice in meeting the needs of Muslim pupils. An advisory teacher in each Local Education Authority could be given special responsibility for this.

Church Schools

7. Where a church school plans to admit up to 15 per cent of pupils who do not belong to the same denomination, those places should be open to all faiths, not just to Christians. This would improve choice for Muslim parents and also enrich the cross-cultural and inter-faith understanding of the church school.

8. Where Muslims make up a large majority of the population of a particular Church of England or other voluntary school, the Diocesan board of education should explore the possibility of re-establishing that school either as a Muslim voluntary-aided school or as a multi-faith school.

9. Local Education Authorities should explore with Diocesan Boards and other religious groups the potential of establishing multi-faith schools, as a way of meeting the needs of those parents who want a multicultural but faith-based education.

Single-Sex Schooling

10. Local Education Authorities should explore the possibility of providing single-sex education as an option available to parents in regions where there are significant numbers of Muslim pupils.

State-Maintained and Independent Muslim Schools

11. Stronger links should be developed between Muslim and non-Muslim schools, whether the former are independent, State-funded or simply community schools with a large preponderance of Muslim pupils. At the pupil level, such links might take the form of school visits; pen-pal or email exchanges; joint sporting, debating or extra-curricular activities; and other twinning activities. However, there are also benefits in making links at the teaching and

administrative levels.[297] Personal advice services, such as Connections, that are currently enjoyed by the maintained sector should be extended to pupils in non-maintained Muslim schools.

12. Local Education Authorities should seek to create a more inclusive school system by bringing independent Muslim schools wherever possible into the LEA community of schools.

9.1.2   Supplementary Schools

13. Where Muslim pupils attend mosque schools or other supplementary schools on a regular basis, Local Education Authorities and community schools should initiate contacts with these schools in order to increase mutual understanding of educational goals and methods and to encourage closer working relationships. Bradford's practice of encouraging links between mainstream schools and supplementary mosque schools is an example of good practice worth emulating elsewhere.

9.1.3   The Academic Achievements of Muslims

14. The Department for Education and Skills and Local Education Authorities should ensure that factors relating to faith or religion that may affect pupils' achievement levels are taken into account in future planning. The Government should require Local Education Authorities to show in their Educational Development Plans how they intend to raise the achievement levels of minority faith groups, as well as minority ethnic groups.

15. The Department for Education and Skills should commission research on the causes of disaffection among certain groups of Muslim pupils and young people, especially boys, in order to develop strategies (in conjunction with parents and community leaders) to support Muslim pupils at risk of exclusion from community schools.

16. The current effectiveness of the Office for Standards in Education (OFSTED) in dealing with specifically Muslim issues (as opposed to 'Asian' or minority ethnic issues) and helping to raise the achievement levels of Muslim pupils should be examined. More training for registered inspectors should be

---

[297] *The Cantle Report* makes further helpful suggestions about ways to address what it calls "the problem of mono-cultural schools". *The Cantle Report*, p. 35.

provided where necessary, especially on Islamophobia and issues of British Muslim identity.

9.1.4   Muslims in Further and Higher Education

17. The Government should establish a system of student loans that does not involve Muslim students in Higher Education being required to act against Islamic rules on paying and receiving interest.

18. Universities and other institutions of Further and Higher Education should ensure that prayer facilities (including the necessary washing facilities) are provided for Muslims on all campuses; that food in conformity with Islamic dietary requirements is available in student refectories; and that no Muslim students are required on any courses to wear clothing that contravenes Muslim rules regarding modesty and decency. They should also respect Islamic festivals and prayer times in planning events that require student attendance, in particular examinations, and should be aware of the special needs of Muslim students who fast during the month of Ramadan.

19. Universities and other institutions of Further and Higher Education with significant numbers of Muslim students should ensure that students are provided with pastoral support through a Muslim chaplaincy or counselling services. Universities with smaller numbers of Muslim students should ensure that chaplains and counselling services are trained to meet the needs of Muslim students.

20. Universities and other institutions of Further and Higher Education should develop official policies on Islamophobia within their equal opportunities and race relations policies, and should develop sensitive procedures for reporting incidents of religious harassment and discrimination both on and off campus.

21. Universities and other institutions of Further and Higher Education should ensure that there are no obstacles that discourage the recruitment of Muslim students across the full range of courses, or the recruitment and promotion of Muslim academic and support staff.

9.1.5   Muslims Working in the Education System

School Teachers

22. Teacher trainers should investigate the reasons why Muslims, especially Muslim men, are avoiding the teaching profession, so that steps can be taken to improve the desirability of the profession for Muslims.

23. The Department for Education and Skills, Local Education Authorities, schools and Teacher Trainers should establish targets for the recruitment specifically of Muslim teachers, not just teachers from ethnic minorities.

24. Local Education Authorities should carry out ethnic and religious monitoring of promotions to ensure that Muslim teachers and administrative staff are being treated fairly and equally.

School Governors

25. Local Education Authorities and schools should take positive steps to recruit Muslim governors both as parent governors and as community representatives.

Home-School Links

26. Local Education Authorities should survey the opinions of Muslim parents about their children's education and about the preferences they have for different kinds of schooling, whether single-sex, faith-based, multicultural or other. They should also arrange consultation meetings with Muslim parents' groups, mosques, community organisations and young people, to discuss ways to respect Islamic culture and meet the needs of Muslim pupils. They should then develop practices and strategies to support Muslim pupils and should be responsible for providing extra support where necessary.

27. Local Education Authorities and schools should actively encourage home-school links for Muslim families, so that schools can involve parents more fully in the activities of the school and so that the school can take account of parents' wishes.

9.2   Issues of Identity and Islamophobia

9.2.1   Religious and Ethnic Identity

28. The Department for Education and Skills and Local Education Authorities should ensure that all educational statistics are collected on the basis of religion or faith, as well as ethnic background.

29. OFSTED inspectors should be required to report in every school inspection on the way in which maintained schools are supporting the identity of Muslim pupils and meeting their spiritual, moral and other needs. Good practice should be acknowledged and shared.

9.2.2   Islamophobia in Schools and Universities

30. Schools, Local Education Authorities and national bodies should ensure that Islamophobia in all its forms is specifically included in all policies on racism, and that it is incorporated into existing initial and in-service training programmes on bullying and racism. Teachers should be trained to offer support to Muslim pupils who are victims of Islamophobic behaviour and to deal appropriately with the offending pupils.

9.2.3   Knowledge of Islam among Non-Muslims

31. Schools should take all possible steps to check the factual accuracy of representations of Islam in the textbooks and library books they use, and to check that they include pictures of Muslim pupils in a non-tokenistic way in textbooks for all subjects.

32. Local Education Authorities and schools should ensure that where citizenship is taught as a school subject, it is taught in a way which is sensitive to the particular issues that face Muslims as British citizens. This may require the development of specific materials relating to Muslims and Citizenship that schools can use both with Muslim pupils and in the context of developing inter-cultural understanding and respect.

33. Local Education Authorities should ensure that training and support for school governors includes developing sensitivity to, and an understanding of, issues of policy and practice that affect Muslim pupils, especially in such areas as exclusions, equal opportunities, admissions, appeals, and the community use of school premises.

9.3 Curriculum Issues

9.3.1 The Cultural Dimension of the Curriculum

Islamic Literature, History and Art

34. Schools should provide a culturally inclusive curriculum that integrates Muslim contributions into all aspects of the curriculum, especially literature, history and art, so that Muslim pupils can "recognise their identities in the curriculum".[298]

Arabic as a Modern Foreign Language

35. Arabic and community languages should be given full status as modern foreign languages in the National Curriculum, so that schools can meet the expected high take-up of these options among Muslim and other pupils. Taking this request seriously will require that both funds and places on PGCE courses are made available to train teachers of Arabic, and that graduates with qualifications in Arabic are recruited to such courses.

English as an Additional Language

36. Local Education Authorities and schools should ensure that bilingual pupils and those learning English as an Additional Language (EAL) receive appropriate support for their language skills and needs, to help them to achieve their full potential.

37. Local Education Authorities and schools should ensure that EAL material respect Muslim values.

Sex Education, Music and the Performing Arts

38. Teacher training institutions and Local Education Authorities should ensure that teachers working in areas of the curriculum that raise particular issues for Muslims are given specific training to help them to be sensitive to Muslim beliefs and values. This applies specially to the teaching of music, art, dance and sex education to Muslim children.

Religious Education

39. Schools with a significant number of Muslim students should offer Islam as an option for Muslim children studying Religious Education for GCSE.

---

[298] NUT, *Response*, p. 7, para. 42.

40. Where Muslim children attend community schools or church schools, suitable provision should be made for qualified Muslim teachers to provide separate Religious Education lessons, wherever possible.

41. Local Education Authorities should ensure that there is adequate Muslim representation on their Standing Advisory Council for Religious Education (SACRE).

9.3.2 Teacher Training

42. All institutions responsible for initial teacher training should ensure that students are adequately prepared to meet the needs of Muslim pupils and to understand and respond appropriately to issues of cultural diversity in and beyond the classroom. Teachers training should encourage positive perceptions and expectations of Muslim pupils.

43. Local Education Authorities should ensure that teachers, including head teachers, are supported through induction and continuing professional development to develop further skills and increased confidence in meeting the needs of Muslim students. Such training should be an obligatory element, for example, in the National Professional Qualification for Headship (NPQH).

44. The Department for Education and Skills, Local Education Authorities, schools and teacher trainers should ensure that assessment practices respect cultural diversity. Examination questions should not assume a non-Muslim framework of values. A non-standard response to questions about history, literature or other arts and humanities subjects that is written from a Muslim perspective should be respected as valid, in the same way that feminist, Marxist or postmodern responses are accepted.

45. Teacher trainers should seek ways to make training more Muslim-friendly, in order to attract more Muslim teachers. More support should be provided for Muslims training to be teachers in order to encourage long-term commitment to the profession.

Appendix 1: Definitions

"Community schools" are State schools under the control of the Local Education Authority (LEA); the vast majority are co-educational.

"Church schools" are State-funded schools under the control of a church, a diocesan board of education or other religious authority; a higher proportion than for community schools (though still a minority) are single-sex. Church schools may be voluntary aided, voluntary controlled, special agreement or foundation schools. In *voluntary aided* schools, school governors carry responsibility for admissions and the appointment of staff, the cost of building maintenance and improvement is shared between governors and the LEA, and Religious Education follows the Church syllabus. In *voluntary controlled* schools and *foundation* schools, the cost of building maintenance and improvement is met by the LEA, and Religious Education follows the local Agreed Syllabus. However, in voluntary controlled schools, admissions and the employment of staff are managed by the LEA, whereas in foundation schools they are managed by the governors. *Special agreement* schools are very similar to voluntary aided schools; the term refers to a small group of mainly Catholic schools set up by agreement with LEAs before the 1944 Education Act.

"Muslim schools" are mainly independent (i.e. fee-paying) schools, but five now have State funding as voluntary aided schools; at secondary level, virtually all are single-sex.

Religious categories in the UK 2001 National Census: the 2001 census asked an optional question on religious affiliation. The data is disaggregated into the following nine categories: Buddhist, Christian, Hindu, Jewish, Muslim, Sikh, any other religion, no religion and religion not stated.

Ethnic categories in the UK 2001 National Census: the 2001 census contained a 16-point structure: White (British, Irish or Any Other White Background); Mixed (White and Black Caribbean, White and Black African, White and Asian or any other Mixed Background); Asian or Asian British (Indian, Pakistani, Bangladeshi, Any Other Asian Background); Black and Black British (Caribbean, African, any other Black background); Chinese or other ethnic group (Chinese, any other).

"Ethnic minorities": in this report, the use of the term "ethnic minority" as a broad "umbrella" label, is deliberate, to signify reference to a wide variety of ethnic minority groups. Where greater precision is required, reference to specific component groups within the ethnic minority population is made in the text. There is, inevitably, considerable debate and disagreement on the question of race, ethnicity and nomenclature. No specific political or sociological inference should be drawn from the use of related terminology in this report.

"White": as with the term "ethnic minority", the generic label "White" should be used with some caution. The existence of distinctive ethnic groups within the "White" category is gradually being acknowledged. Notably, in the UK 2001 National Census, people of Irish descent are recognised as a separate ethnic group.

Appendix 2: Bibliography

Ahmad, F., "Modern Traditions? British Muslim Women and Academic Achievement", *Gender and Education*, 13:2 (2001), 137–152

Ahmad, F., T. Modood and S. Lissenburgh, *South Asian Women and Employment in Britain: the interaction of gender and ethnicity* (London: Policy Studies Institute, 2003)

al-Attas, S. M. N., ed., *Aims and Objectives of Islamic Education* (London: Hodder and Stoughton, 1979)

Allen, A., *Fair Justice: the Bradford Disturbances, the Sentencing and the Impact* (London: Forum Against Islamophobia and Racism, 2003)

Allen, C. and J. Nielsen, *Summary Report on Islamophobia in the EU after 11 September 2001* (Vienna: European Union Monitoring Centre on Racism and Xenophobia, 2002)

Ansari, H., *The Infidel Within: Muslims in Britain since 1800* (London: Hurst, 2004)

Anwar, M., *British Pakistanis: Demographic, Economic and Social Position* (Coventry: CRER, 1996)

Archard, L., *Race, Masculinity and Schooling: Muslim Boys and Education* (Maidenhead: Open University Press, 2003)

Association of Muslim Social Scientists and other groups, *Muslims on Education: a position paper* (Richmond: AMSS, 2004)

Audit Commission, *Bradford Metropolitan District Council: Corporate Assessment, December 2002* (London: Comprehensive Performance Assessment Project Team, 2002)

Bailey, C., *Beyond the Present and the Particular: a Theory of Liberal Education* (London: Routledge and Kegan Paul, 1984)

Basit, T., *Eastern Values, Western Milieu: Identities and Aspirations of Adolescent British Muslim Girls* (Ashgate: Aldershot, 1997)

Berthoud, R., *The Incomes of Ethnic Minorities* (Colchester: University of Essex, 1998)

Bhattacharyya, G., L. Ison, and M. Blair, *Minority Ethnic Attainment and Participation in Education and Training: the Evidence* (Nottingham: Department for Education and Skills, 2003)

Bhatti, G., *Asian Children at Home and at School* (London: Routledge, 1999)

Bishops' Conference of England and Wales, *Catholic schools and Other Faiths: a consultation paper* (London: Catholic Bishops' Conference of England and Wales, 1997)

Blackburn with Darwen Borough Council, *Faith Schools and Cultural Diversity: Consultation Document* (Blackburn: Education and Lifelong Learning Department, 2001)

Bradford District Race Review Team, *Community Pride, not Prejudice* (Bradford: Bradford Vision, 2001)

Burgess, A., "Co-education – the Disadvantages for Schoolgirls", *Gender and Education,* 2:1 (1990), 91–95

Burgess, S., and D. Wilson, *Ethnic mix: how segregated are English Schools?* (Bristol: CMPO, 2004)

Burnley Task Force, *A Neighbourhood Renewal Strategy for Burnley* (Burnley: Burnley Borough Council, 2003)

Burnley Task Force, *Burnley Speaks, Who Listens* (Burnley: Burnley Borough Council, 2001)

Cabinet Office, *Ethnic Minorities and the Labour Market: final report,* (London, Cabinet Office, Strategy Unit, 2003)

Cairns, J. and R. Gardner, eds. *Faith Schools: Conflict or Consensus?* (London: Kogan Page, 2004)

Church Schools Review Group, *The Way Ahead: Church of England Schools in the New Millennium (the Dearing Report)* (London: Church House Publishing, 2001)

City of Birmingham District Council, *Guidelines on Meeting the Religious and Cultural Needs of Muslim Pupils* (Birmingham: Birmingham Council, 1986)

City of Bradford Metropolitan Council, *Education for a Multicultural Society: Provision for Pupils of Ethnic Minority Communities* (LAM 2/82) (Bradford: Bradford Council, 1982)

City of Bradford Metropolitan Council, *Racist Behaviour in Schools* (LAM 6/83) (Bradford: Bradford Council, 1983)

Cline, T., G. de Abreu, C. Fihosy, H. Gray, H. Lambert and J. Neale, *Minority Ethnic Pupils in Mainly White Schools,* Research Brief No 365 (London: Department for Education and Skills, 2002)

Coles, M. I., *Education and Islam: a new strategic approach* (Leicester: School Development Support Agency, 2004)

Commission for Racial Equality, *Code of Practice on the Duty to Promote Race Equality* (London: CRE, 2001)

Commission for Racial Equality, *Schools of Faith* (London: CRE, 1990)

Commission on British Muslims and Islamophobia, *Addressing the Challenge of Islamophobia* (London: Uniting Britain Trust and Runnymede Trust, 2001)

Commission on British Muslims and Islamophobia, *Islamophobia: a Challenge for us all* (London: Runnymede Trust, 1997

Commission on British Muslims and Islamophobia, *Islamophobia: issues, challenges and action* (Stoke-on-Trent: Trentham Books, 2004)

Connor, H., C. Tyers, S. Davis, and N. Tackey, *Minority Ethnic Students in Higher Education* (London: DfES, 2003)

D'Oyen, F. M. *The Miracle of Life: a Guide on Islamic Family Life and Sex Education for Young People* (Leicester: Islamic Foundation, 1996)

Darr, N., ed., *Muslim Directory, MDUK* (London: Media Ltd, 2003)

De Jong, J. and G. Snik, "Why Should States Fund Denominational Schools?", *Journal of Philosophy of Education*, 36: 4 (2002), 573–587

Department for Education and Employment, *Citizenship: the National Curriculum for England* (London: Qualifications and Curriculum Authority, 1999)

Department for Education and Employment, *Schools Achieving Success* (Cm. 5230) (London: Her Majesty's Stationery Office, 2001)

Department for Education and Skills, *Aiming High: Raising the Achievement of Ethnic Minority Pupils*, Ref DfES/0183/2003 (Nottingham: DfES Publications, 2003)

Department of Education and Science, *Education for All: Final Report of the Committee of Enquiry into the Education of Children from Ethnic Minority Groups, under the chairmanship of Lord Swann*. Cmnd 827 (London: Her Majesty's Stationery Office, 1985)

Eade, J. "Identity, Nation and Religion: educated young Bangladeshi Muslims in London's East End", *International Sociology*, 9:3 (1994), 377–394

Eade, J. and F. Zaman, *Routes and Beyond: Voices from Educationally Successful Bangladeshis* (London: Centre for Bangladeshi Studies, 1993)

Elkins, M. and J. Olagundoye, *The Prison Population in 2000: a Statistical Review*, Home Office Findings 154 (London: Home Office, 2001)

F. Shain, *The Schooling and Identity of Asian Girls* (Stoke-on-Trent: Trentham Books, 2003)

Federation of Student Islamic Societies, *Islamophobia on Campuses and the Lack of Provision for Muslim Students* (London: FOSIS, 2003)

Federation of Student Islamic Societies, *The Future of Higher Education Funding and its Implications for Muslim Students* (London: FOSIS, 2003)

Gearon, L., ed. *Education in the United Kingdom: Structures and Organisation*, (London, David Fulton, 2002)

General Teaching Council for England, *Response to DfES Consultation 'Aiming High: Raising the Achievement of Ethnic Minority Pupils'* (London: GTC, 2003)

Ghadiwala, A. and A. Lasania, *Muslim Girl's Manual of Self-watching* (Bolton: Bolton Muslim Welfare Trust, 1994)

Gillborn, D. and C. Gipps, *Raising the Attainment of Minority Ethnic Pupils, School and LEA Responses* (London: OFSTED, 1999)

Grace, G., *Catholic Schools: Missions, Markets and Morality* (London: RoutledgeFalmer, 2002)

Halstead, J. M. and T. H. McLaughlin, eds., *Education in Morality*, (London: Routledge, 1999)

Halstead, J. M., "Muslim Attitudes to Music in Schools", *British Journal of Music Education*, 11:2 (1994), 143–156.

Halstead, J. M., "Muslim Perspectives on the Teaching of Christianity in British Schools", *British Journal of Religious Education*, 15:1 (Autumn 1992), 43–54

Halstead, J. M., "Muslims and Sex Education", *Journal of Moral Education*, 26:3 (1997) 317–330

Halstead, J. M., "Radical Feminism, Islam and the Single-Sex School Debate", *Gender and Education*, 3:3 (1991), 263–278

Halstead, J. M., "Towards a Unified View of Islamic Education", *Islam and Christian-Muslim Relations*, 6:1 (1995), 25–43

Halstead, J. M., ed., *Parental Choice and Education* (London: Kogan Page, 1994)

Halstead, J. M., *Education, Justice and Cultural Diversity: an Examination of the Honeyford Affair, 1984-85* (London: Falmer Press, 1988)

Halstead, J. M., *The Case for Muslim Voluntary-Aided Schools: some philosophical reflections* (Cambridge: Islamic Academy, 1986)

Haque, M. "Muslim Education in Britain: the King Fahd Academy, London", *Muslim Education Quarterly*, 17:2 (2000) 69–72

Haque, M., "Review of the Progress of Islamic Education", *Muslim Education Quarterly*, 19:4 (2002), 68–73

Harris, F., "Do We Really Want More Faith Schools?" *Education Review*, 15:1 (2002) 32–36

Hashmi, N., *A Muslim School in Bristol: an Overview of the Current Debate and Muslim School Children's Views* (Bristol: University of Bristol, Centre for the Study of Ethnicity and Citizenship, 2003)

Hashmi, N., *From Ethnicity to Religion: the Shifting Identities of Young Muslims in Britain and France* (doctoral dissertation, European University Institute, 2003)

Hawe, K., "Muslim Girls' Schools – a conflict of interests? *Gender and Education*, 6:1 (1994), 63–76

Hewer, C., "Schools for Muslims", *Oxford Review of Education*, 27:4 (December 2001), 515–527

Hewitt, I., "The Case for Muslim Schools", *Issues in Islamic Education*, (London: The Muslim Educational Trust, 1996) 72–78

Hirsch, E. D. Jr, *Cultural Literacy: What Every American Needs to Know* (New York: Vintage Books, 1988)

Homan, R. and L. King, "Mishmash and its Effects upon Learning in the Primary School", *British Journal of Religious Education*, 15:3 (1993), 8–13

Home Office, *Community Cohesion: Report of the Independent Review Team Chaired by Ted Cantle* (London: Home Office, Community Cohesion Review Team, 2001)

House of Lords Select Committee on Religious Offences, *Report of the Select Committee on Religious Offences in England and Wales*, (London: Her Majesty's Stationery Office, 2003)

Humanist Philosophers Group, *Religious Schools: the Case Against*, (London: British Humanist Association, 2001)

Imran, M., and E. Miskell, *Citizenship and Muslim Perspectives: teachers Sharing Ideas* (Birmingham Development Education Centre, 2003)

IQRA Trust, *Meeting the Needs of Muslim Pupils: advice for teachers and LEAs* (London IQRA Trust, 1991)

Islamic Human Rights Commission, *The Hidden Victims of September 11: the Backlash against Muslims in the UK*, (Wembley: IHRC, 2002)

Islamic Human Rights Commission, *UK Today: the Anti-Muslim Backlash in the Wake of 11th September 2001* (Wembley: IHRC, 2001)

J. Hull, "Mishmash, Religious Education and Pluralism", *British Journal of Religious Education*, 12:3 (1990), 121–125

Jackson, R., "Should the State Fund Faith-Based Schools? A Review of the Arguments", *British Journal of Religious Education*, 25:2 (2003), 89–102

Jacobson, J., "Religion and Ethnic Identity: dual and alternative sources of identity among young British Pakistanis", *Ethnic and Racial Studies*, 20:2 (1997), 238–256

Joly, D., *Britannia's Crescent: making a place for Muslims in British Society*, (Aldershot: Avebury, 1995)

Judge, H., "Faith-based Schools and State Funding: a partial argument", *Oxford Review of Education*, 27:4 (2001), 472–473

Kaul-Seidman, L., J. S. Nielsen and M. Vinzent, *European Identity and Cultural Pluralism: Judaism, Christianity and Islam in European Curricula*. Supplement: Country Reports (Bad Homburg, Germany: Herbert-Quandt-Stiftung, 2003)

Klausen, J., "Is There an Imam Problem?", *Prospect,* May 2004.

Kücükan, T., "Community, Identity and Institutionalisation of Islamic Education: the Case of Ikra Primary School in North London," *British Journal of Religious Education*, 2:1 (1998), 32–43

Kymlicka, W., *Liberalism, Community and Culture,* (Oxford: Clarendon Press, 1989)

L. Sheridan, "Religious Discrimination: the New Racism", in Muslim Council of Britain, *The Quest for Sanity: Reflections on September 11 and the Aftermath* (Wembley: Muslim Council of Britain, 2002)

Learning and Culture Scrutiny Committee, *Faith in our Schools* (first draft), Oxfordshire County Council, 2004.

Learning Skills Council, *Further Education and Work Based Learning for Young People: Learner Numbers in England on 1 November 2003* (Coventry: LSC, 2004)

Lewis, P., *Islamic Britain; Religion, Politics and Identity among British Muslims* (London: I. B. Tauris, 1994)

M. A. Khan-Cheema *et al., The Muslims and "Swann"* (London: The Council of Mosques (UK and Eire), 1986)

Mabud, S. A., "Aims and Objectives of an Integrated Science Curriculum for a Multi-faith, Multicultural Country", *Muslim Education Quarterly,* 9:4 (1992), 14–24

Mabud, S. A., "Editorial: Can Muslim Faith Schools Be Divisive?", *Muslim Education Quarterly,* 19:2 (2002), 1–3

Mabud, S. A., ed. *Essays in Memory of Professor Syed Ali Ashraf* (Cambridge: Islamic Academy) *forthcoming*

Mason, M., "Religion and Schools: a Human Rights-based Approach, *British Journal of Religious Education,* 25:2 (2003), 117–128

McDonough, K. and W. Feinberg, eds., *Citizenship and Education in Liberal-Democratic Societies* (Oxford: Oxford University Press, 2003)

Ministerial Group on Public Order and Community Cohesion, *Building Cohesive Communities, a Report of the Ministerial Group Chaired by John Denham* (London: Home Office, 2001)

Modood, T., R. Berthoud, J. Lakey, P. Smith, S. Virdee, and S. Beishon, *Ethnic Minorities in Britain: Diversity and Disadvantage* (London: Policy Studies Institute, 1997)

Murphy, M., "Household and Family Structure among Ethnic Minority Groups", in *Ethnicity in the 1991 Census,* Vol. I (London: Her Majesty's Stationery Office, 1996)

Muslim Educational Trust, *Issues in Islamic Education* (London: MET 1996)

Nasr, S. H., "The Teaching of Art in the Islamic World", *Muslim Education Quarterly*, 6:2 (1989), 4–10

National Association of Schoolmasters and Union of Women Teachers, *Islamophobia: advice for schools and colleges* (London: NAS/UWT, 2003)

National Union of Teachers, *Response to DfES Consultation 'Aiming High: Raising the Achievement of Ethnic Minority Pupils* (London: NUT, 2003)

National Union of Teachers, *The War in Iraq: the impact on Schools* (London: NUT, 2003)

North, C. W., *Islam in Schools and Madrasahs: a Field Study in Sparkbrook, Sparkhill and Part of Small Heath in Birmingham, 1983-85* (Unpublished master's thesis, University of Birmingham, 1986)

Office for Standards in Education, *Handbook for Inspecting Secondary Schools* (London: OFSTED, 2003)

Office for Standards in Education, *Inspecting Independent Schools: the Framework for Inspecting Independent Schools in England under Section 163 of the Education Act 2002. In use from September 2003* (London: Office of Her Majesty's Chief Inspector of Schools, 2003)

Office for Standards in Education, *Inspection of Bradford Local Education Authority, September 2002* (London: OFSTED/Audit Commission, 2002)

Oldham Independent Review Panel, *Oldham Independent Review Panel Report: One Oldham, One Future, under the chairmanship of David Ritchie,* (Oldham: Oldham Borough Council, 2001)

Open Society Institute, *Minority Protection in the EU: The Situation of Muslims in the UK* (Budapest: EUMAP, Open Society Institute, 2002)

Owen, D., A. Green, J. Pitcher and M. Maguire, *Minority Ethnic Participation and Achievements in Education, Training and the Labour Market* (London: Her Majesty's Stationery Office, 2000)

Parekh, B., *Rethinking Multiculturalism: Cultural Diversity and Political Theory* (Basingstoke: Macmillan, 2000)

Parker-Jenkins, M., *Children of Islam* (Stoke-on-Trent: Trentham, 1995)

Penn, R. and P. Lambert, "Attitudes towards Ideal Family Size of Different Ethnic/Nationality Groups in Great Britain, France and Germany", *Population Trends*, 108:3 (2002), 49–58

Purdam, K., and P. G. Weller, eds., *Religious Discrimination in England and Wales: an interim report* (London: University of Derby/Home Office, 2000)

Pye, D., B. Lee, and S. Bhabra, *Disaffection amongst Muslim Pupils. Exclusion and Truancy,* (London: IQRA Trust, 2000)

RAISE Project, *The Achievement of British Pakistani Learners: work in progress* (Stoke-on-Trent: Trentham Books, 2004)

Redbridge Standing Advisory Council on Religious Education, *Muslim Madrasahs in Redbridge*, Briefing Paper 4 (London: Borough of Redbridge, 2003)

Ross A., *Ethnic Minority Teachers in the Teaching Workforce*, IPSE Occasional Paper, (London: IPSE, 2001)

Runnymede Trust, *Addressing Prejudice and Islamophobia* (London: Runnymede Trust, 2001)

Runnymede Trust, *Briefing Paper for GTC Teacher Meeting on Black and Minority Ethnic Issues in Teaching and Learning* (London: Runnymede Trust, 2003)

Runnymede Trust, *Islamophobia: its Features and Dangers* (London: Runnymede Trust, 1997)

Runnymede Trust, *The Future of Multi-Ethnic Britain: Report of the Commission on the Future of Multi-Ethnic Britain, under the Chairmanship of Bhikhu Parekh* (London: Profile Books, 2000)

Sahgal, G., and N. Yuval-Davis, eds. *Refusing Holy Orders: Women and Fundamentalism in Britain* (London: Virago, 1992)

Sarwar, G., *British Muslims and Schools*, (London: Muslim Educational Trust, 1991)

Sarwar, G., *Sex Education: the Muslim Perspective* (London: Muslim Educational Trust, 1992)

Sasano, Y., *The Creation of British Muslim Identity in the Islamic Schools of London*, Unpublished MPhil thesis (Hitotsubashi University, Japan, 2003)

Scott, A., D. Pearce, and P. Goldblatt, "The Sizes and Characteristics of Ethnic Populations of Great Britain", *Population Trends*, 105:4 (2001), 6–15

Shaikh, S., and A. Kelly, "To Mix or Not to Mix: Pakistani Girls in British Schools", *Educational Research*, 31 (1989) 10–19

Shiner, M. and T. Modood, "Help or Hindrance? Higher Education and the Route to Ethnic Equality", *British Journal of Sociology of Education*, 23:2 (2002), 209–232

Tulasiewicz W., and C-Y. To, eds., *World Religions and Educational Practice*, (London: Cassell, 1993)

Underkuffler, L. S., "Public Funding for Religious Schools: difficulties and dangers in a pluralistic society", *Oxford Review of Education*, 27:4 (2001), 577–592

University of Plymouth, *Widening Participation Initiative in Initial Teacher Education* (Plymouth: University of Plymouth, Faculty of Education, 2003)

Weston, R. S., "Food for Thought: Four Issues Confronting a School Governor in a Multicultural Area", *Viewpoints*, 8 (Spring 2001)

British Muslims
and the Labour Market

Table of Contents

List of Acronyms

ACAS	Advisory, Conciliation and Arbitration Service
BAA	British Airports Authority
BT	British Telecom
CIPD	Chartered Institute of Personnel Development
DfES	Department for Education and Skills
DMAG	Data Management and Analysis Group (of the GLA)
DTI	Department for Trade and Industry
DWP	Department for Work and Pensions
EMBS	Ethnic Minority Business Service (Bolton)
EMED	Ethnic Minority Employment Division (of the DWP)
EMES	Ethnic Minority Enterprise Centre (Glasgow)
GLA	Greater London Authority
GSCE	General Certificate of Secondary Education
LFS	Labour Force Survey
LSP	Local Strategic Partnership
ONS	Office for National Statistics
PSA	Public Service Agreement

1. EXECUTIVE SUMMARY

Muslims currently constitute three per cent of the UK population.[1] Census statistics show that Muslims, as a whole, are by far the most disadvantaged faith group in the UK labour market. Muslims are three times more likely to be unemployed than the majority Christian group.[2] They have the lowest employment rate of any group, at 38 per cent, and the highest economic inactivity rate, at 52 per cent.[3]

At 17 per cent, Muslims represent the largest faith group who have never worked or are long-term unemployed, as compared to three per cent of the overall population.[4] Over half of Muslims are economically inactive, compared to a third of all other faith groups.[5] At 68 per cent, Muslim women have the highest level of economic inactivity amongst all faith groups.[6]

Between 1999 and 2009, Pakistanis and Bangladeshis, who are predominately Muslim and who make up almost 60 per cent of the UK Muslim population, will account for 15 per cent of the growth in the working-age population.[7] The challenge for Government, employers, and Muslims themselves, is to tackle the barriers Muslims currently face to ensure that they are integrated into the mainstream labour market.

There are variations in the labour market achievements within the Muslim group. For example, Indian Muslims, who make up nine per cent of the British Muslim population, are on average doing well in schools and in the labour market. However, they are doing less well when compared to Indian Hindus. Pakistanis and Bangladeshis experience significantly higher unemployment, economic inactivity and lower earnings than most other ethnic groups. They disproportionately live in the most disadvantaged wards of the UK and suffer disproportionately from geographic deprivation. Those

---

[1] The UK 2001 National Census, (hereafter, UK 2001 National Census) available at http://www.statistics.gov.uk/census2001/ (accessed on 12 July 2004).

[2] See Figure 2.6.

[3] See Figures 2.2 and 2.6.

[4] Ethnic Minorities Employment Division (EMED), Department for Work and Pensions (DWP).

[5] See Figure 2.6.

[6] See Figure 2.6.

[7] D. Owen and A. Green, *Minority Ethnic Participation and Achievements in Education, Training and the Labour Market,* Centre for Research in Ethnic Relations and Institute for Employment Research, University of Warwick, 2000, pp. 16–17. Over 90 per cent of British Pakistanis and Bangladeshis are Muslim. UK 2001 National Census.

who are in employment are disproportionately represented in a narrow range of low-pay industries and self-employment.[8]

The extent to which religion is a driver for labour market outcomes is not yet known.

This is a significant knowledge gap regarding the situation of Muslims and further analysis is needed to improve understanding of the British Muslim group as a whole. Data by ethnicity is used in this report to highlight the experiences of the Pakistani and Bangladeshi groups as a proxy for the broader group of British Muslims.

Economic inactivity has impacts beyond the individual person who is not in work and can have longer term effects on their partners and families. This can result in long term and generational economic and social disadvantage. In London, where over 40 per cent of the UK's Muslim population live, Pakistanis and Bangladeshis have the highest level of children in workless households, at 30-40 per cent, compared to 20 per cent of their White counterparts.[9]

Muslims represent a very high proportion of the younger age cohort. 90 per cent of Muslims are aged under 50. The average age of Muslims is 28, 13 years below the national average. Official reports into the Bradford, Oldham and Burnley disturbances identified failure in policy and service delivery to meet the needs of young Muslims.[10] Failing to meet the employment aspirations and needs of young Muslims will not only have economic costs but also create potential strains on social cohesion.

The reasons for the level of multiple disadvantage Muslims face are complex, ranging from gaps in mainstream labour market policy and employer practices, poor service delivery and a lack of faith-friendly work environments. Policy must reflect this complexity and aim to integrate Muslim men and women into the mainstream labour market, through local and national, public and private sector initiatives. It should also acknowledge that the faith dimension is an important factor in effectively targeting the most disadvantaged group in the labour market.

Due to the demographic change in the Muslim working-age population, the Government and employers must recognise and respond proactively to the level of disadvantage Muslims face. Policy must aim to integrate Muslims, men and women, into the mainstream labour market, through local and national, public and private sector initiatives.

---

[8] See: Cabinet Office, *Ethnic Minorities and the Labour Market*, London, Cabinet Office Strategy Unit, 2003, (hereafter, *Strategy Unit Report*).

[9] Ethnic Minorities Employment Division, Department for Work and Pensions.

[10] See: Home Office, *Community Cohesion: The Report of the Independent Review Team chaired by Ted Cantle*, London, Home Office, Community Cohesion Review Team, 2001, (hereafter, *The Cantle Report*).

Through changes in labour market policy, it is possible to achieve successful integration, retention and progression. Specific policy measures could fall into three categories:

- First, policies addressing the socio-economic disadvantage of Muslim communities, which recognise that faith can be important for effective delivery to Muslims.

- Second, understanding how existing and changing social and cultural norms impact on the labour market engagement of Muslims.

- Third, tackling the prejudice, stereotypes and disadvantage that arise from a lack of awareness and understanding about Muslims.

There should also be a Government commitment that has one clear aim: to integrate Muslims into the mainstream labour market. Policy-makers need to develop an inclusive and integrated strategy for Muslims, to support their labour market entry and progression and help overcome any barriers they face. This strategy should begin by focusing on geographic disadvantage, a focus that will help alleviate many of the current employment problems faced disproportionately by Muslims in deprived areas. Thereafter, more specific policy measures are needed to address barriers faced by Muslim women and young Muslims.

The benefits of improved labour market integration for Muslims are not just financial. Mainstream labour market integration will ensure long-term economic and social integration for current and future generations of British Muslims, for the benefit of Muslims, the economy and wider society.

2. INTRODUCTION

The UK 2001 National Census (hereafter, 2001 Census) statistics show that British Muslims, as a whole, are by far the most disadvantaged faith group.[11] Their unemployment rates are three times the national average and twice that of any other minority faith group. They have the lowest employment rate of any group at 38 per cent and the highest economic inactivity rate at 52 per cent.[12] British Muslims represent, proportionately, the youngest age cohort in the UK. The average age of Muslims is 28, 13 years below the national average.[13] Making the best use of their skills will be a challenge for Government and employers, as well as for Muslims themselves. Evidence from the past two decades suggests that the continued economic growth alone will not tackle the labour market disadvantage faced by most Muslims. If no intervention is made, their position will at least stay the same if not worsen, thereby further reinforcing social exclusion.

A central obstacle in the examination of the labour market position and experience of British Muslims is the lack of data collected on the basis of religion. The 2001 Census for the first time asked a question on religion. Statistics disaggregated by faith communities from the census are beginning to emerge. In this report, data from the 2001 Census is used to provide employment information of the British Muslim group as a whole. As the British Muslim population is comprised of different ethnic minority groups, data by ethnicity has also been used in this report, courtesy of the Ethnic Minority Employment Division (EMED).

The extent to which religion is a driver for labour market outcomes is not yet known. This is a significant knowledge gap and further analysis is needed to improve understanding of the British Muslim group as a whole. Data by ethnicity is used in this report to highlight the experiences of the Pakistani and Bangladeshi groups, which constitute 60 per cent of the British Muslim population.[14] While it is recognised that not all Pakistanis and Bangladeshis in the UK are Muslim, statistics available for Pakistani and Bangladeshi communities are used as a proxy, to highlight the position of this significant section of British Muslims. This, of course, will leave unexamined the experiences of the remaining 40 per cent of British Muslim communities, including Arab, Afghan, Indian, Iranian, Kosovar, Kurdish, North African, Somali and Turkish Muslims.

---

[11] UK 2001 National Census. Census statistics in the tables in this report were provided by EMED. EMED is a research, anaysis and policy unit in the DWP. Labour market statistics refer to persons in the working age population.

[12] See Figure 2.2 and 2.6.

[13] UK 2001 National Census.

[14] Over 90 per cent of Pakistanis and Bangladeshis in the UK are Muslims. UK 2001 National Census.

This chapter builds on the steps and policy approach taken by the Strategy Unit report, *Ethnic Minorities and the Labour Market* (hereafter, *Strategy Unit Report*).[15] This report emphasised the differing levels of achievement in the labour market across and within all minority ethnic groups, with Indian and Chinese people out-performing White people in some categories. However, it put forward policy recommendations for ethnic minority groups as a whole, with no specific recommendations for individual ethnic groups. Whilst the recommendations are focused interventions, and should produce positive change, targeted emphasis and interventions in employment policy for the most disadvantaged individual ethnic groups have yet to occur.

Policies are not yet targeted by individual faith group. Using the current ethnic categories, targeting by specific ethnic groups allows policy to reach Pakistanis and Bangladeshis, but does not extend to Muslims from other minority ethnic communities. This reach could be achieved by further fine graining of ethnic minority categories, to also cover Afghan, Arab, Iranian, Kosovar, Kurdish, Somali and Turkish Muslims. However, policy must also target Muslims as a whole. While Muslims are not one homogenous cultural or ethnic group, barriers to the labour market which affect Muslims specifically, often affect most Muslims alike. This report suggests that the acknowledgement of the faith dimension is an important factor that should be added to the policy-making process, when appropriate, to ensure the effective delivery of services.

Section three begins by outlining the context of ethnic minority participation in the labour market. It then looks at Muslims in the labour market, their geographical distribution, age profiles and labour market attainment. It compares the labour market position of Muslims with other faith groups and the position of Pakistanis and Bangladeshis with other ethnic groups.

Section four identifies some of the barriers that are faced in entering and progressing in the labour market. These include barriers arising from area deprivation, low educational attainment, childhood poverty and existing engagement in the labour market. The section looks at the impact of an "ethnic penalty" and poses the question of whether there is a "Muslim penalty".

Section five begins by outlining some of the current policy measures that are being taken by Government to address ethnic minority labour market disadvantage. The chapter looks at examples of best practice that aim to tackle labour market disadvantage at three levels. First, improving delivery of policy across Government and at the local level to reach Muslims. Second, improving engagement with, and access to, the labour

---

[15] *Strategy Unit Report.* In 2000, the Prime Minister's Strategy Unit was asked to look into the labour market achievements of ethnic minorities and to recommend action to tackle the barriers they face. The Strategy Unit published its final report in 2003. The Government accepted all its conclusions and committed to implement its policy recommendations.

market. This requires developing aspirations, soft skills and basic skills, and improving qualifications. Third, supporting entry to, and progression within, the labour market. This requires a coordinated approach to assisting people in obtaining work, positive action measures to ensure labour market entry and career support, and in-work support to ensure progress through the labour market.

The objective of this report is to highlight the clear gaps in current policy. Policies designed to improve employment levels for all ethnic minorities, many of whom are already known to be disadvantaged in the labour market, miss the fundamental dimension of faith identity. Tackling the inactivity and unemployment of Muslims requires a new focus to address the scale of multiple disadvantage affecting this group. The different characteristics and profiles within this group, such as young people and women, require targeted policy interventions that meet the needs of Muslim communities.

There is a fundamental need for political commitment at the highest level and a coherent, cross-Government strategy to tackle the disproportionate level of disadvantage faced by British Muslims in the labour market. This requires a policy commitment to integrating Muslims into the mainstream labour market. Central to this will be policies to address the disadvantage faced by Muslims as a result of living in the most deprived wards in the UK. This can lead to high levels of inactivity which affect Muslims and non-Muslims alike in those wards.

Specific policy measures should be adopted to tackle the barriers that result in high levels of inactivity and unemployment of Muslims. In addition, policy must ensure workplaces are sensitive to the needs of faith groups, to encourage Muslims to apply for all employment opportunities and to help them retain and progress within those positions. The benefits of improved labour market outcomes through economic integration for Muslims are not just financial. Economic integration will ensure long-term social and civic integration for future generations of British Muslims.

3. CONTEXT AND BACKGROUND

3.1 Ethnic Minorities and the Labour Market

There are wide variations in the labour market achievements of different ethnic minority groups in the UK. However, all ethnic minorities appear to be disadvantaged in the labour market on a broad range of measures of achievement, including employment and unemployment rates, levels of self-employment and progression in employment.[16] Nonetheless, there are significant differences between and within ethnic groups. Most notably, the Indian and Chinese ethnic groups out-perform their White majority counterparts on many of these measures. However, they are still not doing as well as they should be, given their education and other characteristics relevant to labour market attainment.[17]

The UK, in 2003, had the highest employment rate and the lowest unemployment rate of the major industrialised countries. Since 1997, the Government has set out to provide help and support, to move those who can work from welfare into work and to achieve the goal of full employment in every region of the UK. The total employment level is currently at a record high, having risen by nearly 1.7 million since 1997, and claimant count unemployment has fallen by more than 700,000 since 1997.[18]

The Government acknowledges, however, that there are areas where more progress is needed to tackle the challenges faced by some ethnic minority groups, people with no qualifications and other groups amongst whom economic inactivity is high, such as people living in big cities and those living in rented accommodation.[19] Employment rates amongst all ethnic minority groups are lower than those of the majority White population.[20] Despite economic growth over the past 15 years, the overall employment rate gap between ethnic minorities and White people has remained at around 16 percentage points.[21] The Department for Work and Pension (DWP) and the Department for Trade and Industry (DTI) share a Public Service Agreement (PSA) target to increase the employment rates of people from ethnic minority backgrounds and significantly reduce the difference between their employment rates and the overall employment rates by 2006.[22]

---

[16] See Appendix 1.

[17] *Strategy Unit Report*, p. 4.

[18] HM Treasury, *Full Employment in Every Region*, London, 2003, pp. 33–35, (hereafter, *Full Employment in Every Region*)

[19] *Full Employment in Every Region*, pp. 33–35.

[20] *Strategy Unit Report*, p. 5.

[21] *Full Employment in Every Region*, London, pp. 33–35.

[22] *Full Employment in Every Region*, London, pp. 33–35.

The *Strategy Unit report* detailed how the extent and nature of labour market disadvantage differed significantly by ethnic group, with some groups being more disproportionately disadvantaged than others. Across almost all indicators, Pakistanis, Bangladeshis, and African Caribbeans were found to be disproportionately disadvantaged. Within ethnic groups, labour market performance was found to vary considerably according to factors such as gender, generation and geography.

According to the *Strategy Unit report*, there is no single cause for the level of labour market disadvantage faced by ethnic minorities. Social class, culture and family patterns all play a part. Educational underachievement is both a symptom of these factors and an important causal factor. Given the numerous factors involved, the *Strategy Unit report* recommended intervention in areas with cross-departmental policy responsibilities. Policy measures therefore fell into four categories:

- improving the employability of ethnic minorities, by raising levels of educational attainment and skills;

- improving the connection of ethnic minorities to work, by reforming existing employment programmes and tackling specific barriers to work;

- promoting equal opportunities in the workplace; and

- improving delivery, through creating a cross-departmental task force to carry forward this cross-departmental responsibility.[23]

The *Strategy Unit report* looked at the area of ethnic minority labour market disadvantage, but did not disaggregate by individual ethnic groups and create targeted policy initiatives accordingly. Similarly, the use of census categories such as Black African, does not allow policy to tease out the differences in the experiences, for example, of Somalis, Nigerians or Zimbabweans. Ethnic categories at present do not account for Afghan, Arab, Iranian, Kosovar, Kurdish, North African, Somali and Turkish communities. Therefore, current ethnic minority categories will not help identify disadvantage in the labour market faced by different faith groups, including Muslims.

3.2   Muslims and the Labour Market

This section outlines the context of Muslim participation in the labour market, their geographical distribution, age profiles, and labour market attainment. It compares the position of Muslims with other faith and ethnic groups.

---

[23] *Strategy Unit Report*, pp. 7–9.

Geographic settlement patterns

The current picture of geographic settlement across the UK continues to reflect "on-entry" settlement patterns of clustering in the UK's major cities and conurbations by ethnic minorities.[24]

As shown in Figure 2.1, over 80 per cent of Muslims live in the five major conurbations of Great Britain, compared to 50 per cent of the general population. The conurbations are Greater London, West Midlands, West Yorkshire, Greater Manchester and East Midlands. While such clustering reflects little population drift outside of the original settlement areas, it is uncertain if this is through religious or cultural preference or limited access and affordability of alternative housing. Similar conurbation settlement patterns are also found with the Hindu and Sikh communities. However, as highlighted later in this report, theses two groups do not suffer the same level of employment disadvantage as Muslims. Hindu and Sikh communities may be clustering in more affluent parts of these conurbations, resulting in this variation in employment.

Approximately 40 per cent of Muslims live in Greater London (607,000 people).[25] Muslims represent the second largest faith community in London and make up 8.5 per cent of its population. They are concentrated in a small number of London boroughs. A quarter of London's Muslims live in Tower Hamlets and Newham, where the average household non-employment rate is approximately 30 per cent. In comparison, approximately, 53 per cent of Hindus live in London, (292,000 people).[26] One third of London's Hindus live in Brent, Barnet, Ealing and ·Harrow, where the average household non-employment rate is approximately 15 per cent.[27]

Research shows that, while people from ethnic minority groups are more likely to live in cities, this is particularly true for those groups that have difficulty in finding employment, such as those with little or no English; recent migrants; and those with a tradition of non-participation in the labour market. The concentration of such groups in particular wards, and their unemployment or inactivity there, suggests a skills mismatch in their area of residence. The areas with the lowest ethnic minority employment rates (Glasgow, Tower

---

[24] A. Power, *Barriers to Social Housing for Asians*, Bradford, Bradford City Council, June 2001. See also: D. Owen and P. Ratcliffe, "Estimating local change in the population of minority ethnic groups, 1981–1991", Working Paper No. 1, in *Changing spatial location patterns of ethnic minorities in Great Britain*, 1981–1991, Coventry, Centre for Research in Ethnic Relations, 1996.

[25] E. Howes, *2001 Census Key Statistics: Ethnicity, religion and country of birth*, London, Greater London Authority, October 2003, p. 31, (hereafter, Howes, *Census Key Statistics*)

[26] Howes, *Census Key Statistics*, p. 30.

[27] See: Howes, *Census Key Statistics*, p. 32; and D. Gaffney and B. Armstrong, *Workless household with dependent children in London: Output area maps from the 2001 Census*, London, Greater London Authority, p. 12.

Hamlets, Oldham, Bradford and Blackburn & Darwen) are also the areas where the largest minority ethnic groups are Pakistanis and Bangladeshis.[28]

Figure 2.1 Geographic distribution by religion

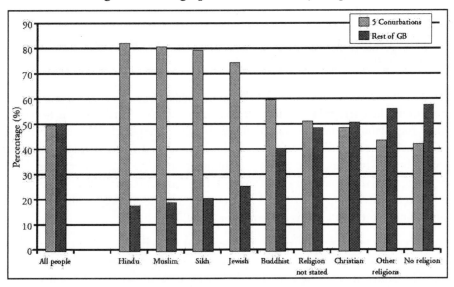

Source: Ethnic Minority Employment Division, Department for Work and Pensions, 2004

Age profile

The age structure of all ethnic minority groups is relatively young. The average age of Muslims in the UK is 28, 13 years younger than the national average. Eighty-nine per cent of Muslims are under 50.[29] Over one third of Pakistanis and Bangladeshis are aged under 16, the youngest age cohort in the UK. This youthful age profile, combined with the highest birth rates amongst all groups, not only means that half the growth in the working-age population between 1999–2009 will come from ethnic minorities, but more specifically, nearly one third of that growth will come from the Pakistani and Bangladeshi

---

[28] HM Treasury, *Full Employment in Every Region*, London, HMT, 2003, pp. 33–35.

[29] UK 2001 National Census.

groups.[30] Therefore, between 1999–2009 approximately 15 per cent of the growth in the UK working-age population will come from British Muslims.

This fundamental shift in the religious demographic profile of the current and future working-age population of the UK has major implications for employment and integration policies and practices. Policy will need to make positive changes in the light of this demographic shift if the UK is to benefit economically and socially through integrating Muslims into the mainstream labour market.

Employment, unemployment and economic inactivity rates

To determine the current labour market position of British Muslims, it is necessary to compare their labour market attainment levels with other faith groups. This can be measured using a range of indicators, including employment and unemployment rates, economic inactivity rates, occupational attainment, and income and earnings levels.[31] Data disaggregated by faith on the level of full-time and part-time working hours would have further helped to detail the current labour market position of British Muslims, but unfortunately this data was not available.

The 2001 census, for the first time, collected data on religion and therefore allows a comparison to be made between the positions of different faith groups. There are 967,000 Muslims of working age. The following data shows that Muslims have the lowest labour market achievements when compared to other faith groups:

- Muslims have an employment rate of 38 per cent, the lowest of all faith groups and almost half that of the Christian group.[32]

- At 15 per cent, the unemployment rate for Muslims is the highest of all faith groups and is approximately three times that of Christians and Hindus.[33]

---

[30] D. Owen and A. Green, *Minority Ethnic Participation and Achievements in Education, Training and the Labour Market*, Centre for Research in Ethnic Relations and Institute for Employment Research, University of Warwick, 2000, pp. 16–17, esp. Table 2.7. Between 1999 and 2009, the working age population in the UK is projected to increase by 963,500 people (a growth of 2.7 per cent); while that of UK minority ethnic groups is expected to increase by 507,700 people (to 2,880,400), equivalent to 52 per cent of the total projected increase. At the same time, the working age population of UK Pakistanis and Bangladeshis is expected to increase by 146,200 people (to 628,100); equivalent to 15 per cent of the total increase in the working-age population, or 28 per cent of that for UK Minority ethnic groups.

[31] See Appendix 1.

[32] See Figure 2.2.

[33] See Figure 2.6.

- Over 50 per cent of all Muslims are economically inactive, as compared to one-third of Christians, Hindus, Jews and Sikhs.[34]

- Muslim women have the highest economic inactivity rate of all faith groups. Sixty-eight per cent of Muslim women are economically inactive, compared to 28 per cent of Christian women and about 35 per cent of Hindu and Sikh women.[35]

- Of young people aged 16-24, Muslims have the highest unemployment rate of all faith groups. Some 17.5 per cent of Muslims in this age category are unemployed, as compared to 7.9 per cent of Christians and 7.4 per cent of Hindus.[36]

As data disaggregated by faith has previously not been available, to begin to explain this multifaceted level of labour market disadvantage of Muslims requires looking at ethnic categories. As 60 per cent of Muslims are from the Pakistani and Bangladeshi ethnic minority groups, data for these groups will be used to examine the disadvantage faced by Muslims.

Over the past 15 years, the gap in economic activity rates between ethnic minorities and the White majority has remained consistently at around 17 percentage points, even though within this period the UK economy experienced economic growth.[37] The benefits of economic growth in the mid-1990s were not shared across all minority ethnic groups. Employment and unemployment differentials narrowed for some ethnic minority groups, such as Indians, relative to their White counterparts. However, no significant improvement in employment prospects could be observed for Bangladeshi and African Caribbean men. Their employment rate hardly rose at all, at any stage in the recovery.[38]

Amongst those who are economically inactive are persons who have "other" responsibilities, such as looking after the home or full time education. One third of all economically inactive people are inactive because they are looking after family or the home.[39] In all, 37 per cent of economically inactive Muslims fall into this category. Fifty-two per cent of economically inactive Muslim women are looking after the home. Some 45 per cent of economically inactive Muslim men are students.[40]

---

[34] See Figure 2.6.

[35] See Figure 2.3.

[36] Figures provided by EMED, DWP, 2004.

[37] See Figure 2.7.

[38] J. Wadsworth, "The Labour Market Performance of Ethnic Minorities in the Recovery", in R. Dickins, P. Gregg and J. Wadsworth (eds.), *The Labour Market Under New Labour: the State of Working Britain II,* London, Centre for Economic Performance, 2003.

[39] Figures provided by EMED, DWP, 2004.

[40] Figures provided by EMED, DWP, 2004.

In a recent study, one sixth of British adults aged 17-59 were found not to have either a job or a working partner. Those at high risk of economic inactivity were people with low qualifications and skills, those living in areas of weak labour market demand, and certain ethnic minority groups. Pakistanis and Bangladeshis have been described as being "seriously at risk of non-employment compared to White people".[41] The *Strategy Unit report* also found that Pakistanis and Bangladeshis (together with Black Caribbeans) face the greatest labour market disadvantage across all ethnic groups.[42]

These statistics also show that Muslims as a faith group face disadvantage in the labour market. While much of this can be explained by education and disadvantage in relation to geography and deprivation, what is uncertain is to what extent religion and cultural preference can explain it. What is clear is that Pakistanis and Bangladeshis as ethnic groups, and Muslims as a faith group, are the furthest away from full integration in the labour market.

Figure 2.2 Employment rates by religion

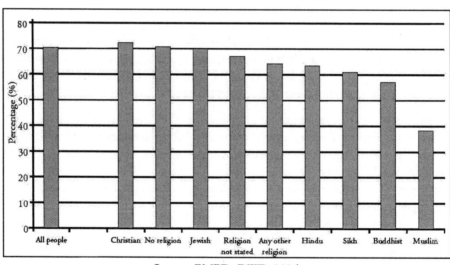

Source: EMED, DWP, 2004

---

[41] R. Berthoud, *Multiple Disadvantages in Employment*, Joseph Rowntree Foundation, 2002.

[42] *Strategy Unit Report*, p. 4.

Figure 2.3 Economic inactivity rates of women, by religion

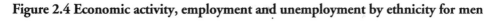

Source: EMED, DWP, 2004

Figure 2.4 Economic activity, employment and unemployment by ethnicity for men

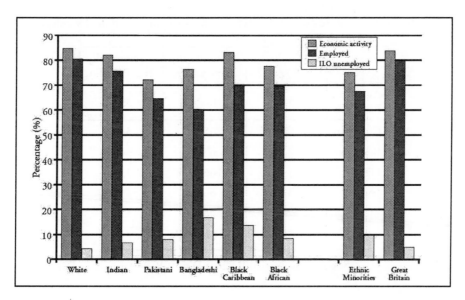

Source: Labour Force Survey (hereafter, LFS), Autumn, EMED, DWP, 2003

2.5 Economic activity, employment and unemployment by ethnicity for women

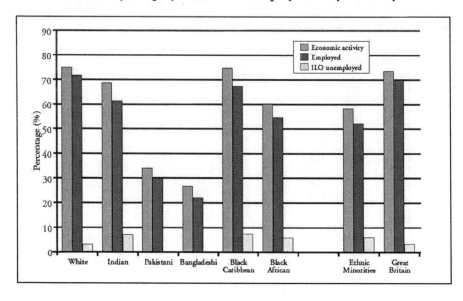

Source: LFS, Autumn, EMED, DWP, 2003

Figure 2.6 Economic activity, inactivity and unemployment by religion

	Unemployed (%)	Economically Active (%)	Economically Inactive (%)
ALL PEOPLE	5.0	66.5	33.5
Christian	4.3	65.5	34.5
Buddhist	7.9	63.0	37.0
Hindu	5.4	66.9	33.1
Jewish	3.8	66.1	33.9
Muslim	14.6	48.3	51.7
Sikh	6.9	66.2	33.8

Source: Census 2001, EMED, DWP, 2003

Figure 2.7 Economic activity by ethnic group

	Economically Active (%)
White	76
Indian	68
Pakistani	44
Bangladeshi	38
Black Caribbean	65
Black African	56
All Ethnic Minorities	58
Great Britain	75

Source: LFS, EMED, DWP, 2003

Muslim women

The economic inactivity rate of Muslim women is almost double that of other faith groups. Figures disaggregated by gender show 68 per cent of Muslim women are economically inactive, as compared to less than 30 per cent for Christian women and approximately 35 per cent of Hindu and Sikh women.[43]

Statistics for Pakistani and Bangladeshi women have shown that they have the lowest employment rates compared to other ethnic groups. A study comparing the labour market experiences of ethnic minority women with majority White women found that the experiences of Indian women were very similar to those of White women and that the experiences of Pakistani and Bangladeshi women were the furthest away from those of White women. The gap in the employment levels of Pakistani and Bangladeshi women compared to White women is 48 per cent.[44] Over the period 1992–2003, there was an increase in the proportion of White women working full time, as well as in the number of most ethnic minority women working full time. Among ethnic minority groups, Black Caribbean women aged 19-59 had the highest levels of full-time working, at 45 per cent (in 2000-02), while Pakistani and Bangladeshi women had the lowest, at 14 per cent and nine per cent respectively (in 2000-02). Even when comparing part-time work activity, White women had a much higher level of part-time

---

[43] See Figure 2.3.

[44] A. Dale, *Ethnic Differences in Women's Employment: The Changing Role of Qualifications,* unpublished, p. 20, (hereafter, Dale, *Ethnic Differences in Women's Employment*).

working aged 19-59, at 28 per cent. Pakistani and Bangladeshi women again had the lowest levels, at 12 per cent and six per cent respectively.[45]

There are also differentials in labour market outcomes of Pakistani and Bangladeshi women within the same generation. Recent research into patterns of education and employment for different ethnic groups found qualifications are playing an increasingly important role in explaining the employment levels of women from ethnic minority groups. Evidence suggests there is increasing polarisation between women with a degree, as compared to those without a degree, for all ethnic groups. This polarisation is especially large for Pakistani and Bangladeshi women. Those Pakistani and Bangladeshi women who had obtained a degree had more positive employment outcomes. However, not all Pakistani and Bangladeshi women with graduate qualifications entered employment. Pakistani and Bangladeshi women without a degree had the greatest negative outcomes to employment.[46] Greater understanding of the barriers that Muslim women may face in entering higher education or employment is needed.

A study of the experiences of South Asian women found virtually all women across religious, ethnic, employment and age divides agreed that employment and educational opportunities should be available for all women if they want to pursue these avenues. Second-generation Muslim women were found to identify preference to have careers, not just jobs, on the basis of social acceptability on the grounds of religion.[47] Those who had difficulty in language fluency, or in managing caring responsibilities, or who encountered resistance within their own families found it difficult to gain or sustain employment.[48]

There is a need for policy to encourage Muslim women into the mainstream labour market. Targeted policy is not only needed here to foster gender equality, which is highly necessary in itself, but is also due to the level of unemployment and inactivity for Muslims as a group. Encouraging dual income households, in a culturally sensitive way, would be one way of tackling severe economic inactivity and disadvantage.

The level of economic disadvantage Muslims face requires policy to encourage and support dual income households. Policy should ensure that there are measures in place to support not only the female partners of Muslim men who already have employment, but also those women whose male partners are not currently employed, through

---

[45] J. Lindley and A. Dale, "Ethnic Differences in Women's Demographic, Family Characteristics and Economic Activity Profiles 1992 to 2002", in *Labour Market Trends*, April 2004, p. 160.

[46] Dale, *Ethnic Differences in Women's Employment*, p. 20.

[47] F. Ahmad, T. Modood, S. Lissenburgh, *South Asian Women and Employment in Britain: Interaction of Gender and Ethnicity*, London, Policy Studies Institute, 2003, pp. 21–23, (hereafter, Ahmad et al, *South Asian Women and Employment in Britain*).

[48] Ahmad et al, *South Asian Women and Employment in Britain*, pp. 21–29.

assisting both in entering the labour market. Facilitating female labour market entry could be of financial and social benefit to the family unit as a whole. Their entry into the mainstream labour market may encourage and support the entry of future generations into the mainstream labour market.

Women from all ethnic minority groups are currently under-represented in the self-employed sector.[49] There may be cultural preferences which may restrict employment by some Muslim women into the mainstream labour market.[50] Other possible barriers, examined later in this report, include lack of soft skills, lack of training, and childcare responsibilities. If this is the case, other opportunities to become economically integrated through other forms of employment should be explored, such as self-employment and home working.

Muslim youth disengagement and social exclusion

There are 281,000 Muslims aged between 16-24. Seventeen per cent of Muslims in this group are unemployed. This is the highest unemployment rate of all faith groups aged 16-24. Pakistanis and Bangladeshis represent high numbers in the younger age cohort. They also represent a disproportionate number of young people who are not in "education, training or employment". While it is in part characteristic of young people not to engage in mainstream provision, it is a matter of concern when they are excluded from such provision in disproportionate numbers.

The "disturbances" in Bradford, Oldham and Burnley in summer 2001 were a clear indication of Pakistani and Bangladeshi youth unrest. While the nature of these violent outbursts was complex, a high level of non-engagement in education, training and employment was cited as a key concern for this group. The Cantle report recommended greater tailoring of services to meet the needs of this group.[51]

Glasgow offers an example of an attempt to provide a more tailored service to ethnic minorities. Glasgow City Council has employed two "Ethnic Minority Youth Development Workers" to liaise with this group and encourage them to enter education, training or employment. However, there is still a growing number of young Pakistani Muslim men, some of whom are recent graduates, who are not engaging in mainstream employment services. One possible reason for this may be the geographic clustering of Pakistanis and Bangladeshis in areas of the city that are not adequately

---

[49] *Strategy Unit Report,* p. 24.

[50] See: C. Brown, *Black and White Britain,* London, Policy Studies Institute, 1984; I. Bruegel, "Sex and Race in the Labour Market", in *Feminist Review,* p. 32; T. Jones, *Britain's Ethnic Minorities,* London, Policy Studies Institute, 1993; and Ahmad et al, *South Asian Women and Employment in Britain.*

[51] *The Cantle Report,* 2001, p. 11.

reached by this service. To deliver this service more effectively, there needs to be a better understanding of the barriers this group faces in accessing such tailored employment services.

Due to the growing number of young Muslims about to enter the working-age population, the challenge for government is to secure an integrated mainstream labour market by engaging this group, through mainstream service delivery, to help them realise their own potential in an increasingly ethnically and religiously diverse labour market.

While the UK has not seen further disturbances since 2001, anecdotal evidence suggests that young Pakistanis and Bangladeshis, both male and female, are still excluded from mainstream education and employment. Those who are not in employment may be at greater risk of social exclusion and related problems. For example, anecdotal evidence from local service providers highlights the rising "drug problem" in Tower Hamlets, specifically amongst the young Bangladeshi population, as one of great concern.[52] If local services delivery is not enhanced to tackle this soon, the drug problem may well become intractable.

Self-employment rates

The rate of self-employment is high amongst all Asian ethnic minority groups.[53] It is not known the degree to which this tendency towards entrepreneurialism is a cultural preference or a result of experience, or fear of, discrimination in the paid employment sector. High levels of self-employment should not be taken to indicate labour market success, especially for Pakistanis and Bangladeshis, who have the lowest net pay of all ethnic minority groups. For example, 52 per cent of Bangladeshi male workers are to be found in the restaurant industry (compared with only one per cent of White males), while one in eight Pakistani male workers is a taxi driver.[54] Both sectors involve longer than average hours worked, lower than average financial return and, as a result, there is a potential for long-term exclusion from the mainstream labour market and society. For example, the 2001 Scottish Census found the Pakistani population, the largest ethnic minority group in Scotland, was nearly seven times more likely than White people to work 50 hours a week[55] or more.

It is not known if Muslims chose to enter self-employment after attempts to enter mainstream labour market have failed, nor the degree to which Muslims are trapped in a cycle of low paid self-employment because they face barriers to entering the

---

[52] Representative of NAAFAS, a local advisory organization in Tower Hamlets helping the community deal with and overcome the drug problem. January, 2004.

[53] *Strategy Unit Report,* p. 24.

[54] *Strategy Unit Report,* p. 24.

[55] Scotland 2001 National Census.

mainstream labour market. High levels of self-employment, such as those of Pakistanis and Bangladeshis, should not limit the wider employment opportunities of future generations in this group. There should be no negative assumption that they will "carry on the family business" or are in less need of support and encouragement from teachers and careers advisers to explore other employment aspirations they may have.

Government currently provides support and advice to those seeking to enter or already in self-employment through its Business Links network in the Department for Trade and Industry. Government must ensure support is available equally to all ethnic and faith groups to help facilitate entry into a wider range of sectors.

One barrier for Muslims wishing to establish their own company is that financial support and loans available for business start-ups are not currently Sharia-compliant and therefore may limit Muslims' access and ability to finance self-employment. Recent changes in tax rules from the Treasury on the levying of stamp duty have enabled banks to provide Sharia-compliant mortgages.

4. BARRIERS TO THE LABOUR MARKET

4.1   Direct Barriers

Area deprivation

The Government, in the *Full Employment in Every Region* report, found that geographic location was a significant factor in explaining high levels of unemployment and inactivity.[56] A significant proportion of the disadvantage in the labour market faced by Pakistanis and Bangladeshis is a result of the areas in which they live and the fact that employment opportunities in those areas are limited.

Muslims are disproportionately concentrated in the most deprived local authorities of the UK. Some 57 per cent of Muslims live in the most deprived 20 per cent of local authorities, compared to 28 per cent of the population as a whole.[57]

The employment rates of Muslims vary by region. However, for Pakistanis and Bangladeshis, who are disproportionately concentrated in the most deprived wards of these deprived areas (such as Tower Hamlets and Newham), the level of geographic and employment disadvantage is greater still. A large part of this is due to the fact that current housing settlement patterns reflect "on-entry" settlement, where manufacturing jobs existed.[58] Many of the first generation of Muslim migrants were employed in industries that have since disappeared, with little to replace them for second- and third-generation Muslims.

The Government has put in place several "area-based initiatives" in response to the fact that some geographic areas face disproportionate levels of unemployment and deprivation. To improve labour market outcomes for Muslims, it is important to address the multi-faceted level of deprivation in the areas where they live. The degree to which Muslims are disproportionately disadvantaged by this – and whether current area-based initiatives, and the targets they have established, are sufficient in addressing it – also needs to be assessed. All areas in the UK, at regional and local levels, have Government targets to meet. The degree to which these targets are met in areas of Muslim concentration should be assessed to enable policy-makers to know how effective current targets are in these areas.

Muslims have tried to improve their economic situation even in some of the most deprived areas, mainly through entering self-employment in retail and catering, and starting up small businesses. The degree to which entering this limited range of sectors

---

[56] HM Treasury *Full Employment in Every Region,* London, HM Treasury, 2003, pp. 33–35.

[57] Index of Multiple Deprivation, UK 2000 and 2001 National Census.

[58] *Strategy Unit Report,* p. 17.

in these deprived areas further perpetuates their economic disadvantage is unknown. It is important to understand whether this has created a cycle of disadvantage, in which Muslims themselves become trapped, further adding to the geographic disadvantage.

The Government has recognised that strategies designed to regenerate deprived areas need to connect a number of individual issues.[59] Current levels of unemployment and inactivity suggest that there is a need for greater coordination of national and local institutions to respond to the multiple levels of disadvantage and deliver better services.

Jobcentre Plus, the Government's national employment service, has tried to address the need for better service delivery in deprived areas through operating a separate target structure in the most deprived areas. In these areas the Job Centre Plus provider gains twice as many points per person assisted into employment compared to other areas in the UK, the objective being to create greater incentives in those areas to meet employment targets.[60] However, changing the target structure will not, in itself, necessarily improve service delivery. Addressing the needs of people in these areas, including Muslims, will help enhance service delivery and improve outcomes for people in these areas.

Clustering and concentration in deprived areas is a complex problem. Despite low levels of employment opportunity, Muslims may choose to continue to reside in such deprived areas due to established cultural and religious ties and preferences, such as proximity to the local mosque or Islamic schools and familial and social ties. Any policy attempt to support Muslims moving to neighbouring affluent areas with greater employment opportunities will need to take account of these issues. Positive measures should be explored in this area. For example, planning applications for faith institutions such as mosques, schools and cultural centres or cemeteries could be an opportunity for local authorities to encourage the building of such institutions in more affluent areas, to help movement out of the most deprived areas. However, any such policy intervention will have to be applied with due care to cultural and religious sensitivities.

Education and qualifications

Human capital levels[61] account for much of the difference in labour market outcomes for all groups.[62] Education is an important element of human capital. The proportion of pupils who gain five or more GCSE grades A*-C is much lower amongst Pakistani and

---

[59] *Strategy Unit Report,* p. 86.

[60] See: *Full Employment in Every Region,* London, HM Treasury 2003, pp. 33–35.

[61] Human capital encompasses the sum of skills, knowledge, experience and educational qualification that a person possesses. Definition from the *Strategy Unit Report,* 2003, p. 152.

[62] *Full Employment in Every Region,* pp. 33–35.

Bangladeshi pupils than amongst Indian and White people. White pupils receiving five or more A-C grade GCSEs outnumbered Black pupils by 16 percentage points and Pakistanis and Bangladeshis by over ten percentage points.[63] Forty per cent of British Muslims do not have any GCSE grades A*-C.[64]

A key indicator of pupil attainment is economic disadvantage.[65] Concentration in lower social classes can impact on education attainment. Raising educational attainment of some ethnic minority pupils may be particularly challenging. Pakistanis, for example, are nearly twice as likely as White people to fall under the socio-economic classification of semi-skilled or unskilled.[66] Other causal factors that impact on the attainment of Pakistanis and Bangladeshi pupils include low levels of income, poor parental education, lack of English language fluency, unemployment, low teacher and parental expectations and religious discrimination.[67]

Within the working population, 44 per cent of Bangladeshis and 32 per cent of Pakistanis have no qualifications; for all other groups the figures are between 15 and 20 per cent. At present 20 per cent of White people hold a first degree or equivalent level qualification, compared to 12 per cent of Pakistanis and seven per cent of Bangladeshis.[68] Research into the participation of ethnic minority students in undergraduate study found that Pakistanis and Bangladeshis are under-represented when compared to their numbers among 16-24 year-olds.[69]

Labour market experiences and the effects of inactivity

All ethnic minority groups have a higher proportion of the population which has never worked or is long-term unemployed, as compared with the proportion for the population as a whole.[70] Again, this is disproportionately true of Pakistanis and Bangladeshis, where 16 and 17 per cent respectively have never worked or are long-

---

[63] Department for Education and Skills, *Youth Cohort Study: The Activities and Experiences of 19 Year Olds: England and Wales,* DfES, 2002.

[64] Information provided by EMED, DWP, 2004.

[65] See: D. Gillborn and H. Mirza, *Educational Inequalities,* London, Ofsted 2000, HMI 232.

[66] Interim *Strategy Unit Report,* p. 80.

[67] *Strategy Unit Report, 2003,* p. 58.

[68] Education and Training Statistics for the United Kingdom, London, DfES, 2002, cited in G. Bhattacharyya, L. Ison and M. Blair, *Minority Ethnic Attainment and Participation in Education and Training: The Evidence,* RTP01-03, London, DfES, 2003, table 6, p. 30.

[69] H. Conner, C. Tyers, S. Davis, N.D. Tackey, *Ethnic Minority Students in Higher Education: Interim Report,* London, DfES, 2003, RR 448.

[70] EMED, DWP, 2004.

term unemployed. This is around six times the proportion for the population as a whole (three per cent).[71]

Nearly a quarter of all Muslims are employed in the wholesale or retail trade.[72] Forty per cent of Muslims are in the lowest occupations groups, as compared to less than 30 per cent of Christians. Broken down by gender we see that 36 per cent of Muslim men are in the highest occupations group compared to the 75 per cent of Jewish men.[73]

Child poverty

In households with dependent children, income poverty is strongly associated with childhood poverty. Three-quarters of Pakistani and Bangladeshi children live in households earning less than half the average income for the UK.[74] Statistics available for London show that the highest proportion of children growing up in "workless households" are from the Pakistani and Bangladeshi groups. Forty per cent of Bangladeshi and 30 per cent of Pakistani children are growing up in workless households, compared to 20 per cent of White children.[75]

A study by the Greater London Authority (GLA) found the percentage of workless households with children in London was the highest of any region of England. Forty-two per cent of Bangladeshi children and almost 34 per cent of Pakistani children in Inner London were in a workless households, compared to 27 per cent of White children.[76] Childhood poverty can have a disproportionate impact on Muslim communities.

Soft skills

One consequence of the unemployment, economic inactivity or self-employment of their parents' generation is that young Pakistanis and Bangladeshis seeking to enter employment may find themselves without many of the necessary soft skills, such as job-seeking skills and links to the wider labour market. Therefore, this younger cohort may in some cases have higher education levels than their parents and yet still face the same

---

[71] EMED, DWP, 2004.

[72] EMED, DWP, 2004.

[73] Occupations are classified as falling into nine standardised categories. These have been averaged into three groups: High – including managers and senior officials; Medium – including administrative and skilled trades: Low – including sales and customer service occupations.

[74] DWP, *Households Below Average Income*, 1994/95–2000/01, London, Department of Work and Pensions, 2002.

[75] EMED, DWP, 2004.

[76] D. Gaffney, *Workless Households with dependent children in London: Output area maps from the 2001 Census*, Data Management and Analysis Group (DMAG), Greater London Authority, October 2003, pp. 8–10.

level of unemployment and disengagement. This creates a gap in connectivity with the labour market, as this group has limited awareness and understanding of how they can translate their education and skills into employment possibilities, and this in turn can generate frustration and social tension where they are unable to realise their aspirations.

Evidence from interviews with voluntary youth organisations in Glasgow suggested that, due to high levels of self-employment by their parents, young people were "taking on the family business" even when they had no desire to do so. In many cases, even those young people who had degree-level qualifications were unable to find suitable employment.[77] This could be the result of a lack of relevant soft skills.

Interviews with career councellors who engage with Pakistanis and Bangladeshis suggest that there is a need to provide greater information and advice on the range of employment opportunities available, the qualifications needed for different occupations and the different options to improve existing skills levels. They suggest that, while some have high levels of qualifications, others seek employment in areas where they do not currently hold the appropriate qualifications or training.[78]

Pakistani and Bangladeshi graduates were found to be experiencing "engagement fatigue" from trying to access employment commensurate to their skills but with little success. Youth development workers reported noticing this as having a "knock-on" effect onto the siblings of these graduates. The graduates were suggesting that with their limited success at accessing graduate-level employment, there was little point in their siblings paying for university education and then also not finding work.[79]

4.2 The "Ethnic Penalty"

Statistical analysis can be used to estimate which proportion of labour market achievement between ethnic minority groups and their White majority counterparts is determined by variables such as education, economic environment, age and fluency in the English language. However, even after these key variables have been accounted for, significant differences in the labour market achievements of ethnic minorities remain.

Regression studies have shown that ethnic minorities remain disadvantaged in terms of employment and occupational attainment even after key factors are taken into account. Ethnic minority men have been persistently disadvantaged in terms of earnings, relative to their White majority counterparts, with Pakistani and Bangladeshi men facing the greatest disadvantage. "Like-for-like" regression analysis shows that Pakistani and

---

[77] Interview with a youth worker in Glasgow, December 2003.

[78] Interview with career counsellors in London, January 2004.

[79] Interview with a youth development worker in Glasgow, December 2003.

Bangladeshi men are the most disadvantaged amongst all ethnic minority groups relative to White men. Key factors, such as age, education, recency of migration, economic environment and family structure, can explain just £21 of the £150 wage gap between Pakistani and Bangladeshi men and White men. This can be compared to £9 of the £116 wage gap for Black men and £5 of the £23 wage gap for Indian men.[80]

4.3   A "Muslim Penalty"?

In addition to an "ethnic penalty", it is possible that disadvantage in the labour market may result from the fact that a person is of a particular faith group, if they have discernable and identifiable religious characteristics, values and practices that shape their interaction with the labour market. Alternatively, disadvantage may be faced by a faith group due to the presence of prejudice and stereotypes that may exist about that faith group and may reflect negatively upon the group and people's attitudes towards that group. A combination of these factors may exist where Muslims are concerned and may in part explain their low levels of labour market participation. The combination of these factors can be identified as the "Muslim penalty".

In the absence of statistical analysis to estimate what proportion of gross differences in the labour market achievement between Muslims and other faith groups is determined by factors such as education, economic environment, age and fluency in the English language, it is not possible to determine the absolute presence of such a penalty. Further research is needed to understand the influence of religious and cultural issues in shaping the employment outcomes for Muslims.

The impact of faith identity may be different for different faith communities. Furthermore, a difference in the impact of faith background on employment may differ according to the extent to which faith identity is visible or requires accommodations. For Muslims, accommodations in the workplace include space for prayers, allowing time for prayer, especially on Fridays, and being flexible around the holy month of Ramadan. Other ways in which faith impacts on work life may be more subtle, such as the avoidance of after-work drinks, though these can play an important role in building networks within organisations and with company clients.

Laws prohibiting religious discrimination in employment in Britain only came into effect in December 2003.[81] Until this point, there was no clear requirement for

---

[80]   R. Berthoud, "Ethnic Employment Penalties in Britain", *Journal of Ethnic and Migration Studies*, no. 26, 2000, pp. 389–416.

[81]   Employment Equality (Religion or Belief) Regulation 2003, No 1660, implementing EU Council Directive 2000/78/EC of 27 November 2000 establishing a general framework for equal treatment in employment and occupation.

employers to be aware of, or accommodate, the needs of Muslims. The employment rights of Muslims, and the obligations upon employers under the new legislation on religious discrimination, should be disseminated to all Muslims still in full-time education. This would undoubtedly improve awareness of employment rights, once Muslims move into employment, and will result in greater numbers accessing and integrating into the wider labour market through assurance that their religious affiliation and observance will not hinder their choice of employment, as their rights are protected.

There is a knowledge gap in our understanding of the presence, nature and shape of workplace religious discrimination encountered by Muslims. We do not know the differences between the experience of those who are visibly Muslim or assert a Muslim identity and those who do not. At the same time, we also do not have a clear understanding of how cultural and religious values of Muslims influence their labour market choices. These "influences" can be wide ranging, from community and family expectations, which can be different for men and women, to prejudices about employers, either through negative experiences or assumptions, to more general preference of "working from home"[82] or working alongside others from similar faith or ethnic groups. These factors may also vary between first and second generations. In order to be effective, policies must be informed of the role of religious values and cultural values, where they differ and correspond.

Religious values and principles can be an important resource used by Muslims to challenge cultural values. In relation to Muslim women, anecdotal evidence from voluntary organisations suggests it is not always culturally acceptable for them to be in active employment outside the home.[83] This is not a religious precept, as Islamic law does not forbid women to enter employment. In fact, religious values could play an important part in promoting economic integration and challenging existing cultural preferences on the issue of Muslim women's entry into employment. However, cultural sensitivity and preference should be respected as much as possible, and no alternative set of values should be imposed. Any policy response in this area should incorporate the views of a wide range of Muslim organisations on this issue.

We do not know the degree to which Muslim female economic inactivity is a result of cultural values or of the personal preferences of women, who prefer to remain in the home and look after their children. Research suggests that, for those born in the UK, the second generation, preferences are changing. The *Dale study* also found that some

---

[82] A. Dale, E. Fieldhouse, N. Shaheen, and V. Karla, *The Labour Market Prospects for Pakistani and Bangladeshi Women*, Occasional paper, Manchester: The Cathie Marsh Centre for Census and Survey Research, 2000, (hereafter, A. Dale et al., *Labour Market Prospects*).

[83] Interview with Muslim women's organisation in London, January 2004.

women in the younger age cohort were determined to find ways in which to manage childbearing combined with a career, while others felt they were unable to find paid work due to insufficient qualifications.[84]

However, while such cultural preference may be relevant considerations in understanding Muslim women's level of engagement with the labour market, these would not explain the level of economic inactivity of Muslim men.

The Strategy Unit report outlined the level of disadvantage faced by Muslims, but stated that religion may simply be a proxy for other factors determining employment, such as education and fluency in English.[85] The report referred to research which stated that:

> unemployment risk does vary significantly by religion. Even controlling for a range of factors, Sikhs and Indian Muslims remain almost twice as likely to be unemployed as Hindus. Pakistani Muslims are more than three times as likely as Hindus to be unemployed. Sikhs, Pakistani and Bangladeshi Muslims experience particular under-representation in professional employment, with this area showing higher concentrations of Hindus and Indian Muslims. In terms of earnings, Muslim men and women are over-represented in the lowest income band. Almost a quarter earning less than £115 per week, compared to around one in ten Sikhs and Hindus. Yet despite over-representation among low earners, Indian Muslims actually record the highest share within the highest income band.[86]

Statistical analysis is needed to explore whether a residual "Muslim penalty" exists after key factors have been accounted for. The above evidence suggests the presence of a possible "Muslim penalty" may have different effects for different ethnic groups within the Muslim community. Due to the variance in outcomes between Pakistanis and Bangladeshis and Indian Muslim groups, it is difficult to conclude at this stage that there is a "Muslim penalty", and if there is, that it has a blanket negative effect. The degree to which the variance in outcomes within Indian groups (Indian Hindus, Muslims and Sikhs) and between Indians, Pakistanis and Bangladeshis is a result of their varying human capital levels is uncertain.

From this limited and complex picture it is clear that Indian Muslims' labour market achievements are different from those of Pakistanis and Bangladeshis. Limitations in data availability mean that it is not possible to ascertain whether, with the exception of Indian Muslims, other Muslim communities encounter the same levels of labour market disadvantage as Pakistanis and Bangladeshis. However, it is known from the

---

[84] Dale et al., *Labour Market Prospects*, p. 23.

[85] *Strategy Unit Report*, p. 32.

[86] *Strategy Unit Report*, p. 32, citing: M. Brown, „Religion and Economic Activity in the South Asian Population', *Ethnic and Racial Studies*, vol. 23, No. 6, 2002, p. 1045.

census that the employment rate for Muslims as a faith group is less than 40 per cent, which is almost half that of the majority Christian group.

Researchers have raised the question of whether the visibile identity of some Muslim men and women are barriers to labour market entry. Interviews of Muslim women who wear a *hijab* found a consensus among these women that wearing the hijab to a job interview raised doubts in the mind of an employer as to how well the applicant would "fit in". In some cases questions were also raised as to the image that would be presented to customers.[87]

While further research is needed to determine the nature and scale of a "Muslim Penalty" and other religious discrimination, policy makers must address the fundamental issue of the faith diversity of the labour market.

---

[87] Dale et al., *Labour Market Prospects*, p. 36.

5. The Policy Framework

5.1 Current Policy Measures by Government

Government employment measures and policies supporting ethnic minorities

The Strategy Unit report set out detailed analysis of the multiple and complex causes of labour market disadvantage for ethnic minorities and gave clear policy recommendations of how their labour market achievements could be improved. It set the goal of removing, within ten years, the disproportionate labour market disadvantage faced by ethnic minority groups.[88]

The recommendations of the *Strategy Unit report* fall to departments responsible for economic policy in its widest sense. A cross-departmental ministerial Task Force (hereafter, DWP Task Force) oversees implementation of the recommendations.[89] As the policy recommendations are carried forward, a more in-depth understanding of ethnic disadvantage is likely to be uncovered. As new evidence and understanding emerges, scope exists for more targeted policy interventions to be created. The DWP Task Force and Jobcentre Plus have recently put in place a number of policies to improve the employment rate for ethnic minorities:

- Jobcentre Plus have a new target structure[90] that focuses on the 258 wards with a high concentration of ethnic minorities and unemployment.

- The Ethnic Minority Outreach programme, a community-based initiative, is designed to engage ethnic minorities with Jobcentre Plus services and improve links between communities and employers.

- A "Flexible Fund" of £8m will now be available to Jobcentre Plus district managers in areas of high ethnic minority concentration and unemployment, to use flexibly according to local needs.[91]

- Specialist employment advisers provide advice to employers on increasing the diversity of their workforce.

- The DWP, through Jobcentre Plus, delivers employment programmes that provide tailored support to all working-age claimants.

---

[88] *Strategy Unit Report*, p. 3.

[89] The DWP Task Force is chaired by the Minister for Work, with membership spanning the lead Whitehall departments, the Commission for Racial Equality and employer organisations. The DWP Task Force will exist until spring 2006.

[90] *Full Employment in Every Region*, p. 21.

[91] *Full Employment in Every Region*, pp. 33–35.

- The DWP is currently enhancing delivery of their programmes, to deliver more tailored support to ethnic minority clients by taking account of specific ethnic minority needs, such as language and cultural preference.

Need for Government employment measures and policies supporting Muslims

As outlined in the previous sections of this chapter Muslims on average face a disproportionate level of labour market disadvantage compared to other faith groups. As the majority of British Muslims are also from ethnic minority communities, there is currently a gap in employment policy for ethnic minorities, in that it does not address this overlapping faith dimension. There is no evidence to suggest the current level of labour market disadvantage faced by Muslims will change without direct policy intervention. The challenge for policy is to address this gap and have a goal to integrate Muslims into the mainstream labour market, to help them realise their aspirations in employment through improving their labour market entry, retention and progression levels. This requires changes to existing mainstream policy and the addition of specific targeted policy measures around employment.

Government has service delivery targets for all current policies. However, the degree to which these targets are met evenly on the ground, especially in deprived areas, should be assessed. Effective delivery of mainstream services, appropriate targets, as well as specific policies for Muslim women and young Muslims, should significantly improve employment integration possibilities for Muslims.

Through changes in employment policy, successful labour market integration, retention and progression of Muslims is possible. The Government and employers must therefore recognise and respond proactively to this level of disadvantage, due to the demographic change in the working-age population. Initiatives must be delivered with flexibility by local institutions on the ground in the most deprived areas.

Specific policy measures could fall into three categories: first, policies addressing the socio-economic disadvantage of Muslim communities, where recognising faith can be important for effective delivery to Muslims; second, understanding the impact of existing and changing social and cultural norms impacting on the labour market engagement of Muslims; third, tackling the prejudice, stereotypes and disadvantages that arise from a lack of awareness and understanding about Muslims.

It is important for Government to work with Muslim communities, to ensure shared ownership of all policies supporting integration into the mainstream labour market and to introduce positive action measures where appropriate. The benefits of improved labour market outcomes through economic integration for Muslims are not just financial. Economic integration will ensure long-term social and civic integration for future generations of British Muslims.

All of these approaches are discussed in more detail in the following sections. These describe, with examples of best practice, how enhanced and improved policy can be delivered presently, to improve labour market outcomes for Muslims. Improvement of service delivery, through enhanced cross-departmental and local-level cooperation, is an essential and cross-cutting factor. Policies should then be developed, or extended, to improve labour market accessibility for Muslims and to better support their entry into the labour market.

5.2   Improving Service Delivery

Improved cross-departmental and local-level cooperation

The evidence put forward in this chapter suggests that tackling the disadvantage faced by Muslims, as in the case of ethnic minorities, requires cross-departmental cooperation. The remit of the DWP Task Force should therefore now include a new focus on tackling the specific disadvantage of Muslims. This would serve a dual purpose: to ensure effective policies for Pakistanis and Bangladeshis, who comprise 60 per cent of the UK Muslim population, and also for other Muslims in the UK, the majority of whom are also ethnic minorities. The DWP Task Force should therefore ensure that any new policies it creates are targeted at removing labour market barriers for individual ethnic groups. With this added emphasis on Muslims, it could develop a clear approach to removing labour market barriers faced by this faith group, ensuring that the labour market needs of ethnic minorities who are also faith minorities are met effectively.

Previous sections of this chapter have also highlighted the scale of geographical disadvantage faced by Muslims. Improving service delivery for people in deprived areas requires a cross-departmental commitment. Employment policy on faith communities, as on race, is influenced and affected by various departmental responsibilities. Recent policy initiatives suggest an improved level of understanding of geographic deprivation and the need to tailor services to meet the needs of people in these areas.[92] In particular, the DWP is now beginning to promote the need for local areas with concentrations of ethnic minorities to exercise flexibility of approach when delivering their labour market services.

Local areas with high levels of labour market disadvantage require a coordinated delivery and approach by local service providers. The current mechanism in place at the local level to bring together local service providers is the Local Strategic Partnership

---

[92]   Office of the Deputy Prime Minister, *A New Commitment to Neighbourhood Renewal: National Strategy Action Plan*, available on the website of the Social Exclusion Unit, at www.socialexclusionunit.gov.uk/publications/reports/ html/action_plan, (accessed 2 November)

(LSP).[93] The LSP is under the authority of the Office of the Deputy Prime Minister. It coordinates local delivery to promote effective partnership and to ensure a more comprehensive and holistic approach to meet the needs of local people.

There are organisations at the local level that have understanding and expertise of the employment needs of Muslims. Their work can be identified as examples of best practice. Some of these organisations are discussed later in this report. However, it can be difficult to share such best practice between Government departments, or at the local level. One reason for this is that none of the organisations identified have representation on the LSP or other local coordination bodies. Such organisations should be able to share their local knowledge and experience of how to identify specific Muslim disadvantage and how to improve labour market outcomes for Muslims with all local service providers. This collective approach would help avoid duplication in the work undertaken by individual bodies to improve their understanding of the needs of Muslims.

Such a collective approach would ensure that race, faith and other issues affecting labour market outcomes for individuals in these groups are kept central to local delivery planning by all LSP members. Therefore, information on engagement, capacity building, education, childcare, transport, gender and age-specific issues, religious observance and cultural practices and their effect on Muslims could be shared and receive strategic cross-departmental commitment. Sharing knowledge in this way should not just be confined to the LSP level but should also be spread regionally.

LSPs, working with local Learning and Skills Councils, try to ensure that skills training matches the immediate and long-terms needs of local employers. The National Employment Panel's Fair Cities project will pilot a demand-led initiative to train unemployed or inactive members of local working-age populations in areas of great deprivation. The initiative aims to secure local jobs for local people. It is envisaged that the project will help to meet the immediate and future skills needs of local employers. Such forward planning will allow for skills training for future employment opportunities and improve connectivity to the labour market.

Every district covered by Jobcentre Plus has a target for increasing the number of people in work in those areas. Achieving this target is the responsibility of Jobcentre Plus and the local authority. However, improving labour market outcomes in areas of high unemployment and inactivity requires widely sharing this target with other local agencies responsible for employment. Adopting such a measure would provide greater incentive for local agencies to collectively tackle the multiple barriers to labour market

---

[93] Local Strategic Partnerships is a Government body that tackles key issues that require a whole range of local organisations to work together – issues such as crime, jobs, education, health and housing.

entry and therefore benefit Muslims as they, like ethnic minorities, face multiple barriers to labour market entry.

In Birmingham, the local authority, Jobcentre Plus and members of the LSP have recently agreed to share responsibility for this target. While it may be too early to assess success of this measure, any proposal that seeks to underpin collective responsibility of the target with coordinated local service delivery is taking a step in the right direction.

Sharing responsibility for achieving the local employment target in this way effectively takes the commitment of the DWP Task Force down to local authority level. It should also ensure cross-departmental responsibility and accountability at the local level for meeting the needs of the local working-age population. More crucially, it should ensure that commitment to improving labour market outcomes and overcoming the multiple levels of disadvantage in employment faced by Muslims and other disadvantaged communities is shared by all local service providers. This sharing of responsibility for the target across local agencies in disadvantaged areas should be supported by a wider change to the setting of targets for these areas by the Treasury.

5.3 Improving Engagement with, and Accessibility to, the Labour Market

Due to the barriers outlined in this chapter, employment entry can be particularly difficult for Muslims. In part, this is because they are largely concentrated in the most deprived areas of the country, where labour market demand is more fragile. However, jobs are nonetheless available in areas that are short distances away.

In order to improve the engagement of Muslims with the labour market, and to enable them to better access employment opportunities, policy needs to better address ways to further the aspirations of Muslims, through careers advice, developing their skills and improving their access to education and training. Policy must also take on board a more holistic approach to labour market entry and encompass measures to meet the specific employment needs of Muslim women, in particular work experience and childcare provision.

Aspirations and broadening horizons

Aspiration requires individuals being proactive about their future and making informed choices about the economic activities in which they would like to participate.

In order to broaden the horizons of Muslims seeking employment, it is necessary to ensure that information about the benefits of labour market integration, and the rewards it can bring, are given to both first and second-generation Muslims. It is also important that they should be made aware of the contribution that they can make to the labour market and to wider society. Thereafter, they should be encouraged to realise their employment aspirations and be given appropriate support, including training. Career counselling plays a crucial role in this process.

The Connexions Service and Careers Service have responsibility to provide support, careers advice and guidance to young people aged 13-19, and to help young people aged 16-17 find employment. They work closely with Jobcentre Plus to ensure young people receive appropriate advice to facilitate smooth transition into employment. However, it is important that these services provide greater connectivity for Muslims seeking to enter into employment. The need for Muslims to improve connectivity to the labour market as early as possible is vital if they are to have a chance of success in the labour market. In most cases, employment opportunities in their current areas of residence are limited.

Many members of society who are out of work may still be able to contribute in very positive ways and should be encouraged to do so. There is a sizeable number of first-generation Muslims who are now in the 50-65 age range who are out of work.[94] Even if individuals in this group do not find appropriate employment, they continue to have skills which could be utilised to benefit wider society. For example, voluntary work in the local Muslim and non-Muslim community in education, social care or community activities would help them remain active members of society and ensure wider social integration. This may also have a positive effect on younger members of the Muslim community and encourage them to be active in economic and social life.

Preparing individuals for employment is important if Muslims are to find appropriate employment and then retain and progress within employment. However, a large proportion of employed Pakistanis and Bangladeshis are currently found in a disproportionately narrow range of employment sectors, which are also low-paid and offer limited prospects for advancement. Concentration in such narrow sectors result in this group not realising their full economic and aspiration potential, which can lead to economic disadvantage and wider social exclusion. To improve labour market accessibility for Muslims, policy must seek to improve access to training, work experience placements and childcare provision, while giving enhanced outreach services.

Development of skills

Policies on the preparation of Muslims for labour market entry must focus on the development of both hard and soft skills. Soft skills are aimed at personal development and include confidence building and raising awareness of the benefits of economic

---

[94] Current mandatory employment programmes such as New Deal are for people aged between 18-49 only. For those over 49, employment programmes are voluntary.

integration for the individual and their families. They help individuals to realise their potential and prepare them for the labour market.

However, programmes to improve soft skills must be delivered in a manner that is culturally sensitive and appropriate for all. Inappropriate or insensitive service delivery can lead to individuals avoiding engagement with service providers. One survey found that 89 per cent of Muslim women felt mainstream public services did not meet their needs.[95] There may be cultural reasons as to why Muslim women do not access mainstream services. This may be due to their own personal choice or the choice of family members. Greater cultural sensitivity in the delivery of services could help to ensure Muslims take the first step towards considering, and then preparing themselves for labour market integration, in a culturally appropriate manner that would satisfy the concerns of both themselves and their families.

There is good practice in this area that suggests that, with some encouragement, women and younger Muslims can improve their skills levels and successfully enter employment and self-employment. One such example of good practices in the development of soft skills comes from Amina, a Muslim Women's organisation in Glasgow.

Amina has had success in providing intermediary support and guidance to Muslim women. They help with the first stages of confidence building and interaction with others in a culturally sensitive manner. They provide support and guidance on training and advocacy, together with group working and skills development, to improve the future employment prospects of Muslim women. They also complement and support other Government initiatives, by providing advice and referrals on access to public services and to the labour market, including Jobcentre Plus. They refer Muslim women onto ethnic minority organisations delivering labour market programmes and initiatives specifically targeted to the younger female ethnic minority group. These services are provided through a "drop-in" surgery and a telephone help-line. Feedback from service users suggests that both they and their families are happy that their cultural needs are accommodated in the delivery of these services.

Although development of soft skills is an important pre-requisite for accessing employment, lack of basic hard skills is a key barrier to employment. Individuals with poor basic skills, such as literacy and numeracy, are up to five times more likely to be unemployed and far more likely to have low-paid, low-skilled jobs.[96] Therefore, the need to increase basic skills is imperative to increasing an individual's ability enter employment.

---

[95] Centre for the Study of Child and Society and the Muslim Network, *The Needs of Muslim Women*, Glasgow, Centre for the Study of Child and Society and the Muslim Network, 1995.

[96] *Strategy Unit Report*, p. 52.

The current Department for Education and Skills (DfES) policy initiative aims to improve the basic skills levels of language fluency, literacy and numeracy for the UK working-age population. The DfES has also announced that they will be improving the delivery of language training by reaching out to faith groups. The first roll-out of this service will be to the Muslim community. It will be delivered through targeting community faith leaders and encouraging them to promote language fluency training to the communities they serve.

Brent Employment Zone,[97] an employment initiative led by the private sector, has recognised the clear need to help ethnic minorities improve their language skills, in order to improve their labour market outcomes. The group has sought to increase the employability of members of the local inactive and unemployed population. They have funded an effort directed at improving the English language fluency of those who accessed their outreach facility, to help these people enter employment.

The degree to which language fluency is a barrier to employment for Muslims is uncertain. For first generation economically inactive Muslims, many of whom are now of (or nearing) retirement age, improving their English language fluency may not greatly increase their labour market opportunities. Nonetheless, increasing their language fluency would certainly benefit their social integration. For younger Muslims, the majority of whom are UK-born and educated, it appears unlikely that their labour market inactivity is largely due to a lack of English language fluency. However, this is a complex picture, as Muslims continue to enter the UK through migration. Language fluency for employment and social integration should continue to be a priority.

Education and training

The single most critical determinant of lifelong human capital levels is the quality of schooling a person receives. However, the educational attainment levels of the Pakistani and Bangladeshi groups are the second poorest in the country. In proportionate terms, the Indian ethnic group out-perform White people by about ten percentage points, while the majority White group out-perform Pakistanis and Bangladeshis by over ten percentage points, although this gap is narrowing.[98]

Improving this picture will require greater emphasis on raising educational attainment, for those still of compulsory schooling age, and improving access to further education. The Strategy Unit report contains various recommendations for the Department for Education and Skills on how to improve this picture for ethnic minority groups, an effort that will largely affect those still within schools. There are specific factors that

---

[97] Brent Employment Zone is a public-private partnership employment service led by the organisation Working Links.

[98] *Strategy Unit Report,* 2003, p. 53.

can impact on the attainment level of Muslim pupils. These will be examined in a separate section of this publication.

Pupils in full-time education need to be made aware of the recent legislation prohibiting religious discrimination in employment and the accommodations that need to be made by employers for members of different faith groups. This should reassure those who will become part of the working age population that, should they wish to enter employment, they will be protected from religious discrimination and they can seek accommodation of their religious observance from their employers.

Those who are no longer in education are largely reliant upon employers and those organisations delivering workforce development to improve their skills base. The Workforce Development Agenda[99] is a positive policy measure to increase skills levels of people already in work. It seeks to improve the skills levels of people in lower-skilled positions and to facilitate their progress into higher employment opportunities. For the many Muslims who are concentrated in narrow employment sectors and in self-employment, the Workforce Development Agenda may be beneficial in increasing their skills levels and broadening their employment opportunities. However, the number of Muslims that access and benefit from this service needs to be assessed.

Even when ethnic minorities do improve their education and skills levels, the provisions currently on offer do not then help connect individuals to the labour market. In particular, work experience placements and help with overcoming other barriers can be difficult to secure. Work experience placements can also help prepare employers for a more diverse workforce. However, in 2002 only three per cent of 16-19 year olds in Modern Apprenticeships were from ethnic minority backgrounds. There remains a need to understand more clearly what happens to young Muslims after they leave full-time education and programmes such as the Modern Apprenticeships. In particular, it is important to ensure that they are able to progress within their chosen careers.[100]

Labour market entry

A holistic approach to the multiple barriers faced by Muslim groups is needed to ensure labour market entry and all-round improvement in their labour market prospects. The Bolton-based Ethnic Minority Business Service (EMBS)[101] and the

---

[99] The Workforce Development Agenda is a programme in the Department for Education and Skills to improve the skills levels of people already in employment.

[100] Black Training and Enterprise Group, *Modern Apprenticeships and Race Equality,* Black Training and Enterprise Group, 2003, p. 17.

[101] EMBS has been highlighted here as an example of best practice as Indian, Pakistani and Bangladeshi Muslims make a significant proportion of those who access their services.

Ethnic Minority Enterprise Centre (EMEC) in Glasgow provide examples of best practice in this area.

The EMBS was created by the Chief Executive of Bolton Metropolitan Council, as part of a strategy to improve service delivery for ethnic minorities in Bolton following evidence that members of these communities were not accessing mainstream business service providers. Established in 1987 to provide self-employment and business advice to ethnic minorities, it played a key role in helping many ethnic minority men and women set up or expand their own businesses. The EMBS delivers business advice through outreach services, workshops and one-to-one support. The success of this ethnic minority-led organisation in reaching and understanding the needs of minority communities and helping to tailor service delivery accordingly, led the Council to extend the EMBS remit to also include employment training and support. The service is proving highly successful.

Coming from a business background, the EMBS understands and communicates with local businesses and is aware of local labour market needs. Crucially, through contacts with faith and cultural organisations within the minority communities, it is able to understand, and communicate effectively with the local ethnic minority communities. It is able to support, encourage and help train and facilitate employment and work experience placements for its ethnic minority clients. Through this approach, it has been able to help ethnic minorities realise their employment aspirations. The EMBS has been a crucial element in diversifying the local public and private sector labour market. While its clients are from all age backgrounds, the greatest proportion are from the younger age cohorts. The EMBS meets the needs of local employers through supporting ethnic minority recruits with the appropriate skills to access local jobs. Understanding of this demand-led focus ensures that ethnic minorities seek training and employment in areas that are commensurate to their skills, and for which jobs are available locally.

This holistic model of service delivery through an ethnic minority provider has been replicated by the neighbouring Blackburn and Darwen Council.[102] In assessing the success of these two initiatives, however, it is important to remember that they are in the same region as Oldham and Burnley. In these towns, there is no such holistic employment and business training initiative that would be sensitive to ethnic minorities.

In Glasgow, a similar initiative to the EMBS can be found in the Ethnic Minority Enterprise Centre (EMEC). This too has been successful in attracting young ethnic minorities who are otherwise not in education, training or employment. The EMEC has

---

[102] The initiative is called the Business Resource Centre.

established employment links with large local employers, such as British Airports Authority (BAA). It identified ethnic minorities that matched the skills needed by BAA.

Due to the success of this initiative, BAA have entered an agreement to advise the EMEC directly of any future recruitment opportunities that arise and also to run workshops with other EMEC clients.

Outreach services exist to reach out to communities that do not access mainstream services. In April 2002, the DWP launched the "Ethnic Minority Outreach" service.[103] Based within the five ethnic minority conurbations of Greater London, West Midlands, West Yorkshire, Greater Manchester and East Midlands, the service is delivered by organisations that are able to demonstrate their knowledge of, and ability to work with, ethnic minority communities. They aim to find innovative ways of helping ethnic minorities overcome the barriers they face in the labour market. While it may be too early to judge the effectiveness of this service, the need for such an outreach function to help facilitate initial engagement with mainstream services is clear.

There is a need to improve the capacity of such outreach services and ensure they are coordinated to help public services providers meet the needs of the Muslim community on the ground.

Meeting the employment needs of Muslim women

In addition to the other factors mentioned in this section, Muslim women would benefit, in particular, from improved access to work experience and to childcare provision. For Muslim women, work experience is particularly important to help alleviate the cultural concerns they or their family might have. It is known that Pakistani and Bangladeshi women are more likely to have more dependent children.[104] Therefore, a short period of employment would help them experiment with the use of formal or informal childcare. The same experience would also allow all Muslim women to assess whether employment is something they could, and would want to, participate in in the immediate term, or whether they would want to prepare for employment when they no longer have childcare responsibilities.

---

[103] Outreach services provide help with job searching, interview techniques and filling application forms.

[104] For Pakistani and Bangladeshi families, the average number of children per household is 2.42 and 2.63 respectively, whereas for White families it is 1.8. "Average Number of Dependent Children in the Family Aged under 19 by Ethnicity", ONS, *Labour Force Survey*, London, Office of National Statistics, Autumn 2001.

The National Employment Panel's evaluation of the New Deal for Lone Parents[105] recommended a one-week employment course called "Discovery Week". This would allow single parents to gain advice and support through greater interaction with providers, to gain valuable labour market experience and to become used to the work pattern alongside that of caring for small children. This in turn would help to improve their personal confidence, while assuring financial support through the in-work benefits available. It would also allow the employer to gain greater understanding of this potential labour market client. If extended to economically inactive Muslim women, the "Discovery Week" could provide a valuable employment experience for this group.

A lack of available and affordable formal childcare can act as a barrier to labour market participation for women. However, the use of formal childcare is lower amongst ethnic minorities than for the White majority. While 87 per cent of working White parents use formal childcare services, only 79 per cent of Black parents and 68 per cent of Asian parents do so.[106] In London, where over 40 per cent of the UK's Muslims live, childcare costs can be much higher than elsewhere.[107] Initiatives are being taken forward to help increase the availability of affordable childcare for ethnic minorities who want the service. In Stratford, East London, a training centre for childcare workers has been established. Due to the high numbers of ethnic minorities living in the area, they have had considerable success in increasing the number of ethnic minorities becoming childcare workers.

There is also need for effective childcare policies that adequately take into account the specific religious and cultural needs of Muslims. A recent study into the childcare needs of ethnic minority mothers found a need for cultural and religious sensitive childcare services for Muslim clients, such as employing staff from a variety of ethnic and faith backgrounds.[108] However, the survey also found that Muslim women had identified

---

[105] B. Verwaagen, *What Works – Final Report of Recommendations*, Steering Group on Lone Parents, National Employment Panel, DWP, April 2003.

[106] These statistics do not account for latent demand for formal childcare. Department of Education and Skills, *Repeat Study of Parental Demand for Childcare*, DfES Research Report No. 348, 2002.

[107] See, for example, The Daycare Trust's 2003 survey of the cost of nurseries, childminders and after school club. Available at www.daycaretrust.org.uk/article.php?sid=138 (accessed on 12 July 2004).

[108] Department of Trade and Industry, *Diversity and Difference ME Mothers and Childcare*, London, Women and Equality Unit, DTI, January 2004, (hereafter, DTI, *Diversity and Difference*).

much positive change in childcare services that had taken place and that they did not view the greater use of childcare as compromising their traditional Muslim values.[109]

5.4   Supporting Entry to, and Progression within, the Labour Market

Proactive policies are needed to ensure Muslims are not disadvantaged by their faith identity when trying to enter and progress within the mainstream labour market. It is important to ensure Muslims are able to enter the labour market and, once they are in employment, able to progress within it. To achieve this, policy must adopt proactive employment measures through setting targets, promoting faith diversity in the workplace, providing in-work support and enhancing career development.

Positive action measures: "Targets not quotas"
Acceptance of ethnic and faith diversity in the labour market should deliver positive change for Muslims in the long-term. However, the employment gap between ethnic minorities and their majority White counterparts has remained persistent over the last 15 years, despite attempts by mainstream interventions to change this. Targeted positive action measures to minimise the gap are now clearly necessary.

At present, the Home Office has race employment targets to increase the number of ethnic minorities at all levels across the Civil Service. Building on this approach a target for faith groups disadvantaged in the labour market should be adopted. Muslims are one such group. The best way forward would be to introduce a system of "targets, not quotas". A targeted employment initiative would help Muslims enter employment commensurate to their skills, without giving them "special treatment" due to their faith backgrounds. This should leave no room for suggestions of preferential treatment.

One example of good practices of positive action is Birmingham City Council. Despite the high numbers of Pakistanis and Bangladeshis in their local working-age population, the Council found, through ethnic monitoring records, that few were employed by the local authority. It recognised the limitations of mainstream employment initiatives, targeting all ethnic minorities, and introduced an initiative called "Bridges into the Future: Positive Action for Pakistanis and Bangladeshis."

This initiative includes a target for increasing the numbers of Pakistanis and Bangladeshis employed by the local authority. It facilitates the crucial first step of work experience and training in employment for many in this group who otherwise face multiple barriers to labour market entry. The programme has been running for four years and has directly helped to increase employment outcomes for those who

---

[109] DTI, *Diversity and Difference.*

participate. It goes further than just entry-level success and also ensures that the new recruit benefits from staff development, while building capacity within the organisation to improve the workplace culture and organisational structure to encourage diversity. It is envisaged that this holistic approach to employment will improve the working environment for these groups and encourage them to remain and progress within the local authority.

A further step to improving employment retention levels has been the acknowledgement of minority religious holidays. Birmingham local authority was the first in the UK to publish annual religious holiday calendars, which are circulated to all departments, highlighting when Muslim and other religious holidays are to occur. E-mail reminders are circulated to senior staff when these holidays are approaching, to ensure they prepare appropriate staff coverage when Muslims want to take annual leave. Such measures improve relations between Muslim employees and their employers and help such employees feel valued.

Faith diversity in the workplace

New laws prohibiting religious discrimination allow employees to seek accommodation of their faith needs from employers.[110] As yet, the degree to which Muslims request and access religious observance provisions, such as using a prayer room during work hours and requesting annual leave for Muslim holidays, is not known, as this has never been surveyed or monitored.

The Chartered Institute of Personnel Development (CIPD) has produced guidance giving practical information on direct and indirect discrimination and religious observance for personnel officers in the public or private sectors.[111] This includes details about the observance of religious holidays and religious practices, such as prayers during work hours. It also covers detailed issues related to social interaction at events during and outside working hours that may indirectly disadvantage or exclude Muslims. For example, "the after-work drinks in the pub", while a common social event for the majority of workers, may be uncomfortable for Muslims.[112] Similarly, the employment Advisory, Conciliation and Arbitration Service (ACAS) has produced a Code of Practice outlining steps that can be taken by employers to accommodate

---

[110] The Employment Equality (Religion or Belief) Regulations 2003, No 1660.

[111] The Change Agenda, *Religious Discrimination, An Introduction to the Law,* Chartered Institute of Personnel and Development, 2003.

[112] The Change Agenda, *Religious Discrimination, An Introduction to the Law,* Chartered Institute of Personnel and Development, 2003.

religious observance. This includes suggesting flexibility over hours worked during the Islamic festivals of Eid and Ramadan.[113]

There is a considerable weight of evidence supporting empirical links between good "corporate social responsibility" practice and high performance.[114] Acknowledging and accommodating faith diversity can also deliver positive benefits for businesses. There is an economic case for employing Muslims and individuals from other minority faith communities in industries that have to operate throughout the Christian holiday periods of Christmas and Easter, when those who are celebrating request annual leave.

For example, First Group, a private organisation providing public transport, found difficulty in work coverage over the Christmas period until they diversified their workforce. Through consultation with their employees, they found that their Muslim employees were more than happy to work over Christian holidays and, in return, their fellow non-Muslim counterparts were happy to cover Ramadan and Eid festivals.

Facilitation of such employment flexibility was recognised by senior management and filtered down to employees, and it achieved consensus. As a result, the measure was extended to also acknowledge the need for long periods of annual leave for Muslims wishing to perform the *Hajj*. First Group now allows employees to take their annual leave in a four-to-six week slot every three years, which accommodates the *Hajj* requirement of Muslims.[115]

The consultation exercise adopted by First Group ensured that there was informed understanding between employees of all faiths. This level of informed understanding between fellow work colleagues and flexibility by employers has helped to create a positive working environment of shared understanding of religious observance.

Evidence from organisations such as British Telecom (BT) has shown positive benefits from placing equality and diversity at the core of a business. All BT employees undertake a course, called "Valuing our Difference", to improve their awareness of the needs of different ethnic groups.[116] They found this type of across the board training equipped their employees with greater understanding of fellow employees and their diverse client base.

---

[113] Advisory Conciliation and Arbitration Service (ACAS), Religion of Belief in the Work Place, London, ACAS, 2003.

[114] P. Emery and T. Hoskins, *Achieving High Performance CSR at the Heart of Business*, London, The Virtuous Circle and The Work Foundation, 2004.

[115] First Group, Scotland.

[116] University of Glasgow, *Developing a Strategic Approach to Employment Issues for Glasgow's BME Communities*, Glasgow, University of Glasgow, 2002.

However, despite these instances of good practices, more still needs to be done to ensure that all employers and all employees, not just Muslims, recognise the value of shared understanding of religious diversity in employment. There is great value in the public and private sector partnering with Muslim organisations representing the diverse religious needs of the community, to ensure employers fully understand and appreciate the religious and cultural nuances involved when discussing the issue of Islam, the Muslim community and employment.

The Faith Communities Unit in the Home Office, alongside the Department of Trade and Industry (DTI), should promote faith diversity in the workplace, by working with employer organisations and Muslim and other faith organisations. To this end, the DTI has joined forces with several Muslim organisations to ensure that employers and employees are aware of the implications of the new religious discrimination legislation. They are also taking a positive proactive approach through publicising the positive contribution of Muslims in the area of employment to the British economy.[117]

However, more needs to be done to provide individual employers with advice and guidance on preparing their working environment for the needs of Muslims. For over 50 years, the Jewish community has produced guidance for employers and employees on the religious observance needs of the Jewish community.[118] As the Muslim community is relatively new in the UK, proactive work in the form of such awareness building needs to be carried out and the take-up and utilisation of such a service should be promoted.

Award schemes already exist to reward employers for recognising and valuing diversity, gender and disability.[119] However, no such scheme yet exists for recognising faith diversity. Due to the disproportionately young age cohort of Muslims in the UK, and the demographic shift in the growth of the working age population, a rapid awareness-building campaign is a priority if Muslims are to be encouraged to enter the mainstream labour market.

---

[117] For example, in 2003 there was a joint initiative by the Department for Trade and Industry and the Muslim Welfare House Trust (a voluntary Muslim organisation) to raise awareness of the benefits of faith diversity.

[118] The Board of Deputies of British Jews, *Jews in Employment: A Practical Guide*, London, The Board of Deputies of British Jews.

[119] Investors in People is an organisation that provides quality assurance and development to employers involved in the standard for the benefits of being an Investor in People. See: Investors in People website at www.iipuk.co.uk (accessed on 12 July 2004).

Career development

Ethnic minorities with high levels of education still find difficulty in accessing senior positions.[120] Difficulty in access to, and progression in, senior positions can be the result of a multitude of factors. These include a lack of human capital, limited knowledge of how to approach such opportunities, limited knowledge of how to fill in senior management application forms, and discrimination. This may, in part, be because many of their parents were self-employed, unemployed or economically inactive, and were therefore unable to give soft skills advice on labour market employment to their children.

The University of Bradford recognised that its ethnic minority graduates were not able to access graduate employment opportunities commensurate to their education levels. They therefore introduced a graduate mentoring scheme in collaboration with the neighbouring Huddersfield, Leeds and Leeds Metropolitan Universities. The measure is a positive action initiative, designed to develop the competitiveness and employability of ethnic minority undergraduates and graduates through a tailored programme of guidance and career development. They also offer practical help with job-search strategies, work placements and personal development.

In-work support

To address the poor levels of progression within employment for the majority of ethnic minority groups, central Government recently put in place measures to help improve the skills, and thereby the progression levels, of public sector ethnic minority employees.

The PATHWAYS initiative, operated through the Cabinet Office and the Home Secretary's Race Employment Targets, focuses on recruitment and progression for ethnic minorities in the Civil Service. There are procedures and mechanisms in place to facilitate progression, such as mentoring.[121] However, while the introduction of these measures is to be commended, their design appears to indicate that they will not benefit the most disadvantaged ethnic groups, or Muslims. For example, the Home Office employment target is set by the overall number of ethnic minorities in the local population. However, this does not take into account the disproportionate number of Pakistanis and Bangladeshis in the younger age cohort within the local population. Thus, while the overall percentage of Muslims in London is 8.5 per cent, their percentage in the working-age category is much higher.

The Home Secretary's race employment target may, therefore, be met by departments, but this could be achieved through the employment of Indian and Chinese ethnic

---

[120] *Strategy Unit Report*, p. 29.

[121] The PATHWAYS Programme in the Cabinet Office encourages more ethnic minority staff with potential to reach the senior levels of the Civil Service, known as the Senior Civil Service.

minority groups. While this is not an undesirable outcome, as the Strategy Unit report details, these groups achieve labour market success on most measures.[122] This monitoring measure should be utilised to detail the progression of individual ethnic groups – and not simply combine the outcomes of all ethnic minorities together. These targets should, therefore, be disaggregated by individual ethnic groups and focused on those who are underrepresented. Ethnic monitoring by individual ethnic group, using the UK 2003 National Census categories, now operates in all public sector organisations. Due to the increased understanding of economic disadvantage faced by individual ethnic groups, the Home Secretary's Race Equality Target should now be adjusted to set targets for individual ethnic groups.

Between 1999–2009, one-quarter of the working-age population will come from the Pakistani and Bangladeshi community.[123] Therefore, the Government needs to ensure that work environments in the public and private sector are prepared for and able to attract, and retain, a diverse faith workforce.

---

[122] *Strategy Unit Report*, p. 22.

[123] D. Owen and A. Green, *Minority Ethnic Participation and Achievements in Education, Training and the Labour Market*, Warwick: Centre for Research in Ethnic Relations and Institute for Employment Research, 2000, pp. 16–17.

6. RECOMMENDATIONS

6.1 Strategy to Integrate Muslims into the Mainstream Labour Market

Due to the increasing number of Muslims in the working age population, the Government should commit to one clear aim: to integrate Muslims into the mainstream labour market. To this end, policy makers need to develop an inclusive and integrated strategy for Muslims, to support their labour market entry and progression and help overcome any barriers they face.

1. In developing an inclusive and integrated strategy for Muslims, policy-makers should begin by focusing on geographic disadvantage, to help alleviate many of the current employment problems faced disproportionately by Muslims in deprived areas. Thereafter, more specific policy measures are needed to address barriers faced by Muslim women and young Muslims.

2. The Government should set targets for deprived areas to increase service delivery overall, thereby delivering improved outcomes for all residents in those geographic areas, including Muslims.

3. The Government should adopt positive action measures to increase the number of Muslims in employment.

4. The Government should develop and encourage measures to ensure that workplaces and work environments are "faith friendly".

5. The Government, to ensure effectiveness of policies, should communicate the agenda for this strategy for Muslims with a diverse range of Muslim and non-Muslim organisations.

6.2 Research

In order to better address the barriers to mainstream labour market integrations encountered by British Muslims, there is a clear need for further research:

6. The Government should commission research to gain more understanding of Muslims in the UK, across geography, gender and age. This research should evaluate why their labour market experiences are so different from those of other faith groups, and the extent to which these differences can be explained by factors other than religion.

7. The Government should also commission research on the employment situation of self-employed Muslims. This research should aim to develop understanding of the factors that influence and determine the choice of Muslims to enter self-employment. It should also explore the impact of self-employment by Muslims on their wider economic and social progression, examine how Muslim women could be encouraged to enter employment and look at how their religious and cultural needs can be met in the workplace.

8. Building on the policy change permitting *Shariah* compliant mortgages, the Treasury and the Department for Trade and Industry should assess whether the absence of other Shariah complaint financial products restricts employment and self-employment opportunities for Muslims; and if so, it should explore possibilities to introduce more *Shariah* compliant financial products, such as career development and business start-up loans.

6.3   Tackling Geographic Disadvantage

Government employment strategy and policy on Muslims should, as a priority, focus on geographic disadvantage, which disproportionately affects Muslims in the UK.

9. The Treasury should adopt a new target structure for the most disadvantaged areas in the UK. This should take the form of an area-based employment target, which all agencies in the area must work collectively towards, to improve employment outcomes for all residents in those geographic areas, including Muslims.

6.4   Muslim Representation and Consultation

10. The Government should ensure that Local Strategic Partnerships in areas that have high Muslim concentration – and that are characterised by high levels of unemployment, inactivity and concentration in low-skilled employment sectors – include a Muslim or ethnic minority organisation that has demonstratedexternal success in meeting the employment needs of Muslims.

11. The Department for Education and Skills and the Department for Work and Pensions should ensure that support is available to mosques and other Muslim community organisations, to build awareness of the benefits of education and employment integration for all Muslims.

12. The Government, to ensure the effectiveness of its policies, should communicate the agenda for this strategy to a diverse range of Muslim and non-Muslim organisations.

6.5   Connecting Young Muslims to the Labour Market

There is a specific policy need to enhance mainstream services from the Department for Education and Skills and the Department of Work and Pension to ensure that young Muslims progress from education into employment. The DfES and DWP should:

13. Ensure that schools, through careers advisors, head teachers and governors, provide Muslim pupils with informed advice about the wide range of employment opportunities available to them.

14. Ensure that the Connexions and Careers Services disseminate information about employee rights and employer obligations, and guidance on religious observance, to all pupils in full-time education.

15. Ensure that the Connexions and Careers Services provide and help Muslim pupils gain valuable work experience while still in full-time education.

16. Ensure greater access to intermediary services that meet the needs of different faith groups.

6.6   Connecting Muslim Women to the Labour Market

To address the specific barriers to employment faced by Muslim women, action must be taken by several Government departments:

17. The Department for Trade and Industry's Women and Equality Unit should work with employers to improve understanding of the employment, childcare and cultural preferences of Muslim women.

18. The Department for Education and Skills should provide support and advice on entry and affordability of higher education to Muslim women, to ensure they are able to make an informed choice of whether or not to continue to higher education.

19. The Department for Work and Pensions should offer the "Discovery Week" to economically inactive Muslim women.

20. The Office for National Statistics should monitor Muslims women' responses to the question on attitudes to employment in the Labour Force Survey.

6.7   The DWP's "Ethnic Minority Outreach" Service

The DWP's "Ethnic Minority Outreach" service should be enhanced to meet the needs of Muslims through faith sensitive delivery of this service. The enhanced service should provide:

21. Improved understanding amongst Muslim communities of the benefits and value of wider labour market integration.

22. Greater engagement with young Muslims, to understand their needs and help realise their aspirations.

23. Greater engagement with agencies involved in drugs, crime and social exclusion prevention, to help overcome obstacles Muslim individuals face.

24. Improved employment, training and business support advice for Muslims.

6.8   Private Sector Recruitment and Employment Policies

Private sector employer practices need to be enhanced to ensure Muslims are proactively recruited and that their work environment meets the needs of Muslims:

25. Umbrella organisations, such as the Confederation of British Industry and the Institute of Directors, should identify best practice examples of how to recruit Muslim employees and disseminate this to their members.

26. The Confederation of British Industry and the Institute of Directors should also encourage their members to make it a priority to have cultural and religious awareness procedures in their work places and to give these measures senior level support. They should also be encouraged to invest time and resource into creating "faith friendly" work practices and positive action measures.

6.9   Public Sector Recruitment and Employment Policies

Public sector employer practices need to be enhanced to ensure Muslims are proactively recruited and that their work environment meets the needs of Muslims:

27. The Faith Communities unit should build on Government employment targets to increase the number of ethnic minorities at all levels of the Civil Service by ensuring government also adopts a "Faith Groups Employment Target", to increase the number of Muslims at all levels in the Civil Service.

28. The Government should ensure that recruitment exercises by the public sector actively encourage Muslims recruits.

29. The Government should ensure that existing public sector performance management outcomes include an additional measure to ensure that there are no significant differences in recruitment, retention, progression and satisfaction levels for employees from different faith groups.

30. The Government should ensure all public sector organisations carry out a faith monitoring survey to gain more information about the religious identities and needs of their employees.

31. The Government should develop and encourage measures to ensure that all workplaces and work environments in the public sector are "faith friendly".

6.10 Coordination Between the Public and Private Sectors

The Government should encourage better coordination between the public and private sectors, to develop recruitment and employment policies that better meet the needs of Muslims and allow for the sharing of best practice. This approach should, as a priority, also include representatives of Muslim organisations.

32. The Chartered Institute of Personnel Development (CIPD), the Department for Trade and Industry (DTI) and Muslim organisations should work together to create and disseminate greater understanding and awareness of the need for employer flexibility, capacity building and the benefits to be gained from Muslim economic integration.

33. Public and private sector organisations should develop an award scheme that rewards employers for adopting positive action measures and for valuing religious diversity in the workplace,

34. The Government should encourage both public and private sector organisations to develop mentoring schemes that attract mentees from different faiths, to help improve their connection to the labour market.

Appendix 1: Definitions

Ethnic categories in the 1991 Census: the UK 1991 National Census contained a nine-point structure of ethnic categories: White, Black (African, Caribbean), South Asian (Indian, Pakistani, Bangladeshi), Other (Chinese, other Asian, Other).

Ethnic categories in the 2001 Census: the UK 2001 National Census contained a 16-point structure: White (British, Irish or Any Other White Background); Mixed (White and Black Caribbean, White and Black African, White and Asian or any other Mixed Background); Asian or Asian British (Indian, Pakistani, Bangladeshi, Any Other Asian Background); Black and Black British (Caribbean, African, any other Black background); Chinese or other ethnic group (Chinese, any other).[124]

Ethnic minorities: The term "ethnic minority" is used in the *Strategy Unit report* to denote people of South Asian, Black African and Black Caribbean origin. In this report, the use of the term "ethnic minority" as a broad "umbrella" label, is deliberate, to signify reference to a wide variety of ethnic minority groups. Where greater precision is required, reference to specific component groups within the ethnic minority population is made in the text. There is, inevitably, considerable debate and disagreement on the question of race, ethnicity and nomenclature. No specific political or sociological inference should be drawn from the use of related terminology in this report.

White: as with the term "ethnic minority", the generic label "White" should be used with some caution. The existence of distinctive ethnic groups within the "White" category is gradually being acknowledged. Notably, in the UK 2001 National Population Census, people of Irish descent are recognised as a separate ethnic group.[125]

Religious categories in the 2001 Census: the UK 2001 National Census asked an optional question on religious affiliation. The data is disaggregated into the following categories: Buddhist, Christian, Hindu, Jewish, Muslim, Sikh, any other religion, no religion and religion not stated.

Ethnic penalty: net differences in achievement between ethnic groups are often referred to as "ethnic penalties". Some scholars use the term to emphasis the importance of discrimination in explaining the persistence of net differences in labour market achievement and others to refer to "all the sources of disadvantage that might

---

[124] UK 2001 National Census.

[125] UK 2001 National Census.

lead to an ethnic minority group to fare less well in the labour market than similarly qualified Whites."[126]

"Muslim penalty": refers to an identifiable net difference in the labour market achievement of Muslims, as compared to non-Muslims who are similarly qualified. Statistical analysis is needed to explore whether such a "Muslim penalty" exists, after key factors have been accounted for.

Employment: The Labour Force Survey[127] determines the status of individuals, depending on their answers to a number of questions about their recent labour market activity:

> **Employment:** people are counted as "in work" if they have carried out one hour or more of paid work in the reference week for the survey; are temporarily away from their job; are on a government-supported training programme; or are an unpaid family worker.

> **ILO unemployed:** people are counted as ILO unemployed if they are not in work and have actively sought work during the last four weeks and are available to start within the next two weeks; or have found a job and are waiting to start in the next two weeks.

> **Economic inactivity:** individuals who are not in work and who do not meet the ILO definition of unemployment are counted as economically inactive.

---

[126] *Strategy Unit Report.*

[127] The Labour Force Survey (LFS) is a quarterly sample survey of households living at private addresses in Great Britain. Its purpose is to provide information on the UK labour market that can then be used to develop, manage, evaluate and report on labour market policies. The questionnaire design, sample selection, and interviewing are carried out by the Social and Vital Statistics Division of the Office for National Statistics (ONS) on behalf of the Statistical Outputs Group of the ONS.

Appendix 2: Bibliography

Advisory Conciliation and Arbitration Service (ACAS), *Religion of Belief in the Work Place* (London: ACAS, 2003)

Ahmad, F., T. Modood and S. Lissenburgh, *South Asian Women and Employment in Britain: Interaction of Gender and Ethnicity* (London: Policy Studies Institute, 2003)

Berthoud, R., "Ethnic Employment Penalties in Britain", *Journal of Ethnic and Migration Studies,* 26 (2000), 389–416

Berthoud, R., *Multiple Disadvantages in Employment* (York: Joseph Rowntree Foundation, 2002)

Bhattacharyya, G., L. Ison and M. *Blair, Minority Ethnic Attainment and Participation in Education and Training: The Evidence,* Research Topic Paper (London: DfES, 2003)

Black Training and Enterprise Group, *Modern Apprenticeships and Race Equality* (London: Black Training and Enterprise Group, 2003)

Brown, C., *Black and White Britain* (London: Policy Studies Institute, 1984)

Brown, M., "Religion and Economic Activity in the South Asian Population", *Ethnic and Racial Studies,* 23:6 (2002), 1045

Bruegel, I., "Sex and Race in the Labour Market", *Feminist Review* 32 (1989), 49–68

Cabinet Office Unit, *Ethnic Minorities and the Labour Market* (London: Cabinet Office Strategy Unit, 2003)

Centre for the Study of Child and Society and the Muslim Network, *The Needs of Muslim Women* (Glasgow: Centre for the Study of Child and Society and the Muslim Network, 1995)

Chartered Institute of Personnel and Development, *The Change Agenda, Religious Discrimination, An Introduction to the Law* (London: Chartered Institute of Personnel and Development, 2003)

Conner, H., C. Tyers, S. Davis, N.D. Tackey, *Ethnic Minority Students in Higher Education: Interim Report,* Research Report No. 448 (London: DfES, 2003)

Dale, A., E. Fieldhouse, N. Shaheen and V. Karla, *The Labour Market Prospects for Pakistani and Bangladeshi Women,* Occasional paper (Manchester: The Cathie Marsh Centre for Census and Survey Research, 2000)

Department for Education and Skills, *Repeat Study of Parental Demand for Childcare,* Research Report No. 348 (London: DfES, 2002)

Department for Education and Skills, *Youth Cohort Study: The Activities and Experiences of 19 Year Olds: England and Wales* (London: DfES, 2002)

Department of Trade and Industry, *Diversity and Difference ME Mothers and Childcare* (London: Women and Equality Unit DTI, January 2004)

Department of Work and Pensions, *Households Below Average Income, 1994/95–2000/01* (London: DWP, 2002)

Dickins, R., P. Gregg and J. Wadsworth (eds.), *The Labour Market Under New Labour: the State of Working Britain II* (London: Centre for Economic Performance, 2003)

Emery, P. and T. Hoskins, *Achieving High Performance CSR at the Heart of Business* (London: The Virtuous Circle and The Work Foundation, 2004)

Gaffney, D. and B. Armstrong, *Workless Households with dependent children in London: Output area maps from the 2001 Census* (London: Greater London Authority, Data Management and Analysis Group (DMAG), October 2003)

Gillborn D. and H. Mirza, *Educational Inequalities: Mapping Race, Class and Gender* (London: Ofsted, 2000)

HM Treasury, *Full Employment in Every Region* (London: HMT, 2003)

Home Office, *Community Cohesion: The Report of the Independent Review Team chaired by Ted Cantle,* (London: Home Office Community Cohesion Unit, 2001)

Howes, E., *2001 Census Key Statistics: Ethnicity, religion and country of birth* (London: Greater London Authority, October 2003)

Jones, T., *Britain's Ethnic Minorities* (London: Policy Studies Institute, 1993)

Lindley J. and A Dale, "Ethnic Differences in Women's Demographic, Family Characteristics and Economic Activity Profiles 1992 to 2002", *Labour Market Trends,* April 2004

Office of National Statistics, "Average Number of Dependent Children in the Family Aged under 19 by Ethnicity", *Labour Force Survey* (London: Office of National Statistics, Autumn 2001)

Owen, D. and A. *Green, Minority Ethnic Participation and Achievements in Education, Training and the Labour Market* (Warwick: Centre for Research in Ethnic Relations and Institute for Employment Research, University of Warwick, 2000)

Owen, D. and P. Ratcliffe, "Estimating local change in the population of minority ethnic groups, 1981–1991", Working Paper No. 1, *Changing spatial location patterns of ethnic minorities in Great Britain, 1981–1991* (Coventry: Centre for Research in Ethnic Relations, 1996)

Power, A., *Barriers to Social Housing for Asians* (Bradford: Bradford City Council, June 2001)

The Board of Deputies of British Jews, *Jews in Employment: A Practical Guide* (London: The Board of Deputies of British Jews, 2004)

University of Glasgow, *Developing a Strategic Approach to Employment Issues for Glasgow's BME Communities* (Glasgow: University of Glasgow, 2002)

Verwaagen, B., *What Works – Final Report of Recommendations of the National Employment Panel's Steering Group on Lone Parents* (London: National Employment Panel, DWP, April 2003)

British Muslims
and the Criminal Justice System

Table of Contents

List of Acronyms

ACPO	Association of Chief Police Officers
BAWP	British Association of Women Police
CAP	Complaint Access Point
CJA	Criminal Justice Act
CPS	Crown Prosecution Service
CSV	Community Service Volunteers
FAIR	Forum Against Islamophobia and Racism
HAT	housing action trust
HMP	Her Majesty's Prison)
HMSO	Her Majesty's Stationery Office (Government information service)
IHRC	Islamic Human Rights Commission
IPPC	Independent Police Complaints Commission
NCWMP	National Council for the Welfare of Muslim Prisoners
NOMS	National Offender Management Service
NPS	National Probation Service
PSAs	Public Service Agreements
RIMS	Racist Incident Monitoring Scheme
RRA	Race Relations Act
RR(A)A	Race Relations Amendment Act 2000
SOVA	Society of Voluntary Associates

1. EXECUTIVE SUMMARY

A feeling of confidence that the legal system provides justice and fair process is central to a sense of belonging and inclusion in a society. The majority of Muslims come into contact with the criminal justice system as (direct or indirect) victims of crime. However, whether they are victims, witnesses, suspects, offenders, prisoners or employees, Muslims face particular challenges in their interaction with the criminal justice system.

Pakistanis and Bangladeshis, who make up 60 per cent of Muslims in the UK, are more likely than other ethnic groups to be victims of crime, including racially motivated crime. They also have the lowest satisfaction levels with public-initiated police contact, and the lowest levels of confidence in the police. Unlike in other public services, Muslims who have had contact with the Crown Prosecution Service, the Prison Service and the Probation Service are more likely to feel they will be discriminated against than those who have not had contact with these services. Muslims make up three per cent of the UK population but nine per cent of the population of prisoners.

This report argues for more nuanced policies that are sensitive to the specific needs of Muslims. A pre-condition for developing such policies is better data collection. At present, accurate statistics on Muslims' experiences of the criminal justice system are not available, because the statistics that are available are mainly disaggregated on the basis of a restricted number of categories, based on race and/or ethnicity. To remedy this situation, this report recommends that, where data on ethnicity is collected, it should at least include Pakistani and Bangladeshi as distinct categories. Wherever possible, however, data should also be collected on the basis of religion or faith identity.

An understanding of Muslims and the criminal justice system cannot ignore the impact of anti-terrorism legislation and policing on Muslim communities. The gap between the number of stops and searches and the number of actual arrests that lead to charges and convictions is fuelling a sense within Muslim communities that they are being unfairly policed. At the same time the incarceration without trial of detainees at HMP Belmarsh, under anti-terrorism legislation, further undermines Muslim's confidence in the criminal justice system. Perceptions of unfair treatment by the police should be a real cause of concern. These perceptions can influence how people engage with the police, how much trust they have in policing and how secure they feel in their daily lives.

The challenge that the Police Service faces is finding ways in which anti-terrorism policing can take place, while also building confidence with Muslim groups at the same time. Engagement by criminal justice agencies with local Muslim communities is central to meeting this challenge. This engagement must involve a broad cross section of the Muslim community, including women, young people and those marginalised within the Muslim community. The concerns of these various groups should be built into local crime-reduction strategies.

Confidence in criminal justice agencies would, of course, also increase with greater employment of Muslims in all areas. Employment targets for the recruitment of ethnic minorities should include specific targets for Pakistanis and Bangladeshis. Particular attention should be paid to the effective recruitment and subsequent retention of police officers. In local areas with a significant number of Muslims, consideration should be given to introducing specific targets for the recruitment of Muslim police officers. Diversity training for those working in the criminal justice system should also enhance trainees' understanding of the faith diversity of the UK.

Monitoring of faith or religious identity can also be an important step towards ensuring appropriate and effective service delivery by agencies in the criminal justice system. With the introduction of a religiously aggravated element to crime, under the Anti-Terrorism Crime and Security Act (2001), the Crown Prosecution Service is increasingly considering the religious identity of victims. Within the Prison Service, monitoring of the religion or faith of prisoners has enabled prisons to better cater to the needs of Muslim prisoners. The religion of an offender may also be relevant in developing suitable cognitive skills programs that address offender behaviour. However, although the Probation Service has an increasing focus on diversity issues, less attention has been paid to developing programmes for Muslim offenders.

There are many ways in which volunteers contribute towards the criminal justice system. Agencies should support, encourage and facilitate voluntary participation by Muslims as lay visitors, independent custody visitors at police stations or members of prison boards. However, for Muslims to act as representatives on boards and forums related to criminal justice, there needs to be a greater focus on providing them with training about criminal justice issues. The practical, emotional and psychological support provided to victims of crime may need to take the victim's faith into consideration. Muslims can be victims of racially and religiously motivated hate crime and also of crime in general. Victim-support services therefore need to be sensitive to the specific needs of Muslims and other faith communities.

There are examples of good practices among the many Muslim organisations and community groups that provide services for Muslims. However, at present, mainstream organisations that receive Government funding refer clients to unfunded Muslim organisations, which provide welfare services tailored to meet the needs of Muslims. Because they do not receive government funding, Muslim community and voluntary sector groups report a lack of capacity as a key barrier to greater participation. Any strategy for increasing the confidence of Muslims in the criminal justice system must explore capacity building to facilitate participation.

2. INTRODUCTION

In the criminal justice arena, a particular focus on the experiences of Muslims has generally been omitted, because debates around issues such as policing, community and criminal justice and victimisation have taken place through the lens of race and ethnicity – but not religion. Although the vast majority of Muslims in Britain belong to minority ethnic groups, the 2001 Home Office *Citizenship Survey* clearly shows the interconnected nature of religion and ethnicity, suggesting that both should be considered when addressing criminal justice policy issues.[1] This report considers the broad range of ways that Muslims interact with the criminal justice system, both as members of minority ethnic communities and as members of their wider faith community.

Many positive criminal justice-related policy developments are currently taking place within the UK Government. These include the creation of a Civil Renewal Unit, seeking to promote and support local people in solving the problems that affect their communities; the formation of a Faith Communities Unit, aiming to encourage and facilitate faith communities' involvement in the voluntary and criminal justice sectors; and the issuing of a series of important strategy documents by the Home Office, such as *A New Deal for Victims and Witnesses.*[2]

This chapter aims to examine such recent developments and to suggest ways in which these new initiatives might be more inclusive of British Muslim communities.

There are many reasons why a particular focus upon British Muslim communities in relation to criminal justice policy is timely and important. Statistics published by the Home Office and agencies of the criminal justice system suggest that Muslims face specific challenges as victims, witnesses, suspects, offenders, prisoners and employees. Recent findings from the British Crime Survey show that Pakistanis and Bangladeshis, who comprise almost 60 per cent of UK Muslims, are significantly more likely than

---

[1] C. Attwood, G. Singh, D. Prime and R. Creasey, *Home Office Citizenship Survey: people, families and communities,* London, Home Office, 2001 (hereafter, Attwood et al, *Home Office Citizenship Survey*).

[2] The Civil Renewal Unit has been set up by the British Government to promote the Home Secretary's agenda for civil renewal, working across the Home Office and the Government. The Faith Communities Unit was created to lead Government engagement with faith communities, so that the Government will recognize and utilize the experience, skills and diversity of faith communities. *A New Deal for Victims and Witnesses* is a national strategy for new initiatives to help crime victims and witnesses. This includes the ongoing development of the Witness Service by Victim Support, the introduction of Victim Personal Statements and the provision of information to victims by the Crown Prosecution Service. Further details of all of these projects can be found on the Home Office website at http://www.homeoffice.gov.uk/justice/victims/index.html (accessed 21 September 2004).

White or Black people to be the victims of household crime.[3] They are also significantly more likely to be the victims of racially motivated attacks than Indians, Blacks or Whites.[4] However, Pakistanis and Bangladeshis also indicate the lowest satisfaction with public-initiated police contact and the lowest levels of confidence in the police.[5]

Research suggests that a lack of confidence in the police is common across minority ethnic groups in the UK. For example, a study by Docking reveals that minority ethnic groups share a perception that police discriminate against or stereotype them. Young people in these minorities said they believe that they are more likely to be stopped and searched than White people. This study also found that older people from minority ethnic groups felt that the police did not take them seriously when they reported crimes, and they felt that the police did not trust them.[6]

The Home Office *Citizenship Survey* also reveals that – unlike in other public sector services, such as education and health – minority ethnic groups who have had contact with the police, the courts, the Crown Prosecution Service, the Prison Service and the Probation Service, are more likely to feel that they will be discriminated against than those who have not had any contact with these organisations.[7] Moreover, 28 per cent of Pakistanis and Bangladeshis said that they would be discriminated against by the police, as opposed to four per cent of White respondents. And 19 per cent of Pakistanis and 16 per cent of Bangladeshis said that they would be discriminated against by the Prison Service, as opposed to four per cent of White respondents.[8]

The terrorist attacks in the US on 11 September 2001, and the subsequent government response to the threat of terrorism in the UK, have involved a number of significant

---

[3] According to the 2001 National Census, over 90 per cent of Pakistanis and Bangladeshis in the UK are Muslim. Also, 43 per cent of Muslims are Pakistanis, and 17 per cent of Muslims are Bangladeshis, so that these two ethnic groups make up 60 per cent of the Muslim population in England and Wales. 2001 UK National Census, *Ethnic Group by Religion*, available at http://www.statistics.gov.uk/census2001/profiles/commentaries/ethnicity.asp (accessed 21 September 2004), (hereafter, UK 2001 National Census).

[4] A. Clancy, M. Hough, R. Aust, and C. Kershaw, *Crime, Policing and Justice: the experiences of ethnic minorities, Findings from the 2000 British Crime Survey: Home Office Research and Statistics 223*, London: Home Office, 2001, p. 2, (hereafter, Clancy et al *Crime, Policing and Justice*).

[5] Clancy et al *Crime, Policing and Justice*, p. 2.

[6] M. Docking, "Public Perceptions of Police Accountability and Decision-Making", in *Home Office Online Report* 38/03, 2003, available at http://www.crimereduction.gov.uk/activecommunities49.htm (accessed 21 September 2004).

[7] Attwood et al, *Home Office Citizenship Survey*, p. 47.

[8] Attwood et al, *Home Office Citizenship Survey*, p. 43.

consequences for British Muslim communities. Anti-Muslim sentiment and Islamo-phobia, which have long existed within western societies, were heightened in the aftermath of the atrocities that were committed.[9] Muslim men, women and children, as well as Muslim places of worship, became the targets of hate crime.[10] In the current situation, Muslim communities are living in a state of heightened anxiety, as evidenced by their requests for greater police protection and their adoption of precautionary strategies to try and avoid becoming the targets of hate crime.[11]

The implementation of the Terrorism Act (2000), and the introduction of the Anti-Terrorism Crime and Security Act (2001), which was hurriedly put together in the aftermath of the terrorist attacks of 11 September 2001, has important implications for Muslim communities. The new anti-terror laws have been criticised as being both draconian and ineffective in improving national security.[12] These laws, which will inevitably be used disproportionately against Muslims, create a unique challenge in relation to UK Muslim communities. The Government must balance the need for greater surveillance against the need to maintain Muslims' confidence in the criminal justice system.

There is an increasing perception among Muslims that they are being targeted unfairly by the police, and, in particular, that they are being disproportionately stopped and searched. Direct evidence of the number of Muslims who have been targeted by the police, either as part of wider anti-terror operations or due to more general policing initiatives, is generally unavailable, due to the data-gathering methods of agencies of the criminal justice system. Statistics tend to be collected on the basis of race and/or ethnicity, so that individuals' religious affiliations are rarely recorded. According to recent Home Office statistics, whereas the number of White people stopped and searched under the Terrorism Act (2000) increased by 118 per cent from 2001-02 to 2002-03, the number of Asians stopped and searched increased by 302 per cent.[13] This

---

[9] See: E. Said, *Orientalism*, Harmondsworth, Penguin Books, 1978.

[10] See: Islamic Human Rights Commission, *The Hidden Victims of September 11th: prisoners of UK Law*, London, IHRC, 2002 (hereafter, IHRC, *The Hidden Victims of September 11th*).

[11] B. Spalek, "Hate Crimes against British Muslims in the Aftermath of September 11th", in *Criminal Justice Matters*, 2002, 48, 3, 2002, pp. 20–22.

[12] See Liberty's critique of the anti-terror laws and their impact upon Muslim communities, *Reconciling Security and Liberty in an Open Society: Liberty Response*, August 2004. available on the Liberty website at http://www.liberty-human-rights.org.uk/resources/policy-papers/2004/liberty-and-security.pdf (accessed 21 September 2004), (hereafter, Liberty, *Reconciling Security and Liberty*).

[13] Home Office, *Statistics on Race and the Criminal Justice System – 2003. A Home Office publication under section 95 of the CJ Act 1991*, London, Home Office, 2004, p. 2, (hereafter, Home Office, *Statistics on Race and the Criminal Justice System – 2003*).

is likely to have an impact upon Asians' confidence in policing and in the wider criminal justice system in general.

The Prison Service is the only agency of the criminal justice system to collect data on the religious identity of prisoners, due in part to the Prisons Act (1952), which states that members of other religious groups have the same right to practice their faith as Christian prisoners. This data reveals that the number of Muslims in prison doubled between 1993 and 2000, whereas the number of all Christians grew more slowly, falling from 75 per cent of the total prison population in 1993 to 59.5 per cent in 2000.[14] On 30 June 2002, there were 5,379 male Muslim prisoners, compared to 430 Sikh and 256 Hindu male prisoners.[15]

Social and economic deprivation appears to be a factor behind the large number of Muslim offenders. Statistics in relation to Pakistani and Bangladeshi communities, as well as other Muslim ethnic communities, reveal that they are much more likely than other groups to be living on low incomes, with almost 60 per cent of the one million people in this group living in low-income households.[16] The statistics indicate that the link between social exclusion and crime is well-established.[17]

In light of the issues highlighted above, this report considers the broad range of ways that Muslims interact with the criminal justice system, as victims, witnesses, suspects, offenders, prisoners and employees.

Section three of this report highlights how difficult it is to get accurate statistics illustrating Muslims' experiences of the criminal justice system. Statistics on offenders, suspects, victims, witnesses and employees tend to be collected on the basis of race and/or ethnicity, and monitoring of religious or faith identity rarely takes place. This focus upon racial categories makes it difficult to substantiate any claims of discrimination or bias that members of Muslim communities might be experiencing within the criminal justice system, since Muslims do not overwhelmingly belong to any one particular race. This statistical problem is compounded by the difficulty in trying

---

[14] F. Guessous, N. Hooper and U. Moorthy (2001) *Religion in Prisons, 1999 and 2000, England and Wales,* London, Home Office, 2001, 15/01, p. 1, (hereafter, Guessous et al, *Religion in Prisons, 1999 and 2000*).

[15] Home Office, *Prison Statistics England and Wales – 2002. CM5996,* London, Home Office, 2003, p. 133, (hereafter, Home Office, *Prison Statistics England and Wales – 2002*).

[16] Department for Work and Pensions, *Family Resources Survey, 2000/2001,* London, DWP, 2003, (hereafter, DWP, *Family Resources Survey, 2000/2001*).

[17] D. Farrington "Human Development and Criminal Careers", in M. Maguire, R. Morgan and R. Reiner (eds) *The Oxford Handbook of Criminology* (2nd edn), 1997 Oxford, Clarendon Press, pp. 361–408, (hereafter, Farrington, *Human Development and Criminal Careers*).

to gain information about particular ethnic groups who are likely to be Muslim, such as Pakistanis and Bangladeshis.

Since April 2003, a 16-point system of ethnic monitoring, based on the system adopted in the 2001 UK National Census, has been in effect. Although this new system allows for the compiling of information that is more detailed than in the past, statistics about offenders, suspects, victims, witnesses and employees of the criminal justice system, and any targets that are set, are likely to be presented according to a modified five-point scale, which uses the categories "Black, White, Asian, Chinese and Other" (one category), and "Mixed". This means that the experiences of particular Muslim communities will continue to be subsumed within very general racial groupings. For instance, Pakistanis' and Bangladeshis' experiences are likely to continue to be merged with Indians' experiences within a general "Asian" category. As a result, in Section three, this report recommends that a more nuanced approach to the presentation of data should be introduced, so that the experiences of specific ethnic groups can be made visible. In particular, where data is available regarding Pakistanis and Bangladeshis, this should be separated from the general Asian category. This report also stresses that religious or faith identity should be monitored more often, so that religious affiliation, as well as ethnicity, would help to inform policy and practice.

Section four examines policing issues with respect to Muslim communities. Of particular concern is how anti-terror legislation seems to have influenced Muslims' perceptions of the Police Service. Representatives from a wide range of Muslim organisations argue that there is little acceptance amongst Muslims that anti-terrorism legislation should mean the disproportionate policing of members of their communities. Perceptions of policing within Muslim communities include the notions that they are being criminalised, that police officers are operating "religious profiling" when deciding whom to stop and search, and that young Muslims are being unfairly targeted. At the same time, there is a perception that some police officers are Islamophobic. Cases of alleged police abuse or mistreatment quickly become common knowledge amongst Muslim communities, and these cases have the potential to detrimentally affect the community's relationship with their local police forces. Nonetheless, when it comes to community involvement in policing issues, there are some cases of good practice, such as the Muslim Safety Forum, which should be more widely reproduced.

Section four of this report also highlights that police forces should be encouraged to recruit more Muslim police officers, as this would boost Muslims' confidence in policing. Particular attention should be paid to the recruitment and retention of female police officers, who face multiple discrimination. Much like the changes being implemented within the Police Service due to the *Macpherson report*, new policies should include tackling Islamophobia and anti-Muslim prejudice.

Section five looks at the Crown Prosecution Service and the courts. It highlights how the Crown Prosecution Service is increasingly considering the religious identity of victims, since the Anti-Terrorism Crime and Security Act (2001) introduced a religiously aggravated element to crime. So far, there have been relatively few prosecutions of religiously aggravated criminal cases, as can be seen from the annual report on racially and religiously aggravated crime, published by the Crown Prosecution Service. Nonetheless, the majority of the victims in these cases are Muslim.[18] Section five of this report also stresses that – while a considerable amount of research has examined direct or indirect discrimination in the courts, and the extent to which minority ethnic communities feel they are treated equally – the focus of these studies has been on ethnicity and not religious identity. Research on ethnicity should, at the very least, disaggregate statistics, to show any disadvantage experienced by Pakistanis and Bangladeshis. Research should also look at Muslim communities and their perceptions and experiences of the courts.

Section six of this report illustrates that, in the last few years, there has been a significant increase in the number of male Muslim prisoners. In response to this growing inmate population, many changes have been implemented within prisons to better cater to the needs of Muslim prisoners. For example, in 1999, the Prison Service appointed a Muslim adviser, whose work has involved a focus upon three areas: Friday prayers, access to Imams and *halal* diet. In 2003, for the first time, full-time Muslim chaplains were also employed. A multi-faith ethos has also been pursued in the Prison Service Chaplaincy. A Chaplaincy Council has been created, and its members include Prison Service faith advisers from a variety of different religions. The Chaplaincy Council provides a forum for consultation on a broad range of prison issues.

Despite these changes, difficulties remain. For example, the authenticity of *halal* food has been questioned, in spite of official assurances. This issue is of crucial concern for Muslim prisoners, and it has become a frequent source of frustration. Meanwhile, because prison staff members are often ignorant of the spiritual and practical aspects of Islam, these workers may get the impression that religious requests are a privilege rather than a necessity. Such an attitude among prison staff may lead to the inappropriate treatment of Muslim inmates.

Section six also examines offender rehabilitation programmes within prisons, and looks at whether these might be tailored to engage Muslim offenders more effectively by incorporating considerations of their religious identities. Similar to the Sycamore Tree programme that is run through chaplaincy departments for Christian prisoners, a programme could be developed by representatives from Muslim communities, run by

---

[18] Interview in April 2004 with Seamus Taylor, Head of Equality and Diversity, Crown Prosecution Service (CPS), Equality and Diversity Unit, London.

Imams, to help challenge offenders' rationalisations and to help provide offenders with a clear moral framework from which to re-build their lives. Muslim representative bodies and Islamic theological colleges/bodies should encourage members of their communities to help rehabilitate Muslim offenders, as currently, prison issues tend not to be high priority for many Muslim organisations.

Section seven looks at the work of the Probation Service. The report argues that it is of vital importance for the Probation Service to have knowledge about the number of Muslim offenders with whom it is in contact, as well as the nature of the communities that those individuals belong to, so that appropriate responses to Muslim offenders can be put together. This means that the Probation Service should adopt a system of ethnic and religious monitoring, so that it can make informed decisions about practice and policy regarding Muslim offenders. The Probation Service should also examine the sensitivity and responsivity of the services used by Muslim offenders. For example, the service should consider the issue of whether probation hostels offer *halal* food. Staff should also be properly trained in faith issues, since the race awareness training programmes that are currently offered are unlikely to give faith issues the level of focus that is required.

Section eight examines the role of partnerships between the Police Service and other statutory and voluntary agencies in reducing crime, and their relevance for Muslim communities. The section also looks at the role of volunteers working in the criminal justice system. It is argued that, even though statutory guidance under the Crime and Disorder Act (1998) makes community safety partnerships responsible for involving faith communities in their work, faith communities are rarely consulted by the lead agencies undertaking crime and disorder reduction partnerships. Section eight highlights the enormous diversity of the Muslim population in Britain and the need for engagement with a broader range of Muslim groups for consultation. This should include voices that are often marginalised, such as women's groups and young Muslims.

One way of engaging with the wider Muslim community is to encourage, support and facilitate their participation as volunteers. Volunteers are considered to bring the community perspective to bear on community justice-related issues. Clearly, Muslim volunteers, whether acting as members of Muslim charities, welfare and support services, or other Muslim organisations – or as individuals – have much to offer the criminal justice and community safety sectors. Currently, however, the involvement of Muslims in mainstream criminal justice-related initiatives is relatively low, and many obstacles lie in the way of gaining greater Muslim involvement. Researchers have found that participation in local crime prevention activities is most common among individuals who are fairly concerned about crime, but it is more likely to occur where crime levels are low. In high-crime areas there is likely to be very little participation by the wider community in community justice initiatives. Social exclusion and inequality is high amongst Muslim communities, and many Muslims live in socially and economically deprived areas. The stress factors associated with living in areas with high rates of crime and disorder are likely to deter Muslims from volunteering their services to the criminal justice system.

Muslim faith groups that run services for their local communities are also likely to be poorly funded, relying mostly on voluntary donations, which means they are unlikely to have the resources to work with the criminal justice sector. Muslim groups usually do not receive public resources, because funding for local housing, welfare and crime reduction initiatives cannot be used to support religious projects, only projects based on race and/or ethnicity. It would be unrealistic to expect greater involvement of Muslim service providers in community and criminal justice if there are no better ways for them to raise funds. The situation could be improved via the Active Community Unit, which could explore ways of helping Muslim groups to secure funding. Greater collaboration between Muslim specialist service providers and mainstream providers should also be encouraged.

Section nine looks at the issue of Muslims as victims of crime. This section of the report points out that the majority of Muslims who come into contact with the criminal justice system will have been affected by crime, either because they are a direct victim or an indirect victim – someone who has seen a crime, is related to a victim or is a friend of the victim.[19] As the report shows, Muslim communities are not only likely to experience racist crime, but also crime that is motivated by religious hatred. It is therefore of vital importance to investigate the incidence of religious hate crime and its impact upon victims, so that adequate services can be developed to cater to victims' needs.

The risk of being a victim of crime is not equally distributed amongst the general population. Muslim communities, whose members are more likely to experience social and economic deprivation, are also at high risk of experiencing a wide range of different crimes, which may or may not include a racist and/or Islamophobic component. It is therefore important that the needs of Muslim victims are adequately researched and addressed. Organisations that offer help and support to the victims of crime also need to examine their core values more closely, and find ways in which to better accommodate the experiences and perceptions of Muslim communities – as well as other faith communities. Although agencies that help victims may focus upon providing practical, emotional and psychological support, there is also the issue of spiritual healing and support. Spiritual support presently seems to be denied to people, yet it may be of great benefit to many individuals. It should be remembered that, even

---

[19] OSI Roundtable on British Muslims and the criminal justice system. *NB. OSI held a roundtable meeting in London, 8 June 2004, hosted by the Diversity Forum, Victim Support, to invite critique of this chapter in draft form from invited experts.*

though people may not regularly attend prayer meetings, they may nonetheless identify themselves as being part of a religious community. Mainstream victim support organisations should therefore consider widening the range of organisations that they suggest people contact to include the option of spiritual support.

3. DOCUMENTING EXPERIENCES OF MUSLIMS IN THE CRIMINAL JUSTICE SYSTEM

The Home Office recently published a report based on the findings of the *2001 Citizenship Survey,* which addresses aspects of religion and self-identity and civil participation in society.[20] That report highlights the interconnected nature of religion and ethnicity, and stresses that religious affiliation and ethnicity should be considered together, rather than separately, when carrying out research and when making policy decisions. The report also shows that religious affiliation is often a much more fundamental aspect of the self-identity of members of minority ethnic groups, as compared to White Christians. In contrast to the 17 per cent of White respondents who said that religion was important to their self-identity, 44 per cent of Black and 61 per cent of Asian respondents deemed religion as important. For Muslims, religion was ranked second only after family in terms of the importance to their self-identity.[21]

The system of race and ethnic monitoring presently in place in the criminal justice system therefore has a number of policy, practice and research implications for Muslim communities. These can be linked to wider debates. First, it could be asked whether the current system of monitoring might be further improved, so as to better monitor, and develop policies for, a wider range of Muslim ethnic communities. Second, it could be asked how extensively religious identity should also be monitored by agencies of the criminal justice system, and how this should be carried out.

This section shows that agencies of the criminal justice system tend to monitor race and ethnicity, rather than religious identity, of offenders, suspects, victims, witnesses and employees. Until very recently, a nine-point system of race and ethnic monitoring was used to gather statistics. It was based on the categories used by the UK 1991 National Census (hereafter, 1991 Census). However, the ways in which statistics are often collected and analysed is based on a modified four-point scale that includes "Black, White, Asian and Chinese and Other" (Chinese and Other being one category). This focus upon racial identity, rather than ethnicity, makes it difficult to substantiate any claims of discrimination or bias that Muslim communities might be experiencing within the criminal justice system, because Muslims are racially and ethnically diverse, and do not belong overwhelmingly to any one category.

April 2003 saw the introduction of a 16-point race and ethnic monitoring system, based on the system adopted in the UK 2001 National Census (hereafter, 2001 Census). The aim of this change is to provide a single common system for collecting

---

[20] M. O'Beirne, *Religion in England and Wales: findings from the 2001 Home Office Citizenship Survey,* London, Home Office, 2004 (hereafter, O'Beirne, *Religion in England and Wales*).

[21] O'Beirne, *Religion in England and Wales,* p. 18.

data on race and ethnicity in all agencies of the criminal justice system.[22] However, the new 16-point system of classification raises similar issues to those found under the nine-point system of ethnic monitoring. The new system does mean that more detailed information can be compiled in relation to individuals' ethnicities. But statistics in relation to offenders, suspects, victims, witnesses and employees of the criminal justice system, and any targets that are set, are likely to be presented according to a modified five-point scale, which focuses on the racial categories of "Black, White, Asian, Chinese and Other and Mixed".

This means that, under the new system, the experiences of particular Muslim communities will continue to be subsumed within these racial classifications. For instance, Pakistanis' and Bangladeshis' experiences are likely to continue to be merged with Indians' experiences within a general Asian category. This report therefore recommends that agencies of the criminal justice system, as well as the Home Office, should release data that relate to specific ethnic communities, and that specific targets should be set for these specific communities. In particular, data in relation to Pakistanis and Bangladeshis should be separated out from the general Asian racial category. Furthermore, this chapter stresses that, following the lead taken by the Prison Service, religious identity should also be increasingly monitored.

3.1   The Collection of Data on Ethnic and Faith Groups

The monitoring of minority ethnic groups' experiences of the criminal justice system has been done largely through the lens of race and ethnicity, and the issue of religious identity has rarely been addressed. This is due, in part, to the secular nature of the race relations movement. Researchers who have documented racial disadvantage and discrimination have, for many years, argued that public bodies should routinely assemble information about ethnicity (but not religion) in order to monitor disadvantage, and to ensure that their policies and practices do not disadvantage particular communities.

Local authorities were the first public agencies to begin ethnic monitoring in the late 1970s. The Race Relations Act (1976) was a powerful impetus here, because it extended the law to cover indirect, as well as direct, discrimination. Furthermore, Section 7 of that act gives local authorities specific responsibilities for ethnic monitoring.[23] At the same time, Section 95 of the Criminal Justice Act (1991) led to new measures to establish

---

[22]   Home Office, *Statistics on Race and the Criminal Justice System – 2003*, p. 4.

[23]   M. Fitzgerald and R. Sibbitt, "Ethnic Monitoring in Police Forces: a Beginning", in *Home Office Research Study 173*, London, Home Office, 1997, (hereafter, Fitzgerald and Sibbitt, *Ethnic Monitoring in Police Forces*).

consistent ethnic monitoring within agencies of the criminal justice system.[24] More recent legislation, under the Race Relations (Amendment) Act (2000) (RR(A)A), stipulates that those providing public services ensure that their policies and services are fair. The specific duties require key bodies to prepare and publish a Race Equality Scheme, which should demonstrate how they will promote race equality for staff and for the public that they serve. These bodies also have to set out their arrangements for assessing and consulting on proposed policies, to monitor for any adverse impact of their policies on the promotion of race equality and to ensure public access to information and services.

Official ethnic monitoring of suspects and offenders on a national basis first took place within the Probation Service and the Prison Service. But the Probation Service received poor returns on ethnicity, apparently due to concerns that this information might be used against minority ethnic groups rather than for them. The Prison Service, therefore, was the first agency of the criminal justice system to collect detailed data on the race and ethnicity of prisoners, a practice it began in 1985.[25] Ethnicity was initially determined through a combination of self-assessment by the prisoner and observation by the prison officer. In 1992, however, the Prison Service implemented a new system, which required prisoners to classify themselves. This system of classification mirrored the nine-point structure of the 1991 Census.[26] In March 2003, the Prison Service introduced the new ethnic categories based on the 16-point classification used in the 2001 Census.[27] Statistics based on this count have not yet been published.

The Prison Service is the only agency of the criminal justice system that also monitors religious affiliation. When prisoners arrive at a prison, they are asked to self-classify their religion.[28] This is due in part to the Prison Act (1952), which provides that

---

[24] Home Office, *Statistics on Race and the Criminal Justice System – 2003*.

[25] Fitzgerald and Sibbitt, *Ethnic Monitoring in Police Forces*.

[26] Home Office, *Statistics on Race and the Criminal Justice System – 2003*. See also: Appendix 1 Definitions: ethnic categories in the 1991 census.

[27] V. Hollis, I. Cross, and T. Olowe, *Prison Population Brief, England and Wales, October 2003*, London, HMSO, 2003. See also: Appendix 1 Definitions: ethnic categories in the 1991 census.

[28] The prison service use the following categories: Anglican (Anglican, Church in Wales, Church of England, Church of Ireland, Episcopalian), Roman Catholic, Free Church (Baptist, Celestial Church of God, Church of Scotland, Congregational, Methodist, Non-Conformist, Pentecostal, Presbyterian, Quaker, Salvation Army, United Reformed Church, Welsh Independent), Buddhist, Hindu, Jewish, Church of Jesus Christ of the Latter-day Saints, Muslim, Sikh, Other (Protestant, Jehovah's Witness, Greek/Russian Orthodox, Seven Day Adventist, Ethiopian Orthodox, Spiritualist, Chrisadelphian, Christian Scientist), Other non-Christian religions (Pagan, Druid, Taoist, Jain), Unrecognised Religions (Rastafarian, Nation of Islam), No religion (Atheist, Agnostic). See: Guessous et al, *Religion in Prisons, 1999 and 2000*.

members of other religious groups have the same right to practice their faith as Christian prisoners. This data reveals, for example, that Muslims form eight per cent of the prison population.[29]

At the local level, the police have collected information on ethnicity for many years, partly due to the information given by witnesses about the physical appearance of offenders. Local police forces have also been increasingly operating within an environment involving working partnerships and voluntary and statutory consultation arrangements with representatives of various ethnic groups. This has created the need for the collection of data on ethnicity, and, for this reason, local monitoring initiatives have been put together since the early 1990s. At the national level, a number of developments have led to an increased focus upon ethnic monitoring by the police.

Section 95 of the Criminal Justice Act (1991) requires that, every year, the Home Secretary must

> publish such information as he considers expedient for the purpose of (a) enabling persons engaged in the administration of criminal justice to become aware of the financial implications of their decisions, or (b) facilitating the performance by such persons of their duty to avoid discriminating against any persons on the grounds of race or sex or any other improper ground.[30]

This led to the issuing of Home Office Circular 70/1992 to all chief constables, which highlighted that additional monitoring would be necessary in order to fulfill the requirements of the act.[31]

Other important developments during this time include the Royal Commission on Criminal Justice, in 1993, which argued that a national system of race and ethnic monitoring should be implemented in the Police Service, in order to establish how minority ethnic communities are treated by the criminal justice system and to ensure that practices and procedures do not disadvantage particular groups. A joint working party involving the Association of Chief Police Officers (ACPO) and the Commission for Racial Equality (CRE) in 1993 also issued a strategic policy document, which included discussion of how ethnic monitoring is to be covered. At the same time, the Police Inspectorate introduced a Performance Indicator requiring all forces to provide

---

[29] Home Office, *Prison Statistics England and Wales – 2002*, p. 127.

[30] Home Office, *Statistics on Race and the Criminal Justice System – 2003*, p. iv.

[31] Fitzgerald and Sibbitt, *Ethnic Monitoring in Police Forces*, p. 9.

ethnicity statistics on their use of stop and search powers under the Police and Criminal Evidence Act (1984).[32]

While it was agreed that the data collected must be comparable to the 1991 Census nine-point structure, in some instances, this would not be possible. For example, in stop and search situations, this might not always be practical, as it would require police officers to ask people to classify themselves. It was decided that police officers in the street should use a four-point scale, modified from the 1991 Census nine-point structure, consisting of "Black, White, Asian and Other". It was argued that, based on a person's visual appearance, a police officer could group them into these basic categories.[33] This system would retain comparability with the 1991 Census codes, and the fuller nine-point scale could still be used in situations where it was feasible to do so. In 1996, mandatory ethnic monitoring came into effect in all police force areas, for stops and searches, arrests, cautions and homicides. The classifications were based on the police officer's visual perception of the suspect/victim, using the four-point scale.[34]

The Probation Service's data on race and ethnicity was first systematically collected in 1992, using the following categories: "Black, White, Other (please specify) or Refused". This data was gathered based on the question: "Where would you say your ethnic group comes from?" Results have been mapped based on the 1991 Census nine-point structure, or based on the four-point system referred to above.[35] The creation of the new National Offender Management Service (NOMS) in June 2004 has implications for data collection for the Probation and Prison Services. In the future, the probation part of NOMS may follow on from the Prison Service's lead and start to collect data on the religious identity of offenders.

From April 2003, all agencies of the criminal justice system were to begin collecting data on offenders, suspects, victims, witnesses and employees, based upon self-classification, using the 16-point classification system employed in the 2001 Census. This will make it possible to create a single common system for the collection of race and ethnic data in all agencies.[36] One result of this change is that, in addition to the visual assessment using the four point classification, it is mandatory for all police forces to record ethnicity based on the self-assessment of the suspect, using the 16-point

---

[32] Fitzgerald and Sibbitt, *Ethnic Monitoring in Police Forces*, p. 9. See also: *Policing and Racial Equality: a practical guide to the ACPO strategic policy document "Setting the Standards for Policing: meeting community expectations"*, Commission for Racial Equality, London, 1993.

[33] Asian in this context refers to individuals who are of Indian, Pakistani or Bangladeshi origin. Home Office, *Statistics on Race and the Criminal Justice System – 2003*, p. 12.

[34] Home Office, *Statistics on Race and the Criminal Justice System – 2003*.

[35] Home Office, *Statistics on Race and the Criminal Justice System – 2003*, p. 11.

[36] Home Office, *Statistics on Race and the Criminal Justice System – 2003*, p. 12.

classification.[37] However, it is sometimes impractical to secure cooperation from suspects or arrestees in classifying their own ethnicity.[38]

Crown and magistrates' courts have been asked to include information on the ethnicity of defendants in all new cases received from October 2001, based on information supplied to them by the police. Currently, information from magistrates' court is limited, due to the absence of a single national computer system, though steps are being taken to expand coverage. The Crown Prosecution Service has also agreed to introduce ethnic monitoring to all of their casework decisions. However, this is dependant upon the successful operation of new IT systems, which were to begin implementation in 2004. Staff will rely on ethnic data collected by the police.[39]

3.2 Monitoring Employees Working within the Criminal Justice System

Following race relations legislation, as well as Section 95 of the Criminal Justice Act (1991), agencies of the criminal justice system also collect data about the ethnicity of employees, this being according to the 16-point classification system since April 2003. However, the reports that agencies issue about the minority ethnic representation within their organisations, and the ethnicity targets that are set, tend to be presented according to the modified four point system ("White, Black, Asian and Other"), and, increasingly, according to the modified five-point system ("White, Black, Asian, Other and Mixed").

Similarly, statistics published by the Home Office in relation to the representation of minority ethnic practitioners within the Police Service, the Prison Service, the Probation Service, the Crown Prosecution Service and the Lord Chancellor's Department Headquarters, under the Home Office publication *Statistics on Race and the Criminal Justice System*, are according to the following categories: "White, Black, Asian, Other and Mixed". Statistics on the Crown Court staff are presented only slightly differently, according to the categories of "White, Black, Asian, Mixed, Chinese and Other".

However, for Magistrates' Court, statistics on staff do reveal the number of Bangladeshi, Indian and Pakistani employees. For example, for the period 2001-02, there was a total of 50 Pakistani Magistrates' court staff, as opposed to 143 Indian and

[37] Home Office, *Statistics on Race and the Criminal Justice System– 2003*, p. 12.

[38] Institute for Criminal Policy Research, *Race and the Criminal Justice System: an overview to the complete statistics 2002–2003*, London, Criminal Justice System, Race Unit, Home Office, 2004, p. 5.

[39] Home Office, *Statistics on Race and the Criminal Justice System – 2003*, p. 4.

19 Bangladeshi staff.[40] Similarly, information about the number of Bangladeshi, Indian and Pakistani barristers in independent practice and Queen's Counsel is also provided. For example, for the period 2001-02 there were 91 Pakistani barristers in independent practice, as opposed to 221 Indian and 30 Bangladeshi barristers.[41] Nonetheless, information about the specific ethnicities of the judiciary, magistracy and solicitors is not provided – instead, the following general racial categories are used: "White, Black, Asian, Mixed and Other".[42]

Within the Police Service, the Macpherson Inquiry into the death of Stephen Lawrence,[43] together with the HM Inspectorate of Constabulary report, *Winning the Race,* gave heightened focus to the need to pay greater attention to the recruitment, retention and career development of minority ethnic police officers.[44] The Government has established a national target of seven per cent for minority ethnic officers by 2009.[45] Most forces have some proactive recruitment measures in place. Personnel departments have collected data according to the nine-point format, and departments now collect data using the 16-point format. However, for the purposes of analysis, police forces use a modified five-point scale ("White, Black, Asian, Other, Mixed").[46] Targets are therefore set according to this modified scale, rather than being directed particularly at Pakistani and Bangladeshi, or other Muslim, communities.

Since April 2003, the Probation Service has been using the 2001 Census 16-point classification system for ethnic monitoring of staff and offenders.[47] However, the way in which ethnic representation amongst the workforce has been presented in publications, such as *The Heart of the Dance* (2003), has been according to the more general four-point format. Using this format, the National Probation Service has acknowledged that a disproportionately low number of Asians are employed, compared to African/African-Caribbean staff, and the service has set itself a goal of increasing

---

[40] Home Office, *Statistics on Race and the Criminal Justice System – 2003,* p. 79.

[41] Home Office, *Statistics on Race and the Criminal Justice System – 2003,* p. 81.

[42] Home Office, *Statistics on Race and the Criminal Justice System – 2003,* pp. 76–81.

[43] *The Stephen Lawrence Report,* Report of an Inquiry by Sir William MacPherson of Cluny, Cm. 4262-I, London, HMSO, 1999.

[44] Her Majesty's Inspectorate of Constabulary, *Winning the Race: embracing diversity,* London, HMIC, 2000.

[45] Home Office, *National Policing Plan for 2003–2006,* London, Home Office, 2002, p. 27, (hereafter, Home Office, *National Policing Plan for 2003–2006*).

[46] J. Cotton and C. Smith, *Police Service Strength England and Wales March 31ˢᵗ 2003,* London, Office of National Statistics, 11 March 2003, p. 6, (hereafter, Cotton and Smith, *Police Service Strength England and Wales March 31ˢᵗ 2003*).

[47] Home Office, *Statistics on Race and the Criminal Justice System – 2003.*

Asian representation in its workforce by 20 per cent.[48] However, no specific targets for Bangladeshis/Pakistanis have been considered.

Within HM Inspectorate Reports on race equality, the ethnic composition of Probation Boards is referred to as "minority representation", so it is not possible to know exactly what communities are being referred to here.[49] Thus, the publication *Towards Race Equality* highlights how, by 2001, minority representation on Probation Boards was 16 per cent of the total board membership. This report also refers to the selection of 18 minority ethnic Probation Board members, who are to act as diversity advisers to all Probation Boards. However, further information about the ethnicity of these individuals is not given.[50]

The Prison Service also sets targets for the percentage of minority ethnic representation in general. According to the HM Prison Service Annual Report 2004, the service met its target for 2003–2004 of ensuring that 5.5 per cent of its staff came from minority ethnic groups.[51]

The Crown Prosecution Service presents employment statistics according to two basic categories: White and minority ethnic. According to data issued by the Crown Prosecution Service Human Resources Department, out of all staff members who provided details on their ethnic background in 2004, 14.1 per cent belonged to minority ethnic groups.[52] Statistics issued by the Home Office in relation to the Crown Prosecution Service are more detailed. According to the Home Office, for the period 2001/02, while the proportion of ethnic minorities within the Crown Prosecution Service rose from 9.2 per cent to 12.2 per cent, there was a decline of 6.9 per cent for Asians.[53] A staff survey is also carried out every two years by the Crown Prosecution Service, and recently it has included a question regarding the religious identity of

---

[48] National Probation Directorate, *The Heart of the Dance: a diversity strategy for the National Probation Service for England and Wales 2002–2006*, London, National Probation Directorate, 2003, p. 11, Objective 1.2.1 "To increase the existing Asian Representation (250) within the NPS workforce by 20 per cent", (hereafter, National Probation Directorate, *The Heart of the Dance*).

[49] HM Inspectorate of Probation, *Towards Race Equality: Follow-up Inspection Report*, London, HM Inspectorate of Probation, 2004, (hereafter, HM Inspectorate of Probation , *Towards Race Equality: Follow-up Inspection Report*).

[50] HM Inspectorate of Probation, *Towards Race Equality: Follow-up Inspection Report*, p. 41.

[51] HM Prison Service, *Annual Report and Accounts April 2003–March 2004*, London, HM Prison Service, 2004, p. 49.

[52] Statistics obtained from the Pay and Performance Team, Human Resources Department, Crown Prosecution Service (CPS), "CPS Staff in Post: ethnic background by level as at 1st April 2004", p. 1.

[53] Home Office, *Statistics on Race and the Criminal Justice System – 2003*, p. 75.

employees.[54] Results are not yet available. According to statistics issued by the Home Office, for the period of 2001/02, four per cent of senior grade employees working within the Lord Chancellor's Department Headquarters were Asian; there were also five Asian district judges, 15 Asian recorders and two Asian circuit judges.[55]

Victim Support, a network of affiliated charities that run court and community-based services aimed at helping the victims of crime, collects data about the race and ethnicity of staff, volunteers and trustees, using the 16-point system of classification. In 2003, for those volunteers who gave information about their ethnicity, 1.1 per cent were Pakistani, 0.2 per cent were Bangladeshi and 1.5 per cent were Indian. In 2003, for those members of staff who provided details about their ethnic background, 0.6 per cent were Pakistani, 0.5 per cent were Bangladeshi and 1.7 per cent were Indian.[56] Victim Support wants the ethnicity of volunteers and staff to reflect not only the wider general population, but also to reflect the ethnic composition of the local communities that volunteers and staff serve.[57]

The fact that agencies of the criminal justice system predominantly use very general racial categories when presenting data and setting targets for minority ethnic representation among employees has some important limitations. Although it is known that people from minority ethnic backgrounds are under-represented in all grades as employees in the Police Service and the Prison Service, and in all senior posts in all criminal justice agencies, the extent of under-representation of specific communities, and of Muslims in general, has not been assessed.[58]

Moreover, while some areas of the criminal justice system – such as the Probation Service and Victim Support – have been extremely successful in recruiting minority ethnic staff, it may be the case that the increased level of recruitment has not come from Muslim communities specifically. Indeed, the statistics issued by Victim Support serve to illustrate this point, because the representation of Pakistanis and Bangladeshis, amongst both volunteers and members of staff, is much lower than that of Indians. Thus, although minority ethnic representation has increased, Muslim representation may not have significantly increased. In fact, it may have stayed the same, or even decreased.

---

[54] Interview with Seamus Taylor, Head of Equality and Diversity, CPS Equality and Diversity Unit, April 2004, London.

[55] Home Office, *Statistics on Race and the Criminal Justice System – 2003*, pp. 79–80.

[56] Victim Support, *Ethnicity of Volunteers and Staff for 2003*, London, Victim Support, Research Department, National Office, 2003, p. 1.

[57] Interview with Fiona Richmond and Ben Smith of Victim Support, National Office, London, March 2004.

[58] Home Office, *Statistics on Race and the Criminal Justice System – 2003*, p. 8.

For those agencies of the criminal justice system where minority ethnic representation among staff has been substantially improved, some important examples of good policy and practice may be drawn and passed onto other agencies of the criminal justice sector. However, for this to be effective, there needs to be greater specificity in terms of identifying exactly which minority ethnic groups have benefited, and creative ways must be found to increase the representation of groups that are under-represented.

Where Pakistanis and Bangladeshis are grouped together with Indians within a broader Asian or South Asian category, the particular difficulties faced by Pakistani and Bangladeshi communities can be obscured, because these groups experience more socio-economic deprivation, and higher offence and incarceration rates, than Indian groups. At the same time, any criminal justice policy targets that are set to give benefits to members of the general category "Asian" may not reach the more-deprived Pakistani and Bangladeshi communities. Instead, targets may be reached through the greater involvement of Indian communities. This is a problem because, it has been argued, the social and economic profile for Indians is similar to the White population – though according to data from the 2001 Census, 12.7 per cent of Indians are Muslim.[59]

In order to increase the representation of Muslims among their employees, agencies of the criminal justice system should collect and use more detailed data for any reports that they issue, and for any proactive targets that are set. First, where data is available regarding the number of Pakistanis and Bangladeshis who work for a particular agency, this should be explicitly presented, so that statistics relating to Pakistani and Bangladeshi employees are separated from those relating to Indian employees. Agencies should also consider setting targets according to Pakistani and Bangladeshi representation, keeping them distinct from any overall Asian target. Second, agencies should consider broadening the ethnic monitoring of staff, to include other minority ethnic groups. Finally, agencies should consider carrying out surveys of the faith or religious affiliation of staff, in order to obtain a better picture of Muslim representation among staff.

3.3   Monitoring Victims of Crime

It is not only important to reconsider the collection of statistics covering the race and ethnicity of criminal justice system employees, offenders and suspects. The ethnic monitoring of victims is also important. Most police forces record the ethnicity of victims, and they are currently moving towards using the 16-point format. Following the

---

[59] Clancy et al., *Crime, Policing and Justice.* See also 2001 UK National Census, *Ethnic Group by Religion,* available at http://www.statistics.gov.uk/census2001/profiles/commentaries/ethnicity.asp (accessed 21 September 2004).

implementation of the Police Performance Assessment Framework in April 2004, which includes a measure on detection rates by victim ethnicity for offences of violence against the person, victims' ethnicity will increasingly be classified in a more standardised manner.[60] Details of victims' ethnicity might then be passed on to the Probation Service's victim liaison officers, staff of the Crown Prosecution Service and Victim Support staff and volunteers – all of whom may be providing help and support to these individuals.

According to the HM Inspectorate of Probation report *Towards Race Equality*, there has been no central work by the National Probation Service to facilitate local access by probation areas to victim monitoring information that is held by the police or the Crown Prosecution Service. Out of 42 probation areas, 35 areas had no data at all on the race and ethnicity of victims, while four others were attempting to build up monitoring arrangements. Only three areas had achieved a comprehensive monitoring of victims: Dyfed-Powys, Nottinghamshire and County Durham.[61] The HM Inspectorate of Probation report, *Valuing the Victim*, highlights the need for a nationally based agreement with the police.[62]

Data on victims' ethnicity is collected by the Witness Services and the Victim Supportline run by Victim Support. However, Victim Support has not yet put in place a national system for gathering this data. Currently, a project is underway that will look at the kinds of statistics that are collected within the local victim support schemes, and this will include demographic information relating to victims supported.[63] Information about victims' ethnicity is recorded by some local support schemes. For example, in Northamptonshire, the County Racist Incidents Officer at Victim Support collects statistics about the ethnicity of victims of racist incidents who report these incidents directly to them. These statistics are compiled in six-monthly formats and include the following ethnic identities: Bangladeshi, Pakistani, Somali, Indian, Travellers and Kosovar.

Data about minority ethnic groups' experiences of victim support is also collected via Witness Support and Satisfaction surveys, carried out by the Home Office. These

---

[60] The Police Performance Assessment Framework is an initiative by the Home Office, Association of Chief Police Officers and the Association of Police Authorities. It sets out a set of indicators for assessing the performance of the police forces.

[61] HM Inspectorate of Probation, *Towards Race Equality: Follow-up Inspection Report*, p. 19.

[62] HM Inspectorate of Probation, *Valuing the Victim: an inspection into national victim contact arrangements*, London, HM Inspectorate of Probation, 2004, (hereafter, HM Inspectorate of Probation, *Valuing the Victim*).

[63] E-mail correspondence with a policy officer Victim Support, 30 July 2004.

surveys include a booster sample of minority ethnic groups.[64] However, for the 2002 Witness Satisfaction Survey, an insufficient number of minority ethnic witnesses were interviewed. The small sample size meant that it was impossible to draw any firm conclusions about differences in the satisfaction or experiences of specific minority ethnic groups. Data relating to ethnicity is limited here, and is presented according to a general four-point format: "White, Black, Asian and Other"[65] Victim Support is about to implement a national Victim Satisfaction Survey, which will include the use of the 16- point system of race and ethnic monitoring.[66] It is important that, where data is available regarding Pakistani and Bangladeshi communities, they are publicly released.

The British Crime Survey offers a further means for documenting Muslim communities' experiences of crime and the criminal justice system. The annual British Crime Survey allows policy makers to look at a wide range of crime-related issues, including the levels of crime reporting to the police, attitudes towards the police, attitudes towards the criminal justice system and individuals' fear of crime. Unlike the Witness Satisfaction Survey or the data collected by police, the data obtained by the British Crime Survey is not reliant upon people officially reporting their experiences to agencies of the criminal justice system. As a result, this survey can capture the experiences of a wider range of individuals.

From January 2001, the British Crime Survey has included an annual minority ethnic boost sample. This is because a sample of the general population will not contain a sufficiently large number of individuals of minority ethnic identity. Researchers designing and implementing the British Crime Survey argue that greater disaggregation of minority ethnic groups is desirable. However, due to the need for cost-effectiveness, and given the size and geographical distributions of the diverse communities, this has not happened. Although researchers argue that they would like to differentiate between Pakistani and Bangladeshi groups, at present the two groups are combined, because the numbers are too small to support reliable statistical analysis.[67] This problem of sample size highlights an important difficulty in introducing greater specificity into the monitoring of ethnicity, a point addressed in more detail later in this chapter.

---

[64] The Witness Satisfaction Survey was carried out by the Home Office (in 2000 and 2002) in order to explore and monitor witnesses' experiences of the key agencies of the criminal justice system, these being the police, the CPS/prosecution lawyers, defence lawyers, court staff, judges and magistrates, Victim Support and the Witness Service. Witnesses are recruited from Crown Court centres and Magistrates Courts. See: H. Angle, S. Malam, and C. Carey, *Witness Satisfaction: findings from the Witness Satisfaction Survey 2002, Report 19/03*, London, Home Office, 2003 (hereafter, Angle et al, *Witness Satisfaction*).

[65] Angle et al, *Witness Satisfaction*.

[66] E-mail correspondence with Ben Smith, Policy Officer, Victim Support, 30 July 2004.

[67] Clancy et al Crime, *Policing and Justice*, p. 2.

3.4   Confidence in the Criminal Justice System

The Government is currently tackling the issue of confidence in the criminal justice system. Results from the British Crime Survey show that people from minority ethnic groups are more likely than the rest of the population to believe that the criminal justice system as a whole is doing a good job. However, it is also clear that their experiences of criminal justice are very different from White people. For example, minority ethnic groups are more likely to show confidence in the courts, judiciary, magistracy, the Crown Prosecution Service and probation services than the White majority, but they are less likely to have confidence in the police and prison services.[68] A study by the Home Office shows that, although a lower proportion of minority ethnic respondents (58 per cent, compared to 63 per cent of the overall sample) are confident about how crime is dealt with in the area where they live, a higher proportion of minority respondents (53 per cent, compared to 47 per cent overall) are confident about the way crime is dealt with nationally.[69]

The *2001 Citizenship Survey* findings indicate that minority ethnic groups believe they will be treated worse than people from other races by the criminal justice system, especially the police, prison service, courts and the Crown Prosecution Service.[70] The Home Office has introduced Criminal Justice System Public Service Agreements (PSAs) in order to boost the efficiency of the criminal justice system. One key target that has been set is in relation to increasing the number of crimes for which an offender is brought to justice, since there is a large gap between the number of offences that are recorded and the number that lead to an offender being arrested and punished. Two further, related targets are: the need to raise public confidence in the criminal justice system and the need to increase, year-on-year, the satisfaction of victims and witnesses. Public confidence and satisfaction is considered important because it is argued that the justice system relies on public co-operation and involvement to function effectively. These targets have been published in a framework document, *Improving Public Satisfaction and Confidence in the Criminal Justice System,* which is aimed at local Criminal Justice Boards and outlines the approach agreed by the National Criminal

---

[68]   Home Office, *Statistics on Race and the Criminal Justice System – 2003*, p. 9.

[69]   B. Page, R. Wake, and A. Ames, *Public Confidence in the Criminal Justice System: Home Office Research Findings 221,* London, HMSO, 2004, p. 1.

[70]   Attwood et al, *Home Office Citizenship Survey,* p. 5.

Justice Board. The document provides guidance on developing local plans for improving public satisfaction and confidence.[71]

Agencies of the criminal justice system have also been given national and local targets in relation to increasing public confidence in the effectiveness of the criminal justice system. A national target of a three per cent increase in Black and minority ethnic groups' confidence in the effectiveness of the criminal justice system in bringing offenders to justice has been set. This will be measured by comparing data supplied by the British Crime Survey 2005-06 with data supplied by the 2002-03 British Crime Survey. The Government also plans to introduce local targets for increased confidence in areas where there are high Black and minority ethnic populations, including London, West Midlands, Greater Manchester, West Yorkshire, Thames Valley and Leicester. Local data will be collected via the introduction of a new local crime survey.[72]

The introduction of PSAs, and targets to boost minority ethnic communities' confidence in the criminal justice system, is a significant and positive development. Nonetheless, the Government's targets seem to be set in relation to Black and minority ethnic groups in general, which means that it will not be possible to see what groups in particular show an increase in confidence. Particularly in relation to the impact of anti-terror legislation on British Muslim communities, it would be useful to know if Muslim communities' confidence has been increased as a result of any measures that have been introduced via the local criminal justice boards, especially in areas where there is a high proportion of Muslims. Here again, there needs to be a re-consideration of the system of ethnic monitoring in place. Authorities must consider whether, either via the British Crime Survey or local crime surveys, data that is collected, presented and analysed about ethnicity might be more specific. Additionally, consideration needs to be paid to the issue of religious identity and whether this should also feature in measures to boost minority ethnic groups' confidence in the criminal justice system.

3.5   Improving the Monitoring of Ethnic Groups

The collection of data on race and ethnicity within the criminal justice system have, over the years, become more nuanced, especially with the current movement towards standardisation, through the adoption of the 2001 Census 16-point scale. However,

---

[71]   The National Criminal Justice Board was created in 2003, and is responsible for supporting 42 local criminal justice boards to deliver the Criminal Justice System PSAs. The Board also has responsibility for combating inequality and discrimination in the criminal justice system, and for communication across the system.

[72]   Home Office, *Improving Public Satisfaction and Confidence in the Criminal Justice System Framework Document,* London, Home Office, 2003.

the examples discussed in the previous sections highlight how a more nuanced form of monitoring is necessary, over and above any classification of faith or religious affiliation that may be introduced. In particular, greater specificity in terms of the ethnic categories that are used – and greater specificity in the ways in which data is subsequently analysed and research statistics are presented – would be advantageous for better assessing the specific situation of Muslims in the UK.

Where criminal justice agencies use the full nine-point or, more recently, the 16-point classification systems, data should be available regarding the experience of Pakistanis and Bangladeshis, who constitute almost 60 per cent of the Muslim population in Britain.[73] This means that it might be possible to get an accurate picture of the issues related to criminal justice facing Pakistanis and Bangladeshis, and it may be possible to set targets specifically for these communities within current monitoring systems.

This approach, however, has some important limitations. First, not all Bangladeshis and Pakistanis are Muslims. According to data from the 2001 Census, 92 per cent of Bangladeshis and Pakistanis living in the UK are Muslim. Second, the present system of monitoring does not reveal any information about the 40 per cent of British Muslims from outside of these communities. Finally, whilst, in theory, the nine- or 16-point race and ethnic monitoring formats are encouraged by the Home Office and agencies of the criminal justice system, in practice, race seems to be the predominant focus. The collection of statistics, the presentation of this data and the ways in which research is conducted and statistically analysed is according to a modified four-point system of racial classification, which uses the categories "White, Black, Asian and Other" – though, more recently, under the 16-point system of monitoring, the "Mixed" category is increasingly being introduced.

With respect to research reports related to crime and criminal justice, whereas some studies will feature the experiences of Pakistanis and Bangladeshis, other reports will subsume these groups within a broader Asian or South Asian category. For example, prison statistics published by the Home Office are sometimes presented according to the categories "White, Black, South Asian, Chinese and Other", but, in other cases, these statistics are presented in a more nuanced format, using the nine-point or 16-point structures. Statistics about the male population under sentence, by ethnic group and offence type, are presented according to the four basic categories.[74] However, the incarceration rates of male and female British nationals are presented according to the more detailed format. The more specific statistics reveal that the incarceration rate per

---

[73] Both the nine-point and 16-point systems include the ethnic categories Indian, Pakistani, Bangladeshi. See Appendix 1: Definitions.

[74] Home Office, *Prison Statistics, England and Wales – 2000*, London, Home Office, HMSO, 2001, p. 113, (hereafter, Home Office, *Prison Statistics England and Wales – 2000*).

100,000 of the general population is 126 for Indians; 329 for Pakistanis; and 193 for Bangladeshis. But according to more general statistics, the overall incarceration rate for the category Asian is 199.[75] The decision of whether to use racial or ethnic categories seems to be related to sample sizes and issues of statistical significance. In situations where the samples are too small to draw firm conclusions about the experiences of Pakistanis or Bangladeshis, the general Asian category will be used instead.

The British Crime Survey generally avoids combining Indian, Pakistani and Bangladeshi groups into a single Asian category. As a result, the survey does contain information about Pakistanis' and Bangladeshis' experiences of crime and justice. Still, the available information is rather limited, and statistics from the British Crime Survey are also often presented according to the general categories of "Asian, Mixed Background, Chinese/Other, Black and White". For example, in a report stemming from the British Crime Survey 2001/2002, *Ethnicity and Drug Use,* findings are presented according to the categories "Asian, Mixed Background, Chinese/Other, Black and White". Sample size appears again to be a major limitation, because the authors argue that, due to the small numbers of people engaged in drug use across the different ethnic groups, it is not possible to explore links between drug use, ethnicity, social disadvantage and exclusion. Nonetheless, they argue that once two or more similar survey years are available, data might be combined, to allow further investigation.[76]

Yet, even if the Asian category is divided into Pakistani and Bangladeshi subgroups for the purposes of statistical analysis, this still leaves unexplored the experience of the remaining 40 per cent of Muslims who are from other minority ethnic communities, such as Afghan, Arab, Iranian, Indian, Kosovar, Kurdish, Turkish and Somali Muslims. Indeed, the research report on the *Citizenship Survey* (2001) specifically highlights the diversity of the Muslim faith community, and Muslim research participants indicated that they were from 11 of the 15 ethnic groups listed in the study.[77] This means that there is a significant case for looking beyond Pakistani and Bangladeshi experiences, so that a wider range of Muslim groups are also recognised, and so that policies and targets that are set on improving the disadvantage and discrimination experienced by minority ethnic groups can include the diverse range of Muslim communities living in Britain.

The Race Relations Amendment Act (RR(A)A) 2000 requires that those providing public services ensure that their policies and services are fair. Specifically, the act

---

[75] Home Office, *Prison Statistics, England and Wales – 2000,* p. 115.

[76] R. Aust and N. Smith, "Ethnicity and Drug Use: key findings from the 2001/2002 British Crime Survey", in *HM Prison Service Annual Report and Accounts,* London, The Stationery Office, 2003.

[77] O'Beirne, *Religion in England and Wales,* p. 8.

requires key bodies to prepare and publish a Race Equality Scheme, which should involve an examination of policies and procedures in terms of whether they may have a negative impact upon minority ethnic groups. The scheme should also set out a format for ensuring that any forms of discrimination are addressed. In addition, the act requires key bodies to describe their arrangements for assessing and consulting on proposed policies, to allow monitoring for any adverse impact of the proposals on the promotion of race equality and to ensure public access to information and services. It would appear that the RR(A)A 2000 might act as the legislative mechanism through which agencies of the criminal justice system should consider monitoring the experiences of a wider range of minority ethnic communities and implementing policies aimed at those specific communities.

There is also a very practical reason for the documentation of a wider range of minority ethnic groups. Voluntary welfare organisations working within, and for, these diverse communities may need to have details about where their service users are located within the criminal justice system. Under the present system of ethnic monitoring, however, such information is generally unavailable. For example, the IQRA Trust recently received a request from a Somali organisation wanting to locate Somali prisoners, so as to be able to help them whilst they are incarcerated. However, details regarding the whereabouts of Somali prisoners are not easily available, either under the ethnic monitoring or the religious monitoring systems of classification used by the Prison Service.[78] Another example involves the Aziziya Mosque in Stoke Newington, which was keen to help members of the Turkish community who are in prison, many of whom are non-English speakers.[79] Again, details about Turkish prisoners are not easily available, so it is very difficult for welfare groups to establish contact with these prisoners.

While collecting information about the specific ethnicities of individuals being processed by the criminal justice system would undoubtedly be of practical benefit, in many instances, this approach also has some important limitations. Such information may not easily translate into the compilation of research statistics in relation to these communities, due to the low numbers of individuals belonging to these diverse groups. According to the 2001 Census, the minority ethnic population constitutes 4.6 million people, or 7.9 per cent, of the total UK population of 58.8 million. However, those individuals classified as "Other Asian", "Black African", "Black Other" and "Other" constitute just 1,061,141 individuals, or 1.8 per cent of the total population. This means that it may not be possible to carry out valid statistical analyses in relation to each individual community, and so communities may inevitably have to be grouped

---

[78] Interview with Salah el-Hassan, Director of the IQRA Trust, April 2004, Birmingham University.

[79] Interview with Salah el-Hassan, Director of the IQRA Trust, April 2004, Birmingham University.

together according to various aspects of their class/ethnic/religious identities. This point takes us to the issue of monitoring the religious identity of offenders, suspects, victims, witnesses and employees within the criminal justice system.

3.6   Religious Monitoring

The focus upon ethnicity means that the role of religion in individuals' lives, and the significance of their religious identity, has been largely omitted in policy-making terms. Whilst direct and institutional racism by the police, the courts and the penal system has been documented, and policies have been implemented to tackle these issues, discrimination on the grounds of religion has rarely been addressed. The racist murder of Stephen Lawrence led to the publication of the *Macpherson Report* (1999), which defined institutional racism as "unwitting prejudice, ignorance, thoughtlessness and racist stereotyping which disadvantages minority ethnic people". The need to tackle institutional racism within public services has led to the implementation of new policies, training procedures and recruitment targets. A report commissioned by the Runnymede Trust found that "Islamophobia" is endemic to British society:

> The term Islamophobia refers to unfounded hostility towards Islam. It refers also to the practical consequences of such hostility in unfair discrimination against Muslims and to the exclusion of Muslims from mainstream political and social affairs.... Islam is seen as violent and aggressive.[80]

Islamophobia leads to both covert and overt discrimination that disadvantages Muslim communities. Anti-Muslim sentiment and Islamophobia have increased in the aftermath of the terrorist atrocities of 11 September 2001.[81] In a survey looking at the effects of the events of 11 September on discrimination and implicit racism in five religious and seven ethnic groups, religion was found to be more important than ethnicity in indicating which groups were most likely to experience racism and discrimination.[82] Moreover, this research indicates the existence of "modern" and implicit religious discrimination. The phrase "modern religious discrimination" indicates that prejudice against religious communities continues to exist in a "post-civil rights, politically correct era". "Implicit" religious discrimination refers to daily life situations in which covert religious prejudice, such as being treated rudely or not being

---

[80]   Commission on British Muslims and Islamophobia, *Islamophobia, a challenge for us all*, London, The Runnymede Trust, 1997, p. 10.

[81]   IMRC, *The Hidden Victims of September 11th*.

[82]   L. Sheridan, R. Gillett, E. Blaauw and F.W. Winkel, *Effects of the Events of September 11th on Discrimination and Implicit Racism in Five Religious and Seven Ethnic Groups*, Leicester, University of Leicester School of Psychology, 2003, p. 19, (hereafter, Sheridan et al, *Effects of the Events of September 11th*).

taken seriously, can be experienced.[83] British White People also reported a rise in post-11 September discrimination, and of the White people in the study who said they faced religious discrimination, almost half were Muslim.[84]

These reports and surveys highlight the difficulty of approaching the documentation of Muslim communities' social and criminal justice experiences solely through the lens of ethnicity. As O'Beirne's report on the *Citizenship Survey* (2001) makes clear, religious affiliation is a fundamental aspect of the lives of many individuals belonging to minority ethnic groups, and so approaching diversity predominantly through the strand of ethnicity fails to take into consideration people's religious identities and their social experiences in relation to their faith.[85] Indeed, according to the Commission on the Future of Multi-Ethnic Britain, Muslims have become disillusioned with an anti-racism movement that refuses to combat Islamophobia.[86] Specific attention should be paid to the negative stereotyping of Muslims and the direct and indirect discrimination they face.

Monitoring is an essential tool for identifying discrimination. It is important to consider points at which data on religious identity might be collected within the criminal justice system, so that religious affiliation, as well as ethnicity, might help to inform policy and practice. Based on discussions with individuals who work in the criminal and community justice fields, there appears to be an assumption among government agencies and the voluntary support sector that asking people for information about their religious affiliation is intrusive. These workers seem to feel that questions about religion might serve to damage the relationship between the client and the service provider. However, there is no research to either validate or dismiss this assumption. As a first step, it is important for service providers to carry out research into whether their clients perceive religious monitoring to be overtly intrusive, or whether a significant proportion of clients would welcome such monitoring. At the same time, however, adequate protections must be put into place, to prevent abuse of such potentially sensitive data.

Following on from this point, each agency of the criminal justice system should carefully consider the points at which religious monitoring might take place. The 2001 Census included a voluntary question about religious identity, and agencies might be able to adopt this format. Alternatively, the format used by the Prison Service, which is more detailed, might also be used. Monitoring religious identity would enhance our knowledge about a wide range of crime and criminal justice issues, and this would have

---

[83] Sheridan et al, *Effects of the Events of September 11th*, p. 13. and 19.

[84] Sheridan et al, *Effects of the Events of September 11th*, p. 20.

[85] O'Beirne, *Religion in England and Wales*, p. 1.

[86] Commission on the Future of a Multi-ethnic Britain, *The Future of Multi-ethnic Britain: the Parekh Report*, London, Profile Books, 2000, p. 62.

some important practical benefits. For example, faith communities involved in the re-settlement of prisoners have argued that it would help them if statistics could be made available regarding the re-offending rates of particular faith communities.[87] Currently, however, statistics about this topic are compiled on the basis of an ethnic monitoring system.

There are three developments within criminal justice that might lead to an increased focus upon religious monitoring.

First, police forces will do more to monitor the religious identity of victims, particularly in the context of religiously aggravated offences. Where local partnerships between the police and other statutory and voluntary agencies begin to focus upon religiously aggravated crimes, then local police forces may feel increased pressure to monitor the religious identity of victims. This will also help agencies cater to victims' needs more specifically, and, where these details are passed on to the Crown Prosecution Service, the Probation Service and Victim Support, they can be used as the basis from which to inform service delivery.

Second, the merger of the Prison and Probation Services into the new NOMS (National Offender Management Service) will enable the probation part of the new service to consider monitoring the religious identity of offenders that it manages. Since the Prison Service already collects data about the religious identity of prisoners, the probation wing of NOMS might consider the extent to which it will be possible to use the Prison Service's categories and systems of monitoring. These statistics can then be used in order to draw conclusions about Muslim offenders and to inform practice and policy decisions, an issue we will return to later on in this report.

Third, from April 2003, Crown Prosecution Service areas will be required to submit the standard Racist Incident Monitoring Scheme (RIMS) forms in cases of religiously aggravated offences. When appropriate, these forms will have to be clearly marked to identify that the case involves a religiously aggravated offence.[88] See section five for further details about RIMS.

---

[87] Meeting of Chaplaincy Council, November 2003, Interview with Salah el-Hassan, Chairman of the IQRA Trust, April 2004, Birmingham University.

[88] Crown Prosecution Service, *Racist Incident Monitoring Scheme (RIMS): Annual Report 2002–2003*, London, CPS, p. 35, (hereafter, *RIMS Annual Report 2002–2003*).

3.7 Researching Muslims' Experiences, and Perceptions, of Crime and Criminal Justice

At the moment, Muslims' experiences and perceptions are not being directly explored by agencies of the criminal justice system. As was explained in the preceding sections, this is due, in part, to the system of race and ethnic monitoring that is currently in place. This system uses very general race categories to monitor individuals' experiences. Therefore, as was explained, Muslims' experiences are subsumed within broader categories and generally remain hidden. Religious monitoring is rarely carried out.

There is an urgent need for detailed research to examine the following core issues:

1. Anti-Muslim sentiment, Islamophobia and discrimination in Muslims' daily lives.

2. Muslims' perceptions of the risk they face in being the victims of religious/racist hate crime, racially/religiously aggravated offences and discrimination and prejudice.

3. the extent to which Muslim communities are being unfairly targeted by the new anti-terror powers.

4. Muslims' perceptions that they are being unfairly targeted by anti-terror legislation.

5. Muslims' perceptions of, and confidence in, the correctional services – the police, the Crown Prosecution Service, the Probation Service and the Prison Service.

The voices of young Muslims and women are particularly likely to be marginalised through the existing consultation processes that are now in use, so research should specifically focus on their experiences.

Muslim organisations have been, and remain, active in monitoring Muslims' experiences of Islamophobia. For example, the Islamic Human Rights Commission (IHRC) documented the rise in aggression against Muslims following the 11 September attacks in the United States. Information was collected from a wide range of Muslim organisations, and victims were also directly reporting incidents to the IHRC. According to the IHRC report, Muslims experienced malicious phone calls and death threats, and women and children in particular experienced physical and verbal abuse. The IHRC documented 188 cases of verbal and written abuse, 20 cases of discrimination, 108 cases of psychological pressure and harassment and 344 serious crimes of violence.[89] The Forum

---

[89] IMRC, *The Hidden Victims of September 11th*.

Against Islamophobia and Racism (FAIR) has also logged Islamophobic incidents using a wide range of sources, including reports in both the Muslim and mainstream media and reports that were brought directly to the organisation.

There is now a need for more extensive research. Large-scale surveys should specifically focus on Muslim communities, to record Muslims' experiences and perceptions of the criminal justice system, as well as their feelings of (un)safety and their experiences of victimisation. The data needs to be carefully analysed, so that there is better understanding of how perceptions and experiences differ according to variables such as age, class and gender. This analysis might employ national or local crime surveys. The British Crime Survey might be one mechanism through which such statistics can be delivered.

Despite the wide diversity of Muslim communities, it might be argued that certain oppressive structures and discriminatory practices in relation to Muslims' faith identity frame individual lives. In the aftermath of the terrorist attacks in the United States on 11 September 2001, and in the course of the subsequent fight against terrorism, it can be argued that the documentation of the experiences of crime amongst Muslim communities is crucial, and the British Crime Survey might be an effective tool for doing this. By classifying individuals according to their religious affiliation, it may be possible to produce a booster sample consisting of a diverse range of Muslim communities, so that statistically valid results might be obtained in relation to these communities' experiences of crime and the criminal justice system. As will be argued later on in this report, Muslims' perceptions of policing include the notion that they are being unfairly targeted by the police as part of the ongoing fight against terrorism, but we need to have more extensive research that examines this issue.

The British Crime Survey, through the inclusion of a booster sample of Muslim communities, could help to systematically research this issue. However, such national crime surveys significantly undercount sensitive topics like hate crime.[90] Furthermore, researchers within the Home Office might argue that it is too costly or impractical to carry out a survey that specifically samples Muslim communities. Therefore, local crime surveys – carried out in partnership between Muslim organisations and universities, or other organisations, such as the CRE, might be a better, and more realistic – way forward.

Local crime surveys could target cities in which there are significant numbers of Muslims, including London, Birmingham, Manchester and Bradford. They can include questions about a wide range of issues, such as attitudes towards the

---

[90] B. Bowling, *Violent Racism: victimisation, policing and social context,* revised edition, Oxford, Oxford University Press, 1999, (hereafter, Bowling, *Violent Racism*); and S. Walklate, "Appreciating the Victim", in R. Matthews and J. Young (eds.), *Issues in Realist Criminology,* London, Sage, 1992, pp. 102–118.

community; attitudes towards crime; attitudes towards the police; experiences with crime, as a victim or a witness; and experiences with the police and other agencies that deal with crime. Specific information can also be sought regarding details of the offence, the offender and the impact of the crime on the victim. Muslim organisations can be involved in the design and evaluation of surveys, and they are crucial in terms of establishing trust and trying to get a high response rate from research participants.

An examination of Muslims' perceptions of, and confidence in, the correctional services might then be used as the basis from which to set targets to increase Muslims' confidence levels, as, currently, the government's targets seeking to boost minority ethnic communities' confidence in the criminal justice system do not relate specifically to Muslims. There is also a need for qualitative research that explores, in-depth, Muslims' experiences and perceptions of crime, criminal justice and community justice. In particular, the experiences of Muslim youth need to be further explored. There are currently only a limited number of studies looking at the experiences of both perpetrators and victims.[91]

---

[91] See: M. Quraishi, *Muslims and Crime*, London, Ashgate, 2005 (forthcoming); A. Wardak, *Social Control and Deviance: A South Asian Community in Scotland*, London, Ashgate, 2000; and C. Webster, "Youth Crime, Victimisation and Harassment: The Keighley Crime Survey", in *Community Studies*, No 7, Bradford, Bradford and Ilkley Community College, Department of Applied and Community Studies, 1994.

4. Policing Muslim Communities

Following the passage of the Police Reform Act (2002), the first annual National Policing Plan for the Police Service in England and Wales has been published by the Home Secretary, in consultation with the Association of Chief Police Officers, the Association of Police Authorities and other key stakeholders.[92] This plan outlines a set of national priorities for the Police Service, as well as the indicators against which performance will be judged. It provides the framework within which chief police officers and police authorities should prepare their own local three-year and annual policing plans.

National priorities are closely linked to the Home Office PSA (Public Service Agreement) targets. Target one requires the Government to reduce crime and the fear of crime. Target four is to improve the level of public confidence in the criminal justice system. This includes increasing the confidence of minority ethnic communities and increasing, year-on-year, the satisfaction of victims and witnesses, whilst respecting the rights of defendants.[93] Underpinning these priorities are two larger goals that the Government expects all forces to aim for as part of a national effort:

- community engagement and civil renewal; and
- countering terrorism and the threat of terrorism.[94]

Both these goals should serve to reinforce each other if the task of policing is to be done effectively.

4.1 Building Community Confidence in the Police

Official data shows that police are using the new powers granted them under anti-terrorism legislation to target a large number of individuals, who are being stopped and searched – even though the vast majority are not subsequently arrested. According to statistics released by the Home Office, whereas the number of pedestrians stopped and searched under section 44(2) of the Terrorism Act (2000) increased from 946 in 2001/02 to 4,774 in 2002/03, only seven arrests were made in connection with these stops.[95] The number of Asians, Black people and "other minority ethnic" people who

---

[92] Home Office, *National Policing Plan for 2003–2006.*

[93] Home Office, *National Policing Plan for 2003–2006*, Annex A.

[94] Home Office, *Policing: Building Safer Communities Together, a consultation exercise*, London, Home Office, 2003, p. 1.

[95] Home Office, *Statistics on Race and the Criminal Justice System – 2003*, p. 28.

have been stopped and searched rose significantly during 2002-03.[96] Muslims feel that they have been directly targeted by the state.[97] This is likely to influence their confidence in the police and the wider criminal justice system. At the same time, the incarceration without trial of detainees at HMP Belmarsh, under anti-terror legislation, further undermines Muslims' confidence in the criminal justice system, because many feel that the principle of due process underpinning British justice is being significantly compromised here.[98]

According to Home Office statistics, there has been a substantial rise in the number of Asians, Black people and those classified as "other minority ethnic" people stopped and searched during 2002/03. Across all police forces, there has been a 36 per cent rise in the number of Asians, a 38 per cent increase in the number of Black people, and a 47 per cent increase in "other minority ethnic" groups stopped and searched under the Police and Criminal Evidence Act (1984).[99] Under the Terrorism Act (2000), whereas the number of White people stopped and searched increased by 118 per cent from 2001-02 to 2002-03, the number of Black people stopped and searched rose by 230 per cent, and the number of Asians stopped and searched increased by 302 per cent.[100]

There is growing perception within the Muslim community that the police are increasingly targeting them in stops and searches. Ethnic data on stops and searches are recorded according to a four point format: "Black, White, Asian and Other". Statistics specifically in relation to Muslim communities are not available. Between 2000–2001 and 2001–2002, while the number of stops and searches recorded by the Metropolitan Police fell by eight per cent for White people, stops and searches of Black people rose by 30 per cent and stops and searches of Asians, who include Indians, Pakistanis and Bangladeshis, rose by 40 per cent. In England and Wales, excluding the Metropolitan Police Service, statistics show that, whereas the number of stops and searches for White people fell by an average of two per cent, stops and searches rose by an average of six per cent for Black people and 16 per cent for Asians.[101] The Government has set up a

---

[96] Home Office, *Statistics on Race and the Criminal Justice System – 2003*, p. 28.

[97] Interview with the Chairman of the Islamic Human Rights Commission, March 2004, London. Interview with Rashid Skinner, Muslim community representative, March 2004, Bradford.

[98] See: Forum Against Islamophobia and Racism, *Anti-Terrorism, Crime and Security Act 2001 Review. A Submission from FAIR*, London, FAIR, 2003, (hereafter, FAIR, *Anti-Terrorism, Crime and Security Act 2001 Review*).

[99] The *Police and Criminal Evidence Act 1984* is the main piece of legislation that regulates the use of stop and search powers by police officers in England and Wales.

[100] Home Office, *Statistics on Race and the Criminal Justice System – 2003*, p. 28.

[101] Home Office, *Statistics on Race and the Criminal Justice System– 2003*, p. 5.

Stop-and-Search Action Team in response to the significant rise in stops and searches carried out against minority ethnic groups.[102]

Interviews with a wide range of Muslim community leaders and organisations (including An-Nisa Society, Forum Against Islamophobia and Racism, Islamic Human Rights Commission, IQRA Trust, and the Muslim Council of Britain), indicate that there is little acceptance amongst Muslims that anti-terrorism legislation should mean the disproportionate policing of members of their communities. Perceptions of policing within Muslim communities include the notion that community members are being criminalised, that police officers are operating "religious profiling" when deciding whom to stop and search and that young Muslims are being unfairly targeted. At the same time, there is a perception that police officers are Islamophobic. Cases of police abuse and mistreatment – such as the controversial arrest of a Muslim in Tooting, where police officers were allegedly racist, Islamophobic and heavy handed[103] – have quickly become common knowledge in Muslim communities. These incidents have the potential to detrimentally affect Muslim communities' relationship with their local police forces.

There is also a perception that the criminal justice system is concerned more with the political control of Muslim communities than with their safety and protection, and that police officers often seek informants from communities for anti-terrorism activities rather than for issues relating to crime and disorder. And there is anxiety that Muslims are being spied on by the authorities, which makes the Muslims very distrustful of any engagement in civil/public life, causing many to retreat within their own communities.[104]

The perceptions that Muslims have of the police should be an area of concern and focus in their own right. Perceptions will influence how people engage with the police, how much trust they have of policing and how secure they feel in their daily lives. There needs to be an attempt to reconcile the claims made by senior police officers with the lived experiences and subjectivities of Muslim communities. Further research is therefore necessary, in order to examine how common these poor perceptions of the criminal justice system are amongst Muslim communities – whether they are widespread throughout the UK, or whether they are to be found in particular areas, such as London. Muslims' perceptions of policing also need to be explored across

---

[102] Home Office, *Government and police must engage communities to build a fairer criminal justice system*, Home Office Press Release 220/2004, London, Home Office, 2 July 2004.

[103] H. Muir, "Inquiry into Arrest of Muslim Suspect", *The Guardian*, 24 January 2004.

[104] This information has been obtained through interviews that were conducted with representatives of the Forum Against Islamophobia and Racism, the Islamic Human Rights Commission, the IQRA Trust, An-Nisa Society February–March 2004. See also *Anti-Terrorism, Crime and Security Act 2001 Review;* and Liberty, *Reconciling Security and Liberty.*

gender, class, age and ethnic groups, and there is a need to investigate whether encounters with the criminal justice system leave Muslims with a better or worse perception. As highlighted earlier on in this report, the British Crime Survey, or local crime surveys, might be used to document Muslims' perceptions.

A key challenge for the Muslim community and the police is to find ways in which to pursue anti-terrorism policing while at the same time building confidence with Muslim groups. Police engagement with local communities can take place on many different levels. Every police force in England and Wales has a police authority, which must ensure that community consultation takes place regarding the ways in which a particular area is policed and regarding policing priorities that a particular police force adopts. Police authorities can also work with local police forces on community engagement. They have helped develop many important initiatives that seek to build the trust of local communities and to increase community involvement in policing.[105]

Examples of good practices in community involvement should be more widely reproduced. For example, in Balham, South London, Special Constable Farhad Ahmed has set up a crime prevention and advice centre in the Tooting Islamic Centre. The crime centre, which acts as a contact point for the local South Asian Muslim community to liase with the police, is the first of its kind in the country.[106] The Government has sought to stress the importance of such initiatives, and publicise them, through the creation in 2003 of a National Centre for Policing Excellence, whose remit is to identify, develop and spread good practice in operational policing, so that police forces can learn from each other.

Research shows that different communities have different needs, and so it is necessary to employ a wide variety of means of interaction.[107] This research found that, while all participants wanted to have more information about an individual's rights, especially in relation to being stopped by the police, people from minority ethnic groups thought that they were more likely to need this information, as they were more likely to be stopped. In light of the increasing numbers of stops and searches Muslims are likely to

---

[105] A. Myhill, S. Yarrow, D. Dalgleish, and M. Docking, "The role of police authorities in public engagement", in *Home Office Online Report 37/03*, 2003, available at http://www.crimereduction.gov.uk/activecommunities50.htm (accessed 21 September 2004), (hereafter, Myhill et al., *The role of police authorities in public engagement*).

[106] Home Office, *Policing: Building Safer Communities Together, a consultation exercise*, London, Home Office, 2003, p. 11.

[107] See: Myhill et al *The role of police authorities in public engagement*, chapter 4. For example, different age groups preferred different methods of publicity and consultation. Younger age groups favoured TV, newspapers, the Internet and email. People in the 30-59 age range, and also some of those aged 60 or more, were enthusiastic about public meetings.

face under the anti-terrorism legislation, it is important that Muslims receive accurate and accessible information about their rights when they are stopped and searched.

A key organisation working with the Metropolitan Police Service is the Muslim Safety Forum.[108] The Forum is an important mechanism through which Muslims' concerns about police tactics and approaches are regularly raised. For example, the issue of the heavy-handed police tactics used in the case in Tooting was brought up at a Safety Forum meeting with the Metropolitan Police Service. The police officer investigating the allegations of abuse in this case also attended a Forum meeting. Another example of where the Muslim Safety Forum has played a significant role in community safety issues is in relation to the recent advertising campaign warning people to be vigilant due to the threat from terrorism. The Muslim Safety Forum argued for the withdrawal of a poster showing an image that resembled the mostly covered face of a Muslim woman. A new poster was subsequently distributed. The Muslim Safety Forum is also one organisation that has been asked to work with the Home Office Stop and Search Action Team, which is looking at how police powers are being used.

Officials need to engage in greater consultation with Muslim representatives, from a broader range of Muslim communities, and the London initiative of the Muslim Safety Forum should be encouraged in different cities where there is a significant Muslim population. Part of the process of consultation should include a focus upon examining how policing can meet the demands of countering terrorism while at the same time increasing the involvement of Muslim communities – not just in the war on terrorism but also in issues that affect local communities, such as street and property crime and neighbourhood incivilities.

Under the Police Reform Act (2000) a new independent body to investigate complaints about the Police Service has been established. One responsibility of this body, called the Independent Police Complaints Commission (IPCC), is to improve access to the police complaints system. To do this, the IPCC has set up arrangements with a number of local and national organisations – such as the Citizens Advice Bureau – that agreed to become Complaints Access Points (CAPs). At the CAPs, people can make complaints about the police and can find out information about the IPCC. It is possible for mosques and Muslim community centres to become CAPs, so that people from the local communities that they serve have a place where they can make complaints about the police. Indeed, the Churches Criminal Justice Forum, an organisation whose remit includes sharing experiences and information about criminal justice issues and different religious needs,

---

[108] The Muslim Safety Forum is comprised of representatives from a variety of Muslim groups and associations, including the Al-Khoei Foundation, the Union of Muslim Organisations, the Regent's Park Mosque, the Islamic Human Rights Commission and the IQRA Trust. The Metropolitan Police Service regularly consults the Muslim Safety Forum with respect to criminal justice and community safety issues.

has in the past helped to develop a church-based, third-party reporting scheme for complaints relating to racism by police officers.[109]

4.2 Recruitment of Police Officers

There would naturally be more confidence in policing if there were greater involvement of Muslims in all parts of the policing process. The Government is seeking to achieve a "truly representative Police Service," and it has set a national target of increasing the proportion of minority ethnic officers from 2.6 per cent on 31 March 2003 to seven per cent by 2009.[110] The Government is also seeking to improve the retention rate and rate of progression of minority ethnic staff, by rooting out racism and creating "an environment in which racist attitudes and behaviour are freely and openly challenged".[111] These policies are a response to the Macpherson report.[112]

Following the lead taken on tackling racism in the Police Service, decisive action is now necessary to challenge anti-Muslim attitudes. In particular, police forces in local areas where there is a large Muslim population should consider introducing targets for the number of Muslims that they seek to recruit, so that their force reflects the Muslim identities of the local population. The Home Office is encouraging every force to use members of local communities as assessors,[113] which means that communities become involved in the selection of their own police officers. It is important that police forces consider Muslim assessors in areas where there is a substantial Muslim population.

The recruitment of Muslim women police officers merits special attention, especially because women officers remain a minority group within the Police Service. In 2003, women made up approximately 44 per cent of the economically active population, but they represented only 19 per cent of police strength.[114] According to a report of the Fawcett Society's Commission on Women and the Criminal Justice System, women

---

[109] For further details of this scheme, see the Metropolitan Police Service Race and Hate Crime section.

[110] Home Office, *National Policing Plan for 2003–2006*, p. 27.

[111] Home Office, *Dismantling Barriers*, Equality and Diversity Team, Police Personnel Unit, Home Office, 2004, available at http://www.homeoffice.gov.uk/crimpol/police/equality/index.html (accessed 21 September 2004), (hereafter, Home Office, *Dismantling Barriers*).

[112] Home Office, *Dismantling Barriers*.

[113] Assessors will be part of selection panels when recruiting police officers.

[114] Cotton and Smith, *Police Service Strength England and Wales 31ˢᵗ March 2003*, p. 5.

police officers are concentrated in the lowest ranks. Only five out of the 43 Chief Constables in England and Wales are women.[115]

There are no statistics available on the number of Muslim women police officers. Muslim women police officers are, effectively, balancing a number of often competing demands and expectations that are linked to their gender, ethnicity, faith identity and professional roles. The conflict among these demands helps to explain why so few join the Police Service. Interviews with Muslim women police officers suggest that, within their own communities, there exist cultural expectations about the type of work women should do, and policing carries little status.[116] According to a British Association of Women Police (BAWP) report, entitled *The Gender Gap*, the cultural barriers to Muslim women joining the police are further exacerbated by the low progression rates for minority ethnic women.[117] It therefore takes a very committed and strong woman to break cultural norms and family expectations by joining the Police Service.

Out on the streets, Muslim women police officers face abuse from many angles. They report experiencing abuse from Muslim community members, who question these women's loyalty to the community and suggest that they have "betrayed" their fellow Muslims by joining what is perceived to be a racist and Islamophobic Police Service.[118] Muslim women officers also experience racist, sexist and Islamophobic abuse from members of the wider general public. They are also likely to be harassed for being police officers as they carry out their duties. Whilst Muslim women police officers accept that this is an inevitable aspect to their work, the sexist, racist and Islamophobic abuse that they face from some of their own colleagues is intolerable.[119]

Women also report being discriminated against in terms of career opportunities and promotion.[120] However, they are unlikely to proceed with formal disciplinary procedures, because there is a low level of confidence in the effectiveness of these procedures and there is the added fear that lodging complaints might further stigmatise them. Other, more informal, types of support have been pursued through networks, such as the Black, Asian and Muslim Police Association, and organisations for women specifically, like the BAWP. These networks and Muslim women police officers have

---

[115] The Fawcett Society, *Women and the Criminal Justice System,* London, The Fawcett Society, 2004, p. 9.

[116] Interviews with four Muslim women police officers in February and April 2004.

[117] British Association of Women Police, *The Gender Gap,* London, BAWP, 2001 (hereafter, BAWP, *The Gender Gap*).

[118] Interviews with four Muslim women police officers in February and April 2004.

[119] Interviews with four Muslim women police officers in February and April 2004.

[120] Interviews with four Muslim women police officers in February and April 2004.

also sought assistance through alliances with those senior White police officers who are regarded as being "sympathetic" to race and gender issues.

Some police forces have introduced a policy whereby Muslim women can wear their *hijab* when they are in uniform and carrying out their duties. This policy, by itself, however, is unlikely to increase the number of Muslim women police officers, as there needs to be a wider change in police culture and practice. Interviews with Muslim women police officers suggest that they are unlikely to opt to wear a *hijab* in a working environment in which they encounter sexist, racist and Islamophobic harassment.[121] Indeed, in the absence of any adequate training about British Muslim identities in the Police Service, allowing women police officers to wear the *hijab* may only serve to "demonise" Muslim women further, because other police officers are unlikely to understand the role of the veiling. Instead, officers are likely to be prone to the type of misunderstandings that prevail in wider society.

The effective recruitment and subsequent retention of Muslim women police officers must begin with detailed research into Muslim women's perceptions of the Police Service and their reasons for not wanting to become police officers. Research is also needed to better understand the experiences of Muslim and minority ethnic women working in the Police Service, to examine how long they stay in the Police Service and the reasons why they decide to leave.

The BAWP report, *The Gender Gap*, highlights many ways in which the Police Service can become more inclusive of women officers in general, and minority ethnic women officers in particular. One recommendation is the establishment of fully funded mentoring schemes for women police officers.[122] This does not mean, however, that Muslim women police officers should be automatically linked to other female or Asian members of staff. Connecting women with "sympathetic" senior male police officers might actually change the work environment more effectively. Another recommend-dation is to reconsider lengthy, residential training courses. Some on-site training could instead be replaced through greater use of information technology and distance learning packages, which allow for home study. This change could boost the number of Muslim women applying to join the Police Service, as the idea of having to undergo residential training is off-putting to many.[123]

In conjunction with the BAWP, the Home Office recently launched a number of advertisements in the national press, to challenge misunderstandings that women might hold about policing, including misperceptions about height limits, age and

---

[121] Interviews with four Muslim women police officers in February and April 2004.

[122] BAWP, *The Gender Gap*.

[123] BAWP, *The Gender Gap*.

fitness requirements. Advertisements also appeared in several women's magazines, such as *Marie Claire, Cosmopolitan, Red* and *She.* These advertisements featured female police officers discussing their careers and experiences.[124] It might be beneficial to apply this approach to the particular issue of Muslim women and policing, by designing advertisements featuring Muslim women police officers and by targeting the Asian and Muslim press. These advertisements could stress how Muslim women police officers have managed to balance the many demands placed upon them, and they could include the routes to promotion, thereby enhancing the status of policing. Again, the BAWP could play a significant role here.

A Home Office study looking at attitudes towards a career in the Police Service reveals that a variety of perceptions discourage individuals from minority ethnic groups from joining the police. These perceptions include: concerns that they would have to work in a racist environment; concerns that they would face prejudice from both colleagues and the general public on a daily basis; concerns that the sense of isolation that minority ethnic police officers would feel in a predominantly White male culture would lead them to having to deny their cultural identity in order to fit in; concerns that there would be pressure from the local community to decide where their loyalties are; and, for Asian Muslim women with strong religious beliefs, concerns about whether the job is appropriate for a woman.[125]

The Home Office study also asked respondents to recommend some steps that the Police Service might take in order to increase the likelihood that they would apply to join the police. Respondents suggested that more needs to be done in terms of dealing with racism. They also said that the ways in which the police handle stops and searches needs to be addressed. There could be a similar study researching the attitudes of Muslims, particularly Muslim women, towards a career in the Police Service.

4.3   Training of Police Officers

According to the HM Inspectorate of Constabulary report, *Diversity Matters,* "training has a key role in equipping staff with the skills necessary to handle effectively both the external and internal aspects of diversity".[126] This particular report found that, whereas

---

[124] BAWP, *The Gender Gap,* p. 11.

[125] V. Stone and R. Tuffin, *Attitudes of People from Minority Ethnic Communities towards a Career in the Police Service,* Police Research Series Paper 136, London, Home Office Research, Development and Statistics Directorate, 2000.

[126] HM Inspector of Constabulary, *Diversity Matters: Executive Summary,* London, HM Inspector of Constabulary, 2003, p. 1, (hereafter, HM Inspector of Constabulary, *Diversity Matters: Executive Summary*).

most race and diversity training programmes in the Police Service focus appropriately on race issues, the training needs of wider diversity issues are not being sufficiently identified or addressed. Police forces reported that the requirements of the RR(A)A (2000) provided key motivation for a specific race focus in diversity training, even though there is an increasing recognition of the broader range of diverse communities.[127]

At present, race and diversity training is delivered throughout the Police Service via a number of different approaches, and there is an absence of national guidance and standards. Attempts have been made at setting standards of content and outcome. Partly in response to the Stephen Lawrence Inquiry, the Police Service devised Community and Race Relations Occupational Standards. However, so far, there has not been widespread compliance with these standards.[128] Nonetheless, pressure for further standardisation is likely to increase through the current adoption of National Occupational Standards,[129] which are aligned to the newly implemented National Competency Framework.[130] The Police Training and Development Board has agreed to set a national strategy to promote learning in the Police Service. A target has been set that by April 2006, 95 per cent of courses offered nationally, regionally and locally will be mapped against National Occupational Standards.[131]

Police race and diversity training packages need to pay greater attention to the issue of British Muslim identities and the needs of Muslim communities. The Police Training and Development Board should give national direction, and there should be feedback from local communities about the impact of training on practice. It is also important to consider developing methods of assessment that measure the learning of each individual trained.

Any training programme should ensure that Muslims are not "otherised" through discussions that only focus on the differences between Muslim communities and broader "mainstream" society. Instead, the broad range of Muslim identities should be

---

[127] HM Inspector of Constabulary, *Diversity Matters: Executive Summary*, p. 14.

[128] HM Inspector of Constabulary, *Diversity Matters: Executive Summary*, p. 14.

[129] National Occupational Standards describe performance in terms of what needs to be achieved to reach recognized levels of competence. They form the basis of a wide range of vocational qualifications. See *Diversity Matters: Executive Summary*, p. 20.

[130] The introduction of a National Competency Framework (already piloted in some areas) is planned across the Police Service. The Framework is designed to provide standard definitions of role tasks and a means of measuring an individual's performance against them. See Her Majesty's Inspector of Constabulary, *Diversity Matters: Executive Summary*, p. 20.

[131] Police Training and Development Board, *National Learning Strategy to Promote Learning in the Police Service, 2004*, available at http://www.policereform.gov.uk/ptdb/natlearningstrategy.html (accessed 21 September 2004).

highlighted, and commonalities should be stressed. As part of the research for this paper, interviews were conducted with individuals describing themselves as Muslim, and they each had different interpretations of their own Muslim identity. If one Muslim individual speaks about Islam as part of a training package, the training will not reflect the diverse range of British Muslim identities, and it may serve to reproduce stereotypical images of Islam.

Training packages must therefore seek to engage people to critically reflect on the diverse nature of Islam, as well as the many commonalities of experience between Muslim communities and other communities. Any training package must also include a focus upon gender, since it is likely that Muslim women will have particular requirements from the police. Research indicates that minority ethnic women want the police to understand more about their cultural and religious needs.[132] According to this research, women feel that the police patronise them, stereotype them and listen to any man present before turning to the woman complainant.[133] These issues can be addressed through better training.

According to HM Inspectorate of Constabulary, police training will increasingly need to reflect the local communities that the separate police forces serve. The HM Inspectorate of Constabulary report, *Diversity Matters,* notes that there is presently little evidence of community involvement in identifying police learning requirements, or in designing and evaluating police training programmes.[134] Recommendation 9.5 of the report states that the race and diversity content of training should be restructured, to provide an in-depth understanding of the community that officers will be policing. The report also found that few police forces conduct any kind of community survey to assess whether their performance has improved as a result of training.[135]

The development of effective training requires greater involvement of Muslim communities in the design and evaluation of police training on race and diversity. If policing is to reflect the needs of local communities more specifically – as per the National Policing Plan – then local police forces should do more to engage with the diverse range of Muslim groups when considering training issues. In areas where there is a significant Muslim population, Muslim communities should be involved in the design, development and evaluation of courses delivered by police staff-development and training units.

---

[132] S. Todd, *Seen but not Heard – Women's Experiences of the Police: Report of a Collaboration between Thames Valley Police, Todd Consulting and the University of Surrey,* London, Thames Valley Police, 2002 (hereafter, Todd, *Seen but not Heard*).

[133] Todd, *Seen but not Heard,* p. 9.

[134] HM Inspector of Constabulary, *Diversity Matters: Executive Summary,* p. 9.

[135] HM Inspector of Constabulary, *Diversity Matters: Executive Summary,* p. 131.

5. THE COURTS

This section takes a look at the work of the Crown Prosecution Service and highlights how, now that an anti-religious element can be considered in crimes, the service needs to achieve greater engagement with specific religious communities. This section also focuses briefly upon the courts, noting that there is a lack of research into Muslims' experiences of court processes. Detailed research in this area is urgently needed.

5.1   The Crown Prosecution Service

In 2002, a Crown Prosecution Service Inspectorate reviewed the way in which the service deals with cases having a minority ethnic dimension. The inspectorate found that prosecutors were routinely reducing the seriousness of offences by disregarding the racial element to certain crimes. It recommended further training for prosecutors, more appropriate monitoring of cases and better community engagement.[136] In 2004, a follow-up review of Crown Prosecution Service casework with a minority ethnic dimension found that police identification of racist incident cases has improved. The 2004 review also noted improvement in the overall commitment of prosecution staff to the Racist Incident Monitoring Scheme (RIMS), which gathers information on prosecution decisions and outcomes in all cases identified by the police or Crown Prosecution Service as racist incidents.[137] The review found the level and effectiveness of community engagement had improved significantly, and it noted that a number of worthwhile and innovative initiatives are being pursued. However, the 2004 review noted that, even though such instances are less common, there are still a significant proportion of cases involving a racist incident in which charges are reduced inappropriately.[138]

---

[136] HM Crown Prosecution Service Inspectorate, *Thematic Review of CPS Casework with a Minority Ethnic Dimension*, London, HMCPS Inspectorate, 2002.

[137] HM Crown Prosecution Service Inspectorate, *A Follow Up Review of CPS Casework with a Minority Ethnic Dimension*, London, HMCPS Inspectorate, 2004, (hereafter, HMCPS Inspectorate, *A Follow Up Review of CPS Casework with a Minority Ethnic Dimension*).

[138] HMCPS Inspectorate, *A Follow-up Review of CPS Casework with a Minority Ethnic Dimension*, p. 7.

Following the introduction of a religious element to crime[139] under the Anti Terrorism Crime and Security Act (2001), in April 2002, the Crown Prosecution Service began requiring prosecutors dealing with religiously aggravated cases to submit a summary of the facts and decisions taken in the case to the Director of Public Prosecutions. The Director of Public Prosecutions may ask to see the file, and he can review the case himself if he has any reservation about the decision taken. From April 2003, Crown Prosecution Service areas will be required to submit a RIDS monitoring form for religiously aggravated offences, just as they have had to do for racist incident cases. The RIDS must be clearly marked to identify that the case involves a religiously aggravated offence.[140] So far, there have been relatively few religiously aggravated prosecutions, according to the RIMS annual report on racially and religiously aggravated crime by the Crown Prosecution Service. Nonetheless, the majority of victims involved in cases with a religious element are Muslim.[141]

Whilst community engagement is an important part of Crown Prosecution Service policy and practice, the 2004 Crown Prosecution Service HM Inspectorate review found that, generally, awareness of religious differences is not as developed as it might be, and there may be a tendency to put all minority ethnic communities under the same umbrella. However, very recent developments within the Crown Prosecution Service suggest that religious monitoring and the religious identity of community groups is increasingly being taken into consideration. Victim and witness care units are currently being established in a partnership between the Crown Prosecution Service and the police, with the service taking the lead on this initiative. The units will be monitored in terms of victims' and witnesses' usage, take-up and satisfaction, and religious monitoring will be included. The Crown Prosecution Service is also drawing

---

[139] Some offences can be charged as specific religiously aggravated offences. For these offences, prosecutors have to prove first that the offender committed one of the basic offences (including offences of assault, wounding, harassment, damage and public order offences, such as causing people to fear violence or harassment) and then prosecutors have to prove that the offence was religiously aggravated in one of two ways: either the accused person demonstrated hostility to the victim because the victim was thought to belong to a particular religious group, or the accused person was motivated by hostility towards the victim for the same reasons. See: Crown Prosecution Service, *Racist and Religious Crime – CPS Prosecution Policy*, London, Equality and Diversity Unit and the Policy Directorate, CPS, 2003, p. 5.

[140] *RIMS Annual Report 2002–2003*, p. 35.

[141] *RIMS Annual Report 2002–2003*, p. 36. Breakdown of religion of victims for religiously aggravated offences between 14 December 2001 and 31 March 2003: out of a total of 18 cases, ten involved Muslim victims, two Sikh victims, two Hindu victims, one Jewish, one Jehovah's Witness, one Christian victim and one victim whose religion was not stated.

up a directory of community groups and contacts, including representatives of Muslim communities, which will be available on the Crown Prosecution Service intranet.[142]

5.2   The Court Service

Research has raised serious questions about the prevalence of custodial sentences for minority ethnic defendants in the Crown Court. These concerns have led to an increased focus upon the issue of direct or indirect discrimination in the courts, as well as a focus on the extent to which minority ethnic communities feel they are treated equally.[143] The Department for Constitutional Affairs has recently commissioned research looking at the experiences of minority ethnic magistrates, ethnic diversity and the jury system, ethnic diversity and the tribunal system and minority ethnic families' experience of care proceedings.[144]

Research has focused upon ethnicity and not religious identity. However, the commissioned research on ethnicity should, at the very least, disaggregate statistics to show any disadvantage experienced by Pakistanis and Bangladeshis. If the results of this research indicate significant adverse treatment, then future research may need to place a greater focus on Muslim communities and their perceptions and experiences of the courts.

---

[142] Interview with Seamus Taylor, Head of Equality and Diversity, Crown Prosecution Service Equality and Diversity Unit, London, April 2004.

[143] R. Hood, *Race and Sentencing,* Oxford, Clarendon Press, 1992.

[144] The Department for Constitutional Affairs Research Programme, *Courts and Diversity Programme,* 2004.

6. THE PRISON SERVICE

This section looks at the recent efforts made by the Prison Service to accommodate the needs of Muslim prisoners. It is argued that, despite good progress in areas such as diet and prayer facilities, more attention now needs to be focused upon offender programmes that are run inside prison. The Prison Service should consider whether these programmes could be more inclusive of Muslim prisoners. Muslim communities must also be encouraged to work with the Prison Service, in order to help rehabilitate Muslim offenders.

June 2004 saw the creation of the National Offender Management Service (NOMS), which is intended to provide the end-to-end management of offenders – whether they are serving sentences in prison, in the community, or both – in order to ensure that the whole sentence of the court is planned and delivered in an integrated and effective way. The Prison and Probation services will eventually become delivery arms for NOMS. However, as a date is yet to be established for this transition,[145] the following sections will continue to refer to the Prison and Probation services. Nonetheless, in anticipation of the greater role for NOMS, some recommendations will also be aimed at this particular body.

6.1 Provision for Muslim Prisoners

British prisons today are incarcerating an increasingly diverse ethnic, cultural and religious population. In the last few years, there has been significant growth in the number of male Muslim prisoners. While the number of Muslim prisoners was increasing, the number of prisoners registering as Christian was steadily decreasing.[146] On 30 June 2002, there were 5,379 male Muslim prisoners, compared to 430 Sikh and 256 Hindu male prisoners. The link between social exclusion and crime is well-established, and social exclusion and economic deprivation appears to be a factor in the large number of Muslim prisoners.[147] Statistics for Pakistani and Bangladeshi communities, as well as other Muslim ethnic communities, reveal that they are much

---

[145] "End-to-End Management of Offenders at Heart of NOMS", *Her Majesty's Prison Service News,* 19 August 2004, p. 1, available on the Prison Service website at http://www.hmprisonservice.gov.uk (accessed 2 November 2004).

[146] J. Beckford and S. Gilliat, *Religion in Prison: equal rites in a multi-faith society,* Cambridge, Cambridge University Press, 1998.

[147] Farrington, *Human Development and Criminal Careers.*

more likely than other groups to be living on low incomes, with almost 60 per cent of the 1 million people in this group living in low-income households.[148]

Traditionally, in most prisons, Christian chaplains have provided religious care and services. However, members of other religious groups have the same right to practise their faith as Christian prisoners. The Prison Act (1952) states that the prison chaplain should ensure that every prisoner is able to practise his or her faith. In recent years, the facilities provided for Muslim prisoners have improved. In 1999, the Prison Service appointed a Muslim adviser, whose work has involved a focus upon three areas: Friday prayers, access to Imams and *halal* diets. In 2003, for the first time, full-time Muslim chaplains were also employed. A *Directory and Guide on Religious Practises in HM Prison Service* was issued in 1996, in order to enable staff to cater more adequately to the religious needs of prisoners.[149] The directory describes matters related to worship, sacred writings, diet, dress, ministry and aspects of social functioning, such as the role of families, personal hygiene and race.

The Prison Service Chaplaincy has also pursued a multi-faith ethos. This body has created a Chaplaincy Council, whose members include prison service faith advisers from a variety of different religions. The Chaplaincy Council provides a forum for consultation on a broad range of prison issues and guides and advises the Prison Service Chaplaincy. The National Council for the Welfare of Muslim Prisoners (NCWMP), set up in 1999, is a body consisting of representatives from a number of Muslim organisations. The NCWMP's remit includes: suggesting policy recommendations, via regular meetings with the director general of the Prison Service and meetings with the Chaplaincy Council; supporting the work of the Muslim adviser; and making annual prison visits, in order to assess the quality of the services provided to Muslim prisoners. The NCWMP's work has included assessing the needs, and quality, of facilities provided to detainees held under anti-terror legislation at HMP Belmarsh.

A number of areas continue to concern Muslim prisoners and their representatives. According to the Muslim adviser, due to staff lunch breaks, there has been a shortage of prison officers to escort Muslim inmates, so that they may not be able to go to the place of worship for prayer times.[150] In addition, there are concerns that washing facilities are not available close to prayer rooms, which may also be inadequate in terms

---

[148] Department for Work and Pensions, *Family Resources Survey, 2000/2001,* London, 2001, (hereafter, DWP, *Family Resources Survey, 2000/2001.*)

[149] HM Prison Service, *Directory and Guide on Religious Practices in HM Prison Service,* London, HM Prison Service, 1996.

[150] M. Ahmed, "Muslim Religious Provision in HM Prison Service", in *Prison Service Journal* 137 (September), 2002, (hereafter, Ahmed, *Muslim Religious Provision in HM Prison Service*).

of size, design or location. The authenticity of *halal* food has been questioned, despite official assurances that the food meets *halal* requirements. This matter is of crucial concern to Muslim inmates and a frequent source of frustration.[151] Concerns involving personal hygiene also feature significantly in Muslim prisoners' daily lives. The Prison Service has been advised to build cubical showers, so that individuals do not have to share communal showers, though, in many prisons, there are now curtains or modesty screens.[152]

The NCWMP stresses the large discrepancies in service to be found between the different prison establishments. For example, in HMP Belmarsh, where there are approximately 150 Muslim prisoners, 100 of whom attend Friday prayers, only one full-time Imam is presently employed by the prison. In contrast, at Brixton Prison, where there are around 80 Muslim prisoners, there is one full-time Imam and two relief Imams to support his work. At Feltham Young Offenders Institute there are approximately 135 Muslim prisoners, who are served by one full-time Imam and four relief Imams.[153]

6.2 Staff Training

Anti-Muslim sentiment, discrimination, overt racism and violence, involving members of staff as well as prisoners, are features of prison life.[154] After the death of Zahid Mubarek at HMP Feltham, and other highly publicised incidents at HMP Brixton and Full Sutton, the Commission for Racial Equality (CRE) conducted a formal investigation into the Prison Service, and the director general announced that the service is institutionally racist. The Prison Service has committed itself to working with the CRE to build considerations of race relations into all aspects of its work. A five-year joint Prison Service/CRE action plan, entitled *Implementing Race Equality in Prisons: A Shared Agenda for Change*, was launched in December 2003. The plan will cover

---

[151] Ahmed, *Muslim Religious Provision in HM Prison Service*.

[152] Ahmed, *Muslim Religious Provision in HM Prison Service*.

[153] Interview with Salah el-Hassan, General Secretary of the National Council for the Welfare of Muslim Prisoners, Birmingham, April 2004.

[154] E. Genders and E. Player, *Race Relations in Prisons*, Oxford, Clarendon Press, 1989; R. Burnett and G. Farrell, *Reported and Unreported Incidents in Prisons: Occasional Paper 14*, Oxford, Centre for Criminological Research, 1994; and S. Bryans and D. Wilson, "The Prison Governor: theory and practice", in *Prison Service Journal*, Leyhill, 1998.

areas such as employment, staff development and training, and performance improvement.[155]

Ignorance about spiritual and practical aspects of Islam may lead prison staff to act as if religious requests are a privilege rather than a necessity, and this attitude may lead to the inappropriate treatment of Muslim prisoners. There has been an increased focus upon the need to train staff, to raise their awareness of Islamic issues. A recent study found that most prison officers surveyed were aware of the identity of Muslims, and they knew that Muslim prisoners had particular requirements. Nonetheless, some prison officers appeared to be judgmental of Muslim prisoners who broke Ramadan rules or who chatted to friends during prayers.[156]

6.3   Programmes for Prisoners

Cognitive skills programmes were first introduced in the Prison Service during the early 1990s. The "Reasoning and Rehabilitation programme" was introduced in 1992 and "Enhanced Thinking Skills" in 1993. These programmes started with the premise that the way offenders think, including how they reason and solve problems, is an important factor in their criminal behaviour. To prevent criminal behaviour, these programmes aim to teach offenders the process of consequential thinking, so they will avoid patterns of thinking that lead them to offend.

A recent evaluation study of the effectiveness of prison-based cognitive skills programmes found that those offenders who started a programme but failed to complete it were no less likely to be reconvicted than their matched comparison group, who did not take part in a programme. Moreover, 14 per cent of the young offenders and nine per cent of adult males involved in such a programme failed to complete it, and a substantial proportion of these dropped out through their own choice.[157]

Research is required to determine Muslim prisoners' needs in terms of the cognitive skills programmes currently in place. It is important to examine whether these programmes could be tailored to engage more effectively with Muslim offenders, by incorporating their religious identities. At the same time, the issue of whether other

---

[155] *Implementing Race Equality in Prisons: A Shared Agenda for Change*, HM Prison Service, 2004, available at www.hmprisonservice.gov.uk/abouttheservice/actionplan/ (accessed 21 September 2004).

[156] J. Beckford, *Preliminary Results on Provisions for Muslims in French and British Prisons*, paper presented at the Centre for Ethnic Relations University of Warwick, 12 December 2003, p. 21.

[157] J. Cann, L. Falshaw, F. Nugent and C. Friendship, *Understanding What Works: accredited cognitive skills programmes for adult men and young offenders*, Home Office Research Findings 226, London, Home Office, 2003, p. 4.

programmes could be developed, in addition to the cognitive programmes currently in place, needs to be considered.

For Christian prisoners, there is a programme delivered through chaplaincy departments, called the Sycamore Tree programme. This programme uses a biblical story to illustrate issues similar to those worked on in cognitive programmes. The Sycamore Tree programme is offered in addition to cognitive programmes, and it is only for those who choose to take part. Offenders often use rationalisations to deny or justify their offending activities, but a Muslim chaplain, or other authority figure, can help point out offenders' rationalisations and provide offenders with a clear moral framework from which to build their lives. A chaplain or trainer could use religious stories, and the wisdom that these stories provide could be applied to offenders' everyday lives. In this way, the teachings of Islam can be used to help rehabilitate offenders, so that they are less likely to re-offend upon release from prison.

Although the religious identity of prisoners is monitored by the Prison Service, diversity monitoring with respect to access to, and use of, facilities such as educational courses is carried out in terms of ethnicity, which means that it is hard to know the extent to which Muslim prisoners are, or are not, accessing the available facilities.[158] This report, therefore, recommends that the services that prisoners can access from inside prison should be monitored according to the religious identity of prisoners, to gain a clearer picture of the training and development undertaken by Muslim prisoners. This knowledge will make it easier to formulate policies to tackle any under-representation.

In terms of rehabilitation, a particularly important development consists of Community Chaplaincy schemes, which are a way of involving volunteers of all faiths in the resettlement of prisoners, who can request such help via the prison chaplaincy. Through the Community Chaplaincy Scheme, wide-ranging support is given to ex-offenders when they are released from prison, so that the transition between prison and outside life is eased. This support may include practical help in finding accommodation and work, but it may also include providing spiritual assistance, when this is requested.

Community Chaplaincy schemes, however, tend to feature Christian organisations far more predominantly than Muslim organisations. Indeed, it seems that prison issues are not a high priority for many Muslim groups, and so it is important to gain their help and support. Muslim representative bodies, service providers and Islamic theological colleges/bodies, should encourage Muslim communities to help rehabilitate Muslim offenders. This can mean getting involved in community chaplaincy schemes, as well as getting involved in implementing prisoner programmes.

---

[158] J. Beckford, OSI Roundtable on British Muslims and the Criminal Justice System, London, 8 June 2004.

7. PROBATION WORK AND MUSLIM COMMUNITIES

The following section focuses upon the National Probation Service, which emerged in April 2001. A key aim of the National Probation Service was to achieve consistency of service delivery across the 42 probation areas.[159] It is argued that, despite its increasing focus upon diversity issues, the National Probation Service now needs a greater recognition of Muslim offenders. A series of recommendations are proposed here, including the need to monitor the sensitivity and responsivity of the services used by Muslim offenders. Staff training is also an important concern, because race-awareness training programmes that are currently offered are unlikely to give faith issues the level of focus that is required.

When the Prison and Probation Services are eventually merged into the new NOMS, the change will provide a new opportunity to enhance systems for monitoring the religion of offenders and NOMS staff members. It is of vital importance for NOMS to have knowledge about the number of Muslim offenders that it has contact with, as well as the nature of the communities that those individuals belong to, so that appropriate responses to Muslim offenders can be put together. NOMS should adopt a system of ethnic and religious monitoring, which will allow for better practice and policy decisions regarding Muslim offenders.

NOMS will be responsible for managing both offenders who are in custody and offenders who are being supervised within the community. This means that NOMS can pilot a programme that takes both ethnicity and religious identity into account when looking at Muslim offenders' needs in relation to prison and community work. In 1999, as part of the Government's Crime Reduction Programme, probation services were invited to submit proposals to develop effective programmes targeting a wide range of offenders. These proposals could include STET projects, such as those for Asian and Black offenders.

7.1 Diversity and Race Equality in the Probation Services

A race equality agenda within the probation service has gained increasing significance over the last few years. Following the inquiry into the murder of Stephen Lawrence, HM Inspectorate of Probation published a thematic report entitled *Towards Race Equality,* in June 2000. The report examined the extent to which the probation service promoted and achieved race equality in its employment practices and its work with offenders. The report contained 19 recommendations that addressed policy development, improving the quality of service delivery to offenders, the recruitment

---

[159] See: National Probation Directorate, *The Heart of the Dance.*

and training of staff and performance monitoring. Its publication led to the formulation of a national action plan.[160]

Other important developments include: the publication of *A New Choreography: an integrated strategy for the National Probation Service for England and Wales*,[161] the Race Relations Amendment Act (2000); the publication of *The Heart of the Dance, a diversity strategy for the NPS for England and Wales 2002/2006*;[162] and the follow-up inspection report by the HM Inspectorate of Probation, *Towards Race Equality* (2004), which examined the extent to which the recommendations of *Towards Race Equality* (2000) had been implemented.[163] The pursuit of race equality issues has led to the development of a number of important initiatives, such as the implementation of STET projects for Black and Asian offenders, the promotion of examples of good practice for race equality and the development of links with local minority ethnic communities.[164]

The Probation Service has adopted a broad diversity agenda, which includes addressing issues related to disability, sexuality, gender, age and religion. In February 2004, a Faith Conference was organised to discuss implications of the EU Directive which 200/78/EC of 27 November 2000 establishing a general framework for equal treatment in employment an occupation prohibiting discrimination in employment on the grounds of religion or belief. In the probation area of Humberside, the Probation Service was involved in a project that looked at the religious needs of offenders in hostels.[165]

Clearly, these are important developments taking place within an organisation that has experienced, and is continuing to experience, huge change. In 1998/99, 46 per cent of ethnic minority offenders starting probation were supervised by just five Probation Services: Inner London, Middlesex, North East London, South East London and South West London.[166] However, it is not possible to have an accurate picture of the

---

[160] This action plan combined the targets and recommendations set out in both the thematic inspection report, *Towards Race Equality,* and an earlier report to the Home Secretary, *Developing Minority Ethnic Representation in Probation Services.* For more information see: HM Inspectorate of Probation, *Towards Race Equality: follow-up inspection report.*

[161] National Probation Directorate, *A New Choreography: an integrated strategy for the National Probation Service for England and Wales,* London, National Probation Directorate, 2001.

[162] National Probation Directorate, *The Heart of the Dance.*

[163] HM Inspectorate of Probation, *Towards Race Equality: follow-up inspection report.*

[164] National Probation Directorate, *The Heart of the Dance.*

[165] Interview with Diane Baderin, National Probation Directorate, London, April 2004.

[166] B. Powis and R. Walmsley, *Programmes for Back and Asian offenders on probation: lessons for developing practice,* London, Home Office Research Study 250, 2002, p. 10.

number of Muslims in contact with the probation service, because statistics are collected only on the basis of race and ethnicity.

7.2 Programmes and Training

Programmes for Black and Asian offenders can be classified into two basic types: separate provision and specialist provision. In separate provision, programmes are provided in groups exclusively for Black and Asian offenders, and the work done is the same or similar to that done by White offenders. In specialist provision, Black and Asian offenders are offered interventions that specifically address their perceived needs, where these are seen to be different from those of White offenders. Specialist programmes are likely to have a focus upon empowerment, and there is likely to be an acknowledgment that minority ethnic offenders have encountered both direct and institutional racism, so that specialist forms of rehabilitation are required. Indeed, the South West Probation Training Consortium has published a handbook that gives guidance on the best way to work with Black offenders, and the book includes an explanation of the need to understand racism, as well as an acknowledgement of the differences between Black and White values, learning styles, language and manner.

Some debate has also taken place over the advantages and disadvantages of providing separate group work programmes for Black and Asian offenders. In the probation areas where there is a high proportion of minority ethnic offenders, there needs to be some discussion about whether there could be separate or specialist provision for Muslim offenders, under the *What Works* agenda. This falls into Priority Objective 4, set out in *The Heart of the Dance:* effective and appropriate service delivery. The National Probation Service must ensure that its services are accessible, appropriate, inclusive and responsive to all offenders from minority groups in all aspects of service delivery and policy covering accredited programmes, hostel regimes and general case management.

There may be a cultural/religious context to offences. For example, research on domestic violence against Black women shows that there is often a specific cultural context to this violence, as some men use religion to assert their right to control women.[167] The pervasiveness of Islamophobia in society also means that Muslim offenders are likely to have experienced prejudice not only on the grounds of their race but also due to their faith identity, and the significance of this factor is likely to have increased in the aftermath of 11 September. Even when individuals are not particularly observant of their faith, religion is still strongly linked to culture and how individuals make sense of the world, so that the effectiveness of work with offenders could be

---

[167] A. Mama, *The Hidden Struggle: statutory and voluntary responses to violence against black women in the home,* London, Whiting and Birch Ltd, 1996.

enhanced by focusing upon individuals' faith.[168] Probation officers who have worked with young Muslim men report that they have to negotiate their way between two mutually exclusive worlds – one world influenced by the street and drugs and the other influenced by the home, mosque and work.[169]

Probation programmes tend to be based on cognitive behavioural theories that have been identified as being successful with a wide variety of offenders. It might be argued that this generalist approach does not sufficiently engage with individuals from specific minority communities.[170] Cognitive behavioural programmes generally have significant drop-out rates.[171] By tailoring programmes so that they engage with the individual more closely, it might be possible to obtain better completion rates and, therefore, lower re-offending rates. Probation areas need to consider more closely the possibility of establishing partnerships with Muslim organisations to work specifically with Muslim offenders. This point links to Priority Objective 5 in the *Heart of the Dance* document: communicating and connecting with local communities and working in partnership. This objective includes the following goals:

- the National Probation Service should significantly increase its profile and credibility amongst those groups;

- the National Probation Service should build trust, confidence and close connections with diverse groups, communities and agencies that reflect the local population; and

---

[168] J. McManus, *Friends or Strangers?*, p. 3.

[169] J. Walters, "The Probation Service: working with Muslim communities", in *The Muslim Community and the Criminal Justice System: speeches delivered at the conference, February 3rd 2000*, London, IQRA Trust, 2000 pp. 22–25.

[170] The introduction of the National Probation Service in 2001 signalled a movement towards centralisation and consistency of approach between different probation areas. This led to a reduction in the level of diversity amongst programmes being offered to offenders, since programmes have been increasingly designed to take account of principles of effective practice under the *What Works* initiative. This has stimulated some critical debate and scrutiny of the *What Works* agenda. See G. Mair (ed.), *What Matters in Probation*, Cullompton, Willan Publishing, 2004; S. Farrall, *Rethinking What Works with Offenders: probation, social context and desistance from crime*, Cullompton, Willan Publishing, 2002.

[171] See, for example, J. Cann, L. Falshaw, F. Nugent, and C. Friendship, *Understanding What Works: accredited cognitive skills programmes for adult men and young offenders, Research Findings 226*, London: Home Office, 2003, p. 4, A total of 220 of the young offenders (14 per cent) and 202 of the adult males (nine per cent) failed to complete a cognitive skills programme.

- by 2006, the National Probation Service should established good models of consultation with minority ethnic communities.[172]

In developing offender programmes, it might be beneficial to appoint experts on Muslim communities to act as consultants. It is also important to consider the religious identity of programme deliverers, who should be Muslim if they are running programmes specifically for Muslim offenders. Programme deliverers need adequate training, adequate resources must be made available for programmes, and translators or interpreters may also be required. Some of the programmes that have been developed for Black and Asian offenders have used invited guest speakers, who are usually of a minority ethnic background and who might be successful professionals. A couple of these programmes have also implemented mentoring schemes, whereby mentors are of the same ethnic background as the offender. When considering implementing programmes specifically tailored to Muslim offenders, it would be worthwhile to also explore the possibility of using Muslim speakers.

The National Probation Service must also examine the sensitivity and responsivity of the services used by Muslim offenders. For example, do hostels have *halal* food, and where this is provided, are there questions about its authenticity? Are prayer facilities provided? The expertise of the National Association of Muslim Prisoners can be drawn on here, since this organisation regularly visits prisons in order to examine the sensitivity of the facilities provided to Muslim prisoners.

Probation staff training needs to include an in-depth focus upon faith issues and how these link to culture. The race awareness training programmes that are currently offered are unlikely to give faith issues the level of focus that is required. According to the HM Inspectorate of Probation report, *Towards Race Equality*, whilst there are good practice examples of staff involvement in the planning, development and ownership of diversity training, cultural awareness training is less common.[173] Staff training needs to focus on British Muslim communities and their needs, as well as effective engagement with these communities. In addition, there is a need to examine the way pre-sentence reports are written, to assess how and if biases can occur due to officers' misunderstandings of Islam.

7.3   Recruitment

There are no statistics on the number of Muslims employed in the Probation Service. It is important to improve the monitoring of the ethnicity of staff members according

---

[172] National Probation Directorate, *The Heart of the Dance*, pp. 23–24.

[173] HM Inspectorate of Probation, *Towards Race Equality: follow-up inspection report*, p. 57.

to the 16-point system, because there are still large gaps in the information available here. And once NOMS is fully operational, that agency should consider monitoring the faith identity of employees, to ensure that targets for the employment of ethnic minorities include the recruitment of Muslims. NOMS should also set policies that take "dual discrimination" into consideration. The HM Inspectorate of Probation report, *Towards Race Equality*, highlights how one fifth of minority ethnic probation staff questioned indicated that they felt discriminated against in ways other than racism, including discrimination on the basis of their faith.[174]

Recruitment targets can be set for religious minority groups, so that local staffs more closely reflect the composition of their local communities. Targets can also be set in terms of the number of Muslims in senior positions within NOMS, and innovative initiatives can be taken to improve Muslim recruitment. For example, Muslim advisers can be used on recruitment panels for senior posts. The North East Training Consortium, which is responsible for the recruitment and training of trainee probation officers, published a booklet that included case studies of minority ethnic people joining the probation service.[175] A similar booklet of case studies of Muslims joining the Probation Service can be published by the Probation Training Consortia, which are also responsible for recruiting trainee probation officers.

7.4   Victim Work in the Probation Service

Even though the Probation Service's work is predominantly aimed at offenders, the agency has been involved with victims since the early days of the victims' movement. Probation officers have played an important role in the development of Victim Support schemes, and the first scheme was set up in 1974, as a result of inter-agency discussions about the impact of crime on individuals. However, the Probation Service's work with victims did not have a significant impact on probation practice, as the service's main focus continued to be on offenders.[176]

---

[174] National Probation Directorate, *Towards Race Equality: follow-up inspection report*, p. 53.

[175] North-East Training Consortium "Probation works, do you have something to contribute?", in National Probation Directorate, *Towards Race Equality: follow-up inspection report*, p. 55.

[176] B. Spalek, "Victim Work in the Probation Service", in W. Chui and M. Nellis (eds.) *Moving Probation Forward*, London, Pearson, 2003 (hereafter, Spalek, *Victim Work in the Probation Service*).

The Victim's Charters of 1990 and 1996 have had a pronounced impact on probation work.[177] Policy documents and circulars issued by the Probation Service highlight several areas in which victim-focused work is being applied.[178] This includes giving the victims of sexual and violent offenders a greater voice, by providing them with information about the criminal justice process once the offender has been sentenced to a term of more than 12 months. The Probation Service also seeks to give victims the opportunity to state their views on proposed conditions surrounding the offender's release. And the service acknowledges the need to incorporate a victim's perspective when dealing with offenders. There is even a movement towards developing restorative justice strategies.[179]

The National Probation Directorate has stressed the need to develop local community links, because local groups can provide extra resources to help support the victims of crime more effectively, and they can also provide insights into their communities that might benefit probation practice with victims. At the same time, service uptake from minority ethnic communities is low, so there is an acknowledgement that more needs to be done in promoting probation area services to these communities.[180]

The HM Inspectorate of Probation report on victims, *Valuing the Victim*,[181] recommended that the race and ethnicity of victims contacted by the service should be routinely monitored, in order to be able to examine how well the needs of minority ethnic communities are served.[182] Some probation areas are now beginning to obtain information about victims' ethnicity from the police, at the point of referral, in order to help inform service delivery. However, consideration should be paid to collecting information about the faith identity of victims, so that faith issues can also inform service delivery. This would help the National Probation Directorate to ensure that all victims have equal access to the contact service and that the specific needs of those

---

[177] The Victim's Charter is published by Government, setting out what kind of services that victims should expect to receive from the criminal justice system. Details can be found on the Home Office website at http://www.homeoffice.gov.uk/justice/victims/charter/vicfore.html (accessed 21 September).

[178] See: Home Office, *Probation Service Contact with Victims,* Probation Circular 61/95, 23 August 1995, available on the Home Office website at http://www.homeoffice.gov.uk/docs/vapp.pdf (accessed 2 November 2004). Also guidance provided by the Association of Chef Officers of Probation (ACOP) and Victim Support.

[179] Spalek, *Victim Work in the Probation Service.*

[180] Interview with Pat Brown-Richards, Head of Victim Liaison Unit, West Midlands Probation Area, Birmingham, March 2004.

[181] HM Inspectorate of Probation, *Valuing the Victim.*

[182] HM Inspectorate of Probation, *Valuing the Victim.*

from minority groups are given appropriate consideration, as was recommended by the HM Inspector of Probation.[183]

Victim liaison officers working in areas where there is a high proportion of Muslims need to develop a greater understanding of Muslim communities. Liaison officers need to ensure that they engage with all parts of the Muslim community, including those marginalised within the Muslim community.

An example of good practice is found in the West Midlands Victim Liaison Unit, which has put together an excellent directory of local minority ethnic community groups. This directory serves as a way of informing victim liaison officers about groups that are willing to work with them, and the list includes Muslim community groups, such as the Dudley Mosque and Community Centre, the Tipton Muslim Centre and the Wolverhampton Mosque Trust. This information will enhance the responsiveness of victim liaison units to the needs of minority and Black ethnic communities, as it provides victim liaison officers with the local contacts they need to give advice about culturally sensitive support services for victims from minority ethnic backgrounds. At the same time, this initiative helps to raise the awareness and accessibility of the Probation Service's victim contact work amongst minority ethnic communities.

It is important to replicate this initiative in other probation areas. Examples of good practice can be spread via the National Probation Service or the HM Inspectorate of Probation. While many local organisations are willing to work with victim liaison units, offering general advice and acting as a link with their communities, there seems to be less enthusiasm to give actual support to victims. This hesitancy can no doubt be linked to resource issues.[184]

Specific attention must also be paid to the issue of hate crime. According to the HM Inspectorate of Probation, there seems to be confusion across probation areas about what is meant by "hate crime", with most areas assuming that it consists of racially motivated attacks.[185] Probation staff should have clear guidance about the issue of religious hate crime, so that they can properly address the needs of victims of religiously motivated attacks.

---

[183] HM Inspectorate of Probation, *Valuing the Victim*.

[184] Interview with Pat Brown-Richards, Head of Victim Liaison Unit, West Midlands Probation Area, Birmingham, March 2004.

[185] HM Inspectorate of Probation, *Valuing the Victim*.

8. COMMUNITY PARTNERSHIPS, VOLUNTEERING AND CRIMINAL JUSTICE

8.1 Community Partnerships

The development of partnerships between the Police Service and other statutory and voluntary agencies is a central component of the Government's approach to reducing crime.[186] The Crime and Disorder Act (1998) gave local authorities and the police joint responsibility for the formulation of crime and disorder reduction strategies in each district, borough or unitary local authority area in England and Wales. These strategies set out a range of objectives and targets, which may include reducing offences by youths, tackling drug-related crime and reducing the fear of crime.

Statutory guidance, under the Crime and Disorder Act (1998), gives community safety partnerships the duty to involve faith communities in their work.[187] Yet faith communities are rarely consulted by the lead agencies involved in crime and disorder reduction partnerships. In a survey conducted in 2002 by Jim McManus, out of 200 crime and disorder reduction partnerships, only nine mentioned religious communities as part of their plans. He concludes that there may be a biased, misplaced perception of faith communities, which might affect decision-making at the local and national level, leading to the exclusion of faith communities.[188]

Because funding structures within local government and mainstream services have traditionally been organised, and continue to be organised, around ethnicity rather than religious identity, local government agencies are more experienced and more comfortable in working with groups of a non-religious nature. Faith communities are, therefore, often excluded from partnerships with local government.[189] It is likely that the local authorities, and other agencies involved in the crime and disorder reduction partnerships, do not know what Muslim organisations to contact or what individuals those organisations represent, and they may be suspicious of them.[190]

The Muslim community in Britain is particularly diverse. It is claimed that the Muslim community has 56 nationalities, speaks 70 languages and prays in more than 1,200

---

[186] D. Mullett, *The NACRO Guide to Partnership Working*, London, NACRO, 2001, p. 2.

[187] McManus, *Friends or Strangers?*, p. 2.

[188] J. McManus "Faith Communities and Community Safety", in J. Howarth, *Report of the Fourth Interfaith Meeting held by the Churches Criminal Justice Forum*, 2 November 2002, p. 1, (hereafter, McManus, *Faith Communities and Community Safety*).

[189] McManus, *Faith Communities and Community Safety*, p. 2.

[190] J. McManus argues that some faith communities are particularly stigmatised and regarded as criminally inclined. See: McManus, *Friends or Strangers?*, p. 4.

mosques. Furthermore, there are about 7,000 Muslim organisations in Britain.[191] Muslim councillors, the representatives of local mosques or national organisations that claim to represent the wider Muslim community, do not necessarily reflect grassroots concerns, so there needs to be a more detailed exploration of the broader range of Muslim groups that are available for consultation. It is important to also consider Muslim women's groups, which are often particularly marginalised. Women's voices may not be heard through the usual consultation processes, and while men may act as a useful means for connecting to the women of their communities, direct engagement with Muslim women's groups should be encouraged. At the same time, the voices of young Muslims are likely to be unheard, so greater attention must be paid to establishing links with Muslim youths.

In areas where there is a substantial Muslim population, local councils should consider appointing Muslim community workers, who can help gain the increased engagement of these communities, for social, economic and neighbourhood renewal. There are already examples of the consultation of local faith communities by local authorities, and a February 2002 publication, entitled *Faith and Community: a Good Practice Guide for Local Authorities,* has had a significant impact upon local authorities' dealings with faith communities.[192] Central Government is also increasingly acknowledging the important role that faith communities can play in community justice, and the Home Office Faith Communities Unit publication, *Working Together: co-operation between Government and faith communities,* contains a series of recommendations for Government departments to follow, so that they can improve their engagement with citizens from faith communities. These recommendations include the need to: target carefully, ensuring mailing lists are up to date and appropriate; allow enough time for faith communities to take the initiative and make positive suggestions in response to policy proposals; and pursue "faith literacy" and participate in internal faith awareness training.[193]

Increased dialogue with Muslim faith communities will make it possible to build their concerns into crime-reduction strategies. The Government is seeking to ensure that "the criminal justice system will continue to address the challenge of developing more

---

[191] See: H. Khan, "Unite but follow me: the tragic comedy of Muslim representation", in *Q News,* March 2004, pp. 24–25; and H. Khan "Portfolio: Who Speaks for British Muslims?", *Q News,* March 2004, p. 23; and S. El-Hassan, *A Report on a Consultation with Individuals from the Muslim Community,* London, IQRA Trust, 2003, p. 2.

[192] Home Office, *Working Together: cooperation between Government and faith communities,* London, Home Office, Faith Communities Unit, February 2004, p. 62, (hereafter, Home Office, *Working Together*).

[193] Home Office, *Working Together,* p. 1.

effective community engagement".[194] If crime and disorder reduction strategies are going to take account of Muslim communities, the issue of religious hate crime needs to be included in any targets that are set. Local crime and disorder partnerships offer an ideal opportunity for Victim Support and other victims' services to connect with faith-based communities.[195]

Agencies of the criminal justice system, together with those organisations taking a lead role in crime and disorder partnerships, need to gain a greater understanding of the theological basis of Islam. Greater participation of Muslim organisations can be encouraged by appealing to Islamic beliefs and practices about Muslims' role in the life of society and their role in helping to prevent crime, for example, by helping to rehabilitate offenders. Engaging with Muslim faith communities at a theological level might make it easier to get these communities involved in crime and disorder partnerships.

8.2   Volunteering in the Criminal Justice System and Active Citizenship

Community involvement in the criminal justice system can also take place through volunteering. The involvement of Muslims in mainstream criminal justice-related initiatives is relatively low, and many obstacles lie in the way of changing this situation. Social exclusion and inequality is high amongst Muslim communities, and many Muslim individuals live in socially and economically deprived areas. The stress factors associated with living in areas with high rates of crime and disorder are likely to deter Muslims from volunteering their services to the criminal justice system. At the same time, Muslim faith groups that run services for their local communities are likely to be poorly funded, relying mostly on voluntary donations, so they are unlikely to have the resources to work with the criminal justice sector. This means that, before a greater involvement of Muslim service providers in community and criminal justice can be realistically expected, it is important to find ways of helping them to raise funds.

Within Government, there is a strong emphasis upon active citizenship and community involvement in the delivery of criminal and community justice. A Civil Renewal Unit was recently established to develop the Active Citizenship Centre and ensure that policies and practices consistently take into account the need to advance citizenship, strengthen

---

[194] Blunkett, *Active Citizens, Strong Communities – building Civil Renewal,* The Scarman Trust Forum Lecture, 11 December 2003, London, Home Office, 2003, available at the Home Office website at http://www.homeoffice.gov.uk/docs2/activecitizens.pdf, p. 29, (hereafter, Blunkett, *Active Citizens, Strong Communities*).

[195] OSI roundtable on British Muslims and the Criminal Justice System, London, June 8, 2004.

communities and deliver in partnership with communities.[196] A Faith Communities Unit has also been established, and its remit is to lead Government engagement with faith communities, to ensure that policies and services across Government are delivered appropriately to those communities. The Government has also set up an Active Community Unit, to promote the development of the voluntary and community sector and encourage people to become actively involved in their communities, particularly in deprived areas. The Active Community Unit is responsible for the achievement of the Government's target of increasing voluntary and community sector activity, including community participation, by five per cent by 2006.

The Government is also seeking to "encourage community participation and volunteering within the most disadvantaged communities".[197] The Government sees faith communities as potentially valuable allies in tackling social exclusion, as these communities can provide access to some of the most marginalised groups in society.[198] This is partly why the Government is inviting faith communities to open up their services to other sections of the population, and to apply for statutory funding in the same way as other local welfare providers.[199]

There are many ways in which volunteers contribute towards the criminal justice system. Traditionally, laypersons have been involved in the jury system and in magistracy, both of which share the ideal that a defendant should be judged by their own peers. Volunteers also now work for the Police Service, as special constables. And all Police Forces have Lay Visitors or Independent Custody Visitors, who make unannounced visits to police stations to carry out checks on custody areas. Crime prevention panels undertake campaigns aimed at tackling specific types of crime that affect local areas, and these panels consist of people from the local community.

Volunteers also contribute to the work of the Probation and Prison services through voluntary sector agencies, such as The Society of Voluntary Associates (SOVA), or Community Service Volunteers (CSV). Every prison establishment in England and Wales also has a board of visitors, comprised of volunteers from the local community who are appointed by the Home Secretary. These boards, which are independent, monitor complaints by prisoners and the concerns of staff, and they report to ministers as necessary. Prisons work with Samaritans and about 900 local organisations on a range of activities, including resettlement, drug and alcohol treatment and advice,

---

[196] Blunkett, *Active Citizens, Strong Communities*.

[197] Home Office, *Confident Communities in a Secure Britain. The Home Office Strategic Plan 2004-08*, London, Home Office, CM 6287, July 2004, p. 108, (hereafter, Home Office, *Confident Communities in a Secure Britain*).

[198] Home Office, *Confident Communities in a Secure Britain*.

[199] Home Office, *Working Together*.

befriending prisoners, counselling and relationship support.[200] The National Probation Service also has a significant record in encouraging community involvement, and local probation areas are engaged with a number of local charities and other organisations to provide a wide range of services.[201]

Women's groups, which function largely on the commitment of volunteers, run help lines, refuges and centres for victims of domestic violence and sex crime. Over 11,000 volunteers also provide community-based support to the victims of crime, offer support to witnesses and help run a victim support line for Victim Support Schemes across the country. It is estimated that up to 10,000 volunteers work in the youth justice system.

8.3   Muslim Volunteers and Muslim Service Providers

The use of volunteers is considered a good way to bring the community perspective to bear on community justice-related issues. Clearly, Muslim volunteers, whether as individuals or as members of Muslim charities, welfare and support services or other Muslim organisations, have much to offer the criminal justice system. Although there are many Muslim welfare organisations staffed by Muslim volunteers, involvement in mainstream criminal justice-related initiatives is relatively low.[202] There appear to be a number of factors that need to be considered by policy makers if greater participation by Muslim volunteers is to be developed in this area.

Researchers have found that participation in local crime prevention activities is highest among individuals who are moderately concerned about crime but live in areas where crime levels are low. In high-crime areas, where the fear of crime is also likely to be significant, there is likely to be a low level of participation by the wider community in community justice initiatives.[203] Social exclusion and inequality is high amongst Muslim communities, and many Muslim individuals live in socially and economically deprived areas. The stress factors associated with living in areas with high rates of crime and disorder are likely to deter Muslims from volunteering their services to the criminal justice system.

Muslim faith groups that run services for their local communities are likely to be poorly funded, relying mostly on voluntary donations, and so they are unlikely to have

---

[200] Blunkett, *Active Citizens, Strong Communities*, p. 31.

[201] Blunkett, *Active Citizens, Strong Communities*, p. 31.

[202] See: McManus, *Friends or Strangers?*, p. 2. McManus argues here that Christian agencies are more heavily involved in providing projects than their non-Christian counterparts.

[203] Home Office, *Confident Communities in a Secure Britain*, p. 106.

the resources to work with the criminal justice sector.[204] Projects to fund local housing, welfare and crime reduction initiatives are unlikely to subsidise Muslim groups to meet Muslims' needs, because they have to focus on race and ethnicity, not religion. For example, a housing action trust (HAT) that owns a socially and economically deprived housing estate and has received large sums of money to regenerate the area, including millions of pounds for community development, has rejected proposals that are designed to help Muslim communities in particular. The HAT said it will not finance projects such as Muslim nurseries or women-only Muslim support groups, because the trust cannot fund religious projects.[205]

Groups such as the Muslim Women's Helpline, Mushkil Aasaan, which develops religious and cultural primary care packages that service providers can purchase, and the An-Nisa Society, which offers numerous services, including accredited training in Islamic Counselling, all struggle along on voluntary contributions. Despite many applications for community funding, these groups' Muslim identity, which is so central to the particular services that they offer, has meant that government funding has been difficult to obtain.[206] This attitude can be linked to the historical separation of church and state: Traditionally, religions have been self-financing, depending on bequests, investments, property, charitable trusts and contributions.[207]

Muslim community and voluntary sector groups report a lack of capacity as a key barrier to greater involvement. They find that their capacity restricts them to receiving small amounts of money to fund specific projects. However, even to obtain small grants, they need to know how to go about accessing this money. Many groups are unlikely to know how to get grants and are likely to lack the contacts to find out. Furthermore, even if money is found for specific projects, this does not pay for the costs of office space or administration. Muslim community groups are therefore likely to use their fund-raising energy in trying to find voluntary donations to help pay for their basic operating costs. This means they have less time to put toward accessing funds for specific projects.[208]

The funding problem should be of great concern to the Government, because mainstream organisations that receive government funds will refer their clients to unfunded Muslim organisations. For example, Victim Support Schemes might refer

---

[204] Interview with Khalida Khan, Director of the An-Nisa Society, London, March 2004.

[205] M. Bunting, "The New Anti-Semitism", *The Guardian*, 3 December 2001.

[206] F. Ahmad, S. Sheriff, "Muslim Women of Europe: welfare needs and responses", *Social Work in Europe 2003*, Vol. 8 (1), pp. 2–10, (hereafter, Ahmad and Sheriff, *Muslim Women of Europe*).

[207] E-mail communication with Jane Howarth, Churches' Criminal Justice Forum, 2004.

[208] Interview with Khalida Khan, Director of the An-Nisa Society, March 2004.

Muslim victims to the Muslim Women's Helpline, which provides support to Muslim women for a wide range of issues, including divorce, domestic violence, arranged marriages, sexual abuse and incest.[209] However, this organisation has not as yet received any funding from the Government and relies mainly upon voluntary donations. Muslim welfare organisations have found that the fact that they cater to individuals' religious and spiritual needs means that there is a large demand for their services from, for example, secular women's refuges, mental health services, schools and so forth.[210]

8.4 Encouraging Greater Involvement of Muslims in Criminal Justice and Community Safety

The Active Community Unit carried out a consultation exercise with the voluntary and community sector in 2003. The report stemming from this exercise acknowledges that the minority and Black ethnic sector is comprised of many communities with different needs. At the same time, there is a "need for specialist Black and minority ethnic support, particularly for advocacy, lobbying, campaigning, policy guidance and language assistance. There is support for more active collaboration between specialist providers and more sharing of learning with mainstream providers".[211] The Active Community Unit should focus upon Muslim specialist services and explore ways of helping them to secure funding and other sources of support, by, for example, encouraging greater collaboration between these specialist services and mainstream providers. It is important for the Active Community Unit to examine the agendas of mainstream providers and use these as the delivery mechanisms through which greater collaboration can be encouraged.

The criminal justice system is not well understood, so individuals who might be willing to help are unlikely to know how to go about doing this. The Churches' Criminal Justice Forum and the Prisoners' Advice and Care Trust have published a booklet entitled *What Can I Do?*, which is aimed at people from a faith community and explains about 20 ways in which individuals can lend assistance to the criminal justice system. Muslim communities need a similar booklet, explaining the many ways in which Muslims can volunteer their skills throughout the criminal justice system. At the same time, there should be a greater effort made to train Muslims about criminal

---

[209] B. Spalek, "Muslim Women's Safety Talk and their Experiences of Victimisation: a study exploring specificity and difference", in B.Spalek (ed.), *Islam, Crime and Criminal Justice*, Cullompton, Willan Publishing, 2002, pp. 50–75.

[210] Ahmad and Sheriff, *Muslim Women of Europe*, pp. 2–10.

[211] Home Office, *Voluntary and Community Sector Infrastructure Executive Summary of consultation responses: Final Report*, London, Home Office, Active Community Unit, 2004.

justice issues, so that Muslims can act as representatives on criminal justice-related boards and forums.

The organisers of Islam Awareness Week, which takes place each year, should highlight ways in which Muslims can get involved in the criminal justice system as volunteers. Muslims should be actively encouraged to volunteer for work with offenders or victims, because this would boost community involvement in the criminal justice system. At the same time, Islam Awareness Week should be used as an opportunity to raise the profile of Muslim organisations and community groups whose work relates to criminal and community justice issues.

Clinks is a charity that provides a network for voluntary bodies, religious or secular, working in the criminal justice field. Clinks offers a CD ROM with a directory of organisations that is updated annually and free to members. Muslim groups working in the area of criminal justice should be encouraged to join Clinks.

Muslim volunteer involvement in criminal and community justice would increase if efforts to address justice were more socially inclusive. For example, mainstream organisations should pursue policies aimed at Muslim communities specifically, rather than subsuming Muslims within broader debates and policies on diversity. A socially inclusive process should also involve the establishment of effective partnerships between mainstream organisations and a wide range of Muslim groups.

As an example of good practice here, an excellent initiative has been developed by a local Victim Support Scheme in Nottinghamshire.[212] This particular Victim Support Scheme has developed good links with a locally-based Muslim charity, so that some of the Muslim volunteers belonging to this charity have taken part in training programmes run by Victim Support. Victim Support has many years of experience in helping the victims of crime. By training the volunteers of the Muslim charity, they are empowering them to offer practical and emotional support to the victims of crime from within Muslim communities. This is important because Muslim victims of crime may not seek the help of Victim Support Schemes directly, preferring instead to access services arising from their own communities.

This is an example of how a mainstream organisation, with its own set of values, can engage with a faith community group without imposing its culture onto that community, allowing volunteer members of the community group to continue working within their own spiritual mission and faith identity. It is important to protect minority faith communities from potential coercion by larger organisations – especially where those organisations are secular in nature and will therefore have little appreciation of the importance of faith in Muslims' lives. However, it is important to

---

[212] Interview with Javid Kaliq, Victim Support, Kimberley, Nottingham, March 2004.

bear in mind that greater partnership work is only possible if Muslim groups are adequately funded. At the same time, funding for mainstream services may also be inadequate, since funding for Victim Support is often prone to fluctuation and uncertainty, and not all services are funded to provide training the way it was offered by Victim Support Nottinghamshire.[213]

---

[213] Comments from the OSI roundtable discussion on British Muslims and the Criminal Justice System, London, 8 June 2004.

9. VICTIM AND WITNESS SERVICES AND MUSLIM COMMUNITIES

The majority of Muslims who come into contact with the criminal justice system will have been affected by crime as a direct or an indirect victim. An indirect victim is a person who has seen a crime or is related to the victim or may be a friend of the victim.[214] It is important to consider Muslims' needs as victims of crime and to suggest ways of enhancing criminal justice responses to their victimisation.

9.1 The Impact of Crime on Victims

Much research has explored the consequences of crime upon victims. The research suggests that the process of victimisation is often severe and multi-faceted. Different types of crime, including rape, physical and sexual assault, robbery, burglary and incest, impact upon the victim in a multitude of ways: psychologically, emotionally, behaviourally, financially and physically. The ill-effects may be immediate, or they may linger over weeks, months and years.[215]

Following a number of racist murders in the 1990s, there has been substantial research interest in the impact of racially motivated crime upon victims.[216] For example, according to a local crime survey carried out by Bowling in the London borough of Newham, 21 per cent of Black women, 19 per cent of Asian men, 18 per cent of Asian women and 17 per cent of Black men had experienced some form of racist violence, as compared to eight per cent of White men and seven per cent of White women.[217] Victims' reactions included anger, feeling shocked and being afraid. Bowling further describes how victims' behaviour might change after a crime: they might move house, they might avoid certain places (for example, football matches or the pub), and they might invest in crime prevention items, such as shatterproof glass and fireproof mailboxes.[218]

---

[214] Comments from the OSI roundtable discussion on British Muslims and the Criminal Justice System, London, 8 June 2004.

[215] D. Indermaur, *Violent Property Crime*, Leichhardt NSW, The Federation Press, 1995; R. Janoff-Bulman, "Criminal versus Non-Criminal Victimisation: victims' reactions", in *Victimology: An International Journal* (1985) Vol.10(1-4): 498-511; R. I. Mawby, *Burglary*, Devon, Willan Publishing, 2001.

[216] Clancy et al *Crime, Policing and Justice*, p. 21.

[217] Bowling, *Violent Racism*, p. 196.

[218] Bowling, *Violent Racism*, pp. 216–233.

Research has introduced the notion of a continuum of violence, an idea that acknowledges that victims of racist violence are often repeat victims, so that individuals' everyday lives are framed by the actual, or perceived, threat of racist acts, abuse and violence.[219] The British Crime Survey asks respondents whether they think that an incident of crime that they experienced was racially motivated.[220] Results from the British Crime Survey (1992) indicate that Pakistanis are most likely to regard incidents as racially motivated. Fitzgerald and Hale (1996) found that 31 per cent of Pakistani victims regarded incidents as racially motivated, in comparison to 18 per cent of Indian victims and 14 per cent of African Caribbean victims.[221] The impact of racist crime is particularly severe: findings from the British Crime Survey (2000) indicate that a much larger proportion (42 per cent) of victims of racial incidents said that they had been very much affected by the incident than victims of other types of incident (19 per cent).[222]

9.2 Muslims as Victims of Crime

Muslim communities are not only likely to experience racist crime, but also crime that is motivated by religious hatred.[223] As a result, it is of vital importance to investigate the incidence of religious hate crime and its impact upon victims, so that adequate services can be developed to cater to victims' needs. The British Crime Survey, as well as local crime surveys, could be used to do this. The risk of being a victim of crime is not equally distributed amongst the general population. Victim surveys reveal that people over age 60 are least likely to become crime victims, whilst people aged between 16 and 29 have the highest rates of victimisation for personal crimes of violence and theft.[224] Crime surveys also show that lower income groups are more likely than others to suffer a personal, violent victimisation, including sexual assault, robbery or physical

---

[219] B. Bowling and C. Phillips, "Racist Victimisation in England and Wales", in D. Hawkins (ed.), *Violent Crime: assessing race and ethnic differences,* Cambridge, Cambridge University Press, 2003, pp. 154–170.

[220] The British Crime Survey definition of a racially motivated offence is broadly in line with the definition recommended by the Macpherson Report – "A racist incident is any incident perceived to be racist by the victim or any other person." See: Clancy et al, *Crime, Policing and Justice,* p. 21.

[221] M. Fitzgerald and C. Hale, "Ethnic Minorities, Victimisation and Racial Harassment", in *Home Office Research Study No.154,* London, Home Office, 1996, cited in Clancy et al, *Crime, Policing and Justice,* p. 22.

[222] Clancy et al, *Crime, Policing and Justice,* p. 37.

[223] IHRO, *The Hidden Victims of September 11th.*

[224] C. Mirrlees-Black, P. Mayhew and A. Percy, *The 1996 British Crime Survey,* London, HMSO, 1997, p. 10.

assault.[225] This means that Muslim communities, which are likely to experience social and economic deprivation,[226] are also at high risk from a wide range of different crimes, which may or may not, include a racist and/or Islamophobic component. As a result, it is of importance that the needs of Muslim victims are adequately researched and addressed.

9.3 Victim Services for Muslims

In the *New Deal for Victims and Witnesses,* the Government aims to reduce the adverse effects of crime on victims and witnesses, to encourage more victims and witnesses to come forward and to offer more options to victims and witnesses. The Government also wants to do everything it can to make sure victims and witnesses are treated with respect, in partnership with other public and voluntary organisations.[227]

Although there is no direct evidence to show that Muslims are not accessing mainstream victim support services, indirect evidence suggests that this is the case. This evidence includes accounts given by Muslim welfare service providers, such as the Muslim Women's Helpline and An Nisa Society, as well as accounts given by criminal justice system employees who are one way or another involved in victim support. There is direct evidence that minority ethnic communities do not access certain mainstream services. Racial violence, for instance, is under-reported to the police.[228] However, most referrals to Victim Support come via the police – for example, for the period 2002-03 the police supplied nine out of ten referrals to Victim Support.[229] This means that the majority of victims of racist crime are unlikely to be referred, due to the significant level of under-reporting of this type of crime. Indeed, out of all referrals that were made to Victim Support between 2002 and 2003, only 2,180 were for racially motivated crimes, in comparison to 397,884 referrals for burglary and 73,029 referrals for robbery.[230] Furthermore, in the 2002-03 period, the Victim Supportline[231] took

---

[225] E. Fattah, "Victims and Victimology: the facts and the rhetoric", in *International Review of Victimology,* Vol.1, 1989, pp. 43–66.

[226] *Family Resources Survey, 2000/2001.*

[227] *New Deal for Victims and Witnesses: national strategy to deliver improved services,* London, Home Office Communication Directorate, 2003, p. 3.

[228] Bowling, *Violent Racism,* p. 154.

[229] Victim Support, *Annual Report and Accounts for the year ended March 31 2003,* London, Victim Support, 2003, p. 20, (hereafter, *Victim Support Annual Report and Accounts 2003*).

[230] Victim Support, *Annual Report and Accounts 2003,* pp. 18–19.

[231] This is a national telephone line to provide victims with emotional and practical support.

only 99 calls about racial harassment, as compared to 2,014 calls for domestic violence.[232]

Nonetheless, the Witness Service – which is run by Victim Support, in both Crown Court and Magistrate Court, and which is aimed at providing victims and witnesses with emotional and practical support and information, before, during and after the trial – was accessed fairly well by minority ethnic communities during the same period of time. Thirteen per cent of the people referred to the Crown Court Witness Service between 2002-03 were from ethnic minorities, whilst nine per cent of people referred to the Magistrate Court Witness Service belonged to a minority ethnic community.[233] Some local Victim Support schemes are attempting to encourage greater take-up of their services by employing racist incidents officers, who work in partnership with the police, race equality councils and other agencies. These special efforts by Victim Support are intended to highlight the work that Victim Support does, and also to increase the level of reporting of racist incidents.[234] Anti-Muslim prejudice and religious hate crime should also be included in policy developments within Victim Support, so that Muslims are encouraged to access Victim Support services.

Access to Victim Support is important, because, according to a policy paper by Victim Support, victims have certain, key rights, which include the right to receive information and explanation about the progress of their case, the right to receive compensation and the right to receive respect, recognition and support.[235] One way of combating the discrimination and disadvantage that Muslim victims experience is to ensure that criminal justice agencies give victims their full rights.[236] Mainstream services, such as Victim Support, witness support schemes, domestic violence refuges or counselling/therapy, need to take into consideration particular issues in order to ensure that their services are sensitive to the needs of Muslims.

There may be significant cultural differences in the ways in which Muslims address their victimisation. Many writers have noticed that western society currently seems to be experiencing a "cult of victimhood", whereby individuals are increasingly eager to

---

[232] Victim Support, *Annual Report and Accounts 2003*, p. 22.

[233] Victim Support, *Annual Report and Accounts 2003*, pp. 20–21.

[234] See, for example, the *Stamp Out Racism Report!* leaflet issued by Northamptonshire Victim Support, Northampton.

[235] National Association of Victim Support Schemes, *The Rights of Victims of Crime: a policy paper by Victim Support*, London, National Association of Victim Support Schemes, 1995, pp. 8–10.

[236] Comments from the OSI roundtable discussion on British Muslims and the Criminal Justice System, London, 8 June 2004.

identify themselves as victims.[237] Hundreds of books and articles have been written by, and about, the victims of a wide range of traumatic events, such as murder, rape, incest, kidnapping and war. Talk shows, like *Kilroy* and *Trisha* often involve individuals relaying their experiences of suffering or their sense of outrage at a perceived injustice or form of victimisation.

In contrast to this outspoken, confessional approach, which is increasingly dominant in western society, individuals from more traditional Muslim communities may prefer not to speak or disclose information about negative or traumatic events. Muslims may believe that speaking about victimisation may exacerbate the problem, or at least not help the situation. This is because many Muslims seem to subscribe to the idea that speaking out about a particular issue is only worthwhile if some good will come from it. This more reserved attitude towards victimisation means that many Muslims will be unlikely to approach mainstream organisations for help. It also means that Muslims are likely to be implicitly stigmatised by those organisations and wider society, since the broader cultural value of self-disclosure evident in western society is used as the norm against which Muslim communities are directly or indirectly compared and judged.

Organisations that offer help and support to the victims of crime should examine their core values more closely, to find ways in which the experiences and perceptions of Muslim communities, and other faith communities, can be better accommodated. For example, Victim Support Schemes carry out excellent work, but perhaps the frames of reference/understanding adopted by Victim Support could be culturally and religiously more sensitive. It seems that Victim Support values giving control back to the victims of crime, since crime is seen as taking control away from the victim. This approach contains the assumption that, prior to experiencing crime, people feel that they are in control of their lives. However, it may be the case that individuals who follow a faith, including Muslims, believe that the world is unpredictable, and they have little control over it, because God and other forces are at play.[238]

Although agencies that help victims may focus upon providing practical, emotional and psychological support, there is also the issue of spiritual healing and support. Currently, spiritual support seems to be denied to people, yet it may be of benefit to many individuals. Even people who may not regularly attend prayer meetings may nonetheless identify themselves as being part of a religious community.[239] Indeed, in

---

[237] See: C. Sykes, *A Nation of Victims: the decay of the American character*, New York, St Martin's Press, 1992; F. Furedi, *Culture of Fear: risk-taking and the morality of low expectation*, London, Cassell, 1997; and P. Rock, "On Becoming a Victim", in C. Hoyle and R. Young (eds.), *New Visions of Crime Victims*, Oxford, Hart Publishing, 2002, pp. 1–22.

[238] Interview with R. Skinner, Clinical Psychologist, at the IQRA Trust, London, March 2004.

[239] O'Beirne, *Religion in England and Wales*, p. vii.

recent years in Britain, increasing numbers of people have been seeking alternative/spiritual forms of healing. Mainstream victim support organisations should therefore consider widening the range of organisations that they suggest people contact. Spiritual support and guidance and, in the context of this report, Islamic counselling can be a huge comfort to victims.[240]

Support services for the victims of domestic and sexual violence are secular in nature, which means they lack an appreciation of the centrality of faith in some women's lives. Secular women's refuges, for example, may not be able to provide adequate support, so Muslim women may choose to remain in their abusive domestic environments. It may also be the case that the needs of South Asian Muslim women may be different from the needs of Asian Sikh and Hindu women – and actually more similar to English, Bosnian or Arab Muslim women.[241] Choice is a key issue here, because some Muslim women may specifically want a Muslim counsellor/therapist/refuge, whereas others might prefer to seek help from people outside their own communities.

A Domestic Violence, Crime and Victims Bill is currently going through Parliament. This proposed legislation would aim to strengthen the rights of victims and witnesses. Measures in the bill include providing a new Code of Practice for victims, to replace the last Victim's Charter (1996). The new Code of Practice represents a minimum level of service that victims can expect from agencies of the criminal justice system in England and Wales. The Domestic Violence, Crime and Victims Bill would also allow victims to take their case to the Parliamentary Ombudsman if they feel the code has not been adhered to by the criminal justice agencies.[242] It is important that Muslims are included alongside all other groups in receiving the standards of service laid out in the Code of Practice. It is also important for Muslim communities to be informed of how to go about making a complaint if a service has failed to meet the minimum standards that are expected.[243]

---

[240] Ahmad and Sheriff, *Muslim Women of Europe*, pp. 2–10.

[241] Ahmad and Sheriff, *Muslim Women of Europe*, pp. 2–10.

[242] The *Domestic Violence, Crime and Victims Bill* is available on the website of the UK Parliament at http://www.parliament.uk/. Details on the new Code of Practice for victims, published by the Government, are available at http://www.crimereduction.gov.uk (accessed 21 September 2004).

[243] Comments from the OSI roundtable discussion on British Muslims and the Criminal Justice System, London, 8 June 2004.

10. RECOMMENDATIONS

10.1 Documenting the Experiences of Muslims in the Criminal Justice System

Monitoring and data collection:

Agencies of the criminal justice system should consider the points at which it might be practically possible to monitor the religious identity of offenders, defendants, victims, witnesses and employees.

1. The Home Office, and agencies of the criminal justice system, should consider collecting and presenting data in relation to specific minority ethnic groups, rather than subsuming their experiences within broader categories.

2. Where data in relation to Pakistani and Bangladeshi employees is available, agencies of the criminal justice system should release this information and disaggregate it from the general Asian category, as part of a more specific approach to ethnic monitoring and target setting.

3. The Home Office should consider the possibility of adding a booster sample of Muslims to the British Crime Survey, in order to document Muslims' confidence in the criminal justice system, their trust of, and satisfaction with, the police and their fear of crime.

4. Muslim organisations should consider working in partnership with universities, in order to design and implement local crime surveys and in order to examine Muslims' experiences of crime and criminal justice, their perceptions of the correctional services and their fear of crime.

Policy

5. When setting national and local targets to increase minority groups' confidence in the criminal justice system, via the National and Local Criminal Justice Boards, the Home Office should consider developing a more detailed approach to ethnicity, so that specific communities, particularly Muslim communities, are referred to and not subsumed within a broader Black or Asian category.

6. Policies and action plans for tackling institutional Islamophobia and racism within the criminal justice system should challenge anti-Muslim discrimination within the structures, policies and processes of the system.

Research

7. Agencies of the criminal justice system, as well as voluntary and welfare organisations supporting the victims of crime, should conduct research into

whether religious monitoring is perceived to be intrusive by offenders, defendants, victims and witnesses.

8. The Commission for Racial Equality should use its powers to initiate research into all of the areas touched on in this paper. The main areas here being: anti-Muslim sentiment, Islamophobia and discrimination in Muslims' daily lives; Muslims' perceptions of their risk of being the victims of religious/racist hate crime; racially/religiously aggravated offences; discrimination and prejudice; the extent to which Muslim communities are being unfairly targeted by the new anti-terror powers; and, Muslims' perceptions that they are being unfairly targeted by anti-terror legislation. The voices of young Muslims and women are particularly likely to be marginalised through usual consultation processes, so research should also specifically focus on their experiences.

10.2 Policing Muslim Communities

9. HM Inspectorate of Constabulary should consider reporting on policing issues pertaining to Muslim communities.

10. The National Centre for Policing Excellence should consider highlighting examples of good practice that local police forces might adopt, specifically in relation to Muslim communities.

11. Muslim organisations and local police forces should work together to publish and distribute information about the rights an individual has, if they are stopped and searched, or arrested.

12. Organisations like the Muslim Safety Forum, which works with the Metropolitan Police Service, should be set up in other parts of the country, in particular in those locations where there are significant Muslim populations.

13. Muslim community representatives should consider the possibility of some mosques becoming Complaints Access Points for the new Independent Police Complaints Commission IPCC.

Training

14. The Police Training and Development Board should encourage inclusion of a greater focus upon British Muslim identities and communities within the development of race and diversity training packages. Moreover, police forces must be directed to obtain feedback from local Muslim communities about the impact that training has on actual practice. At the same time, consideration should be paid, and guidance given, on developing methods of assessment that measure the learning of each individual trained.

15. In areas where there is a substantial Muslim population, police forces should include an exploration of Islamophobia, religious discrimination, British Muslim identities and their experiences of crime and the criminal justice system within any training package on diversity issues.

Recruitment and staffing issues

16. Police forces working in areas where there are significant Muslim populations should set targets for the recruitment of Muslim police officers, and to help this process, Muslim assessors should be appointed.

17. The Home Office, together with the British Association of Women Policing (BAWP), should consider placing advertisements promoting careers in the Police Service in Muslim and Asian women's magazines and newsletters.

18. Police forces should focus more attention upon the needs of Muslim women police officers, and the multiple discriminations that they can experience, in order to gain a higher representation of Muslim women in the Police Service. The Gender Mainstreaming Team within the Home Office should consider developing employment targets for the recruitment, retention and promotion of minority ethnic women and Muslim women in the Police Service.

Research

19. The Home Office needs to carry out a research study looking at Muslims' attitudes towards a career in the Police Service.

20. There should be research into the careers and working lives of minority ethnic women police officers, including Muslim women police officers, to examine their experiences of working in the Police Service, to see how long they stay in the Police Service and to examine the reasons why they decide to leave.

10.3 The Courts

21. The Department for Constitutional Affairs should commission research looking at the particular experiences of Muslims in Magistrates and Crown Courts, as well as Muslim families' experiences of care proceedings.

10.4 The Prison Service

22. The Home Office should commission research looking at how sensitive cognitive skills programmes are to Muslim prisoners' needs.

23. The Muslim Adviser to the Prison Service, and the NCWMP, should work with the Prison Service and the Chaplaincy Council in order to find ways of

developing programmes that are delivered through chaplaincy departments and are specifically aimed at Muslim prisoners.

24. Services that prisoners can access should be monitored according to prisoners' religious identity, in order to gain a clearer picture of the training and development undertaken by Muslim prisoners, and can formulate policies to tackle any under-representation.

25. Muslim representative bodies, service providers and Islamic theological colleges/bodies, should encourage Muslim communities to help rehabilitate Muslim offenders by, for example, helping to develop community chaplaincy schemes.

10.5 Probation Work and Muslim Communities

The Probation Service and Offenders

26. The Probation Service should adopt an ethnic and religious monitoring system, from which practice and policy decisions regarding Muslim offenders can be made;

27. The Probation Service should examine Muslim offenders' needs, and whether some offenders would welcome specialist programmes that take into consideration both their ethnic and religious identities;

28. The Probation Service examine the sensitivity and responsivity of the services used by Muslim offenders;

The Probation Service and Staff

29. The Probation Service should offer a training package to members of staff that looks at British Muslim communities, ways of improving engagement with them, Muslims' experiences of crime and the criminal justice system, and the specific needs of Muslim offenders;

30. The Probation Service ensure that proper procedures are in place to monitor the ethnicity of members of staff.

31. The Probation Service should also consider religious monitoring of employees and the possibility of setting targets for the number of Muslim employees. Targets should also be set for the number of Muslims in senior positions and service should consider the use of Muslim advisers.

32. Probation areas must develop a clear understanding of religious hate crime and religiously motivated attacks, and victims' needs should receive appropriate attention and action.

10.6 Community Partnerships and Volunteering in Criminal Justice

33. A body of representatives from a wide range of Muslim organisations should create a database or directory of Muslim community groups that can work in partnership for the purposes of crime reduction.

34. The Faith Communities Unit should carry out a survey of crime and disorder partnerships, in order to investigate the level of consultation with faith community groups.

35. Local councils should consider appointing Muslim community workers, whose role can include gaining the increased engagement of these communities for social, economic and neighbourhood renewal.

36. Following recent legislation under the Anti-Terrorism and Security Act (2001), crime and disorder partnerships should engage with Muslim communities and consider strategies to deal effectively with religiously aggravated crime.

37. The work of the Active Community Unit should include a focus upon finding ways of helping to develop Muslim specialist services, by exploring means of helping them to secure funding and other sources of support. The Active Community Unit should examine the policy agendas of mainstream providers and use these as the delivery mechanisms through which greater collaboration can be encouraged.

38. The Home Office, together with a body of individuals representing a wide range of Muslim organisations, should publish a booklet explaining the many ways in which Muslims can volunteer their skills throughout the criminal justice system. A mechanism should be developed for delivering support and training to individuals from Muslim and other minority communities who wish to take up voluntary posts in the criminal justice system.

39. Islam Awareness Week should highlight ways in which Muslims can get involved in the criminal justice system as volunteers. Muslims should be actively encouraged to volunteer for work with offenders or victims, to boost community involvement in the criminal justice system.

10.7 Victim Services and Muslim Communities

40. It is important to investigate the incidence of religious hate crime and its impact upon victims, so that adequate services can be developed to cater to

victims' needs. The British Crime Survey, and local crime surveys, could be used to do this.

41. There should be an effort to inform Muslim communities about the new *Code of Practice,* which sets out a minimum level of service in England and Wales that victims can expect from agencies of the criminal justice system.

42. Mainstream organisations offering support for the victims of crime should consider the possible impact that secular-based approaches to victimisation have upon clients with spiritual and religious needs. It is important to consider means for offering spiritual and religious help and guidance.

Appendix 1: Definitions

Ethnic categories in the 1991 Census: The UK 1991 National Census contained a nine-point structure of ethnic categories: White, Black (African, Caribbean), South Asian (Indian, Pakistani, Bangladeshi), Other (Chinese, other Asian, Other).

The ways in which statistics are often collected and statistically analysed by the Home Office and agencies of the criminal justice system is according to a modified four-point scale: Black, White, Asian and Chinese and Other (Chinese and Other being one category).

Ethnic categories in the 2001 Census: The UK 2001 National Census contained a 16-point structure: White (British, Irish or Any Other White Background); Mixed (White and Black Caribbean, White and Black African, White and Asian or any other Mixed Background); Asian or Asian British (Indian, Pakistani, Bangladeshi, Any Other Asian Background); Black and Black British (Caribbean, African, Any other Black background); Chinese or other ethnic group (Chinese, Any other).[244]

The ways in which statistics are often collected and statistically analysed by the Home Office and agencies of the criminal justice system is according to a modified five-point scale: Black, White, Asian, Chinese and Other and Mixed

Ethnic minorities: In this report, the use of the term "ethnic minority" as a broad "umbrella" label is deliberate, to signify reference to a wide variety of ethnic minority groups. Where greater precision is required, reference to specific component groups within the ethnic minority population is made in the text. There is, inevitably, considerable debate and disagreement on the question of race, ethnicity and nomenclature. No specific political or sociological inference should be drawn from the use of related terminology in this report.

White: As with the term "ethnic minority", the generic label "White" should be used with some caution. The existence of distinctive ethnic groups within the "White" category is gradually being acknowledged. Notably, in the UK 2001 National Census, people of Irish descent are recognised as a separate ethnic group.[245]

Religious categories in the 2001 Census: The 2001 Census asked an optional question on religious affiliation. The data is disaggregated into the following categories: Buddhist, Christian, Hindu, Jewish, Muslim, Sikh, Any other religion, No religion and Religion not stated.[246]

---

[244] UK 2001 National Census.

[245] UK 2001 National Census.

[246] UK 2001 National Census.

Appendix 2: Bibliography

Ahmad, F. and S. Sheriff, "Muslim Women of Europe: welfare needs and responses", *Social Work in Europe*, 8:1 (2001), 2–9

Ahmed, M., "Muslim Religious Provision in HM Prison Service", *Prison Service Journal*, 137 (2002).

Allen, C., *Fair Justice: the Bradford Disturbances, the Sentencing and the Impact* (London: Forum Against Islamophobia and Racism, 2003)

Angle, H., S. Malam, and C. Carey, "Witness Satisfaction: findings from the Witness Satisfaction Survey 2002", Home Office Report 19/03 (London: Home Office, 2003)

Atwood, C., G. Singh, D. Prime, and R. Creasey, *2001 Home Office Citizenship Survey: People Families and Communities,* Home Office Research Study 270 (London: Home Office, 2003)

Aust, R. and N. Smith, "Ethnicity and Drug Use: key findings from the 2001/2002 British Crime Survey", *HM Prison Service Annual Report and Accounts* (London: The Stationery Office, 2003)

Beckford, J., "Preliminary Results on Provisions for Muslims in French and British Prisons", paper presented at the Centre for Ethnic Relations, University of Warwick, 12 December 2003

Beckford, J. and S. Gilliat, *Religion in Prison: equal rites in a multi-faith society* (Cambridge: Cambridge University Press, 1998)

Bland, G., G. Mundy, G. Russell, and R. Tuffin, "Career Progression of Ethnic Minority Police Officers", *Policing and Reducing Crime Unit* (London: Home Office, 1999)

Blunkett, D., "Active Citizens, Strong Communities and building Civil Renewal", The Scarman Trust Forum Lecture, 11 December 2003

Cann, J., L. Falshaw, F. Nugent, and C. Friendship, "Understanding What Works: accredited cognitive skills programmes for adult men and young offenders", *Research Findings* 226 (London: Home Office, 2003)

Chui, W., and M. Nellis, eds, *Moving Probation Forward* (London: Pearson, 2003)

Clancy, A., M. Hough, R. Aust, and C. Kershaw, *Crime, Policing and Justice: The Experience of Ethnic Minorities. Findings from the 2000 British Crime Survey,* Research Study 223 (London: Home Office, 2001)

Commission on British Muslims and Islamophobia, *Islamophobia, a challenge for us all,* (London: Central Books, 1997)

Commission on the Future of Multi-Ethnic Britain, *The Parekh Report* (London: Profile Books, 2000)

Cotton, J. and C. Smith, "Police Service Strength England and Wales, 31 March 2003" (London: National Statistics Office, 2003)

Crown Prosecution Service Inspectorate, *A Report on the Review of CPS Casework with a Minority Ethnic Dimension* (London: Crown Prosecution Service Inspectorate, 2002)

Crown Prosecution Service Inspectorate, *A Follow Up Review of CPS Casework with a Minority Ethnic Dimension* (London: Crown Prosecution Service Inspectorate, 2004)

Denham, J., *Building Cohesive Communities: A Report of the Ministerial Group on Public Disorder and Community Cohesion* (London: HMSO, 2001)

Department for Work and Pensions, *Family Resources Survey, 2000/2001,* (London: DWP, 2001)

El-Hassan, S., "A Report on a Consultation with Individuals from the Muslim Community" (London: IQRA Trust, 2003)

Fawcett Society, *Women and the Criminal Justice System* (London: The Fawcett Society, 2004)

Fitzgerald, M., "Ethnic Minorities and the Criminal Justice System" (London: HMSO, 1993)

Fitzgerald, M., and R. Sibbitt, 'Ethnic Monitoring in Police Forces: a beginning' Home Office Research Study 173, Research and Statistics Directorate Report (London: HMSO, 1997)

Furedi, F., *Culture of Fear: risk-taking and the morality of low expectation* (London: Cassell, 1997)

Genders, E. and E. Player, *Race Relations in Prisons* (Oxford: Clarendon Press, 1989)

HM Inspectorate of Probation, *Towards Race Equality: Follow-up Inspection Report,* (London: HM Inspectorate of Probation, 2004)

Hollis, V., I. Cross and T. Olowe, "Prison Population Brief, England and Wales October 2003" (London: HMSO, 2003)

Home Office, "Prison Statistics 2000 England and Wales" (London: Her Majesty's Stationery Office, 2001)

Home Office Research Statistics, "Statistics on Race and The Criminal Justice System 2003" A Home Office Publication under Section 95 of the Criminal Justice Act 1991, Home Office Research Statistics (London: Home Office, HMSO, 2004)

Home Office, "Statistics on Race and the Criminal Justice System", A Home Office publication under section 95 of the Criminal Justice Act (London: Home Office, HMSO, 2003)

Home Office, *Improving Public Satisfaction and Confidence in the Criminal Justice System,* Framework Document, July 2003 (London: Home Office, 2003)

Home Office, *National Policing Plan for 2003–2006* (London: Home Office, 2002)

Home Office, *Policing: Building Safer Communities Together, a consultation exercise* (London: Home Office, 2003)

Home Office, *Voluntary and Community Sector Infrastructure Executive Summary of consultation responses Final Report* (London: Home Office Active Community Unit, 2004)

Hood, R., *Race and Sentencing* (Oxford: Clarendon Press, 1992)

Howarth, J., Churches' Criminal Justice Forum, 2004.

Hoyle, C. and R. Young, eds., *New Visions of Crime Victims* (Oxford: Hart Publishing, 2002)

Islamic Human Rights Commission, *The Hidden Victims of September 11th: prisoners of UK Law* (London: Islamic Human Rights Commission, 2002)

Kalunta-Crumpton, A., "The Prosecution and Defence of Black Defendants in Drugs Trials", *British Journal of Criminology* Vol.38:4 (1998), 561-591

McManus, J., "Faith Communities and Community Safety", November 2nd 2002 Report of the fourth interfaith meeting held by the Churches' Criminal Justice Forum, 2002.

McManus, J., *Friends or Strangers? Faith Communities and Community Safety* (London: NACRO, 2001)

Modood, T., R. Berthoud, J. Lakey, P. Smith, S. Virdee, and S. Beishon, *Ethnic Minorities in Britain: Diversity and Disadvantage* (London: Policy Studies Institute, 1997)

Myhill, A., S. Yarrow, D. Dalgleish and M. Docking, "The role of police authorities in public engagement" *Home Office Online Report,* 37/03 (2003)

National Probation Directorate, *The Heart of the Matter: a diversity Startegy for the National Probation Service for England and Wales 2002–2006* (London: National Probation Directorate, 2003)

O'Beirne, M., *Religion in England and Wales: findings from the Home Office Citizenship Study 2001,* Home Office Research Study 274 (London: Home Office, 2004)

Page, B., R. Wake and A. Ames, "Public Confidence in the Criminal Justice System" Home Office Research Findings 221 (London: HMSO, 2004)

Powis, B. and R. Walmsley, "Programmes for Back and Asian offenders on probation: lessons for developing practice" Home Office Research, Development and Race and the CJS, a Publication under Section 95 of the Criminal Justice Act 1991 (London: Home Office Statistics Directorate, HORS 250, 2002)

Quraishi, M., *Muslims and Crime* (London: Ashgate, forthcoming 2005)

Said, E., *Orientalism, Western Conceptions of the Orient* (Harmondsworth: Penguin Books 2003)

Sheridan, L., R. Gillett, E. Blaauw and F.W. Winkel, *Effects of the Events of September 11th on Discrimination and Implicit Racism in Five Religious and Seven Ethnic Groups* (Leicester, University of Leicester School of Psychology, 2003)

Sheriff, S., Presentation to the Victim Support Annual Conference, July 3rd, University of Warwick, 2001

Spalek, B., "Hate Crimes against British Muslims in the Aftermath of September 11th", *Criminal Justice Matters,* 48:3 (2002), 20-22

Stone, V. and R. Tuffin, "Attitudes of People from Minority Ethnic Communities towards a Career in the Police Service" Home Office Research, Development and Statistics Directorate, Police Research Series Paper 136 (London: Her Majesty's Stationery Office, 2000)

Sykes, C., *A Nation of Victims: the decay of the American character* (New York: St Martin's Press, 1992)

Todd, S., *Seen but not Heard – Women's Experiences of the Police,* Report of a collaboration between the Thames Valley Police, Todd Consulting and the University of Surrey (2002)

Wardak, A., *Social Control and Deviance: A South Asian Community in Scotland* (Aldershot: Ashgate, 2000)

Webster, C., *Youth Crime, Victimisation and Harassment. The Keighley Crime Survey.* Paper in Community Studies No 7. Centre for Research (Bradford: Department of Applied and Community Studies, Bradford and Ilkley Community College, 1994)